Elementary Statistics for Psychology Students

■

Charles Hinderliter
University of Pittsburgh at Johnstown

James Misanin
Susquehanna University

The McGraw-Hill Companies, Inc.
College Custom Series

New York St. Louis San Francisco Auckland Bogotá
Caracas Lisbon London Madrid Mexico Milan Montreal
New Delhi Paris San Juan Singapore Sydney Tokyo Toronto

McGraw·Hill
A Division of The McGraw·Hill Companies

Elementary Statistics for Psychology Students

McGraw-Hill's College Custom Series consists of products that are produced from camera-ready copy. Peer review, class testing, and accuracy are primarily the responsibility of the author(s).

67890 GDP GDP 09876543210

ISBN 0-07-029017-2

Editor: Linda DuPlessis
Cover Design: Mark Anderson
Printer/Binder: Greyden Press

CONTENTS

PREFACE

Organization of the Text

This text is written for the beginning psychology student who is taking a first course in statistics. The sequencing of topics gives the student a thorough understanding of how research in psychology proceeds from forming the research hypothesis through collection, organization, description, analysis, and interpretation of data. Basic concepts are clearly defined and integrated throughout the text to impress upon the student the comprehensive nature of statistics. Review exercises at the end of each chapter reinforce this notion by having students integrate material from many or all of the preceding chapters. Statistical applications likely to be encountered in psychological research or to engage the interest of students are presented as *Progress Assessments*. These statistical applications are strategically placed throughout each chapter so that students can immediately assess their progress in mastering the fundamentals of statistics. Answers to the *Progress Assessments* are conveniently located at the end of each chapter. Important terms, concepts, and formulas, also located at the end of each chapter, aid the student in reviewing and mastering the language of statistics. This organization encourages an interactive approach to learning statistics that involves acquiring, applying, and integrating statistical concepts and procedures.

Objectives

One major objective in writing this text was to use straightforward language, a writing style, and an organization that encourage students to be active participants in the learning process. A step-by-step approach to the application of statistics to situations encountered by the beginning student and the professional psychologist is intended to provide students with a working knowledge of key concepts and formulas. It is our hope that this approach will persuade students to view statistics as a useful and applicable resource tool. We believe this view will stimulate students to read the text, work through the material, and interact with their instructors, using them as a source to go beyond the many applications provided in the text. A second objective was to produce a statistics text that would serve as a useful reference source that students could use in most, if not all, of their undergraduate psychology courses. A third objective was to maintain the rigor and thoroughness required for graduate study and, at the same time, provide students entering the job market with the skills necessary to apply statistics to problems they are likely to encounter in the workplace.

Special Features

The following are special features of this text that distinguish it from other undergraduate statistics texts:

1. **Progress Assessments,** set off throughout each chapter, provide students with immediate feedback about their mastery of the material. Students should complete these progress assessments as they read each section and check their answers with those given at the end of the chapter.

2. **Review exercises** at the end of each chapter are included to integrate text material and emphasize the comprehensive nature of statistics. Answers to these exercises are located at the back of the text.

3. The **format** for presenting tables, figures, and statistical results follows the guidelines of the *Publication Manual of the American Psychological Association* (third edition).

4. **Key terms,** defined as they are in the main body of the text and located at the end of each chapter, serve as an in-text study aid.

5. **Nonparametric statistical tests are covered in the same chapter as comparable parametric tests** in order to emphasize the importance of measurement scales, sampling procedures, and population characteristics in data analysis and interpretation.

Study Aids

Because mastery of statistics requires an active learning process, a student workbook and a computerized tutorial have been developed to accompany this text.

Student Workbook (by the authors).   In writing the student workbook, we attempted to integrate and extend the text material. For each chapter of the textbook, there is a comparable chapter in the workbook containing the following five sections:

1. A *Detailed Textbook Outline* to be used as a study guide;

2. *Key Terms and Definitions* to be used as a reference for working the exercises in the workbook chapter;

3. *Mastering the Language of Statistics* to help students build their statistics vocabulary by completing fill-in-the-blank, multiple-choice, and true-false exercises;

4. *Applying Statistical Concepts* to provide students with additional opportunities to apply statistics to the kinds of research they are likely to encounter as psychology students;

5. *Meeting the Challenge of Statistics* to enhance students' understanding of statistical reasoning and decision making by applying statistical procedures and tests learned throughout the text to the same data sets.

Computerized Tutorial. The computerized tutorial is designed for use on IBM or IBM-compatible personal computers. Written in a format that incorporates programmed-text principles, it includes a review of basic algebra and arithmetic, multiple-choice conceptual and applied problems, and graphic demonstrations of statistical concepts.

Acknowledgments

We would like to recognize the many individuals who assisted us in writing this textbook. We are most indebted to our developmental editor, Judy Drucker, for her invaluable recommendations and assistance. Thanks are also due to Scott Hardy, Susan Driscoll, Donald Hull, and Laura Pearson, who were instrumental in the production of this text. We also appreciate Helen E. Misanin's careful and tireless proofreading of all the chapters. Several people who reviewed our chapters also deserve thanks for their helpful comments and suggestions: Barry H. Cohen, New York University; Caroline Davis, York University; Raymond W. Frankmann, Michigan State University; Michael W. Gaynor, Bloomsburg University; Robert C. Haygood, Arizona State University; Michael J. Kalsher, Rensselaer Polytechnic Institute; Donald F. Kendrick, Middle Tennessee State University; Duane R. Martin, University of Texas at Arlington; Thomas E. Nygren, The Ohio State University; Sara Staats, The Ohio State University at Urbana-Champaign; and Shawn L. Ward, Le Moyne College. We are grateful to the Literary Executor of the late Sir Ronald A. Fisher, F.R.S., to Dr. Frank Yates, F.R.S. and the Longman Group Ltd., London for the permission to reprint Table II from their book *Statistical Tables for Biological, Agricultural and Medical Research* (6th Edition 1974).

Dedications

Dedicated to our families and students.

FUNDAMENTALS
of STATISTICS
for Psychology Students

CHAPTER 1

The Meaning and Use of Statistics

*T*his chapter introduces the concept of statistics and explains why it is a required course of study in most undergraduate "science" curriculums. Although usually not required in nonscientific areas, statistical methods have proven to be valuable tools in all disciplines. Like any tools, however, these methods have sometimes been misused and even abused by "the experts." A sound start in the basics of statistics will help you reduce your misuse of statistics to a minimal level and allow you to detect the misuse and abuse of statistics by others.

STATISTICS DEFINED

The term **statistics** is used in a variety of ways. For example, it may refer to information described and collected as numbers, that is, **numerical data**—for example, vital medical statistics, such as blood pressure and heart rate. Statistics also refers to measures of group characteristics of numerical data such as the arithmetic average of entering freshmen's Scholastic Aptitude Test Scores. The term is also used for the branch of mathematics that deals with collecting, analyzing, and interpreting numerical data.

In this book you will study statistics as used in all three of the above-mentioned ways. Emphasis, however, will be given to statistics as a branch of mathematics. This book was not written for statisticians. It was designed for students who need to use statistics as a tool for making decisions in their chosen disciplines—psychology, education, sociology, or other fields of study.

PROGRESS ASSESSMENT 1.1

For the following items determine whether statistics is referred to as numerical data, group characteristics, or a branch of mathematics.

1. The number of points made by each player on your school's basketball team.
2. The average Scholastic Aptitude Test (SAT) scores of the freshman class at your college.
3. Your age, date of birth, and the number of brothers and sisters in your family.
4. Determining whether the grade-point average of students enrolled at your school is typical of students enrolled in colleges throughout the United States and Canada.

WHY STUDY STATISTICS?

One reason for studying statistics is to allow you to evaluate reports based, in part, on statistical analysis. All empirical sciences, that is, those that rely on the examination of data, utilize statistical procedures. Understanding reports produced in these sciences requires that you know something about statistics. When a psychologist announces the discovery of a technique that can improve your memory or a health specialist claims to have hit upon a combination of vitamins that will give you greater energy, you should be able to evaluate these claims. If you know something about the use of statistics, evaluation will be possible.

A second reason for studying statistics is that statistical analyses are critical tools needed to complete research projects correctly. Many of you will take an advanced course in your discipline in which you may be required to complete a research project. Those of you who decide to go to graduate school will probably be required to complete a research thesis. An understanding of statistics is one of many skills needed to start and complete a good research project. As you will learn in your research courses, you should never begin to collect data until you have determined how it should be collected, analyzed, and evaluated. Many students and researchers have wasted weeks and months of their time collecting data that can never be analyzed and thus never reported. As you will see in Chapter 2, the use of certain statistical analyses requires that data be collected in a certain way. Failure to meet these requirements often results in data that cannot be analyzed.

A third reason for studying statistics is that you may enjoy the type of thinking and problem solving involved in a statistics course. We hope that you will use some of the techniques learned in this course to approach problems you encounter outside your statistics class. At some time in your life, you will have to evaluate information to make decisions as a consumer, voting citizen, researcher, personnel director, parent, investment counselor, or in other roles. Knowing something about statistics may help you make these decisions in a way that you might never have explored had you not taken your first statistics course.

PROGRESS ASSESSMENT 1.2

For each of the following items determine whether statistics would be used for evaluating research, for completing research, or for thinking and problem solving.

1. Susan is about to propose a master's thesis examining the effects of handling infant monkeys on their socialization behaviors in adulthood. She carefully designs her study in such a way that she knows beforehand how it will be analyzed statistically.

2. Tom is about to buy a car and amasses statistical information on several makes and models produced over the past five years. He formulates various hypotheses about the best models based on such variables as costs, repairs, and insurance. He then uses statistics to evaluate these hypotheses.

3. You would like to know more about the health risks of smoking. You decide to obtain the original scientific reports to determine, among other things, whether the numerical data were correctly analyzed by the researchers.

TWO FUNCTIONS OF STATISTICS

There are two functions of statistics that can be clearly identified when considering statistics as a branch of mathematics. One is to describe and summarize data that have been collected. The other is to analyze and interpret numerical information. Each of these will be discussed in turn in the sections that follow.

Descriptive Statistics

Statistics that are used to describe and summarize a data set, that is, a collection of numerical information, are called **descriptive statistics.** For example, you can determine the yearly salaries for employees of a particular company, the number of months couples married under the age of twenty-one in a particular community remain married, or your classmates' scores on their first statistics exam. In such cases the numerical data, or the statistics, serve merely to describe your data set.

Statistics can also be used to summarize data efficiently. Simply knowing each of your classmates' exam scores, for example, may not be very helpful if you are interested in how your class performed as a whole. If, however, you can measure how widely the scores are distributed or determine the score that most typifies the data set or marks off the top 90 percent of the exam scores, then you will not only be describing your data set but you will be summarizing it in such a way as to ascertain how the class did as a whole. Descriptive statistical procedures allow you to obtain such measures and make such determinations.

Inferential Statistics

Rarely, however, are you called upon simply to describe data sets or to summarize information that you have collected. Usually you are asked to interpret the information that you have collected, that is, you are asked to give an opinion or to make a judgment about what the information means. Suppose, for example, your statistics professor is using a new textbook in your class. A former student asks you if, at this point in the course, your class is performing as well as classes that used the old textbook. Descriptive statistics and descriptive statistical procedures themselves are not sufficient to answer such a question adequately. The question can be answered only after appropriate analysis involving inferential statistics. **Inferential**

statistics are used to make accurate and efficient judgments about an entire group based upon the analysis of information obtained from a portion of the group. In this case you are being asked to judge if the performance of your class is the same as or different than the performance of classes that used the old textbook.

PROGRESS ASSESSMENT 1.3

Determine whether statistics as described in the following items are being used for descriptive or inferential purposes.

1. Listing the average hits each baseball player on your college team has during a particular season.

2. Determining whether or not the average height of your women's basketball team is typical of the height of players in their league.

3. Evaluating whether or not the practice sessions offered by your college have, in general, improved test scores for the Graduate Record Examination relative to the national average.

4. Reporting the average insurance cost per year of all models of cars at one, five, or ten years of age.

DEFINING GROUPS AND MEASURES

In order to use inferential statistics, you must distinguish between two types of groups and between the numerical data collected from these groups.

Populations and Parameters

A **population** consists of all members of a defined group that possess one or more specified characteristics. Populations may consist of people, places, objects, or events and are limited only by the imagination of the investigator defining the population.

Examples of populations are females enrolled at your university, commercial passenger airplanes now in service throughout the world, the stars in the universe, and human beings. Note from the above examples that populations may be extremely large, such as human beings, or relatively small, such as females enrolled at your university. It may also be a **finite population,** a population that has a limited number of members, such as all commercial passenger planes. It may also be an **infinite population** for which there is no limit to the number of members, such as stars in the universe.

Generally, investigators want to know something about these populations. When dealing with a small population it is sometimes possible to measure every member. For example, if you are enrolled at a small university that has 500 students and want to measure the height of each, it is possible to do so. You may find the average height of all students is 5 feet 10 inches. The measurements you obtain from a population are referred to as **parameters.** Parameters are symbolized by Greek letters. For example, the arithmetic average of some measured characteristic of a population is symbolized as μ (pronounced ''mu''). In the student example in which height is measured, μ equals 5 feet 10 inches. Generally, populations are too large for an investigator to observe each and every member.

In statistics population parameters are usually hypothetical. Through sampling (to be discussed in Chapter 2) and inferential statistics, however, an investigator can make relatively accurate guesses about the population characteristics.

Samples and Statistics

Samples are subsets of populations, that is, they are some portion of the defined population. Just as specific populations can be defined in a variety of ways, so can specific samples. Examples of samples from a population defined as ''students currently enrolled in introductory statistics throughout North America'' may include (1) students enrolled in introductory statistics at your university; (2) students enrolled in introductory statistics in the United States; or (3) students taking introductory statistics in colleges throughout Canada and Mexico.

Once you have selected your sample, you can measure some characteristic of each member of your sample, for example, body weight. Measurements obtained from a sample are referred to as **sample statistics.** English letters are most often used as symbols to refer to such measurements. For example, **sample size,** the number of members in a sample, is designated by the English letter N. Whenever you define your sample, you must also specify its size. If you have selected one hundred individuals for a specific sample, you would indicate its sample size as $N = 100$.

The number of different samples that can be selected from a population and the number of populations that can be defined by an investigator is usually quite large. At least four factors determine the population from which a sample is drawn. These factors are (1) the investigators' interests; (2) the investigators' resources, for example, time, equipment, laboratory space, and funds; (3) ethical concerns involved in studying any organism; and (4) conditions and statistical assumptions that must be met if information obtained from the sample can be used to make inferences about the population. The emphasis in the next chapter will be on this last concern. Statistical analyses are meaningless if samples have not been selected correctly.

PROGRESS ASSESSMENT 1.4

For each of the following items determine whether the defined groups refer to populations or samples.

1. The team statistics for each school in NCAA Division 1 are compiled.

2. Your volleyball team's statistics are compiled as representative of the league's average statistics. Note there are two groups, your team and all teams in the league.

3. The average blood pressure of students in your statistics class is compared to the average blood pressure of students enrolled in your university. Note again there are two groups, students in statistics class and students enrolled in your university.

SUMMARY

This chapter introduces you to the subject of statistics, describing three different ways that the term is used. In this book emphasis is given to statistics as a branch of mathematics. Several reasons why statistics should be studied are presented. A distinction is made between descriptive and inferential statistics, and the corresponding functions of statistics are discussed. A distinction is also made between sample and population. Also mentioned are four factors that determine the population from which a sample is drawn.

KEY DEFINITIONS

descriptive statistics   A branch of mathematics used to describe and summarize data.

finite population   A population which has a limited number of members.

inferential statistics   Statistics used to make accurate and efficient judgments about an entire group based upon the analysis of information obtained from a portion of the group.

infinite population   A population that does not have a limit to the number of members.

N   A symbol used to denote sample size.

numerical data   Information collected as numbers.

parameters   Measurements obtained from populations. Greek letters are used to symbolize parameters.

population All members of a group of people, places, objects, or events that share at least one common characteristic.

sample A subset, that is, a portion, of a defined population.

sample size The number of members in a given sample, symbolized by *N*.

sample statistics Usually referrred to simply as statistics. Refers to measurements of a sample. The symbols used to denote statistics are English letters.

statistics A term that can be used in any or all of the following ways (1) information collected as numbers, that is, numerical data; (2) measures of group characteristics of numerical data of samples; and (3) a branch of mathematics that deals with collecting, analyzing and interpreting numerical data.

REVIEW EXERCISES

For the following items determine

a. which of the three ways statistics is referred to (for example, numerical data)

b. why statistics are being used (for example, evaluating research)

c. whether reference is made to descriptive or inferential statistics

d. if the observed group refers to a population or sample

e. if measurements refer to parameters or statistics.

1. A researcher is interested in determining if college students in the United States are reading books other than those assigned in class. The addresses of 50 students are obtained from one state university in each of the fifty states for a total of 2500 students. Questionnaires sent out ask students to list books they have read other than those assigned as class homework. For the returned questionnaires, the average number of books read by students is calculated.

2. A local newspaper editor wants to determine if people who receive the newspaper delivered to their homes still have a preference for morning over evening papers. (Five years ago, the staff had determined that its subscribers preferred morning papers.) A large number of subscribers were contacted and asked for their preference. Again, more people preferred a morning paper.

3. A psychologist completes a project whereby half of the subjects selected from an introductory psychology course are given a caffeine tablet twenty minutes before measuring their heart rate. The other half of the subjects are given a placebo, a tablet identical to the caffeine tablet except that it does not contain any caffeine. Their heart rates are measured twenty minutes later. The average heart rates of both groups are computed and compared to determine if all college students, whenever treated in this manner, would differ as a function of the presence or absence of caffeine.

ANSWERS TO PROGRESS ASSESSMENTS

1.1　　**1.** numerical data
　　　　2. group characteristics
　　　　3. numerical data
　　　　4. branch of mathematics

1.2　　**1.** completing research
　　　　2. thinking and problem solving
　　　　3. evaluating research

1.3　　**1.** descriptive
　　　　2. inferential
　　　　3. inferential
　　　　4. descriptive

1.4　　**1.** population
　　　　2. your team—sample, teams in league—population
　　　　3. statistics class—sample, university students—population

Data Collection

A s mentioned in Chapter 1, inferential statistics are used by empirical scientists to make inferences about populations by using data collected from samples. The term *empirical science* refers to the procedures used in collecting information to evaluate hypothetical statements about natural phenomena. In this chapter you will learn about the basic concepts involved in collecting data. When collecting data about a specific topic, an investigator must not only decide which method to use, but also which specific group of individuals or events to study. This chapter introduces the terms and procedures used in making these decisions.

SAMPLES

Because a population can rarely be examined in its entirety, a subset or sample is drawn from it. The characteristic of interest—for example, exam scores, IQ, or heart rate—is measured for each member of the sample. Investigators usually then make inferences about the population parameters based on sample measurements called statistics. Because a large number of samples can usually be obtained from any given population, rules for selecting appropriate samples must be followed if valid inferences are to be made about population parameters.

Biased Sample

Imagine that you have decided to make some money selling paperback books at your school which currently has a population of 20,000 students. You have limited funds so you cannot buy an unlimited number of books and you do not have the time to ask all 20,000 students what they like to read. So you select a sample of students to determine the type of books—science fiction, romance, and so on—they are most willing to purchase. Would the students currently enrolled in your statistics course be a good sample of the population of students at your school? Probably not. The students enrolled in your course are most likely to be social or natural science majors. If you hope to sell to humanities majors or education majors, the reports from the sample of students currently enrolled in statistics may not represent what is read by all students. Your sample is this case is a biased sample. A **biased sample** is one that reflects only certain aspects of a population and is not representative of the entire population. How then can you select a sample of students that adequately represents your population?

Random Sample and Sample Size

One method that increases the chances that a sample is representative of the population is selecting a random sample. A **random sample** of a given

All you really need to know for now is that you must carefully select a sample based on thorough consideration of the question being asked in the investigation, of the methods used to examine the question, and of the population from which the sample or samples are to be selected.

PROGRESS ASSESSMENT 2.1

For each of the following, determine (a) if the defined groups constitute populations, random samples, randomized samples, or biased samples. If samples, determine (b) if they are independent or dependent, (c) whether they are selected on the basis of sampling with or without replacement, and (d) the populations they are assumed to represent.

1. An educational psychologist is interested in determining whether or not all first-grade children in the United States know the alphabet at the beginning of the school year.

2. A comparative psychologist obtains fifty chicken eggs of a given strain from a commercial supply house. Half of the eggs are to be incubated in natural light and half are to be incubated under the exact same conditions except that artificial light is to be used. A table of random numbers is used to make the selections.

3. A high-school guidance counselor is interested in determining whether or not seniors would take an evening college history course at a nearby college if transporation were available. Because of the limited amount of time the counselor can devote to this project, only 50 of the 500 seniors are asked if they are interested. The counselor has access to the school's computer and uses a program that selects 50 names in such a way that each name has an equal chance of being selected. The computer program accesses each name from the complete roster.

4. A local advertising executive is interested in learning which radio shows people in a community listen to during their lunch break. A member of the marketing staff goes to different restaurants for the next two weeks and determines which program is being broadcasted during the lunch hour and counts the number of people in the restaurant. Using this method, the number of individuals observed totals 579.

5. An exercise physiologist is interested in evaluating the weight-reducing effectiveness of two exercise routines for young adults between the ages of twenty and twenty-five. One hundred volunteers sign up for help in controlling their weight. On the first day of the program, each volunteer is weighed. Pairs of individuals of equal weights are formed. One member of each pair is randomly assigned to Program A and the other member is assigned to Program B.

> **6.** A newspaper personal-advice columnist asks married readers, "If you had it to do over again, would you marry the same person?" Nine hundred seventy-nine readers reply.

MEASUREMENT

Once samples have been selected, investigators can begin to measure the characteristics of interest, for example, exam score or IQ test score. Because empirical scientists rely on collecting information in a systematic manner, the rules used in collecting this information through observation and measurement must be described. Several critical concepts are involved in collecting data. These concepts are described in the following sections.

Operational Definitions

If investigators are to communicate their findings accurately, they must be able to describe what they do in a manner that later allows others to examine these findings in every detail. In order to do so, empirical scientists frequently use operational definitions. **Operational definitions describe events or characteristics of members of a sample or population in terms of the conditions imposed to produce them, or in terms of measurements used to quantify them.** Such definitions are unambiguous and allow for reliable observation.

For example, phobias can be defined in a variety of ways. Generally, a phobia, at least clinically, is considered to be an irrational fear of a specific object. Although, intuitively, this seems to be a reasonable definition, it is not very usable from an empirical point of view. What do the terms *fear* and *irrational* mean? If you were a clinical psychologist, could you now, on the basis of this definition, empirically study snake phobia, or irrational fear of snakes? No! This definition does not lend itself to observation and measurement.

If you define *phobia* operationally, then you have a definition that lends itself to measurement. Following are some examples of an operational definition of snake phobia: a condition produced by a snake that causes a person to report a feeling of fear, or that causes a physiological change, such as in heart rate, or that causes the person to move away from the snake. In these examples the condition imposed to produce fear was the presence of the snake. The phobia can now be measured in a variety of ways. It can be measured in terms of the person's report, a physiological measure of heart rate, or distance moved from the snake.

Note that you still may have questions about these definitions. You may ask whether a person's report should be verbal or written, or how much and in what direction heart rate must change, or how far a person must move from the snake to indicate fear. Just how the event or characteristic of interest is operationally defined and measured depends upon several factors. Most often, investigators utilize operational definitions that have been reported in the literature. In addition the operational definition is usualy described on the basis of a single criterion, such as fear of snakes as the amount of distance (measured in inches) between the individual and the snake.

A word of caution is needed when forming operational definitions. Operational definitions help investigators communicate effectively by making terms observable and measurable. Just because a term is observable, however, does not necessarily mean it is an accurate and meaningful definition of the characteristic of interest. For example, knowledge of statistics may be operationally defined on the basis of a test score in a statistics class. Your "knowledge of statistics" is readily observable in that anyone can look at your test score and determine your degree of statistical knowledge. If you have a score higher than anyone else, one can assume that you have more statistical "knowledge" than the individual with a lower score. This is true if, and only if, the statistical test truly measures information related to statistical knowledge. Thus, not only must an operational definition make the characteristic of interest observable, it must also agree with conceptual definitions of the characteristic established in the research literature.

In conclusion, operational definitions should be viewed as guidelines by which characteristics can be described and measured. They do not rigidly determine the meaning of the characteristics or event of interest or the manner in which it should be observed and measured. Previous reports and the concerns of the investigator are more likely to determine these issues.

PROGRESS ASSESSMENT 2.2

1. Operationally define the following terms making sure that the term is unambiguous and observable. Note that there are several correct possibilities for each term.
   a. intelligence
   b. academic success
   c. memory
   d. paternal behavior
2. Determine which of the following constitute operational definitions.
   a. *Prejudice* is defined as not liking someone.
   b. *Learning* is defined on the basis of number of errors made by a rat in a particular maze.
   c. *Basketball ability* is defined as the number of baskets made out of twenty attempts.
   d. *User-friendly computer* is defined on the basis of a person's likes and dislikes about the computer.

Variables and Mathematical Concerns

A **variable** is anything that can take on more than one specific value. Variables are classified as qualitive or quantitative.

A **qualitative variable** is one that has no consistent numerically identifiable characteristics yet represents distinct events. Examples include sex (male and female), political affiliation (Republican and Democrat), and grades in a course (*A, B, C, D,* and *F*). Some qualitative variables, such as grades, are ordered whereas others, such as political affiliation, are not. In both cases the specific categories of the variables—for example, *A* and *B,* or Republican and Democrat—are *distinct* events. A person cannot have both an *A* and a *B* in the same course nor can the person be both a Republican and a Democrat. In the grade example letter categories may also reflect more or less of a variable such as academic success, but do not reflect numerically identifiable differences. You do not know how much more success is reflected in a grade of *A* than in a grade of *B*.

A **quantitative variable** is one that is defined on the basis of a numerical measurement of the characteristic of interest. A test score expressed as some percentage of 100, number of points at a basketball game, or weight in pounds are examples. Quantitative variables can be either discrete or continuous.

A **discrete variable** is one that falls only at particular points along a scale. For example, number of children in a household can only be a whole number and constitutes discrete measurement. Other examples include number of traffic tickets of a given individual, scores on a video game, and amount of change in your pockets.

In contrast, a **continuous variable** is one that falls on a continuous dimension where the measured value of the characteristic may fall at any point along an unbroken scale of values. Examples are time units measured on the hand of a stopwatch or temperature in your hometown during the months of December and January measured on a mercury thermometer.

Although mathematical distinctions are made between continuous and discrete variables, in practice, distinctions between these two types of measures are often not made. This is because our measuring devices usually do not permit collecting information on a continuous basis. Although air temperature and time are continuous variables, the accuracy of a thermometer and stopwatch limit the values that can be observed when measuring them.

In cases where continuity in the measured characteristic is assumed, the problems associated with discontinuous measurement of a continuous variable can be dealt with by giving the true limits of a number. The **real limits** of a number are those values equal to the number plus *(upper real limit)* or minus *(lower real limit)* one half of the unit of measurement. If the stopwatch in the previous example allows you to observe time to the nearest 0.1 second, the real limits of any recorded number are determined by adding or subtracting 0.05 [(0.1)/2 = 0.05] seconds from the observed number. If you record 10.5 seconds, the upper limit of this number is 10.55 (10.5 + 0.05) and the lower limit is 10.45 (10.5 − 0.05). Likewise a centigrade thermometer with 1-degree graduations might give you a recording of 0 degrees. Its limits would be obtained by subtracting or adding 0.5, that is, one half the 1-degree unit of measurement. The upper limit of 0 degrees in this case would be 0.5 and the lower limit would be −0.5.

Mathematically, the concept of real limits is very important. When discrete values are given for a continuous variable, you must assume that the value is approximate and really means that the true value of the measured characteristic falls somewhere between the real limits of the given value. If you report that it takes a rat 10.5 seconds to run a maze, what this really means is that it took the rat anywhere from 10.45 to 10.55 seconds. Your best approximation, however, is 10.5 seconds.

In this text the distinction between continuous and discrete measurement is emphasized in those situations needed to determine appropriate graphic representation of data and statistical analyses. Real limits are used primarily when data are organized as discussed in Chapters 3 and 4.

PROGRESS ASSESSMENT 2.3

For each of the following items determine (a) whether it is an example of a quantitative or qualitative variable. If it is a quantitative variable, determine (b) if it is continuous or discrete, and (c) if appropriate, the real limits.

1. Number of points at a football game.
2. Elapsed time measured to the nearest second.
3. Numbers selected in a state lottery.
4. Religious affiliation.
5. Number of individuals in income brackets of $10,000–$20,000 and $40,000–$50,000.
6. Age in months.

Scales of Measurement

Directly related to the concept of measurement are the rules or methods used to assign numbers to describe a specific characteristic of a person, object, or event. These rules are referred to as scales of measurement and include four basic types arranged here on the basis of numerical complexity. The type of measurement scale determines, in part, the statistical analyses that can be performed on the collected data.

Nominal Scale.   A **nominal scale** is a system of numerical notation that places a characteristic of interest into a specific category. Basically, when you assign numbers in this fashion, you are only naming or labeling the events. For example, you can identify different political affiliations as categories such as Republicans, Independents, Libertarians, Democrats, and Others. This example contains five categories, but of course the number of categories is determined by the research question being examined. More often than not, numbers are assigned to different categories, such as 1 for Republican, 2 for Independents, and so on. These numbers constitute a nominal scale. In this case the numbers themselves are used as labels for the individual categories, that is, 1 = Republicans, 2 = Independents, 3 = Libertarians, 4 = Democrats, and 5 = Others. The main characteristic of the nominal scale is that the different categories reflect qualitatively distinct events. You know that the events are different from each other, but you do not know how they differ in a quantitative fashion. No category has more or less of a characteristic than another category. The only thing you know is that the categories are recognized as different events. Most mathematical operations performed on numbers constituting a nominal scale have no meaning.

Ordinal Scale.   An **ordinal scale** is a system of numerical notation in which a number represents the relative amount of a particular observable characteristic. The scale is arranged on the basis of order of magnitude, that is, amount of the characteristic from low to high or high to low. Whenever events can be ranked along a single continuum, you can obtain an ordinal scale.

An ordinal scale only allows you to evaluate events with respect to more or less of the characteristic being evaluated. With an ordinal scale you never know how much more or less one event differs from another. You only know if one event is equal to, less than, or greater than another event. For example, if grades on your first exam in statistics are assigned on the basis of test scores arranged from highest to lowest, an ordinal scale is being used. Actual test scores are not given. Instead, the student with the highest test score is assigned a rank of 1, the student with the next highest score a rank of 2, and so on. You cannot tell how much the student with a rank of 1 differs from a student with a rank of 2 if no other information is given.

As you can see, with an ordinal scale you are ordering things along some dimension from highest to lowest, best to worst, most to least, or longest to shortest. The numbers tell you two things: (1) Each number represents a different event as did the numbers of a nominal scale: (2) the number indicates whether an event represents the same, more, or less of the observed characteristic than another event.

Interval Scale.   An **interval scale** is a scale that has an underlying quantitative dimension where the scale's basic units are equally dispersed throughout the dimension and where each unit represents an equal amount of the characteristic being measured. Not only can you make comparisons of equality, greater than, or less than, but, in contrast to ordinal scales, you can also determine how much or how little two events measured on this scale differ. Examples include scales such as the Fahrenheit temperature scale and calendar time. Although a score of zero is possible with an interval scale, it it considered to be an arbitrary zero. It does not reflect the absence of the event being measured. A temperature of 0° on the Fahrenheit scale does not mean the absence of temperature. In general, interval scales can be described as having an underlying quantitative dimension, divided into equal units, with an arbitrary zero point.

Ratio Scale. A **ratio scale,** the most mathematically complex of the four scales, is a measurement scale that has an underlying quantitative dimension with equal quantitative units and an absolute zero point. Thus, as with an interval scale, a statement can be made about equality and amount of difference between two events measured on a ratio scale. In contrast to an interval scale, a ratio scale has an absolute zero point. The quality of an absolute zero refers to the fact that a score of zero reflects the absence of the characteristic being measured. This quality allows proportional (ratio) comparisons to be made. One can talk about a substance weighing twice as much as or half as much as another if the numerical scores differ by a multiple of 2 as in the case of 5 grams of caffeine versus 10 grams of caffeine. Ratio scales are used most often with physical events such as weight (the scale used in our caffeine example), length, and time.

Scaling and Statistics

In general, the type of scale used affects the statistical analysis that can be applied to the data and also the type of conclusion that can be made about the data analysis. Throughout the text, the type of scale required for each statistical analysis will be listed. At this point take the time to learn the characteristics of each scale. In most cases, your decisions will require distinguishing between nominal and ordinal scales and between these two scales and the other two scales of measurement, interval, and ratio. Generally, statistical analyses that are applicable to data collected on an interval scale are also applicable to data collected on a ratio scale. Consequently, a distinction between these two scales does not need to be made for the purpose of analysis. However, you must distinguish between ratio and interval scales when making interpretations about the data you have collected. Only with ratio data can you talk about proportional differences when making comparisons between groups, for example, fertilizer A causing three times as much plant growth (length) as fertilizer B.

In concluding this discussion of measurement scales, keep two things in mind. First, each successive scale, as listed from nominal to ratio, has the major characteristics of each of the previously described scales. For example, a ratio scale, in addition to having an absolute zero point, has the major characteristics of an interval scale, that is, equal quantitative units that represent equal amounts of the characteristics being measured. Second, measurements obtained with a more numerically complex scale can be converted "down" to a less numerically complex scale, for example, interval down to ordinal. Once measurements are obtained, however, a less complex scale cannot be converted "up," for example, ordinal to interval. Chapter 8 also treats this conversion, in which measurements obtained with ratio scales are converted to an ordinal scale so that appropriate statistical analyses can be performed.

PROGRESS ASSESSMENT 2.4

1. For each of the following items determine (1) if the scale of measurement is nominal, ordinal, interval, or ratio, and (2) if the scale potentially could be converted to an ordinal scale even after the data are collected.
   a. numbers worn by marathon runners
   b. birth weight of humans
   c. time measured in seconds to complete a race
   d. high-school class rank
   e. a movie critic's list of ten best movies
   f. Scholastic Aptitude Test score
2. Determine the scale of measurement associated with *each* number in the following items.
   a. A long-distance runner wearing the number 10 finishes fifth in a time of 225 minutes.
   b. A student ranked first in his gym class by his classmates is 6 feet tall, weighs 175 pounds, and won 25 wrestling matches.

APPROACHES TO DATA COLLECTION

Because all empirical sciences rely on collecting numerical information, or data, discussion of the approaches used to collect and evaluate data is necessary. Although the specific approaches are numerous—experimentation, quasi-experimentation, naturalistic observation, correlational study, and so on—only the two most frequently used approaches, the experiment and the correlational study, will be discussed.

Experimentation

In an experiment, something, such as a teaching technique, is manipulated. The investigator then examines the effect of this manipulation on some characteristic, such as exam performance of each member of a given sample. The characteristic of interest is called the **dependent variable.** The specific manipulation is referred to as the independent variable. The **independent variable** is that which the experimenter manipulates, in this case the teaching technique, to determine if it has an effect on the dependent variable. The collected data are referred to as dependent measures. **Dependent measures** are measures of the characteristic of interest. In this example the exam score is a dependent measure. The symbol used to universally represent the value of a dependent measure in an experiment is the letter **X.** Generally, symbols are not used to represent the independent variable. Instead, the independent variable actually used is listed, for example, *teaching technique.*

Suppose an experimenter who is interested in factors that influence memory decides to manipulate the number of times a list of words is practiced to see how practice affects the ability to remember the words. After approval from an ethics committee, a committee that oversees the subjects' welfare, students in an introductory psychology class are randomly assigned to two groups. One group practices the list one time, whereas the other group practices the list ten times. The investigator measures the number of items from the practiced list each student writes correctly from memory. The independent variable in this example is the amount of practice, which is operationally defined as the number of times students are allowed to practice the list, either 1 or 10. Generally, when an independent variable is manipulated, the manipulations are referred to as **levels** of the independent variable. Note that the independent variable in this case, amount of practice, has two levels, either 1 or 10. The dependent variable, memory, is operationally defined as performance on the written test. Remember that operational definitions are used to make a term unambiguous, observable, and measurable. The dependent measure in this case is the number of correct items on the written test.

The basic goal of an experiment is to determine whether one event or events cause changes to occur in another event or events. Usually the experimenter is looking for those conditions both necessary and sufficient to produce a change in the event studied in the experiment. The specific research problem studied depends upon an individual's training and interest. What characterizes all experiments, however, is that the researcher's interest is formulated as a research hypothesis. A **research hypothesis** states the relationship between the variables of interest in such a way that it can be empirically tested through observation or experimentation. In general, the research hypothesis states how changes in the independent variable cause changes in the dependent variable. In the previous example the research hypothesis may have been that study time does (or does not) improve memory. The major purpose of an experiment is to test a specific research hypothesis.

As you might guess, there are reasons why one experiment is not going to prove or disprove a specific research hypothesis. One reason is that the operational definitions used may not be valid. Memory can be measured in a variety of ways such as multiple choice, listing, or matching. Repeating the above experiment with the same independent variable, 1 practice versus 10, and changing the measure of memory from number of correct items on a written recall test to number of correct items on a multiple choice recognition test could lead to a different outcome. A second and probably more important reason that no one experiment proves or disproves a research hypothesis concerns the statistical logic used to evaluate the data collected in an experiment. Chapter 10, dealing with statistical inference, examines in detail the limitation of statistically evaluating the results of any experiment.

In addition to learning the definitions of dependent and independent variables, you must learn to recognize them when they are described in an experimental report. Statistical analyses are performed on the measures of the dependent variable. The type of statistical analysis performed is determined, in part, by the kind of scale used in measuring the dependent variable and, in part, by the specific manipulation of the independent variable by the experimenter. Just how levels of an independent variable influence the type of statistical analyses performed on dependent measures should become clear when more complex experimental designs are discussed in Chapters 14, 15, and 16.

PROGRESS ASSESSMENT 2.5

For the following items list the (a) levels of the independent variable, (b) dependent variable, (c) dependent measure, and (d) research hypothesis.

1. An investigator is interested in examining the effects of handling puppies during the first week after birth on weight gain during the handling period. Ten litters each having six pups are obtained. Pairs of subjects matched according to weight and sex are then selected. One member of each pair is randomly assigned to a handled group and the other member is assigned to a limited-handling group. Those in the handled group are picked up and gently stoked from head to tail, once every 5 seconds, for a period of 15 minutes each day for 7 days. They are weighed to the nearest 0.1 gram at the end of each handling period. The limited-handling group is simply weighed each day.

2. An animal behaviorist is interested in determining whether or not goldfish can learn the concept of left and right when rewarded to do so. One hundred goldfish are obtained from a local pet store. Fifty fish are randomly assigned to a left group and the other fifty are assigned to a right group. Two identical levers which can be suspended simultaneously in an aquarium are constructed. If the

lever is prodded by a fish, it causes a small food pellet to be dropped into the aquarium. The pellet then can be eaten. For those subjects in the left group, prodding the left lever produces food, whereas prodding the right lever produces nothing. The opposite is true for the right group. Two other groups are included. One of these two additional groups receives food no matter which lever is prodded. The other never receives food in the experimental aquarium. Each fish is placed in the aquarium for 30 minutes on each of 10 days and number of prods at each lever are recorded.

Correlational Study

A second approach to data collection and evaluation that you will encounter in this book involves events which cannot be directly manipulated. For example, a psychologist may wish to study the relationship between high-school grades and deliquency. In such a study the characteristics of a given situation, event, individual, or group of individuals are defined, and information is collected for these defined conditions. This type of study is called a correlational study. A **correlational study** is a method of data collection in which two or more operationally defined dependent variables are measured to see if they are related in a systematic fashion.

The basic correlational study requires that at least two characteristics such as SAT scores and grade-point average in college, be measured. The data obtained by measuring the particular characteristics also are referred to as *dependent measures.* Because two dependent measures are collected, the symbols used to universally represent values of the dependent measures are X and Y. Which of the measures is designated as X or Y is usually determined by the investigator. No independent variable is used in the correlational study.

The correlational study also requires that a research hypothesis be evaluated. The research hypothesis in a correlational study states that events are or are not related to each other in a systematic fashion. In contrast to research hypotheses evaluated through experimentation, research hypotheses evaluated with correlational methods cannot be used exclusively to evaluate cause-and-effect relationships. You may determine, for example, that alcohol consumption is related to cardiovascular problems; however, you cannot determine simply on the basis of one correlational study that drinking alcohol causes these problems. It may be that a factor related to both alcohol consumption and cardiovascular problems is responsible for this relationship. For example, it is very likely that people who react to their environment in a stressful way may be more likely to consume alcohol than people who do not react in a stressful way. Likewise, people who react stressfully may have more cardiovascular problems than those who do not react stressfully. It may be that the way a person reacts to his environment is the cause of both of these events. Alternatively, it may be that people with poor cardiovascular systems tend to react more stressfully than people with good cardiovascular systems. These examples demonstrate the danger of evaluating cause-and-effect relationships with the correlational method.

In summary, the correlational approach requires that at least two events be measured. Determining whether events are related to each other is very important to empirical scientists for at least two reasons. First, knowing that two events are related to each other often leads to experimentation into cause-and-effect relationships. Conversely, if experimentation suggests a cause-and-effect relationship between two factors, then a correlational study of these two factors should reveal a systematic relationship. A second reason for knowing whether two events are related to each other concerns the ability to make predictions. Humans constantly make predictions. The methods used to make these predictions are quite varied. For example, to predict whether or not you should see a particular movie you could read a film critic's review of the movie or base your judgement on your own experience with the producer's previous films. Chapter 8 discusses the details of using the correlational approach to make predictions for such events as college success based on college entrance exams.

One major distinction between the experimental approach and the correlational approach is whether or not the investigator controls events influencing the specific values of the dependent measure. If control is involved, it is an experimental approach. A second distinction is that the experimental approach involves both independent and dependent variables, whereas the correlational approach involves at least two dependent variables and no independent variables. Third and finally, research hypotheses associated with experiments describe cause-and-effect relationships, and research hypotheses associated with correlational studies describe how two measured characteristics change in a systematic fashion. When systematic changes occur, the correlational approach can also be used to make predictions.

PROGRESS ASSESSMENT 2.6

For the following items state (a) the dependent measures used and (b) the research hypothesis investigated.

1. An educational psychologist is interested in determining whether or not the number of hours students report they study is related to their Scholastic Aptitude Test score. A roster of all students enrolled at a particular college is obtained. A questionnaire is sent out to one hundred students whose names are randomly selected from the roster. The questionnaire asks them a variety of questions

such as year in college, age, sex, number of hours (to the nearest half-hour) they study per week, and their total Scholastic Aptitude Test score. Sixty questionnaires are returned; forty students fail to respond.

2. An industrial psychologist at a heavy equipment plant, who is interested in determining whether or not there is a relationship between time of day and number of accidents at the plant, obtains the plant records for the last five years. The total number of accidents that occurred during each half-hour interval each day as the plant works round-the-clock seven days a week are recorded. Midnight is set as the zero point for time of day.

SUMMARY

This chapter introduces you to concepts, definitions, and procedures used in collecting data, specifically the experimental approach and the correlational approach. A first step in collecting data requires that appropriate samples be selected. The terms, *biased, random,* and *randomized samples,* as well as *dependent* and *independent samples* are defined. Other terms you should know before proceeding to the next chapter include *operational definition, quantitative* and *qualitative variables,* and the scales of measurement: *nominal, ordinal, interval,* and *ratio.* You should know the basic features of and be able to compare experimental and correlational designs. It is important to have a basic understanding of these methods because the procedures used to collect data influence the statistical procedures that are used to analyze the collected data.

KEY DEFINITIONS

biased sample   A sample that reflects only certain aspects of a population and is not representative of the entire population.

continuous variable   A quantitative variable whose values fall at any point along an unbroken numerical scale of values.

correlational study   A method of data collection in which two or more operationally defined dependent variables are measured to see if they are related in a systematic fashion.

dependent measures   These are obtained measures of the characteristic(s) of interest in an experiment and a correlational study.

dependent or related samples   Samples selected in such a way that assignment to one sample directly determines which member will be assigned to another sample.

dependent variable(s)   The characteristic(s) of interest in an experiment or a correlational study.

discrete variable   A quantitative variable whose values fall only at particular points along a numerical measurement scale.

independent samples   Samples selected in such a way that assignment to one sample in no way affects how members are assigned to another sample.

independent variable   The variable manipulated in an experiment that is assumed to potentially affect the dependent variable.

interval scale   A scale of measurement that has an underlying quantitative dimension where the scale's basic units are equally dispersed throughout the dimension and where each unit represents an equal amount of the characteristic being measured.

levels   The term used to indicate an investigator's manipulation of the independent variable(s) in an experiment.

nominal scale   A system of numerical notation that places a characteristic of interest into a specific category.

operational definition   A definition of a term based on imposed conditions or based on measurements used to identify the term in such a way that the definition of the term is clear and unambiguous.

ordinal scale   A system of numerical notation in which a number represents the relative amount of a particular observable characteristic.

qualitative variable   A variable having no consistent numerically identifiable characteristics that represent distinct events.

quantitative variable   A variable that is defined on the basis of a measurable numerical value.

randomization   The procedure by which members of a limited pool are randomly assigned without replacement to different samples.

randomized samples   Samples formed when a limited pool is divided in such a way that each member of the pool has an equal chance of being assigned to any division and each set of members has an equal chance of forming any of the divisions.

random sample   A sample selected in such a way that every member of a given population has an equal chance of being selected and that every possible sample of the same size has an equal chance of being selected.

ratio scale   A scale of measurement containing an underlying quantitative dimension divided into equal quantitative units with an absolute zero point.

research hypothesis   A statement describing the relationship between the variables of interest in either an experiment or correlational study that can be tested empirically.

sampling with replacement   A procedure used in selecting random samples whereby each member of the population selected for the sample is placed back into the population before the next member is selected.

sampling without replacement   A procedure used in selecting random samples where once a member of the population is selected for the sample, it is removed from the population.

real limits   The values one-half the unit of measurement above (upper real limit) and one-half the unit of measurement below (lower real limit) the estimated measured discrete value of a continuous variable.

variable   Anything that can take on more than one specific value.

X   Symbol used to represent the individual values of a set of dependent measures.

Y   Symbol used to represent the individual values of a second set of dependent measures.

REVIEW EXERCISES

For the data collected in the following items determine whether reference is made to

   a. descriptive or inferential statistics
   b. populations or samples
   c. parameters or statistics
   d. biased, random, or randomized samples
   e. independent or dependent samples
   f. an experimental design or a correlational design
   g. an independent variable (if so, list the levels of the independent variable)
   h. a dependent variable and/or a dependent measure
   i. a qualitative, discrete quantitative, or continuous quantitative dependent measure
   j. the real limits of dependent measure (if not, give the real limits)
   k. a nominal, ordinal, interval, or ratio scale of the dependent measure
   l. an operational definition of the independent variable and/or dependent variable (if so, list the terms and definitions)
   m. the specific research hypothesis (if so, state the hypothesis)

   Before answering any of the above, read the entire item and then go back to determine the answers.

1. In order to determine if very young rats are capable of learning when given a reward, a psychologist allows one group of 9-day-old rats to suckle from their mother for 30 seconds if they move approximately 10 inches from a start section of an alleyway to the goal section. Fifteen training trials are given. Time to move from one end of the alley to the other (recorded to the nearest second) is used to determine if the rats learn the task. A second group of unrewarded rats are given similar treatment except that rats simply are removed from the apparatus upon reaching the goal section. Their mother is not present.

    Ten rats are assigned to each group based on the following procedure. Ten litters are purchased from a professional animal breeder. At nine days of age, each rat pup in a litter is weighed. Two equal-size males are then selected from each litter. One member is randomly assigned to the rewarded group and the other is assigned to the unrewarded group. The average time to move down the alley is computed for each group. The experimenter analyzes the data to determine if the groups differ in time to run the alley in order to state whether all rats of this particular strain would differ if treated as in this experiment.

2. A psychopharmacologist working for a drug company is asked to evaluate the effects of a new cold tablet on reaction time, that is, the amount of time it takes a person to respond after a given event has occurred. An ad run in the local newspaper explains that the research is to be conducted at an established medical laboratory; that it requires administering a cold tablet when the subjects actually have a cold; and that the subjects remain at the medical facility for a period of forty-eight hours after receiving the tablet. A total of twenty-four people respond to the ad. They are told how much they will be paid and, also, that they must come in to complete some reaction time tasks when they have a cold.

    When the subjects with colds return, they are assigned to a treatment condition. A table of random numbers is used to assign twelve subjects to the cold tablet condition and twelve to a placebo tablet condition. A placebo tablet is a pill that has no active ingredients. Over the ten hours following their treatment, they are given reaction time tasks. Each task takes about twenty minutes to complete. The subjects work twenty minutes and rest forty minutes each hour over the ten-hour interval. The tasks involve playing a video game standardized by a researcher where the score on the game, measured in whole units, is recorded for each subject as a measure of reaction time. High scores reflect fast reaction times and low scores reflect slow reaction times. The experimenter finds average scores for each subject and then analyzes these data to determine if the two groups differ. Based on the statistical analysis, the experimenter claims that the cold tablet reduces reaction time for volunteers willing to participate in such an experimental study.

3. A counseling psychologist at a large state university is interested in determining whether or not the habit of smoking tobacco is related to the habit of smoking marijuana. A list of all 30,000 students enrolled at the university is obtained, and a questionnaire, which maintains the anonymity of the respondent, is sent out. The questionnaire contains questions about age, sex, major, year in college, and the number of tobacco and marijuana cigarettes smoked each month. Twelve thousand of the 30,000 questionnaires are

returned. The data are analyzed in an attempt to determine if college students, in general, show a relationship between number of tobacco cigarettes smoked and number of marijuana cigarettes smoked.

ANSWERS TO PROGRESS ASSESSMENTS

2.1   1. a. population
          b. not appropriate
          c. not appropriate
          d. not appropriate
      2. a. randomized sample
          b. independent
          c. without replacement
          d. all chicken eggs from chickens of the particular strain and supplier
      3. a. random sample
          b. not appropriate
          c. with replacement
          d. the 500 seniors
      4. a. biased sample
          b. not appropriate
          c. with replacement
          d. people in the community who listen to the radio
      5. a. randomized samples
          b. dependent
          c. without replacement
          d. All people twenty–twenty-five years old who want to lose weight and are willing to participate in exercise routines to do so.
      6. a. biased
          b. not appropriate
          c. without replacement
          d. all married readers

2.2   1. a. Intelligence is the test score obtained on a standardized IQ test where high scores reflect greater intelligence.
          b. Academic success is grade point average based on a 4.0 scale with higher scores reflecting greater success.
          c. Memory is the number of previously studied items correctly written.
          d. Paternal behavior is the amount of time a father spends with his children.

2. a. not operationally defined
   b. defined operationally
   c. defined operationally
   d. not operationally defined

2.3   **1. a.** quantitative
         b. discrete
         c. not appropriate
      2. a. quantitative
         b. continuous
         c. $+/-$ 0.5 seconds
      3. a. qualitative
         b. not appropriate
         c. not appropriate
      4. a. qualitative
         b. not appropriate
         c. not appropriate
      5. a. quantitative
         b. discrete
         c. not appropriate
      6. a. quantitative
         b. continuous
         c. $+/-$ 0.5 months

2.4   **1. a.** (1) nominal (2) no conversion
         b. (1) ratio (2) conversion
         c. (1) ratio (2) conversion
         d. (1) ordinal (2) already ordinal
         e. (1) ordinal (2) already ordinal
         f. (1) interval (2) conversion
      2. a. 10—nominal, 5th—ordinal; 225—ratio
         b. 1st—ordinal, 6—ratio; 175—ratio; 25—ratio

2.5   **1. a.** handling or no handling
         b. weight gain
         c. weight in grams
         d. Handling affects weight.
      2. a. left group, right group, both-levers group, and no reward group
         b. left-right discrimination learning
         c. number of prods at each lever
         d. Goldfish can learn to discriminate left and right if rewarded

2.6   **1. a.** number of hours studying each week and SAT score

            b. Number of hours spent studying is related to SAT score.

         2. a. time of day and number of accidents

            b. Time of day and number of accidents are systematically related.

Organizing a Set of Data: Table Format

*T*he reasons for studying statistics were discussed in Chapter 1. In Chapter 2 the methods used to collect data were introduced. Data as originally collected are called **raw data** or **raw scores.** Extracting information from raw data is difficult. This chapter introduces some of the ways in which raw scores can be organized in table format so that information can be more readily extracted.

CONVENTIONS FOLLOWED WHEN CONSTRUCTING A TABLE

The data used in the examples in this chapter will be fictional. Assume the data are collected by a teacher who has given three, 100-point exams to a specific class. Each exam consists of 100 items, each worth 1 point. The data the teacher decides to organize are the total points each student has obtained by midterm. The exams were constructed in such a way that midterm scores could potentially range from a total of 0 through 300 for the three exams. The scores of each student and a specific student identification number are given in Table 3.1.

TABLE 3.1
Midterm Scores of Students Enrolled in Fictional Class Including Identification Numbers (ID #), $N = 64$

ID #	Score	ID #	Score	ID #	Score	ID #	Score
1	210	17	228	33	282	49	243
2	252	18	183	34	225	50	246
3	183	19	249	35	198	51	183
4	216	20	216	36	213	52	216
5	264	21	231	37	213	53	291
6	180	22	279	38	264	54	213
7	237	23	279	39	189	55	189
8	249	24	210	40	222	56	180
9	180	25	147	41	282	57	231
10	255	26	258	42	195	58	195
11	189	27	219	43	219	59	222
12	186	28	192	44	180	60	186
13	222	29	279	45	261	61	237
14	219	30	237	46	136	62	237
15	136	31	147	47	231	63	273
16	297	32	216	48	249	64	225

Before considering topics related to organizing data, carefully examine the format used to construct Table 3.1. Whenever you create a table, remember that others should be able to examine and understand it. Therefore, clarity and neatness count. Several conventions are followed in constructing any table. These conventions are listed below with no one having any greater priority than another.

1. The data presented in the table must be clearly labeled with column headings.

2. Each table should have the word "Table" followed by a specific identification number, such as "Table 3.1." When several tables are presented in a report, they should be numbered sequentially as they appear in the report. The table number is then used to refer to the table in the text of the report.

3. A brief description of the information provided in the table and any abbreviations included in the column headings must be given in a table heading. With few exceptions, the heading and table identification number are presented at the *top* of the table.

4. The specific typing format concerning rules of capitalization and punctuation vary from publication to publication. Rules exist for each and every discipline. It is recommended that you follow the typing format used for tables in this text where, for example, the initial letters of the principal words in the heading are capitalized.

ASSESSING THE NEED TO ORGANIZE DATA

Look at the data in Table 3.1 and try to determine how individuals in the class are doing at midterm. You probably cannot make much sense out of all these numbers. Had only five people taken the tests, assessing their performance by examining the raw scores would be an easier task than assessing that of sixty-four students.

One of the first things to do in evaluating data is to determine whether or not the raw scores need to be organized. If questions asked by an investigator can be answered by simply examining the data, no further organization is needed. This rarely happens, however, as most investigators collect data consisting of tens, hundreds, or even thousands of numbers. Even sixty-four numbers become very difficult to interpret if not appropriately organized. In the example then, you can see that organization of the midterm scores is necessary.

You must now decide what type of organization to give the data. Whenever you organize data you must first keep in mind the reason why the data were collected. In the example, the instructor collected the data to determine the level of subject-mastery of individual students and the patterning of midterm scores for the entire class. A second factor to keep in mind is that data should be organized so that the group patterns in the data are not hidden or exaggerated. For example, in Table 3.1 organizing the raw scores on the basis of an arbitrary student identification number (ID #) does not reveal any group patterns in the class. You cannot tell whether the class in general is performing poorly or well. Obviously a different type of organization is needed. A third factor to keep in mind is that calculations often need to be obtained from the data in its organized form. Thus, some guidelines for organizing data are suggested because they allow calculations to be performed relatively easily.

The purpose of organizing data is to allow an investigator or reader to extract from the data information that is not apparent by simply looking at the raw scores. Although organized data are generally preferred to raw scores, changes can lead to the loss of critical information and can also lead to extracting information that is not truly characteristic of the original raw scores. Some of these problems will be dealt with in the discussion of each of the methods used for organizing data.

PROGRESS ASSESSMENT 3.1

After extensive interviews with parents of children who are three months old or younger, a developmental psychologist randomly selects a group of one-hundred pairs of parents. The parents are asked to carefully observe their children for the next two years. The psychologist is most interested in determining the age (in weeks) when the child utters its first word. The following data are obtained from the forty-five children whose parents actually stayed in the project. The numbers given include a subject code indicating the sex of the specific child and age in weeks at which the child uttered its first word, respectively. Organize the data using a table. Include the subject code and age in weeks when the child first spoke.

1m. 36, 2f. 36, 3f. 76, 4f. 40, 5m. 45, 6m. 48, 7f. 52, 8m. 52, 9f. 56, 10m. 80, 11f. 52, 12f. 68, 13m. 40, 14m. 73, 15f. 58, 16m. 64, 17m. 44, 18f. 36, 19f, 44, 20m. 46, 21f. 48, 22m. 48, 23m. 49, 24f. 46, 25m. 40, 26m. 44, 27m. 70, 28f. 48, 29f. 64, 30f. 78, 31m. 51, 32f. 58, 33m. 48, 34m. 59, 35f. 62, 36f. 46, 37m. 47, 38f. 42, 39m. 43, 40f. 62, 41m. 40, 42f. 51, 43m. 44, 44f. 70, 45f. 36.

TYPES OF TABLES

There are several ways that data can be organized in table format that will enable an investigator or reader to extract information more readily than it can be extracted from the raw scores. In this section these formats and their advantages and limitations are discussed.

Array

One way the midterm scores in the earlier example can be organized is by arranging them in order of magnitude. Arranging the data from the highest numerical value to the lowest is called an **array**. An array of the midterm test scores is presented in Table 3.2.

Generally, arrays are presented as a string of numbers either across a page from left to right or vertically from top to bottom. The note beneath the table heading instructs you to read each column before proceeding to the next. This creates the effect of reading the midterm scores sequentially. Arrays usually contain only the organized raw scores. Student identification numbers are included in Table 3.2 in order to refer to specific items from the array.

Organizing the scores as an array allows you to extract information more easily than you can from the raw data. For example, check Table 3.1 and try to find the highest and lowest score. You can do it, but you will find it a rather tedious task. In contrast, the highest and lowest scores in an array, as seen in Table 3.2, are easily determined. Simply find the

TABLE 3.2
Midterm Scores ($N = 64$) from Table 3.1 Arranged as an Array. Also Given Are Student Identification Numbers (ID#). *Note:* **All information in Column 1 should be read before proceeding to Column 2, Column 2 before Column 3, and so forth.**

Column 1		Column 2		Column 3		Column 4	
ID#	Score (X)	ID#	Score (X)	ID#	Score (X)	ID#	Score (X)
16	297	48	249	14	219	11	189
53	291	50	246	27	219	39	189
33	282	49	243	43	219	55	189
41	282	7	237	4	216	12	186
22	279	30	237	20	216	60	186
23	279	61	237	32	216	3	183
29	279	62	237	52	216	18	183
63	273	21	231	36	213	51	183
5	264	47	231	37	213	6	180
38	264	57	231	54	213	9	180
45	261	17	228	1	210	44	180
26	258	34	225	24	210	56	180
10	255	64	225	35	198	25	147
2	252	13	222	42	195	31	147
8	249	40	222	58	195	15	136
19	249	59	222	28	192	46	136

first and the last scores listed in the array. In the example the first score is 297 which, of course, is the highest score. Likewise the last score listed is 136 and is easily seen as the lowest score. The distance between the highest and lowest score is often calculated for the purpose of summarizing data. This value is known as the **range of the raw scores** and is obtained by subtracting the lower real limit (discussed in Chapter 2) of the lowest raw score from the upper real limit of the highest raw score. For example, the range of the distribution of exam scores is 162 (297.5 − 135.5). The range gives you a rough idea of how variable or dispersed your data are. You will again encounter the range in Chapter 6, when measures of variability are discussed.

The array in Table 3.2, in comparison to raw data, allows the teacher in the example to determine more easily whether or not there are differences among individual students or groups of students in the level of mastery as reflected by midterm scores. Assuming higher scores reflect a better mastery than lower scores, the teacher can quickly look at the scores and determine which student performed the best, the student whose ID number is 16, and those students that performed most poorly, the students identified as numbers 15 and 46.

Although an array allows you to quickly calculate the range and easily see the best and the worst performance, it does not readily show whether there are any group patterns within the data. Careful and detailed examination could reveal such patterns. Remember, however, you are trying to present data so that those who examine it can *readily* see how and why you organized it the way you did. Thus, if you want to organize data in a way that reflects group patterns, an organization other than an array should be used.

PROGRESS ASSESSMENT 3.2

1. Form an array of the data given in Progress Assessment 3.1.
2. Determine the highest and lowest score in your array.
3. Determine the range of the data in your array.

Simple Frequency Distribution

Organizing data as a simple frequency distribution also requires that scores be listed from highest to lowest. However, rather than repeatedly listing identical scores as is done in an array, the number of occurrences of a particular score is listed as frequency. **Frequency** is the number of times a raw score occurs. The table used to organize data on the basis of the number of times each raw score occurs is called a **simple frequency distribution.**

A simple frequency distribution is given in Table 3.3. Note that there are two categories of headings *X* and *f*. The *X* refers to each midterm score that possibly could have occurred between the actual lowest and highest midterm scores. The *f* category refers to frequency. Note the expression $\Sigma f = 64$ at the bottom of Table 3.3. The Greek letter sigma (Σ), a summation symbol, directs you to add the frequencies. Whenever you create a frequency distribution you should add the frequencies and determine if the sum equals *N*, the sample size. This allows you to check for errors in the procedures used in creating a simple frequency distribution. If Σf does not equal *N*, you have either made an arithmetic error in adding the frequencies or you have not accounted for all your raw scores. In the example in Table 3.3, Σf can be found by adding the numbers in the frequency column. The total is 64, the sample size.

A simple frequency distribution can be constructed from raw scores or from an array. In either case you must determine whether or not a score (*X*) occurred and, if it did, how many times it occurred. The conventions used in creating a simple frequency distribution include (1) listing the scores in descending order and (2) including each possible score occurring between the highest and lowest scores actually obtained.

TABLE 3.3
Midterm Scores (X) of Fictional Data Organized as a Simple Frequency (f) Distribution

X	f	X	f	X	f	X	f	X	f	X	f	X	f	X	f
297	1	276	0	255	1	234	0	213	3	192	1	171	0	150	0
296	0	275	0	254	0	233	0	212	0	191	0	170	0	149	0
295	0	274	0	253	0	232	0	211	0	190	0	169	0	148	0
294	0	273	1	252	1	231	3	210	2	189	3	168	0	147	2
293	0	272	0	251	0	230	0	209	0	188	0	167	0	146	0
292	0	271	0	250	0	229	0	208	0	187	0	166	0	145	0
291	1	270	0	249	3	228	1	207	0	186	2	165	0	144	0
290	0	269	0	248	0	227	0	206	0	185	0	164	0	143	0
289	0	268	0	247	0	226	0	205	0	184	0	163	0	142	0
288	0	267	0	246	1	225	2	204	0	183	3	162	0	141	0
287	0	266	0	245	0	224	0	203	0	182	0	161	0	140	0
286	0	265	0	244	0	223	0	202	0	181	0	160	0	139	0
285	0	264	2	243	1	222	3	201	0	180	4	159	0	138	0
284	0	263	0	242	0	221	0	200	0	179	0	158	0	137	0
283	0	262	0	241	0	220	0	199	0	178	0	157	0	136	2
282	2	261	1	240	0	219	3	198	1	177	0	156	0		
281	0	260	0	239	0	218	0	197	0	176	0	155	0		
280	0	259	0	238	0	217	0	196	0	175	0	154	0		
279	3	258	1	237	4	216	4	195	2	174	0	153	0		
278	0	257	0	236	0	215	0	194	0	173	0	152	0		
277	0	256	0	235	0	214	0	193	0	172	0	151	0	$\Sigma f = 64$	

It is usually easier to construct a simple frequency distribution from an array. If an array is of no use to you, however, then it may not be worth the effort to create one in order to produce a simple frequency distribution. You may want to organize the raw scores directly as a simple frequency distribution.

The most efficient way to construct a simple frequency distribution from an array or raw data requires three steps:

1. Go through the array or raw data and find the highest and lowest scores. Then, in descending order, list in the X column of the simple frequency distribution each possible score between the highest and the lowest raw scores.

2. Go back through the array or raw data, read the raw data in the order collected or presented, and for each raw score, place some type of tally mark by its specific X in the simple frequency distribution.

3. After you have gone through the entire array or set of raw data, count the tally marks and place a number at each score equal to the tally marks. This number is the corresponding f for that X. The completed simple frequency distribution should be in a format similar to that of Table 3.3 where the tally marks are omitted.

What is clear from Table 3.3 is that organizing exam scores as a simple frequency distribution provides more information than is readily obtained from the array in Table 3.2. There are other notable differences between the two. In the array, only those scores that are actually obtained by students are listed. In the simple frequency distribution, all possible scores between the highest and lowest obtained scores are listed. Because of this, a more accurate visual impression of how the scores are distributed throughout the scale of measurement is produced with the simple frequency distribution. Also, in contrast to the array, with a simple frequency distribution the number of times each score occurs and which score or scores occur most often can be obtained by inspection.

PROGRESS ASSESSMENT 3.3

1. Form a simple frequency distribution from the data given in Progress Assessment 3.1 or from the array you constructed in Progress Assessment 3.2. Both will give you the same answer.
2. Determine the Σf for your simple frequency distribution.

Grouped Frequency Distribution Based on External Criteria

As you have probably guessed, the simple frequency distribution does not do a very good job in summarizing group patterns that might exist in the data. In addition, when there is a large number of different scores, usually more than twenty, individual scores are not listed as in the simple frequency distribution. Instead the scores are assigned to mutually exclusive classes called class intervals. **Class intervals** are groups that are numerically defined in such a way that any given raw score can belong to one and only one of the groups. These class intevals are then used to construct a grouped frequency distribution. A **grouped frequency distribution** is the organization of data into class intervals with the number of raw scores occurring within a class interval listed as its frequency.

In Table 3.3, there are 162 possible scores between 297 and 136, inclusive. As previously mentioned, this organization does not help you to easily discern group patterns. At another extreme, grouping the data into two arbitrary groups, such as scores above 150 and those at 149 or below, would also not be useful in determining group patterns. Thus, you must decide how many groups are to be used in making the grouped frequency distribution.

Determination of the Appropriate Number of Groups.

Deciding how many groups are to be used in making a grouped frequency distribution is determined, for the most part, on the basis of the goals initially set for organizing the data. For example, suppose the teacher used tests that had been standardized by a particular group of researchers who claimed that differences of twenty points adequately discriminated between individuals demonstrating different levels of mastery. In this case, the teacher would be relying on criteria external to the collected data in determining how patterns in the data should be displayed.

Starting with the highest scores in Table 3.4, the first grouping or class interval includes scores starting with 281 and ending with 300. These values represent, respectively, the lower and upper apparent limits of this class interval. More specifically, the **lower apparent limit** and **upper apparent limit** of a class interval are defined respectively to be the lowest and highest score represented in the interval. In this example, 281 would be the lower apparent limit and 300 would be the upper apparent limit. Individuals having scores within this interval would be assumed to have demonstrated equal mastery. In contrast, individuals scoring between 261 and 280 would suggest a different level of mastery than those scoring between 281 and 300. Individuals scoring between 261 and 280 would also be assumed to have demonstrated equal mastery. These differences and similarities would be assumed to hold throughout the entire scale from 1 to 300. If the teacher accepted these assumptions, then the data would be organized on the basis of these 20-point differences as in Table 3.4.

In creating Table 3.4 from Table 3.2, the number of actual scores between 281 and 300, inclusive, are determined. By examining scores falling between 281 and 300 in Table 3.2 you can see that there are two scores of 282, one score of 291 and one score of 297 giving a sum of four. This becomes the frequency of the interval of 281–300 in Table 3.4. For the interval of 261–280, the sum of frequencies between 261 and 280, is 1 + 2 + 1 + 3 = 7 because there is one score of 261, two of 264, one of 273,

TABLE 3.4
Grouped Frequency Distribution of Fictional Midterm Scores Including Midpoints of Each Interval ($i = 20$)

Class Interval	Midpoint (X')	Frequency (f)
281–300	290.5	4
261–280	270.5	7
241–260	250.5	8
221–240	230.5	13
201–220	210.5	12
181–200	190.5	12
161–180	170.5	4
141–160	150.5	2
121–140	130.5	2
		$\Sigma f = 64$

and three of 279. This procedure is used throughout the entire array until every score is accounted for in making the grouped frequency distribution in Table 3.4.

Organizing the data in this fashion gives nine class intervals. The symbol k indicates the number of class intervals in the grouped frequency distribution. In Table 3.4, $k = 9$. Note that the lowest class interval is 121–140. In a grouped frequency distribution you would not continue down to the very bottom of the scale, 1–20, because no scores exist for this interval.

Conventions Followed When Organizing Data. When grouped frequency distributions are constructed, one convention followed requires arranging the intervals on the basis of descending order starting with the highest group.

A second convention followed requires determining the highest and lowest class intervals on the basis of the actual data and not on the basis of scores that potentially could be obtained. The highest class interval is defined in such a way that the raw score with the highest numerical value is placed into this class. Likewise, the lowest class interval in the distribution must be defined in such a way that the raw score with the smallest numerical value is placed into this class. Table 3.4 stops at the class 121–140 because the lowest midterm score obtained by a student is 136. The table started with the class interval 281–300 in order to include the score 297. Had it been the case that the highest midterm score was 279, the highest class interval in Table 3.4 would have been 261–280. There are situations where either the highest value and/or lowest value of the characteristic being measured has not been determined. In such cases the particular interval is left open at the appropriate limit of the interval. Suppose two students in the example had not taken the second and third exams and the teacher did not know whether they would request make-ups. Their scores might be excluded or a lower interval could be added and written as 120 (and lower) to include these two students. In a situation where the highest score cannot be determined, some designation—for example, the highest score actually measured and in parentheses some indication such as "or higher"—is written as the upper limit of the highest class interval.

A third convention followed is that once you have defined one of the class intervals on the basis of its apparent limits, all other class intervals must be the same size. This is to facilitate the computation of several descriptive statistics that you will encounter in later chapters. If they are not the same size, as with open intervals, some descriptive statistics cannot be computed. Thus, open intervals should be avoided when possible. The size of a class interval can be described on the basis of its width, which is symbolized by i. To determine i a computational formula is usually applied. This formula requires that the lower real limit (**LRL**) of the lowest possible score in the interval be subtracted from the upper real limit (**URL**) of the highest possible score in the interval. In symbols the formula for i of any class interval is as follows:

Formula 3.1

$$i = URL - LRL$$

Recall from Chapter 2 that the real limits of a number can be obtained by adding to and subtracting from the number one-half the unit of measurement used in obtaining the number. Correspondingly, the **upper and lower real limits of a class interval** are one-half the unit of measurement above and below the upper and lower apparent limits, respectively. Thus, the **class interval width** is the distance between the lower real limit of the class and the upper real limit of the class. The i for a class interval with apparent limits of 7 and 11, and a unit of measurement equal to 1, would be obtained by subtracting the lower real limit, 6.5, from the upper real limit, 11.5. This gives you the value 5 for i. Note that the correct value for i would *not* have been obtained had the apparent limits been subtracted ($11 - 7 = 4$). The class interval width divided by the unit of measurement represents the possible number of *different* scores contained within the interval. For example, in a class interval defined as 7–11, i is equal to 5. Since the unit of measurement is one there are five (5/1) different possible scores contained in this interval: 7 is the first score, 8 the second, 9 the third, 10 the fourth, and 11 the fifth.

The Class Interval Midpoint. An important class interval value used in computing several descriptive statistics is the midpoint of the class interval. The **midpoint of a class interval,** symbolized by X', is the middle score value of the class interval. It is obtained by summing the limits, either real or apparent, and dividing by 2. The midpoint of the interval 141–160 in Table 3.4 is 150.5. This can be determined by summing the real limits 140.5 + 160.5, which equals 301, and dividing this sum by 2 (301/2), which equals 150.5.

Each of the class intervals in a grouped frequency distribution always differs from another on the basis of i. Once one midpoint has been calculated, the midpoints for all other intervals are obtained by sequentially adding or subtracting i from the intially obtained midpoint. Each interval thereafter is either increased or decreased by i. For example, as 150.5 is calculated to be the midpoint for the interval 141–160, the midpoint for the interval 161–180 can be determined by adding i (which equals 20) to the midpoint 150.5. This calculation reveals that the midpoint of the interval 161–180 is 170.5. Likewise, the interval below 141–160, that is, 121–140, has the midpoint of 130.5, obtained by subtracting 20 from 150.5. In those cases where you have to determine midpoints of class intervals, it is suggested that you find the midpoint of the lowest class interval and then determine the midpoints of each successive interval by adding i to each respective midpoint. Midpoints of each class interval are also presented in Table 3.4.

Practical Value. Examination of Table 3.4 gives you a very easily read summary of the pattern of how the group is doing. There is a clustering of scores in the middle categories, and as you move to either the high or low end of the distribution, fewer scores are obtained. However, note the trade-off made in organizing the data as a grouped frequency distribution. The actual scores of the collected data can no longer be determined, and the range of the raw scores is distorted in the frequency distribution. Recall that the range of the raw scores was calculated to be 162 (297.5 − 135.5). The range in a grouped frequency distribution is determined by subtracting the lower real limit of the lowest class interval from the upper real limit of the highest class interval. The range determined from the distribution in Table 3.4 is 180, (300.5 − 120.5).

Remember that at the beginning of the example of grouped frequency distributions, the teacher decided to organize the data based on information other investigators suggested, that is, categories based on twenty test-score units. Frequently, the specific number of categories or the category width is not given. The investigator must then use suggested guidelines for creating grouped frequency distributions when external criteria are not available. As you will see in the next section, conventions are usually followed. Each investigator, however, will have to make specific decisions in applying these conventions to data.

PROGRESS ASSESSMENT 3.4

1. Form a grouped frequency distribution based on interval width (i) of size 4 from the simple frequency distribution in Progress Assessment 3.3.
2. For your grouped frequency distribution calculate the following:
   a. the upper and lower apparent limits of the highest class interval
   b. the upper and lower real limits of the highest class interval
   c. k

***Grouped Frequency Distribution in the Absence of Designated
External Criteria.*** When forming grouped frequency distributions on
the basis of raw scores, there are three general recommendations to be
followed:

1. No fewer than ten and no more than twenty class intervals should
   be used, that is $10 \leq k \leq 20$. This is suggested so that when different
   investigators examine similar events, their summaries can be compared relatively easily and with some consistency.

2. The interval width, i, should be selected from the following set of
   values: 1, 2, 3, 5, 10, or multiples of 5 or 10 such as 15, 20, and 25.
   These numbers are usually selected for i because they allow for easier
   calculations than numbers such as 11, 17, or 22.

3. The lower or upper apparent limit of the class intervals should be integer multiples of i. In other words, i divides evenly into the apparent
   lower or upper limits. This is recommended so that calculations involving characteristics at one interval can easily be determined for
   another by modifying the initially obtained value by a multiple of i.

Please note that none of these recommendations is sacred. Every investigator needs to determine whether or not adherence to them organizes
his or her data in a way that answers the questions of interest. More often
than not, following these conventions will result in an efficient and accurate organization of data.

Conforming to these recommendations requires that a few calculations
be made to determine the range, values for i and k, the lower and upper
apparent limits of the lowest class interval, and the apparent limits of the
remaining class intervals.

Determining the Raw Score Range. The first step is to determine
the range of your raw scores. In the example, the range is 162 (297.5 −
135.5). Note that you could calculate the range from either the raw scores
in Table 3.1 or the array in Table 3.3. You will find it easier to work from
an array because the data have been organized,

Selecting Values for i and k. Once the range is known, the second
step in constructing this distribution requires that values for i and k be
selected. Use the following formula to determine i and k:

Formula 3.2   Range/$i \approx k$,

where k is rounded to the next larger whole number.

In a trial-and-error fashion divide the range by several of the preferred
values for interval widths, such as 5, 10, 15, or 20. For example, dividing
162 by 5 quickly tells you that 5 is inappropriate for i. If i equals 5, k equals
33 (162/5 = 32.4 rounded to 33). Applying this procedure for i equal to
10, 15, and 20, respectively, gives values for k of 17 (rounding of 162/10),
11 (rounding of 162/15), and 9 (rounding of 162/20). Thus, of the preferred

interval widths, only 10 and 15 create an acceptable number of intervals. Remember you are trying for no fewer than ten and no more than twenty class intervals. In this case you would use 15 for i because it is preferable to start with a frequency distribution with the smaller number of class intervals. Usually you have two possible values for i. You then have to decide which of the two best summarizes your data. Oftentimes that requires constructing both frequency distributions and then determining which of the two produces the better summary. Construction of frequency distributions is done in a similar fashion no matter what the values of i and k. Construction of a frequency distribution for the data where i = 15 and k = 11 is presented in the following sections.

Establishing the Apparent Limits for the Lowest Class Interval.

After selecting values for i and k, the third step is to determine the apparent limits of your lowest class interval. Remember the previous recommendation that integer multiples of i should be used for either the lower or upper apparent limits. To determine an appropriate lower apparent limit, find the lowest raw score and divide it by the value of i. Take the whole number from this division, that is, drop the remainder, and multiply the whole number by i. This will give you the value of an appropriate lower apparent limit for your lowest class interval. Looking at the array in Table 3.2, you can easily determine the lowest score to be 136. Dividing 136 by i, which is 15, gives you the number 9.07. Dropping the decimal remainder and then multiplying the whole number 9 by 15, that is, i, gives you the appropriate lower apparent limit, 135. Once you have the lower apparent limit, add the value i minus 1 (i − 1) to it. You then have determined the upper apparent limit of the particular interval. In the midterm scores example, 135 is used as the lower apparent limit of the lowest class interval. Adding the value 14 (that is, 15 − 1) to this lower apparent limit produces an upper apparent limit of 149.

Creating the Remaining Class Intervals.

The fourth and final step followed in constructing this distribution is to create the remaining class intervals by adding i to the apparent limits of each successive interval. In the example, the next interval following 135–149 would be 150–164. This is determined by adding 15 to 135 and to 149. Continue to add 15 to each apparent limit until you create a class interval that contains the highest score in your collected data. Examining Table 3.2, you can see that the highest score is 297. As can be seen in the grouped frequency distribution of Table 3.5, you must present all class intervals in a continuous fashion between the class interval that contains the lowest score and the class interval that contains the highest score.

Applying the Format.

As was the case with the grouped frequency distribution presented in Table 3.4, the summary in Table 3.5 reveals a clustering of scores in the middle of the distribution and a decrease in frequency of scores that move away from the center of the distribution. The

TABLE 3.5
Grouped Frequency Distribution of
Midterm Scores of Students Enrolled
in Fictional Class

Class Interval	Frequency (f)
285–299	2
270–284	6
255–269	5
240–254	6
225–239	10
210–224	15
195–209	3
180–194	13
165–179	0
150–164	0
135–149	4
	$\Sigma f = 64$

cautions and trade-offs discussed in relation to the grouped frequency distribution based on external criteria are identical to those associated with grouped frequency distributions formed uniquely from the original data. Care must be taken not to hide, exaggerate, or create patterns of information that do not accurately reflect patterns in the original data.

PROGRESS ASSESSMENT 3.5

Form a grouped frequency distribution based on the simple frequency distribution that you constructed in Progress Assessment 3.3 part 1 by responding to the following questions and problems:

1. What are the highest and lowest raw scores?
2. What are the recommended numbers for k and what are the preferred values for i?
3. What are preferred values for lower apparent limits of class intervals?
4. What is the range of the raw scores?
5. Based on trial-and-error evaluation of the range divided by i, what did you select for k and i? Explain why you made your specific selections?
6. Determine an appropriate lower apparent limit for the lowest class interval.
7. Complete the grouped frequency distribution.

Relative Frequency Distribution

A frequency distribution helps you to extract information from your data more easily than you could from raw scores. Comparing two or more frequency distributions of similar data, especially if sample sizes differ, can be made easier if the frequency distributions are converted to relative frequency distributions. A **relative frequency distribution** is a frequency distribution that also includes a relative frequency column where each frequency is expressed as a percent of the total frequency. In order to transform frequencies to relative frequencies, simply divide the frequency of each score or class interval by the sum of the frequencies (Σf) and multiply this quotient by 100. Table 3.6 is a relative frequency distribution of the exam scores summarized in Table 3.5. You can confirm this by transforming each frequency to a percent frequency and determining whether or not you obtain the same percentages shown in Table 3.6.

PROGRESS ASSESSMENT 3.6

1. Create a relative frequency distribution with $i = 3$ from the grouped frequency distribution in Progress Assessment 3.5.
2. Create a relative frequency distribution with $i = 5$ from the grouped frequency distribution in Progress Assessment 3.5.

TABLE 3.6
Relative Frequency Distribution of Fictional
Midterm Scores Where $i = 15$

Class Interval	Frequency f	Relative Frequency rel f
285–299	2	3.1
270–284	6	9.4
255–269	5	7.8
240–254	6	9.4
225–239	10	15.6
210–224	15	23.4
195–209	3	4.7
180–194	13	20.3
165–179	0	0.0
150–164	0	0.0
135–149	4	6.2
	$\Sigma f = 64$	

Cumulative and Percent Cumulative Frequency Distributions

As you see in Table 3.7, a **cumulative frequency distribution** is a frequency distribution that includes a running total of frequencies at each interval starting at the lowest score or class interval. The values in the cumulative frequency column are determined by summing the frequencies of each successive class interval starting at the lowest interval. In Table 3.7 the first value in the cumulative frequency column is 4 because there were four scores in the interval 135–149. The next value remains 4, based on the sum of 4 and 0. Likewise, since there was a zero frequency in the interval 165–179, the cumulative frequency at 165–179 is also 4, based on the sum of 4 + 0 + 0. The cumulative frequency for the interval 180–194 is 17, that is, 4 + 0 + 0 + 13. Continuing up the distribution, the highest value under the cumulative frequency column is 64, which equals the value of N. If you find your highest cumulative frequency does not equal N, then you have made a mistake in adding the frequencies and need to recalculate the cumulative frequency column.

In addition to the advantages of organizing your data as simple or grouped frequency distributions, the cumulative frequency distribution allows you to readily determine the number of scores falling at or below a particular score or class. For example, if you obtained a midterm score of 255, you can easily see in Table 3.7 that fifty-one students had lower scores. Furthermore, if you convert this value to a percentage, you can determine the percentage of students that had lower scores. This conversion

TABLE 3.7
Cumulative and Percent Cumulative Frequency Distributions of Midterm Scores of Students Enrolled in Fictional Class

Class Interval	Frequency f	Cumulative Frequency cum f	Percent Cumulative Frequency Percent cum f
285–299	2	64	100.00
270–284	6	62	96.9
255–269	5	56	87.5
240–254	6	51	79.7
225–239	10	45	70.3
210–224	15	35	54.7
195–209	3	20	31.2
180–194	13	17	26.6
165–179	0	4	6.2
150–164	0	4	6.2
135–149	4	4	6.2
	$\Sigma f = 64$		

is accomplished in the same way that frequency was converted to relative frequency. The value 51 is divided by the sum of the frequencies (64) and multiplied by 100, yielding a percent cumulative frequency of 79.7 (see Table 3.7). A **percent cumulative frequency distribution** is formed when the cumulative frequency for each class interval is converted to a percent cumulative frequency. Such a distribution allows for efficient calculations of values used to describe the relative standing of an individual within a group.

PROGRESS ASSESSMENT 3.7

1. Create a cumulative frequency distribution with $i = 3$ from the grouped frequency distribution in Progress Assessment 3.5.
2. Create a percent cumulative frequency distribution with $i = 5$ from the grouped frequency distribution in Progress Assessment 3.5.

SUMMARY

This chapter introduces you to ways of organizing data into a variety of tables: arrays, simple frequency distributions, grouped frequency distributions, relative frequency distributions, cumulative frequency distributions, and percent cumulative frequency distributions. The uses and advantages of these various formats are discussed.

KEY DEFINITIONS

array   An arrangement of data organized from the highest numerical value to the lowest.

class intervals   Groups that are numerically defined in such a way that any given raw score can belong to one and only one of the groups.

class interval width   The distance between the lower real limit of the class and the upper real limit of the class.

cumulative frequency distribution   A frequency distribution that includes a running total of frequencies at each interval, starting at the lowest class interval or score.

frequency   The number of times a particular raw score occurs, symbolized by f.

grouped frequency distribution   An arrangement of data organized on the basis of mutually exclusive groups of raw scores, called class intervals. The number of times each raw score occurs within a class interval is determined and listed as the frequency of the interval.

i Symbol for interval width.

$i = URL - LRL$ Formula for obtaining *i*.

k A symbol used to refer to the number of class intervals in a grouped frequency distribution.

lower apparent limit The lowest score value associated with a particular class interval.

midpoint of a class interval The middle score value of a class interval obtained by summing either real or apparent limits and dividing by 2.

percent cumulative frequency distribution A frequency distribution in which cumulative frequency is expressed as a percentage.

range/*i* ≈ *k* Formula used to approximate a value of *k* when forming a grouped frequency distribution.

range of raw scores A value indicating the amount of dispersion among the raw scores. It is obtained by subtracting the lower real limit of the lowest raw score from the upper real limit of the highest score.

raw data or raw scores Data as originally collected.

relative frequency distribution A frequency distribution in which frequency is expressed as a percent of the total frequency.

simple frequency distribution An arrangement of data organized on the basis of the number of times each raw score occurs.

Σ A summation symbol.

upper and lower real limits of a class interval One-half the unit of measurement above and below the upper and lower apparent limits, respectively.

URL and LRL Symbols for the upper real limit and lower real limit of a class interval, respectively.

upper apparent limit The highest score value associated with a particular class interval.

X' Symbol for the midpoint of a class interval.

REVIEW EXERCISES

In the two following exercises determine whether reference is made to

a. populations or samples
b. descriptive or inferential statistics
c. parameters or statistics

   d. biased, random, or randomized samples

   e. independent or dependent samples

   f. experimental design or correlational design

   g. an independent variable, (if so, list levels)

   h. a dependent variable or a dependent measure (if so, specify)

   i. qualitative, discrete quantitative, or continuous quantitative dependent variable or dependent measure

   j. measurement scale of the dependent variable or dependent measure

   k. an operational definition of a dependent variable or measure and independent variable

   l. a specific research hypothesis (if so state the hypothesis)

   m. type of table organization, that is, array, simple frequency distribution, and so forth

   n. range of the organized data

   o. f for the lowest class interval

   p. cumulative f for the second-highest class interval

   q. upper and lower real limits of the lowest class interval

   r. upper and lower apparent limits of the highest class interval

Before answering any of the above, read the entire exercise and then go back to determine the answers.

   1. In addition to calculating midterm scores, the instructor referred to in the beginning of this chapter is interested in determining the better of two computer-aided instruction (CAI) programs purported to help students master statistics. The instructor creates thirty-two pairs of students, matching each pair on the basis of midterm scores as closely as possible. For the remaining half of the term, one member of each pair is randomly assigned to work on computer program A and the other member on program B. All students must attend a three-hour weekly lab where they must work on the computer program. At the end of the term, the instructor looks at grades obtained over four test periods for the second half of the term and organizes these grades in relation to the specific computer programs. The results of the grades for the second half of the semester are shown in Table 3-A. The instructor eventually plans to statistically compare the two groups to determine if one or the other CAI program caused better mastery of the material. The purpose of the comparison is to make recommendations about these CAI programs to all college statistics instructors.

   2. A developmental psycholinguist from Kingston, Ontario, is interested in determining whether or not the age at which a child first utters a word is related to the average number of hours television is left on each week during a child's waking hours. A group of parents randomly selected from the Kingston telephone directory are asked the weekly average number of hours their children are exposed to television during their waking hours and the age at which their first word was uttered. The data are analyzed to determine if there is a relationship between these two variables for Kingston children in general. The weekly average number of hours of TV exposure is listed in Table 3-B.

TABLE 3-A
Data Presented in Table Format Necessary to Answer Review Exercises 1 parts a–r. Program Headings Refer to Specific Groups Given Different Computer-Assisted Instruction Programs and the Total Exam Points Distributed within Each Group.

Program A Class Interval	Frequency f	Relative Frequency rel f	Program B Class Interval	Frequency f	Relative Frequency rel f
285–299	1	3.1	285–299	2	6.2
270–284	0	0.0	270–284	2	6.2
255–269	2	6.2	255–269	4	12.5
240–254	4	12.5	240–254	3	9.4
225–239	8	25.0	225–239	8	25.0
210–224	4	12.5	210–224	5	15.6
195–209	4	12.5	195–209	4	12.5
180–194	6	18.8	180–194	3	9.4
165–179	2	6.2	165–179	0	0.0
150–164	0	0.0	150–164	1	3.1
135–149	1	3.1			
	$\Sigma f = 32$			$\Sigma f = 32$	

TABLE 3-B
Data Presented in Table Format Necessary to Answer Review Exercises 2 parts a–r. Class Interval Heading Refers to Average Number of Hours Children Were Exposed to Television.

Class Interval	Frequency (f)
19–20	1
17–18	2
15–16	1
13–14	1
11–12	5
09–10	8
07–08	14
05–06	8
03–04	4
01–02	1
	$\Sigma f = 45$

ANSWERS TO PROGRESS ASSESSMENTS

3.1   See Table 3-C.

3.2   **1.** See Table 3-D

             2. Highest = 80; lowest = 36

             3. Range = 80.5 − 35.5 = 45.0

3.3   **1.** See Table 3-E.

             2. Σf = 45.

TABLE 3-C
**Subject Code (Including Sex, m or f) and Age in Weeks When Child
Uttered First Word from Data Reported in Progress Assessment 3.1,
N = 45**

Code	Age	Code	Age	Code	Age	Code	Age	Code	Age
1m	36	10m	80	19f	44	28f	48	37m	47
2f	36	11f	52	20m	46	29f	64	38f	42
3f	76	12f	68	21f	48	30f	78	39m	43
4f	40	13m	40	22m	48	31m	51	40f	62
5m	45	14m	73	23m	49	32f	58	41m	40
6m	48	15f	58	24f	46	33m	48	42f	51
7f	52	16m	64	25m	40	34m	59	43m	44
8m	52	17m	44	26m	44	35f	62	44f	70
9f	56	18f	36	27m	70	36f	46	45f	36

TABLE 3-D
**Array of Subject Code and Age (in Weeks) at Which Child Uttered First
Word in Data of Progress Assessment 3.1, N = 45**

Code	Age	Code	Age	Code	Age	Code	Age	Code	Age
10m	80	35f	62	31m	51	20m	46	38f	42
30f	78	40f	62	42f	51	24f	46	4f	40
3f	76	34m	59	23m	49	36f	46	13m	40
14m	73	15f	58	6m	48	5m	45	25m	40
27m	70	32f	58	21f	48	17m	44	41m	40
44f	70	9f	56	22m	48	19f	44	1m	36
12f	68	7f	52	28f	48	26m	44	2f	36
16m	64	8m	52	33m	48	43m	44	18f	36
29f	64	11f	52	37m	47	39m	43	45f	36

TABLE 3-E.
Simple Frequency (*f*) Distribution of Age in Weeks
(*X*) of Children When First Word Was Spoken as
Reported in Progress Assessment 3.1

Age		Age		Age		Age		Age	
X	*f*	*X*	*f*	*X*	*f*	*X*	*f*	*X*	*f*
80	1	71	0	62	2	53	0	44	4
79	0	70	2	61	0	52	3	43	1
78	1	69	0	60	0	51	2	42	1
77	0	68	1	59	1	50	0	41	0
76	1	67	0	58	2	49	1	40	4
75	0	66	0	57	0	48	5	39	0
74	0	65	0	56	1	47	1	38	0
73	1	64	2	55	0	46	3	37	0
72	0	63	0	54	0	45	1	36	4

3.4 **1.** See Table 3-F.

 2. a. Upper apparent limit = 80; lower apparent limit = 77.

  b. Upper real limit = 80.5; lower real limit = 76.5.

  c. $k = 12$.

3.5 **1.** Highest score = 80; lowest score = 36.

 2. Recommended values of k are $10 \le k \le 20$; preferred values for i are 1, 2, 3, 5, 10, or multiples of 5 or 10.

 3. An integer multiple of i.

 4. Range is $80.5 - 35.5 = 45$.

 5. For $i = 3$, $k = 45/3 = 15$; for $i = 5$, $k = 45/5 = 9$. *Note:* Because 3 and 5 are both acceptable values for i using the method for selecting the lower apparent limit of the class interval, answers are presented for both $i = 3$ and $i = 5$.

 6. For $i = 3$, lower apparent limit of the lowest class interval = 36; for $i = 5$, the lower apparent limit = 35.

 7. See Tables 3-G and 3-H.

3.6 **1.** See Table 3-I.

 2. See Table 3-J.

3.7 **1.** See Table 3-K.

 2. See Table 3-L.

TABLE 3-F
**Grouped Frequency Distribution of Age in Weeks
(Class Interval) at Which Child Uttered First Word
for Data in Progress Assessment 3.1, ($i = 4$).**

Class Interval	Midpoint	Frequency (f)
77–80	78.5	2
73–76	74.5	2
69–72	70.5	2
65–68	66.5	1
61–64	62.5	4
57–60	58.5	3
53–56	54.5	1
49–52	50.5	6
45–48	46.5	10
41–44	42.5	6
37–40	38.5	4
33–36	34.5	4
		$\Sigma f = 45$

TABLE 3-G
**Grouped Frequency f Distribution of Age in Weeks (Class Interval)
at Which Child Uttered First Word for Data in Progress Assessment
3.1, ($i = 3$)**

Class Interval	Midpoint	f	Class Interval	Midpoint	f
78–80	79	2	54–56	55	1
75–77	76	1	51–53	52	5
72–74	73	1	48–50	49	6
69–71	70	2	45–47	46	5
66–68	67	1	42–44	43	6
63–65	64	2	39–41	40	4
60–62	61	2	36–38	37	4
57–59	58	3			
				$\Sigma f = 45$	

TABLE 3-H
Grouped Frequency Distribution of Age in Weeks
(Class Interval) at Which Child Uttered First Word
for Data in Progress Assessment 3.1, (i = 5)

Class Interval	Midpoint	Frequency (f)
80–84	82	1
75–79	77	2
70–74	72	3
65–69	67	1
60–64	62	4
55–59	57	4
50–54	52	5
45–49	47	11
40–44	42	10
35–39	37	4
		Σf = 45

TABLE 3-I
Relative Frequency Distribution of Age in Weeks (Class
Interval) at Which Child Uttered First Word for Data in
Progress Assessment 3.1, (i = 3)

Class Interval	Frequency f	Relative Frequency rel f
78–80	2	4.4
75–77	1	2.2
72–74	1	2.2
69–71	2	4.4
66–68	1	2.2
63–65	2	4.4
60–62	2	4.4
57–59	3	6.7
54–56	1	2.2
51–53	5	11.1
48–50	6	13.3
45–47	5	11.1
42–44	6	13.3
39–41	4	8.9
36–38	4	8.9
	Σf = 45	

TABLE 3-J
Relative Frequency Distribution of Age in Weeks (Class Interval) at Which Child Uttered First Word for Data in Progress Assessment 3.1, ($i = 5$)

Class Interval	Frequency f	Relative Frequency rel f
80–84	1	2.2
75–79	2	4.4
70–74	3	6.7
65–69	1	2.2
60–64	4	8.9
55–59	4	8.9
50–54	5	11.1
45–49	11	24.4
40–44	10	22.2
35–39	4	8.9
	$\Sigma f = 45$	

TABLE 3-K
Cumulative Frequency Distribution of Age in Weeks (Class Interval) at Which Child Uttered First Word for Data in Progress Assessment 3.1, ($i = 3$)

Class Interval	Frequency f	Cumulative Frequency cum f
78–80	2	45
75–77	1	43
72–74	1	42
69–71	2	41
66–68	1	39
63–65	2	38
60–62	2	36
57–59	3	34
54–56	1	31
51–53	5	30
48–50	6	25
45–47	5	19
42–44	6	14
39–41	4	8
36–38	4	4
	$\Sigma f = 45$	

TABLE 3-L
Percent Cumulative Frequency Distribution of Age in Weeks (Class Interval) at Which Child Uttered First Word for Data in Progress Assessment 3.1, ($i = 5$)

Class Interval	Frequency f	Percent Cumulative Frequency percent cum f
80–84	1	100.0
75–79	2	97.8
70–74	3	93.3
65–69	1	86.7
60–64	4	84.4
55–59	4	75.6
50–54	5	66.7
45–49	11	55.6
40–44	10	31.1
35–39	4	8.9
	$\Sigma f = 45$	

Organizing a Set of Data: Graphs and Displays

*I*n this chapter you will learn more about how to organize data in ways that reveal more information than can be obtained from raw scores. The chapter deals with methods used to show overall patterns or trends in the data. Although a variety of procedures are used to depict data the discussion focuses on two that reveal group patterns or trends either as a diagram (**graph**) or a pictorial organization of raw data (**display**). Graphs and displays can be constructed from raw scores or data that have already been organized as simple frequency distributions. Graphs can also be constructed from data organized as a group frequency distribution. This chapter provides some examples of each.

Although the basic procedures for constructing graphs and displays are introduced in this chapter, you will encounter these topics in many of the later chapters. As you will see, graphs are not only helpful in extracting information from data, but they can also help you decide how to analyze data.

Specific topics covered in this chapter include the general format used in presenting graphs, decisions made in selecting the appropriate type of graph, and methods used in constructing graphs and displays. Individual characteristics and advantages of each type of presentation are also discussed.

SELECTING AN APPROPRIATE FORMAT

You need to carefully determine which format—graphs, displays, or tables—should be used in presenting data. Rarely would you use more than a single format to depict your data in a formal report. In trying to decide which format to use, create preliminary drafts of each to see which one most accurately reflects the information provided by the data. Careful examination of your drafts should help you decide which of the formats to use.

GENERAL FORMAT OF GRAPHS

If you decide to use a graph format, follow these conventions to depict your data correctly:

1. Describe each graph fully in a figure caption.
2. For each set of scores indicate a clearly identified zero point on the graph.
3. Represent frequencies and the characteristic of interest or events counted on the appropriate axes.
4. Proportion axes correctly.
5. Label the axes properly.

Individual investigators must ultimately decide how these specific conventions should be applied to their data. In most cases, however, investigators closely follow these general conventions in ways described in this chapter. As usual, conventions are not given any priority arrangement and are numbered on an arbitrary basis.

Graphs are always presented as figures. A **figure** is a graph that includes a label number and figure caption describing the information presented in the graph. Figures 4.1 and 4.2 illustrate the general format used in presenting graphs.

Figure Captions

One convention followed in constructing figures is that the word *Figure*, a figure number, and a figure caption are included at the *bottom* of the graph. In contrast, Chapter 3 indicated that table headings are placed at the *top* of tables. This distinction between tables and figures should be maintained. Note also that the figure captions as shown in Figures 4.1 and 4.2 are within the left and right margins of the graph, the letters appearing in block form at least one line under the labels of the horizontal axis. Figure numbers are used so that a reader can refer to a specific graph from the text on the basis of the numbering system. Figures should be numbered sequentially as presented in a report. The figure caption at the bottom of a graph should

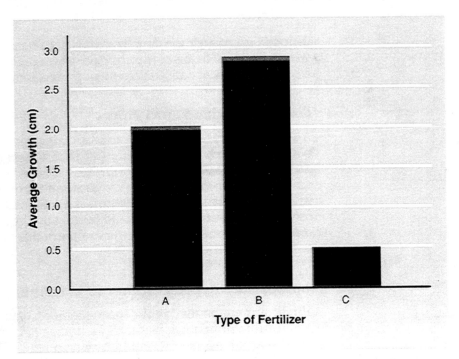

FIGURE 4.1 *Average weekly growth (cm) of plants fed three types of fertilizer.*

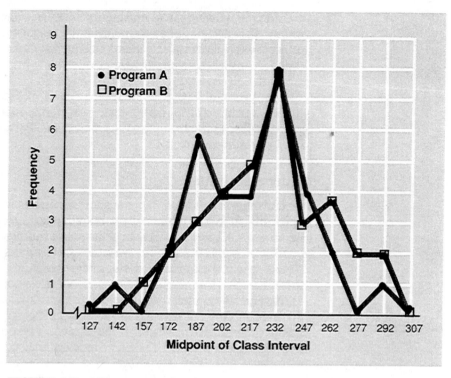

FIGURE 4.2 *Midterm scores of students working on two types of computer-assisted instruction programs, N per group = 32.*

concisely summarize the data presented in the figure. In contrast to tables, where the initial letters of the principal words of the headings are capitalized, typical rules of capitalization and punctuation are used for figures.

Clearly Identified Zero Points

A second convention followed in constructing figures is that the intersection of the **X-axis** (horizontal line) and the **Y-axis** (vertical line) reflects the zero-point for both axes. If you create a graph where the axes are not continuous from the intersection, indicate on the graph that this is not the case. There are many ways to do this, but a frequently used method is to construct a gap through the axes indicating that they are not represented continuously from a zero-point. An example of this marking on an X-axis can be seen in Figure 4.2.

Appropriate Representation of Measures

A third convention used in the construction of a figure is that the dependent measures or frequencies such as average plant growth in Figure 4.1 and frequency in Figure 4.2, must be represented on the Y-axis. Also, the independent variable or events counted, such as type of fertilizer in Figure 4.1 and midpoints of midterm score class intervals in Figure 4.2, must be represented on the *X*-axis.

Correctly Proportioned Axes

The size and division of your axes are determined on the basis of a fourth convention involving a proportion based on the length of the *Y*-axis relative to the length of the *X*-axis and your actual data.

The total length of the *Y*-axis should always be less than the total length of the *X*-axis. An acceptable proportion is one in which the total length of the *Y*-axis is somewhere between 60 and 80 percent of the total length of the *X*-axis.

The highest value at the top of the *Y*-axis should be equal to or slightly larger than the highest value to be plotted on the *Y*-axis. This axis is then divided into equal segments and labeled in a way that allows the divisions to be clearly identified. Be careful not to include so many divisions that they clutter your axis and cannot be read. Also be certain that the divisions are not too few for a reader to reasonably estimate values from your *Y*-axis. Note in both Figures 4.1 and 4.2 that you can clearly read the axes and estimate the values of characteristics displayed in the graphs. For example, in Figure 4.1 it is clear that the average growth in centimeters for plants given type B fertilizer is approximately 2.9 centimeters.

Divisions on the *X*-axis must also be equally spaced and clearly labeled. If the event graphed on the *X*-axis is measured on an ordinal, interval, or ratio scale, the divisions are ordered on the basis of magnitude from left to right. The arrangement of categories for nominal events on the *X*-axis is rather arbitrary.

Because you are organizing data, develop a system that allows some type of organization to be imposed upon the data. For example, if the event graphed on the *X*-axis is nominal, categories may be arranged alphabetically or on the basis of their frequency. If you choose to organize the nominal categories on the basis of their frequency, categories with the highest frequency are placed on the left and arranged toward the right in descending order.

In summary, construction of axes requires the length of the *Y*-axis to be about 60–80 percent of the length of the *X*-axis. All values of the actual data should be represented. There should be equal spacing divisions within each axis and clear labeling of the units of division within each axis.

Properly Labeled Axes

Proper labeling is a fifth convention to be followed in constructing a graph. Note that in each figure discussed so far, the labels of both the *X*- and *Y*-axes are written parallel to the direction of the specific axis. The label must describe what is in your graph, for example, average growth and type of fertilizers in Figure 4.1. Rules for capitalization, centering, and so forth vary from discipline to discipline. Unless a particular discipline requires other rules, follow the examples given in this text.

Note there are two types of labels for each axis: the names of the events represented on the axes, such as frequency and midpoints in Figure 4.2 and the units of measurement associated with the scales involved in observing these events. The units of measurement are the numbers 1–9 on the Y-axis and the numbers 127–307 on the X-axis. For frequency on the Y-axis in Figure 4.1, the units are 0.5 centimeters and for type of fertilizer on the X-axis, the units are the nominal labels A, B, and C.

These five conventions provide you with the basic information needed to represent your data clearly and accurately. To construct the graph that is most appropriate for your data, however, there are certain guidelines that must be followed. These guidelines are discussed in the following section.

SELECTING AN APPROPRIATE GRAPH

In selecting the type of graph to construct it is essential to consider three things: (1) the purpose of organizing your data graphically; (2) whether the characteristic of interest is a discrete or continuous variable; and (3) whether the data collected are frequency data such as the number of *A* grades on a statistics exam, or quantitative measures such as IQ scores or heights of basketball players.

The purposes of organizing data may be to display group patterns, trends in the data, relative standing within a group, or the relationship between characteristics. Each of these purposes would require a different type of graphical representation of the data. The type of graph would also be determined in part by the type of variable, discrete or continuous, being measured. For example, representing the frequencies of different political affiliations would require a different type of graph than the frequencies of test scores on a midterm examination. Finally, data collected as frequencies often require different representation than other quantitative measures. Frequencies of test scores on a midterm examination, for example, would require a different type of graph than a student's test scores obtained on all exams throughout the term.

GRAPHS INVOLVING FREQUENCIES

It should be clear from the examples in the previous section that frequency data can be collected for a variety of different variables and, as such, can be depicted graphically in a variety of forms. Just what form a graph involving frequencies takes will, then, depend on the purpose of the graph and the type of variable observed. In the following sections you will examine the determining factors for a variety of graphs involving frequency data.

Bar Graphs

Assume that your only purpose is to display group patterns and that the events you have measured are discrete. Recall the discussion of a grouped frequency distribution based on external criteria from Chapter 3. Table 4.1 is based on the grouped frequency distribution presented in Table 3.4. This distribution is of midterm scores based on 20-point divisions supplied by researchers examining the effectiveness of tests in determining the level of mastery students reach. Suppose further that these researchers divide the categories on the basis of the grading scale described in Table 4.1. If the instructor decides to make a graph of letter grades and number of students obtaining each grade, a bar graph would have to be used. A **bar graph** is a graph used to display values of discrete variables where the height of each bar represents the frequency of the observed characteristic.

Given that the instructor in the example is interested in displaying group patterns and that the groups are based on discrete measures, in this case, letter grades, a bar graph of this information can be constructed as shown in Figure 4.3.

Notice that the original scale of measurement was changed in order to construct Figure 4.3. Continuous units of measurement, that is, test scores, were converted into 8 discrete intervals, $A, B+, \ldots F$. Note that the last two class intervals are combined as one category, F. The letter grades in Figure 4.3 are placed on the X-axis with F grades placed on the left nearest the intersection of the X and Y-axes. Note also that frequencies are plotted on the Y-axis with 0 starting at the bottom. A space is left between

TABLE 4.1
Grouped Frequency Distribution of Fictional Scores Including Midpoints of Each Interval, Cumulative Frequency, and Percent Cumulative Frequency (i = 20). Modified from Table 3.4.

Class Interval	Midpoint	Grade	Frequency f	Cumulative Frequency	Percent Cumulative Frequency
281–300	290.5	A	4	64	100.0
261–280	270.5	B +	7	60	93.8
241–260	250.5	B	8	53	82.8
221–240	230.5	C +	13	45	70.3
201–220	210.5	C	12	32	50.0
181–200	190.5	D +	12	20	31.2
161–180	170.5	D	4	8	12.5
141–160	150.5	F +	2	4	6.2
121–140	130.5	F	2	2	3.1
			$\Sigma f = 64$		

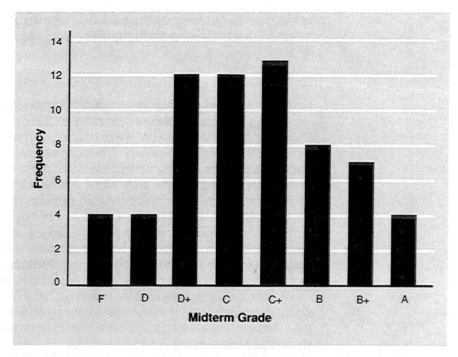

FIGURE 4.3 *Bar graph of midterm grades presented in Table 4.1, N = 64.*

the bars because the categories have been defined as discrete. Vertical bars of *equal width* are placed over each letter category so that the height of the bar corresponds to the respective frequency.

     The advantage of organizing the data in this fashion is that you obtain an immediate visual impression of how the scores are distributed. Clearly you have the largest grouping of scores in the *C* categories and fewer scores as you move toward the *A* and *F* categories.

PROGRESS ASSESSMENT 4.1

Following the five conventions for constructing graphs, create a bar graph for the information in Table 4.1. Use only the five categories *A, B, C, D,* and *F* by combining the frequencies of the plus grades with the non-plus grades. For example, *B+* and *B* should be used for the *B* category.

Histograms

Suppose the instructor did not want to classify the data on the basis of discrete letter grades. Instead, assume a decision is made to display group patterns on the basis of 20-point categories. It could then be argued that the categories are continuous, theoretically ranging from scores of 1 through 300. Since no raw scores fall below 135, there is no reason to represent intervals less than 121–140. If one assumes that these categories are continuous, then a graph, as shown in Figure 4.4, can be used to depict the data. Note that the Y-axis remains exactly the same as the Y-axis in the bar graph, Figure 4.3. An important change, however, is made on the X-axis. Instead of discrete letter categories, the real limits of each class interval appear on the X-axis. A second change from Figure 4.3 is that the bars adjoin each other conveying the assumed continuity of the measured characteristic. The type of graph shown in Figure 4.4 is called a histogram. A **histogram** is a series of adjoining bars of equal width where the height of each bar represents the frequency of a particular interval and the area of the bar corresponds to relative frequency. A histogram is used to present group patterns for frequency data observed for a continuous variable.

PROGRESS ASSESSMENT 4.2

Complete the following for the information provided in Table 4.1:

1. Create a grouped frequency distribution where the class intervals are now combined in such a way that $i = 40$, starting with the interval 121–160.

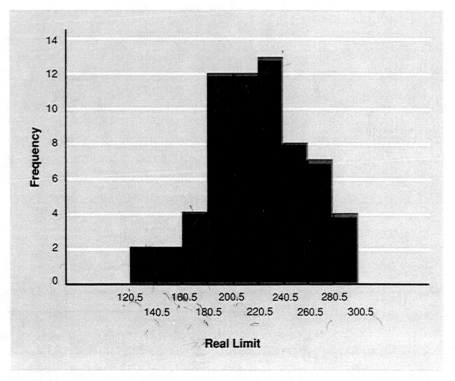

FIGURE 4.4 *Histogram of hypothetical midterm scores where highest possible score was 300, N = 64.*

2. Draw a histogram for the grouped frequency distribution you created in part 1 of this Progress Assessment.

3. Summarize in words any group patterns revealed in your histogram.

Frequency Polygons

An alternative to the histogram is a frequency polygon. **A frequency polygon** is a graph used to represent group patterns for values of continuous variables organized as a frequency distribution. In a frequency polygon, points representing frequencies of each class interval are connected by a straight line to points representing frequencies of adjoining class intervals. Frequency polygons are often used when two or more frequency distributions are compared on the same graph as shown in Figure 4.2. If only one distribution is to be presented, the preference of the investigator usually determines whether or not a histogram or frequency polygon is used. As you will see, histograms and frequency polygons are very similar to each other.

Frequency Polygons versus Histograms. A frequency polygon of the midterm scores of Table 4.1 is shown in Figure 4.5. The major differ-

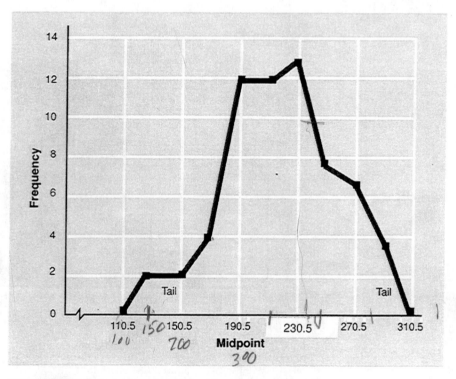

FIGURE 4.5 *Frequency polygon of midterm scores presented in Table 4.1.*

ence between a histogram and frequency polygon is that points are placed over the midpoints of the class interval and connected as a line in the frequency polygon. In contrast, bars are placed over the real limits of the class interval for the histogram. Note that in the frequency polygon the line is extended to the zero frequency at the midpoint of the next occurring interval at both ends of the distribution. The line is specifically extended to 0 at these midpoints because no scores fall at or beyond either of these intervals. By anchoring the polygon to the x-axis the area of any portion of the polygon can be calculated.

Use of the Frequency Polygon.   The frequency polygon is used extensively for statistical purposes. Organizing the data in this fashion reveals group patterns and trends for data assumed to be continuous. In addition, the frequency polygon is important statistically because the area defined beneath any portion of the curve is a direct reflection of the number of scores contained in that area of the curve and corresponds to relative frequency. In other words, percent area under the curve is proportional to percent frequency. For example, in Figure 4.5 the percent area under the curve between the midpoints 110.5 and 310.5 is 100 percent. Likewise you can see in Table 4.1 that the percent frequency between 110.5 and 310.5 also has to be 100 percent. The relationship between percent area of a curve and percent frequency will again be discussed in Chapter 10 as this relationship is the basis for determining probabilities when using frequency distributions and statistical tables.

Symmetry and Skewness.   Because of the extensive use of frequency polygons, some of their characteristics have been rigorously examined. These curves reflect the actual distribution of the raw scores. The curves themselves are often referred to as distributions and are described in relation to their symmetry or skewness. The **tails of a distribution** refer to those areas of the polygon at the left and right extremes of the distribution as marked in Figure 4.5. The shape of the tails, in part, allows you to estimate whether or not a distribution is symmetrical or skewed.

A **symmetrical distribution** is one where the right half of the distribution is the mirror image of the left half. The graph in *section a* of Figure 4.6 represents a symmetrical distribution.

The distribution in *section b* of Figure 4.6 is a negatively skewed distribution. A **negatively skewed distribution** has the longer tail extending to the left toward the zero value of the X-axis. A negative skew is caused by a greater concentration of frequency of scores at the high score values and a trailing of frequencies at the low score values.

A **positively skewed distribution** has the longer tail extending to the right away from the zero value of the X-axis as shown in *section c* of Figure 4.6. Positive skews are the result of a greater frequency of scores at the low score values and a trailing of frequencies at the high score values.

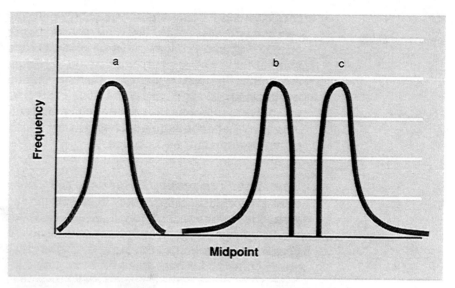

FIGURE 4.6 *Examples of symmetrical (a), negatively skewed (b), and positively skewed (c) frequency polygons.*

As you can see in Figure 4.6, the type of skewness of a distribution is produced as a result of those scores that vary from the majority of your measures. Usually the most important aspect to note about a frequency distribution is whether or not it is symmetrical. The symmetry or lack of it determines, in part, the statistical methods used to summarize and analyze data. You will find further discussion of symmetry in Chapters 5 and 6.

PROGRESS ASSESSMENT 4.3

Use the histogram in Progress Assessment 4.2 to answer the following problems:

1. Convert the histogram for Progress Assessment 4.2 into a frequency polygon.
2. Determine whether the frequency polygon is symmetrical, negatively skewed, or positively skewed. Explain your answer.

Percent Cumulative Frequency Curves

A **percent cumulative frequency curve** is a graphic representation of a percent cumulative frequency distribution where adjoining points connected by straight lines are used to represent the percent cumulative frequency of the observed characteristics. It is often used for the purpose of presenting relative standing of any particular score for frequency data obtained when the variable of interest is a continuous variable. You may recall from Chapter 3 that cumulative frequency refers to a running total of frequencies starting at the bottom of a distribution.

A percent cumulative frequency distribution lists the running total of frequencies expressed in percentage form. The percent cumulative frequency curve is constructed in a manner similar to the frequency polygon except that the points of each class interval are placed over the upper real limits of each interval instead of the midpoints and the line is not anchored to the X-axis at the highest class interval. Also, the label of the Y-axis is "percent cumulative frequency."

A percent cumulative frequency curve constructed from Table 4.1 is shown in Figure 4.7. This type of graph allows a reader to quickly determine the relative standing of any particular score. For example, you can easily determine that about 31 percent of the students have scores at or below 200.5 by examining Figure 4.7. Simply determine where a perpendicular line drawn from 200.5 on the X-axis intersects the percent cumulative frequency curve. Then determine where a line drawn perpendicular from this point intersects the Y-axis as shown in Figure 4.7. In this case the line intersects the Y-axis at a percent cumulative frequency of approximately 31. Thus, 31 percent of the cases fall at or below 200.5. Measures of relative standing will be discussed in greater detail in Chapter 7.

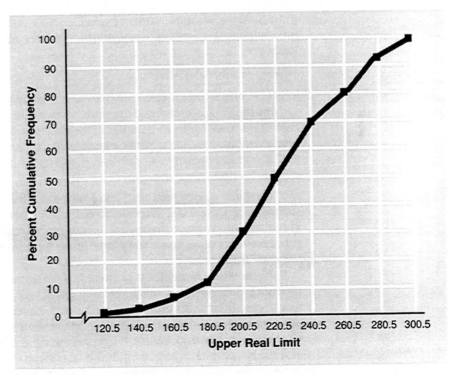

FIGURE 4.7 *Percent cumulative frequency curve of midterm grades presented in Table 4.1, N = 64.*

PROGRESS ASSESSMENT 4.4

For the grouped frequency distribution in part 1 of Progress Assessment 4.2 based on $i = 40$, complete the following items:

1. Create a percent cumulative frequency distribution using a table format.

2. Create a percent cumulative frequency curve for the percent frequency distribution created in part 1 of this Progress Assessment.

3. On the basis of your answer to part 2 of this Progress Assessment, estimate the relative standing of an individual who obtained a midterm score of 220.

GRAPHS INVOLVING QUANTITATIVE MEASURES

For all of the graphs discussed so far, values on the Y-axis always have represented frequencies. Frequency polygons are extremely useful in statistics as they are the basis for determining probabilities. There are many times, however, when graphs are used to display outcomes other than frequency counts, for example, the results of a specific experiment or correlational study. You may recall from Chapter 2, that an experiment involves manipulating an independent variable and obtaining a dependent measure, whereas, a correlational study involves obtaining two dependent measures.

Bar and Line Graphs

In an experiment the dependent variable is usually measured on some type of continuous scale and the dependent measure is used in constructing a graph. As usual, the five conventions discussed previously are followed when constructing graphs summarizing the data collected from an experiment. The independent variable is represented on the X-axis and the dependent variable on the Y-axis.

Bar Graphs. A bar graph is used when the independent variable is assumed to represent a discrete variable. It is constructed exactly as the bar graph used to represent frequencies except that the height of the bars in this case represents some measured aspect of the dependent variable instead of frequencies.

Suppose an investigator is interested in determining the effect of three different fertilizers on average weekly growth of a particular houseplant. The investigator might obtain the arithmetic average for each of the three groups and graph the results. Such an example is given in Figure 4.1. Compare the bar graph in Figure 4.1 representing the effect of different types of fertilizer on plant growth with the bar graph in Figure 4.3 showing the frequency distribution of grades in a specific course. Note that the only difference, albeit an important difference, concerns what is plotted on the Y-axes.

Line Graphs.   If the independent variable is assumed to represent a continuous variable, then a line graph is used to organize the data. A **line graph** is a graph used to display continuous variables where adjoining points, which represent summaries of measured values of specific characteristics, are connected by straight lines. It is used to depict trends in a dependent variable graphed as a function of an independent variable.

Line graphs are constructed in a manner similar to frequency polygons. For the line graph, however, the independent variable is represented on the *X*-axis and the dependent variable on the *Y*-axis. Also, the lines are not anchored to the *X*-axis on a line graph unless a zero value of the dependent measure is obtained.

Generally, line graphs depict a trend in the dependent variable in relation to changes in the value of an independent variable. For example, suppose an investigator is interested in determining if caffeine affects reaction time as measured in seconds. Assume four groups of human subjects are randomly assigned to one of four caffeine dosage groups, 0, 100, 200, or 300 milligrams. In addition assume that each is given a task where the time taken to push a button after hearing a specific tone is recorded to the nearest 0.1 second. After collecting these data, the experimenter obtains the arithmetic average reaction time for each group. The results of this experiment are shown in the line graph in Figure 4.8. The graph indicates that reaction time does not change until a moderate dose (200 mg) of

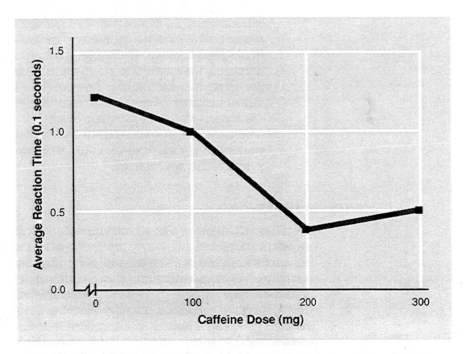

FIGURE 4.8   *Hypothethical example of average reaction time (seconds) recorded after subjects received one of four dosages of caffeine. Note: A 5-ounce cup of brewed coffee contains about 80–150 milligrams of caffeine.*

caffeine is administered. Comparing Figure 4.5 and Figure 4.8 shows the similarities and differences of frequency polygons and line graphs.

PROGRESS ASSESSMENT 4.5

For each of the following experiments: (a) construct an appropriate graph of the information resulting from the experiment, (b) explain why you selected your specific type of graph, and (c) summarize in words the trend or pattern in the graph.

1. An experiment is performed to examine the effects of time on retention of a five-page fictional story composed by an investigator. Five groups of students (each N = 20) from a general psychology class are allowed to study the story for 15 minutes. The five groups are randomly assigned to different retention groups. Each group is tested either 1, 5, 10, 15, or 30 days after the initial study period and the number of errors are recorded. The test consists of 150 multiple choice items each worth 1 point. Arithmetic averages are obtained for each group. The results of this experiment are such that the arithmetic average for the 1-day group is 50, 5-day is 80, 10-day is 95, 15-day is 90, and the 30-day is 98.

2. In a follow-up study this same investigator randomly selects 20 English majors, 20 biology majors, 20 math majors, 20 psychology majors, and 20 physical therapy majors from another section of general psychology. The subjects are given the same story and administered the same test as in the initial study. The test is administered to each group immediately after studying the story. Again number of errors are recorded on the 150-item multiple choice test and the arithmetic average is obtained for each group. The average error score is 35 for English majors, 42 for biology majors, 39 for math majors, 40 for psychology majors, and 22 for physical therapy majors.

Scatter Plots

Recall from Chapter 2 that a correlational study requires obtaining two dependent measures, arbitrarily represented as X and Y, that are measured for each individual in a defined sample or population. Correlational studies usually involve measurement of two continuous variables. If data are organized for the purpose of displaying the relationship between the two variables, then a graph called a scatter plot is used. A **scatter plot** is a graph of pairs of X and Y values of dependent measures obtained in a correlational study. The specific X and Y values measured for each sample member are plotted on their respective axes. Except for the convention of proportioning axes, conventions previously discussed are followed when constructing scatter plots. *In a scatter plot the X-axis and Y-axis are of equal length.*

Figure 4.9 is an example of a scatter plot of hypothetical data obtained by graphing math Scholastic Aptitude Test scores (*X*) and verbal Scholastic Aptitude Test scores (*Y*) of incoming sociology majors at a small liberal arts university. Each and every raw score obtained in the study is represented. For example, the point underscored in the lower left corner represents the *X* and *Y* scores of a student who had a math SAT score of 300 and a verbal SAT score of 400. Scatter plots are useful in evaluating whether or not two events are related to each other in a specific fashion. You will learn more about scatter plots in Chapter 8, which deals with measures of relationship.

PROGRESS ASSESSMENT 4.6

The accompanying data represent average number of hours watching television (*X*) on a daily basis and final number of points (*Y*) out of 400

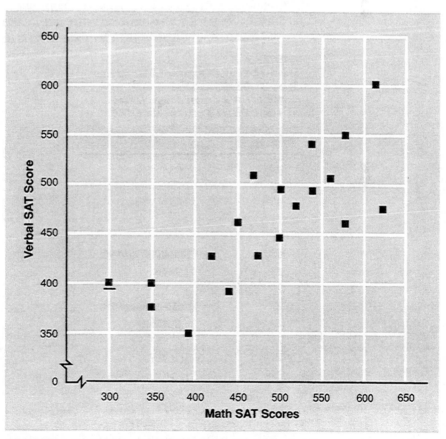

FIGURE 4.9 *Math and verbal SAT scores of incoming sociology majors at a small liberal arts college, N = 19.*

possible in a general psychology class for fifteen subjects.

X:	2	3	8	3	2	5	5	1
Y:	390	200	190	250	300	350	100	400
X:	7	1	6	4	4	1	6	
Y:	150	320	220	270	140	350	250	

1. Make a scatter plot of the data.
2. Summarize in words what the graph reveals.

STEM-AND-LEAF DISPLAYS

A **stem-and-leaf display,** introduced by John Tukey (1977), is a pictorial representation revealing the group pattern using individual raw scores. It includes a label number and a display heading describing the information presented, as shown in Display 4.1.

Stem-and-leaf displays are usually produced from simple frequency distributions or arrays. To maintain the consistency of examples, the array created in Table 3.2 has been reconstructed here as Table 4.2.

For this type of display, the raw data from the array are first divided

DISPLAY 4.1
Stem-and-Leaf Display of Midterm
Scores of Students ($N = 64$)
Enrolled in Fictional Class. Unit
= 1 such that 18 9 equals 189.

Stems	Leaves
13	66
14	77
15	
16	
17	
18	000033366999
19	2558
20	
21	003336666999
22	222558
23	1117777
24	36999
25	258
26	144
27	3999
28	22
29	17

TABLE 4.2
Student Identification Numbers (ID #) and Midterm
Scores (X) from Table 3.2 Arranged as an Array. Each
Score is Divided into a Stem (2 digits) and Leaf (1 digit)
as Indicated by Vertical Line (|) Separating Digits for
Each Score (N = 64).

Column 1		Column 2		Column 3		Column 4	
ID #	X	ID #	X	ID #	X	ID #	X
16	29|7	48	24|9	14	21|9	11	18|9
53	29|1	50	24|6	27	21|9	39	18|9
33	28|2	49	24|3	43	21|9	55	18|9
41	28|2	7	23|7	4	21|6	12	18|6
22	27|9	30	23|7	20	21|6	60	18|6
23	27|9	61	23|7	32	21|6	3	18|3
29	27|9	62	23|7	52	21|6	18	18|3
63	27|3	21	23|1	36	21|3	51	18|3
5	26|4	47	23|1	37	21|3	6	18|0
38	26|4	57	23|1	54	21|3	9	18|0
45	26|1	17	22|8	1	21|0	44	18|0
26	25|8	34	22|5	24	21|0	56	18|0
10	25|5	64	22|5	35	19|8	25	14|7
2	25|2	13	22|2	42	19|5	31	14|7
8	24|9	40	22|2	58	19|5	15	13|6
19	24|9	59	22|2	28	19|2	46	13|6

into two parts, stems and leaves. Each raw score is divided into leading digits (**stems**) and trailing digits (**leaves**). The actual division of the digits is based on an investigator's judgment as a result of working with these displays. The division of the digits is such that the leaf or trailing digits are used to show the patterns of scores.

Note that the raw scores in Table 4.2 are all three-digit numbers ranging from 136 to 297. Dividing each raw score into a 2-digit stem and 1-digit leaf (as marked by the line through each score in Table 4.2) gives the basic structure to your stem-and-leaf display. Also note in Table 4.2 that dividing the raw scores into 2-digit stems reveals that there are few gaps in the actual scores as you proceed down and examine the first two digits. The division that is selected for the stems and leaves should minimize the number of gaps in the stems, and at the same time, it should also preserve any group pattern that exists in the data.

The first gap in the stems in Table 4.2 appears between the scores 210 and 198 in Column 3 where the stem values have a gap of one unit, that is, 21, no 20, then 19. The second gap appears between the raw scores 180 and 147 where stem units have a gap of 3 units, specifically, a stem 18, no 17, no 16, no 15, and then a stem of 14. Once the raw scores have been divided into stems and leaves, a display similar to that of Display 4.1 can be constructed. Note that stem-and-leaf displays have components of tables and graphs.

If you can imagine a histogram tilted 90 degrees to the right on its side, you can see that the height of the leaves make up the bars seen in a histogram and the stems make up the division of the *X*-axis normally seen on a histogram. If you look at the leaves across from the stem of 18, you can see that they are created by taking the last digit of each of the scores—180, 180, 180, 180, 183, 183, 183, 186, 186, 189, 189, 189—and listing them in a row in order of magnitude. Knowing this, you can look at the stem-and-leaf display and determine the entire set of raw scores as you can for a simple frequency distribution. For example, looking at the stem 29 which has leaves of 1 and 7 tells you that the numbers 291 and 297 are used in constructing this portion of the display.

As always, a description of the display of the data is needed. The word "Display" along with a number label, a display heading, and a units scale are included at the *top* of the display enabling anyone reading it to determine the type of data collected. The unit of measurement is given so that a decimal point can be placed in reference to the digit that makes up the leaf of a particular raw score. In this case the leaf of a score 181 was 1; thus the units are ones. Had we been using numbers such as 18.1, using the same stem and leaf division would require that our units would be tenths (Unit = 0.1) and in this example in the display heading, 18 9, would equal 18.9. Labels for the stem and leaf columns are also required, as shown in Display 4.1.

The stem-and-leaf display is an interesting method of presenting data because it allows an investigator whose purpose is to reveal group patterns to maintain the identity of each data point.

PROGRESS ASSESSMENT 4.7

Use the accompanying information—age in weeks when child spoke first word from a study involving 45 children—to answer parts 1 and 2 of this Progress Assessment.

80, 78, 76, 73, 70, 70, 68, 64, 64, 62, 62, 59, 58, 58, 56, 52, 52, 52, 51, 51, 49, 48, 48, 48, 48, 48, 47, 46, 46, 46, 45, 44, 44, 44, 44, 43, 42, 40, 40, 40, 40, 36, 36, 36, 36

1. Create a stem-and-leaf display.
2. Summarize in words group patterns evident in the display.

SUMMARY

This chapter concludes the discussion of organizing data as figures and displays and of the basic conventions followed for constructing both. You have learned about the specific methods used in constructing bar graphs, histograms, frequency polygons, percent cumulative frequency curves, and stem-and-leaf displays. You have also considered the reasons for graphing data and the advantages offered by each type of graph. In Chapter 5 you will examine procedures for extracting information from raw data by using summary statistics that describe the central tendency of a distribution.

KEY DEFINITIONS

bar graph A graph used to display discrete variables where the height of each discrete bar represents the frequency or a measure of each observed characteristic.

display A pictorial organization of raw scores that reveals group patterns or trends.

figure A graph format of data organization that includes a label number and caption describing the information presented.

frequency polygon A graph used to display continuous variables where adjoining points, which represent the frequency of each observed characteristic, are connected by straight lines that are anchored to the X-axis.

graph A diagrammatic representation of group patterns or trends.

histogram A graph used to display continuous variables where the height of each adjoining bar represents the frequency of each observed characteristic and the height and area of which are proportional to total frequency.

leaves The division of trailing digits of raw scores used to create stem-and-leaf displays.

line graph A graph used to display continuous variables where adjoining points, which represent summaries of measured values of specific characteristics, are connected by straight lines. It is used to depict trends in a dependent variable graphed as a function of an independent variable.

negatively skewed distribution An asymmetrical distribution where the greatest frequency of scores occurs for high scores and there is a trailing of frequencies at the low-score values. Its frequency polygon would reveal a tail extended to the left of the graph toward the zero value of the X-axis.

percent cumulative frequency curve A graph used to display continuous variables where adjoining points connected by straight lines are used to represent the cumulative frequency (represented as a percent of the total frequency) of the observed characteristic.

positively skewed distribution An asymmetrical distribution where the greatest frequency of scores occurs for low scores and there is a trailing of frequencies at the high-score values. Its frequency polygon would reveal a tail extended to the right of the graph away from the zero value of the *X*-axis.

scatter plot   A graph showing the points representing each of the *X*- and *Y*-values obtained for the dependent measures of a correlational study.

stem-and-leaf display   A pictorial representation of group patterns using raw scores that includes a label number and a display heading describing the information presented.

stems   The division of leading digits of raw scores used to form stem-and-leaf displays.

symmetrical distribution   A distribution that has left- and right-half mirror images.

tails of a distribution   Those areas of a frequency polygon at the left and right extremes of the distribution.

X-axis   The horizontal axis of a graph.

Y-axis   The vertical axis of a graph.

REVIEW EXERCISES

For the following six exercises identify

a. method of data collection such as experimental, correlational, or just a frequency count

b. independent variable (include levels) and dependent variable, if appropriate

c. dependent measures, if appropriate

d. population or type of sample, such as biased, random, randomized, independent, or dependent

e. terms that are operationally defined, including their definitions

f. characteristics observed or measured as either discrete or continuous variables

g. scale of measurement used

h. the type of graph or display you would use, the labels for the *X*- and *Y*-axes, and your rationale for the type of organization you selected

Read each exercise in its entirety before you answer parts a–h.

1. A developmental psychologist is interested in determining whether young infants prefer to look at pictures of human faces or pictures of squares and triangles. The amount of time (in seconds) infants spend looking at drawings of faces or line drawings of figures is obtained when both figures are presented simultaneously for a two-minute interval. Infants are obtained from a nearby day-care center.

2. A local politician is interested in the makeup of registered voters in a specific district. One thousand addresses are randomly selected and each house is

visited to determine the political affiliation of each person in the household who is of voting age. The frequency is determined of these 1000 households for each of the following categories: Republicans, Democrats, Independents, Libertarians, Others, and Not Registered.

3. From a community of 100,000 households, a local business sends questionnaires to every tenth address listed in a complete mailing directory of the community. The individuals are asked to report their combined yearly incomes anonymously. A total of 5,000 questionnaires are returned. The data are organized as a group frequency distribution and then the results are graphed in a way that group patterns are evident.

4. A local health official believes that exercise is related to academic success. A table of random numbers is used to select one hundred students from a roster of high-school students in the community. The average number of hours spent exercising each week and the grade-point-average based on a 100 percent point system is obtained for each of the one hundred students. A graph of these data points is made to examine the original hypothesis.

5. The dean of students at a large state university is interested in the relative standing of each student in the current freshman class, which numbers 5,000 on academic aptitude as measured by Scholastic Aptitude Test scores. The scores are already organized as a grouped frequency distribution and are graphed to estimate quickly relative standing of any particular student.

6. A junior-high principal has just received the test scores of eighth-grade students who had taken a standardized achievement test with possible scores ranging between 200 and 800. The scores are organized as a simple frequency distribution. The principal would like to organize the data in a way that group patterns are evident and that each individual score is revealed in the organization.

ANSWERS TO PROGRESS ASSESSMENTS

4.1   See Figure 4-A.

4.2   1. See Table 4-A.

2. See Figure 4-B.

3. The majority of cases fall at the middle-most values. Frequencies decrease at lowest and highest score values.

4.3   1. See Figure 4-C.

2. The distribution is symmetrical in appearance as indicated by the fact that the distribution can be divided into relatively equal halves.

4.4   1. See Table 4-B.

2. See Figure 4-D.

3. About 50 percent had lower scores; see perpendiculars in Figure 4-D.

4.5   1. See Figure 4-E.

b. Days can be considered a continuous variable and the experimenter is interested in depicting a trend (how rentention changes over days)

    c. Retention performance decreases up to ten days and then appears to reach an asymptotic level.

  2. **a.** See Figure 4-F.

    b. Major in college is a discrete variable.

    c. Physical therapy majors appear to do best, followed by English majors, and no differences appear among other majors.

4.6   **1.** See Figure 4-G.

  2. Students with higher points in psychology course watch television less than the students with lower points in the psychology course.

4.7   **1.** See Display 4-A.

  2. Most children spoke their first word between 40 and 60 weeks of age; however, four spoke at 36 weeks and eleven uttered their first word between 62 and 80 weeks.

TABLE 4-A
Grouped Frequency Distribution of Fictional Scores Modified from Table 4.1

Class Interval	Frequency f
281–320	4
241–280	15
201–240	25
161–200	16
121–160	4
	$\Sigma f = 64$

TABLE 4-B
Percent Cumulative Frequency Distribution for Data Organized in Table 4-A, Progress Assessment 4.2

Class Interval	Frequency f	Cumulative Frequency	Percent Cumulative Frequency
281–320	4	64	100.0
241–280	15	60	93.8
201–240	25	45	70.3
161–200	16	20	31.2
121–160	4	4	6.2
	$\Sigma f = 64$		

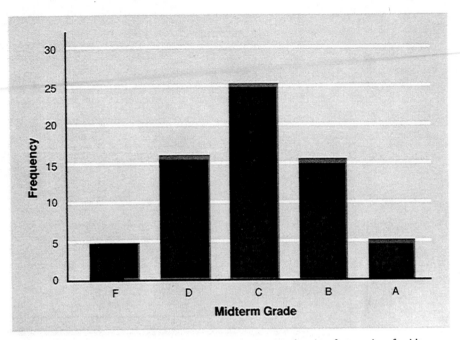

FIGURE 4-A *Bar graph for Progress Assessment 4.1 showing frequencies of midterm grades, N = 64.*

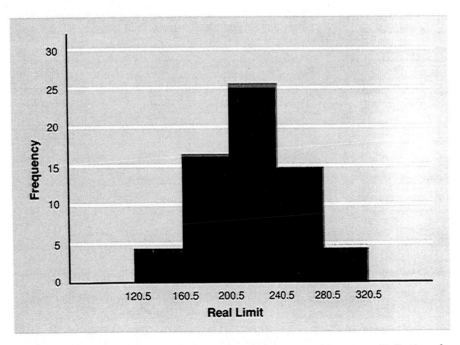

FIGURE 4-B *Histogram of midterm scores based on grouped frequency distribution of part 1 of Progress Assessment 4.2, N = 64.*

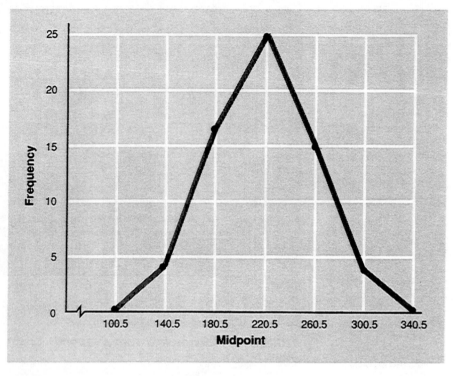

FIGURE 4-C   *Frequency polygon of midterm scores based on grouped frequency distribution of Progress Assessment 4.2, N = 64.*

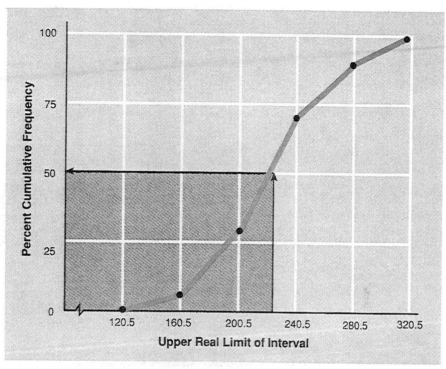

FIGURE 4-D *Percent cumulative frequency curve of midterm scores given in part 1 of Progress Assessment 4.2 where N = 64.*

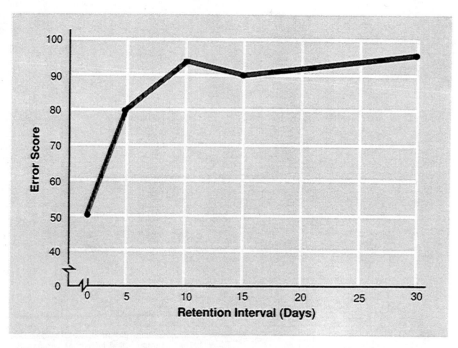

FIGURE 4-E   *Average error scores obtained at 1, 5, 10, 15, or 30-day retention tests. Low scores reflect good retention, N per group = 20.*

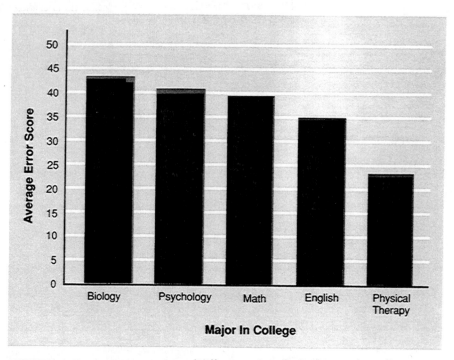

FIGURE 4-F   *Average error scores of different majors obtained on an immediate memory retention test, N = 20. Note: Low scores reflect good retention.*

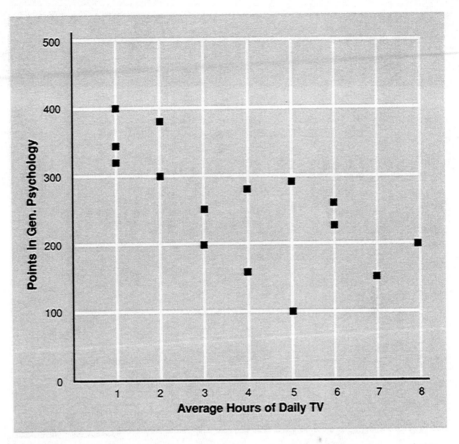

FIGURE 4-G *Average daily hours of watching television and total points out of 400 possible points for 15 students in a general psychology class.*

DISPLAY 4-A
Stem-and-Leaf Display of Age (in Weeks) When First Word Was Spoken. Unit = 1 such that 3 6 equals 36 weeks.

Stems	Leaves
3	6666
4	000023444456667888889
5	112226889
6	22448
7	00368
8	0

Measures of
Central Tendency

In the previous two chapters you found that organizing numerical data into a frequency distribution (Chapter 3) and depicting them graphically (Chapter 4) helped you to get a clearer picture of the patterning of scores or shape of the distribution than would have been possible from inspection of the raw data. But organization provided more than that. It also enabled you to extract information from the data more readily than would have been possible if the data had been left in raw form. The highest and lowest score, the number of times each score occurred, and the score that occurred most often, for example, are readily obtained by inspecting frequency distributions. These scores provide information about how spread out the distribution is and the typicality of the scores. This type of information is necessary for a numerical description of a group characteristic which, at times, is more important than the group pattern.

Oftentimes you may want a score that in some way typifies the distribution. As a college student you may want to know the score on the Scholastic Aptitude Test that is most representative of students in your entering class or you may want to know what salary you can expect to earn after graduation. Similarly, a shoe manufacturer may be more interested in the shoe size that is most typical or popular for a group of college-age males than in the group pattern. In these cases, interest is in a statistic that is most representative of the group characteristic of interest. A statistic that is most representative of the characteristic of interest or most typifies a distribution of scores is called a **summary statistic.**

A summary statistic that most typifies a distribution might be the score that is obtained by most members of the group, the point that divides the distribution in half, or the point about which most of the individual scores tend to cluster. Such scores or points generally tend to be towards the center of the distribution. Summary statistics that tend to be towards the center of the distribution are called **measures of central tendency.** In this chapter we begin our discussion of summarizing data by defining and examining three commonly used measures of central tendency.

MODE

The shoe manufacturer can obtain information about the shoe size most often requested by a group of young-adult male customers by inspecting a frequency distribution of that group's shoe sizes. The shoe size most often requested is, of course, the shoe size with the greatest frequency. This shoe size is referred to as the modal shoe size. The **mode,** then, is the score or measure that occurs most often. In a simple frequency distribution the mode is the score with the greatest frequency, and in a grouped frequency distribution it is considered to be the midpoint (X') of the interval with the greatest frequency. For qualitative data or data measured along a nominal scale, such as religious affiliation, it is the category with the greatest number of entries.

Characteristics of the Mode

The mode is the easiest measure of central tendency to obtain and is most often used when the measure of the sample characteristic or dependent variable is either normally or inherently discrete. Recall from Chapter 2 that a discrete measure is one that can take on only certain values within the limits of the variable. Shoe size is an example of a variable that is normally discrete. You would not find a shoe manufacturer making a size 9 5/6 shoe. Family size is an example of a variable that is inherently discrete. No family can have 3 1/2 children. The mode is also the only measure of central tendency that is appropriate for qualitative data. You would be hard pressed to describe the most typical eye color for Scandinavians other than to name the modal color, that is, the eye color that occurs most often among them.

Limitations of the Mode

Although frequently used in the cases just mentioned, the mode has serious limitations. First, it need not occur. Rectangular distributions, distributions in which all scores have the same frequency, have no mode. Second, there may be more than one mode. Distributions with more than one mode are called multimodal distributions. **Multimodal distributions** are distributions in which the frequencies cluster around two or more nonadjacent scores or class intervals. Third, the mode has poor sampling stability. **Sampling stability** refers to the extent that repeated sampling would lead to the same outcome, in this case the same mode. Fourth, it lacks statistical versatility. **Statistical versatility** refers to the many uses of a summary statistic. A summary statistic that is versatile can be used not only to describe data but also to derive other descriptive measures, and can be used in statistical inference. The mode, which lacks statistical versatility, is used for description and little else.

PROGRESS ASSESSMENT 5.1

1. The following data represent miles walked each day during the month of January by an individual in a fitness program: 8, 5, 7, 6, 9, 3, 2, 1, 6, 5, 8, 4, 2, 6, 3, 5, 5, 7, 6, 4, 3, 4, 7, 5, 4, 0, 5, 1, 3, 2, 4. Find the mode.

2. Find the modal amount of change in the possession of each of eighty fourth graders represented in the simple frequency distribution shown in Table 5-A.

3. The classes shown in Table 5-B represent the ages of residents in a nursing home. Find the modal age.

TABLE 5-A
**Simple Frequency Distribution of
Amount of Change in the Possession
of Each of Eighty Fourth Graders**

Change Possessed X (Cents)	Frequency f
25	3
24	10
23	14
22	26
21	17
20	10

TABLE 5-B
**Grouped Frequency
Distribution of Ages of
Ninety-Three Residents
in a Nursing Home**

Age Class (years)	Frequency f
90–93	4
87–89	5
84–86	8
81–83	11
78–80	18
75–77	16
72–74	14
69–71	10
66–68	6
63–65	1

MEDIAN

The **median,** denoted **Mdn,** is the point in a distribution at or below which 50% of the cases fall. Accordingly, it is also called the 50th percentile and symbolized P_{50}. Although median implies middle, it is not the point halfway between the highest and lowest score. The **midrange** is the halfway point between the highest and lowest score. The midrange is not a commonly used measure of central tendency. The median is the halfway point only with respect to the number of scores falling on each side of it. In an array with an uneven number of scores, for example, it is the middle score. Thus, for the array 9, 9, 9, 7, 6, 5, 5, 4, 1, the median is 6 whereas the midrange is 5. In an array containing an even number of scores, the median is halfway between the two center scores. Thus, for the array 9, 9, 9, 7, 6, 5, 5, 4, 1, 1, the median is 5.5 whereas the midrange is again 5. Calculating the median for data organized into a frequency distribution is somewhat more involved.

Computing the Median of a Frequency Distribution

The median of the grouped frequency distribution in Table 5.1 is computed using the computational Formula 5.1.

Formula 5.1

$$P_{50} = LRL_p + i\left(\frac{[n_{bp} - n_{LRL}]}{f}\right)$$

The letters LRL_p designate lower real limit of the interval containing P_{50}. This interval can be located by determining how many scores constitute half of the sample, that is, the number of scores that should fall at or below P_{50} (n_{bp}), in this case, $0.5 \times 50 = 25$, and counting up the frequency column until you reach the interval that would contain the point below which half of the scores would fall. In this example that interval would be 21–25 since 23 scores fall below its lower real limit and 33 scores fall below its upper real limit. Thus, LRL_p equals 20.5.

The interval width, i, you should recall, equals the distance between the lower real limit and the upper real limit of the class interval. In this example that distance equals 5.

TABLE 5.1
Grouped Frequency Distribution of Scores on a Difficult 50-Point Statistics Exam

Class	Frequency f
46–50	1
41–45	0
36–40	4
31–35	5
26–30	7
21–25	10
16–20	18
11–15	3
06–10	1
01–05	1
	50

The letters n_{LRL} denote the number of scores falling below the lower real limit of the interval containing P_{50}, that is, 23 in the present problem. The symbol f, you recall, refers to frequency; here it refers to the frequency of the interval containing P_{50} that is, in this case $f = 10$. Therefore,

$$P_{50} = 20.5 + 5(\frac{[25 - 23]}{10}) = 21.5$$

Formula 5.1 can also be used to compute the median of a simple frequency distribution. For a simple frequency distribution, the real limits refer to those of the scores and i equals 1.

Characteristics of the Median

The median has both greater sampling stability and greater statistical versatility than the mode. Although it is not used to derive other descriptive measures or to make inferences about population parameters, it is used in nonparametric statistical formulas that permit you to make inferences about the shapes of populations.

Because the median is sensitive to and dependent upon only the number and not the value of the scores falling above and below it, it is the most appropriate measure of central tendency for skewed distributions, such as scores on a difficult statistics exam or the salaries earned by college graduates.

Also, because the median is *not* sensitive to the value of the scores falling above and below it, it can be computed for data sets in which the value of extreme scores are unknown and for open-ended distributions, that is, distributions in which the highest or lowest score or class is indeterminable. For example, because of time considerations, often there are limits put on the number of trials given in a learning experiment. Each of a group of subjects may be permitted 25 trials to learn a list of words. If a subject does not learn the list in 25 trials, he is assigned a number greater than 25, that is, > 25. Suppose that for seven subjects in a learning experiment the number of trials required to learn the list of words is as follows: 14, 16, 17, 19, 21, 25, > 25. A mode for these data does not exist but the median is 19. In the next section you will find that the median is the only measure of central tendency that can be obtained for these data.

PROGRESS ASSESSMENT 5.2

1. Find the median of each of the following data sets:

    Data Set A: 1, 4, 6, 2, 8, 3, 6, 9.
    Data Set B: 2, 3, 7, 8, 3, 10, 6, 13, 12.

2. Find in Table 5-C the median number of freshmen enrolled in elementary statistics courses in 120 small U.S. colleges during the spring semester.

TABLE 5-C
Grouped Frequency Distribution of
Number of Freshman Enrolled in
Elementary Statistics Courses in 120
Small U.S. Colleges during the
Spring Semester

Number of Freshman Class Interval	Frequency f
90–99	1
80–89	6
70–79	6
60–69	8
50–59	12
40–49	14
30–39	24
20–29	36
10–19	10
0–9	3

MEAN

Another summary measure that typifies a distribution is called the mean or arithmetic average. The **mean** or **arithmetic average** is operationally defined as the point in the distribution about which the sum of the raw score deviations equals zero. It is symbolized $\bar{X}$ (pronounced "X-bar"). A **raw score deviation** is the distance a score is from the mean in raw score units. A raw score deviation can thus be symbolized, $X - \bar{X}$. These symbols can be used in a defining equation. A **defining equation** is the symbolic expression of an operational definition. Recall from Chapter 2 that an operational definition is a statement of what something is in unambiguous terms. Thus, the defining equation for the mean is expressed as follows:

Equation 5.1 $$\Sigma(X - \bar{X}) = 0$$

Computing $\bar{X}$ for Raw Data or an Array

The mean for a data set can be obtained by dividing the sum of all the scores (ΣX) by the number of scores (N). The computational formula for the mean of raw data or an array can, therefore, be expressed as follows:

Formula 5.2 $$\bar{X} = \frac{\Sigma X}{N}$$

Consider the following array: 5, 4, 3, 2, 1. These five scores sum to 15. Thus, $\bar{X} = 15/5 = 3$. According to the defining equation for the mean, if the mean is subtracted from each of the five scores in the array and these differences, that is, the raw score deviations, are summed, the sum should equal zero. Subtracting the mean from each score in the array yields the following raw score deviations: $+2, +1, 0, -1, -2$. As you can see, scores larger than the mean yield positive raw score deviations, and scores smaller than the mean yield negative raw score deviations. It is quite obvious that the sum of these raw score deviations equals zero. It can be shown algebraically that this holds true for each and every data set or distribution of scores.

Computing the Mean for Frequency Distributions

When raw data or an array is organized into a simple or grouped frequency distribution, Formula 5.2 is not directly applicable. The X column in a simple frequency distribution may, for example, contain scores that were not actually obtained in sampling, and the scores actually obtained are listed only once in the X column. Thus, ΣX cannot be computed simply by adding up the numbers in the X column. Consideration must also be given to the number of times each score occurred, that is, the formula for computing $\bar{X}$ from data organized as a simple frequency distribution must also involve the information provided in the frequency (f) column. The same holds true for data organized as a grouped frequency distribution. In addition, because information about the individual scores is no longer available when data are presented as a grouped frequency distribution, some score must be designated to represent all the scores within a given class interval. In the following sections, Formula 5.3 is translated into a formula for obtaining the mean from data organized as either a simple or grouped frequency distribution.

Simple Frequency Distributions.   When raw data or an array is organized into a simple frequency distribution, computational Formula 5.2 translates into the following:

Formula 5.3
$$\bar{X} = \frac{\Sigma fX}{\Sigma f}$$

This formula directs you to multiply each value in your score (X) column by its corresponding frequency, sum the obtained (fX) values, and divide that sum (ΣfX) by the sum of the frequencies (Σf). An application of this formula is demonstrated in Table 5.2, which depicts data from a hypothetical learning experiment with rats.

Note that unlike the procedure for obtaining $\bar{X}$ for raw data or an array, the X column is not summed. This is because these values, as you recall, represent all *possible* (not obtained) scores between the highest and the

TABLE 5.2
A Simple Frequency Distribution of the Number of Errors (X) Made by Forty Rats in a Maze Learning Experiment

Number of Errors X	Frequency f	fX
5	6	30
4	8	32
3	16	48
2	0	0
1	10	10
	40	120

$$\bar{X} = \frac{\Sigma fX}{\Sigma f} = \frac{120}{40} = 3$$

lowest obtained scores, and they are listed only once. In the experiment there were actually no rats that made a score of 2 and there were 16 rats that made a score of 3, whereas in the X column both 2 and 3 are listed once. Thus, the literal use of Formula 5.2 to find the mean of a frequency distribution would lead to an erroneous value. In such cases Formula 5.2 *must* be translated into Formula 5.3 to find an appropriate value for the mean.

Grouped Frequency Distributions.   Formula 5.3 can also be used to find the mean of a grouped frequency distribution. In such cases, the X in the formula refers to the midpoint (X') of the class interval. The midpoint of the class interval is considered to be the score most representative of the scores within the interval. The use of Formula 5.3 to find the mean of a grouped frequency distribution is illustrated in Table 5.3.

PROGRESS ASSESSMENT 5.3

1. Find the mean of the following data set: 3, 6, 7, 2, 1, 8, 8.
2. Use Table 5-D to find the mean number of boxes of Girl Scout Cookies sold by thirty scouts in a small community.

Using Transformed Scores to Compute the Mean

There are several advantages to transforming scores. Recall from Chapter 3 that transforming the frequencies of a simple frequency distribution to percent cumulative frequencies enables you to determine at a glance the

TABLE 5.3
Grouped Frequency Distribution of Scores on a Difficult 50-Point Statistics Exam

Class	Midpoint X'	Frequency f	fX'
46–50	48	1	48
41–45	43	0	0
36–40	38	4	152
31–35	33	5	165
26–30	28	7	196
21–25	23	10	230
16–20	18	18	324
11–15	13	3	39
06–10	08	1	08
01–05	03	1	03
		50	1165

$$\bar{X} = \frac{\Sigma fX'}{\Sigma f} = \frac{1165}{50} = 23.3$$

percentage of scores falling at or below any given score or the relative standing of the score in the distribution. Two additional advantages of transforming scores are that they make computations simpler and reduce the likelihood of errors. These advantages can be appreciated by recomputing the mean of the data in Table 5.3 using transformed scores. In order to successfully use transformed scores to compute the mean, you must first understand what effect the operations used in the transformation have on the mean of the distribution.

Effect of Transforming Scores on the Mean. The effect on measures of central tendency of adding, subtracting, multiplying, or dividing each score in a distribution by a constant is easy to remember since whatever you do to the scores in a distribution by a constant you also do to the measures of central tendency. The mean of the scores 1, 2, and 3 is 2. If you multiply each of these scores by the constant 2, the mean of the transformed scores, that is, 2, 4, and 6, is 4, or the original mean multiplied by 2. Accordingly, if the scores 1, 2, and 3 were divided by 2 or the constant 2 were added to or subtracted from each score, the corresponding means of the transformed scores would be 1, 4, and 0. You should verify these results by performing these operations on the original data set (1, 2, and 3) and computing the means for scores transformed by division, addition, and subtraction.

PROGRESS ASSESSMENT 5.4

1. Find the mean of 0.5, 1, and 1.5, that is, the scores 1, 2, and 3 divided by 2.

2. Find the mean of -1, 0, and $+1$, that is, the scores that result when 2 is subtracted from 1, 2, and 3, respectively.

3. Find the mean of 3, 4, and 5, that is, the scores that result when 2 is added to 1, 2, and 3, respectively.

4. What would be the mean of the transformed scores if the transformation involved subtracting 5 from each score in a distribution with a mean = 15, and then dividing each of the $X - 5$ scores by 2?

Computational Procedures Using Transformed Scores. If you have verified that whatever you do to the scores in a distribution, by adding, subtracting, multiplying, or dividing by a constant, you also do to the mean, then you are ready to use transformed scores to find the mean of the distribution in Table 5.3. The first two steps in transforming the scores of a grouped frequency distribution that involve subtraction and division can be done in your head and, hence, to save time they should not be done in practice. However, to provide you with a clear understanding of the transformation procedure, the results of these operations appear in Table 5.4.

You should recognize the X' values in Table 5.4 as the midpoints of the class intervals. The values in the column headed X'' are those obtained

TABLE 5-D
Simple Frequency Distribution of Number of Boxes of Girl Scout Cookies Sold by Thirty Scouts in a Small Community

Number of Boxes Sold X	Frequency f
29	1
28	2
27	4
26	7
25	10
24	5
23	0
22	1

TABLE 5.4
Grouped Frequency Distribution of Scores on a Difficult 50-Point Statistics Exam Where X' Is the Midpoint, X'' Is X' – the Midpoint of the Interval 21-25, and X''' Is X''/i

Class	Midpoint X'	$X' - 23$ X''	$X''/5$ X'''	Frequency f	fX'''
46-50	48	25	5	1	5
41-45	43	20	4	0	0
36-40	38	15	3	4	12
31-35	33	10	2	5	10
26-30	28	5	1	7	7
21-25	23	0	0	10	0
16-20	18	-5	-1	18	-18
11-15	13	-10	-2	3	-6
06-10	8	-15	-3	1	-3
01-05	3	-20	-4	1	-4
				50	3

$$\bar{X}''' = \frac{\Sigma fX'''}{\Sigma f} = \frac{3}{50} = 0.06$$

$$\bar{X}' = \bar{X}'''(i) + X'_{sub} = 0.06(5) + 23 = 23.3$$

when the first operation, subtraction, is performed on the midpoints. To get these values you *subtract the midpoint* of the class 21-25, that is, 23, from all the midpoints in the X' column. Any midpoint can be selected. The midpoint to be subtracted should be selected from a class near the center of the distribution. This keeps the values resulting from the second operation, division, at some minimal level.

The column headed X''' contains values obtained when the second operation, division, is performed. To obtain these X''' values, the values in column X'' are divided by the width of the class interval, i. In the present example, $i = 5$. In practice, all you have to do is pick a frequency near the center of the distribution and put a zero next to it. Then you go up the column in which you put the zero by 1's and down the column by -1's; this will give you an X''' column (See Table 5.4).

Find the mean of these transformed scores in the usual manner, that is, multiply the transformed scores by their corresponding frequencies, sum these products, and divide the obtained sum, $\Sigma fX'''$, by the sum of the frequencies, Σf. The obtained value is the mean of the transformed scores.

To get the mean of the original scores (X') in the distribution, you must transform the mean of the X''' values by reversing the operations performed on the midpoints. You initially subtract a midpoint from all other midpoints and divide these differences by the width of the class interval. Reversing these operations requires that you first multiply the mean of the X''' values by the width of the class interval, i, and then add to this quotient the midpoint subtracted (X'_{sub}). In the example the obtained value of the mean of the X''' values is 0.06. We multiplied this by 5, which is the value for i, to get 0.3. We then added to 0.3 the midpoint that was subtracted from every other midpoint to form the X'' column, that is, 23, to get the value, 23.3, for the mean of the original scores in the distribution. This value, of course, is the same value that was obtained in Table 5.3, where we computed the mean of the distribution using the original midpoints.

We encourage you to use transformed scores in computing the mean for frequency distributions for a number of reasons:

1. As mentioned previously it simplifies the computation, since the values that you must work with can be made whole numbers that are equal to or less than ten.

2. Working with small whole numbers reduces the chances of making errors. This is true even if you use a calculator or computer, since both require entering data.

3. The transformation procedure described here also provides you with a method for simplifying the computation of other summary statistics, such as those discussed in Chapter 6, and aids in reducing the likelihood of errors in those computations.

4. Working with transformations now will make you more at ease in using similar transformations as measures of relative standing, which you will encounter in Chapter 7.

5. A thorough understanding of the transformation procedure will aid you in understanding the logic of various tests used to make inferences about population parameters such as those examined in Chapter 14.

PROGRESS ASSESSMENT 5.5

For the frequency distribution in Table 5-E, which organizes data collected on the spelling ability of 100 third graders, transform the scores using the procedure just described and compute the mean of the distribution using the transformed scores.

Characteristics of the Mean

You can tell from using the computational Formulas 5.2 and 5.3 that, whether or not the formulas are used on the original or transformed scores, the mean takes into consideration and depends upon every score in the data set or distribution. It would be impossible, therefore, to compute the mean of a set of scores when some of the scores are missing or unknown. Let us refer here to the example involving the number of trials needed to learn a list of words by the seven subjects discussed in the section on the

TABLE 5-E
Grouped Frequency Distribution of the
Number of Words Spelled Correctly by
100 Third-Grade Children before Being
Eliminated in a Spelling Bee

Class	f
45–49	2
40–44	0
35–39	6
30–34	8
25–29	9
20–24	13
15–19	22
10–14	19
5–9	16
0–4	5

median. Since the exact value of one of the scores was indeterminable, you could not compute the mean in such an instance.

As you will recall, those trial numbers were: 14, 16, 17, 19, 21, 25, >25. For the same reason, you could not compute the mean of a data set organized into the form of an open-ended frequency distribution. This, however, is not a serious limitation since, as Chapter 3 mentions, organizing data into open-ended distributions is not encouraged.

When all the data are available, however, the mean is the most often used measure of central tendency. It is the preferred measure of central tendency for quantitative variables that are or nearly are symmetrical. It is preferred not only because it takes into consideration every score and the number of times each score occurs, but also because it has much better sampling stability than other measures of central tendency and because it is statistically versatile. The mean describes the central tendency of a sample and allows you to derive other important descriptive statistics, such as some measures of dispersion that you will encounter in the next chapter. It is also used in statistical inference. The sample mean is the only measure of central tendency that is an unbiased estimate of the corresponding population parameter, in this case the population mean, μ, (pronounced "mu").

THE MEANING OF UNBIASED ESTIMATE

An **unbiased estimate** of a population parameter is a statistic that on the average equals the parameter. This meaning of *unbiased* can be illustrated by considering the population of scores: 1, 2, 3, 4, 5. Although this may be an unrealistic size for a population it will suffice for our purpose. Think

TABLE 5.5
All Possible Random Samples (N = 2) of Condor Eggs and Corresponding Means with the Following Numbers of Eggs Laid: 1, 2, 3, 4, 5

Possible Samples (N = 2)					Corresponding Means				
1,1	2,1	3,1	4,1	5,1	1.0	1.5	2.0	2.5	3.0
1,2	2,2	3,2	4,2	5,2	1.5	2.0	2.5	3.0	3.5
1,3	2,3	3,3	4,3	5,3	2.0	2.5	3.0	3.5	4.0
1,4	2,4	3,4	4,4	5,4	2.5	3.0	3.5	4.0	4.5
1,5	2,5	3,5	4,5	5,5	3.0	3.5	4.0	4.5	5.0

of the numbers as representing the number of eggs laid by five remaining females of the nearly extinct California condor. All possible random samples of size 2 (N = 2) and the means of those samples are shown in Table 5.5. The first number of the pairs of numbers to the left represent the first sample element selected from the population, and the second number represents the second element selected. Sampling was with replacement.

You compute the mean of the population in the same manner that you compute the sample means, that is, by summing all the scores and dividing by the number of scores in the population, in this case five. Thus, the mean of the population referred to in Table 5.5 is $(1 + 2 + 3 + 4 + 5)/5$ = 3. If you now compute the average of the means in Table 5.5, you find that this average is also 3 and by definition is an unbiased estimate of the population parameter, μ. Although the term *"average"* can have a variety of meanings, in the definition of an unbiased estimate, and throughout this text, it is used synonymously with *mean*. The average of the means, then, refers to the mean of the means. In this case, it is found by summing all the means and dividing by the number of means, that is, 75/25 = 3.

SELECTING A MEASURE OF CENTRAL TENDENCY

Although the mean, unlike the other measures of central tendency, is an unbiased estimate of its corresponding population parameter, there are times when other considerations cause you to choose a different measure of central tendency to describe a data set. This chapter both alludes and makes direct reference to a variety of factors that you should consider when deciding what measure of central tendency best suits your purposes. To reiterate, here are the factors that should be considered in choosing a measure of central tendency:

1. Type of variable, that is, continuous or discrete.
2. Type of data, that is, quantitative or qualitative.
3. The scale of measurement, that is, nominal, ordinal, interval, or ratio.
4. Shape of the distribution, for example, symmetrical or skewed.

5. The versatility of the statistic and the purpose for which it is intended, for example, description only, to derive other measures, or statistical inference.

6. Sampling stability of the measure, that is, its reproducibility.

7. Availability or determinability of the scores.

8. Time and effort required for computation.

RELATIONSHIPS AMONG MEASURES OF CENTRAL TENDENCY

Of course, there are times when it is desirable to compute all three measures of central tendency. Refer again to Table 5.3. The frequency distribution in this table is the same as that in Table 5.1, which was shown to have a median equal to 21.5. The mean for this distribution is computed in Table 5.3 to be 23.3. The midpoint (X') of the interval with the greatest frequency, that is, the mode of this distribution, is 18. Thus, the three measures of central tendency differ substantially.

These three measures taken together can provide summary information about that distribution that cannot be gotten from any single measure of central tendency. If the three measures are identical, then the distribution is a symmetrical, unimodal distribution. When the distribution is unimodal and skewed, the relative position of three measures of central tendency provides information as to the direction of the skew. The median almost always takes a central position with respect to the mean and mode, and the direction of the skew is almost always in the direction of the mean. Thus, if the mean is larger than the median as it is in the distribution in Tables 5.1 and 5.3, the distribution is skewed to the right, or positively skewed. If the mode is larger than the median; the distribution is skewed to the left, or negatively skewed.

PROGRESS ASSESSMENT 5.6

1. Name the most appropriate measure of central tendency for each of the following distributions:

    a. number of papers published by professors at a small university

    b. scores on an extremely easy English examination

    c. quiz grades for a small class in which no two students are likely to get the same grade

    d. the intelligence quotients (IQ's) of ten-year-olds

    e. hat sizes for adult males

2. Give the direction of the skew for each of the following distributions:

    a. a distribution in which the mean is larger than the mode

    b. a difficult statistics exam

> **c.** a distribution in which the median is smaller than the mode
>
> **d.** a distribution of the number of library books stolen by students at a large university
>
> **3.** For each of the following tell if the mean is most likely larger, smaller, or equal to the mode:
>
> **a.** a distribution with a mean = 50 and median = 35
>
> **b.** a distribution with a mode = 15 and a median = 10
>
> **c.** a distribution with a median = 25 and mode = 25

SUMMARY

The summary statistics introduced in this chapter are measures of central tendency. The definitions and characteristics of the three most commonly used measures of central tendency—mode, median, and mean—are presented along with procedures for computing these statistics. A procedure for transforming scores is introduced to make computations of the mean simpler and to decrease the likelihood of errors in computation. The meanings of unbiased statistic and statistical versatility are explained. The mean is the most versatile of the three measures of central tendency, being used for description, for deriving other statistics, and in statistical inference. Also, the mean is the only measure of central tendency that is an unbiased estimate of its corresponding population parameter.

KEY DEFINITIONS

defining equation The symbolic expression of an operational definition.

Mdn A designation for the median.

mean or arithmetic average The point in a distribution about which the sum of the deviations equals zero.

measures of central tendency Scores or points towards the center of a distribution that typify the scores in the distribution.

median The point in a distribution at or below which 50% of the scores fall.

midrange The point halfway between the highest and lowest score.

mode The score or measure that occurs most often in a distribution. For a grouped frequency distribution, it is the midpoint of the interval with the greatest frequency.

μ (pronounced "mu") Symbol for the mean of a population.

multimodal distributions Distributions in which the frequencies cluster around two or more nonadjacent scores or class intervals.

P_{50} The fiftieth percentile; another expression for the median.

$P_{50} = LRL_p + i([n_{bp} - n_{LRL}]/f)$ A computational formula for the median.

raw score deviation A deviation of a score from the mean in raw score units.

sampling stability A reference to the extent that repeated sampling will lead to the same outcome.

statistical versatility Reference to the many uses of a statistic. A summary statistic that is versatile can be used for description, in other statistical derivations, and in statistical inference.

summary statistic A sample measure that in some way summarizes or typifies a distribution.

$\Sigma(X - \bar{X}) = 0$ Defining equation for the mean.

unbiased estimate A statistic that on the average equals the corresponding population parameter.

$\bar{X}$ (pronounced "X-bar") The symbol for the mean of a sample.

$\bar{X} = \Sigma X/N$ The computational formula for the mean of raw data or an array.

$\bar{X} = \Sigma f X/\Sigma f$ The computational formula for the mean of a frequency distribution. For grouped frequency distributions, X refers to the midpoint (X') of the class interval.

REVIEW EXERCISES

1. The number of students attending a general psychology class for ten successive class days were 41, 46, 44, 42, 43, 43, 45, 47, 46, 46.

   a. Rearrange the data into an array.

   b. Specify the sample size.

   c. Specify the type of graph that would most appropriately depict the data.

   d. Determine the mean, median, and mode.

   e. Judging by the values of the mean, median, and mode, determine the direction of skew.

   f. What would the mean be if each score in the distribution was multiplied by 4?

2. The following data represent the number of hours worked daily by a college student in a work-study program during the month of April: 2, 4, 1, 2, 7, 1, 2, 4, 6, 1, 2, 2, 2, 3, 4, 5, 2, 3, 1, 2, 3, 4, 5, 6, 7, 5, 4, 3, 3, 3.

   a. Organize the data into a simple frequency distribution.

   b. Plot a frequency distribution of the data.

   c. Looking at the figure, determine the direction of skew.

   d. Determine the mode of the distribution.

   e. Using Formula 5.1, compute the median of the distribution.

   f. Compute the mean of the distribution.

   g. Does the direction of skew judged by examining the three measures of central tendency agree with your answer to part c?

   h. What would the mean be if 5 were added to each score in the distribution?

3. The following data represent the number of hours of TV watched by each of 90 students during the fall semester: 91, 160, 211, 271, 36, 67, 132, 144, 156, 177, 152, 169, 188, 209, 211, 233, 206, 241, 242, 350, 328, 301, 272, 299, 245, 268, 187, 206, 155, 156, 121, 143, 92, 98, 118, 123, 72, 77, 49, 50, 158, 169, 157, 174, 177, 182, 211, 222, 233, 234, 215, 249, 255, 279, 284, 286, 151, 161, 172, 199, 197, 203, 194, 132, 100, 118, 135, 156, 185, 196, 167, 173, 177, 179, 214, 236, 244, 247, 69, 103, 181, 159, 169, 174, 178, 200, 123, 137, 149, 179.

   a. Organize the data into a group frequency distribution with $k = 11$ and the lower real limit of the lowest class $= 29.5$.

   b. Construct a frequency polygon for the frequency distribution in part a.

   c. Determine the mode.

   d. Compute the median.

   e. Compute the mean using the method of transformed scores.

ANSWERS TO PROGRESS ASSESSMENTS

5.1	**1.** 5
	2. 22
	3. 79
5.2	**1.** 5, 7
	2. 34.08
5.3	**1.** 5
	2. 25.57
5.4	**1.** 1
	2. 0
	3. 4
	4. 5
5.5	18.25
5.6	**1.** median
	b. median
	c. mean
	d. mean
	e. mode
	2. a. right
	b. right
	c. left
	d. right
	3. a. larger
	b. smaller
	c. equal

Measures of Dispersion

*T*he mean, median, or mode, which you encountered in the previous chapter, summarizes and describes only one feature of a data set or distribution, namely its central tendency. No one of these measures in and of itself is sufficient to distinguish one distribution from another. Consider, for example, the following samples of quiz grades for two students, A and B. Student A on twelve quizzes earned the following grades: 75, 71, 72, 75, 77, 75, 79, 78, 74, 73, 76, 75. Student B on the same twelve quizzes earned the following grades: 72, 60, 75, 65, 75, 75, 75, 85, 75, 78, 75, 90. Neither the mean, median, nor mode, all of which equal 75 for both sets, makes a distinction between Student A's grades and Student B's grades. Furthermore, since both distributions are symmetrical distributions, even the three measures together do not distinguish one distribution of grades from the other. Yet looking at these two data sets, it is quite obvious that they differ substantially. Student B has earned both higher and lower scores than Student A. You can say Student B's scores are more dispersed than Student A's scores.

In this chapter you are introduced to a variety of measures of dispersion. A **measure of dispersion** is a summary statistic that describes how dispersed or spread out scores in a distribution are or how variable the distribution is. Some measures of dispersion have limited descriptive use, whereas others have the statistical versatility that enables them to be used not only to describe a distribution of scores but also how to derive other descriptive measures and to make inferences about population parameters. Your concern with dispersion, then, should be not only how to describe or measure it but also how to make meaningful inferences from sample data about population characteristics in the face of it.

THE RANGE AS A MEASURE OF DISPERSION

Since in the example Student B has both higher and lower scores than Student A, Student B's range of scores is greater than that of Student A. The range of Student B's scores is 31; the range of Student A's scores is 9. You will recall from Chapter 3 that the range of distribution of scores equals the difference between the upper real limit of the highest score and the lower real limit of the lowest score. The range, then, is a measure of how spread out or dispersed the scores in a distribution are. It is typically used as a measure of dispersion for quantitative data, such as family size, for which the mode is the most appropriate measure of central tendency.

The range, as a measure of dispersion, has both advantages and disadvantages. Its major advantage is that it is the easiest of all the measures of dispersion to compute. One major disadvantage is that it is most sensitive to extreme scores in a distribution because its computation depends solely upon those scores. For example, if Student A's highest score had been 90 instead of 79, the range would have been 20 instead of 9. Another major disadvantage of the range is that it is not statistically versatile, which, as you recall from Chapter 5, means that it has limited descriptive use.

OTHER RANGE STATISTICS

90
85
78
75
75
75
—
75
25
25
72
68

60

A measure of dispersion that is not highly sensitive to and dependent upon extreme scores is the interquartile range. The **interquartile range** measures the distance between points in a distribution that mark off the lower and upper 25 percent of the scores. In other words it is the range of the middle 50 percent of the scores. The points that mark off the lower and upper 25 percent of the scores are referred to as the **first** and **third quartiles** and are symbolized Q_1 and Q_3, respectively. Consider the following array of Student A's scores: 79, 78, 77, 76, 75, 75, 75, 75, 74, 73, 72, 71. Scores 74 through 76 comprise the middle 50 percent of the scores. The interquartile range of these scores is obtained in the usual manner, namely, by computing the distance between the upper real limit of the highest of these scores and the lower real limit of the lowest of these scores. The points, Q_3 and Q_1, that mark off the upper and lower 25 percent of the array are 76.5 and 73.5, respectively. The interquartile range, then, is 76.5 − 73.5 = 3. A more detailed procedure for obtaining quartiles will be presented in the next chapter.

Half of the interquartile range, $(Q_3 - Q_1)/2$, is called the **semi-interquartile range** or the **quartile deviation.** This measure of dispersion is commonly used when the median is the most appropriate measure of central tendency, for example, for skewed distributions such as the distribution of scores on a very difficult exam. The interquartile range and the quartile deviation, like the range, have the disadvantage of limited statistical versatility. In addition, both of these measures could eliminate the scores that lend the most variability to the data. For example, two data sets with quite different ranges could have identical interquartile ranges. The range of Student A's grades is 9, whereas the range for Student B's grades is 31. The interquartile range for each of these data sets is, however, 3.

PROGRESS ASSESSMENT 6.1

1. Determine the interquartile range of the following array: 12, 12, 10, 9, 8, 8, 7, 7, 7, 6, 6, 5, 4, 4, 3, 1.
2. Determine the interquartile range of the following data: 13, 16, 12, 14, 3, 1, 7, 10, 2, 15, 12, 4, 8, 15, 14, 1, 2, 5, 12, 10.

DEVIATION MEASURES OF DISPERSION

The need to find a measure of dispersion that takes into consideration all the scores in a distribution and, at the same time, is statistically versatile led statisticians to consider deviation scores as a means of measuring variability. A deviation score, as you recall from the previous chapter, is the distance of a score from the mean in raw score units. A meaningful measure of dispersion, then, would be the average distance the raw scores are from the mean. The larger this average, the more dispersed the scores are. By definition of the mean, however, the sum and, hence, the average of the raw score deviations equal zero for any distribution. It thus follows that some operation or set of operations must be performed on the raw score deviations if they are to be used to derive a measure of dispersion that will enable you to distinguish one distribution from another.

Average Deviation

One set of operations that leads to a meaningful measure of dispersion, called the **average deviation,** is to sum and average the absolute values of the raw score deviations. The **absolute value of a score** is a value irrespective of sign ($+/-$). You will recall that raw score deviations may be positive or negative depending whether the raw score is above or below the mean, respectively. Thus, the absolute value of a raw score deviation, denoted by $|X - \bar{X}|$, indicates the distance, but not the direction (above/below), of the raw score from the mean. For example, whereas the raw score deviation of Student A's lowest exam score, which was earned on the second exam, is $71 - 75 = -4$, the absolute value of that raw score deviation is $|71 - 75| = 4$. The corresponding absolute raw score deviations for all of the grades of Student A are 0, 4, 3, 0, 2, 0, 4, 3, 1, 2, 1, 0. Those for Student B are 3, 15, 0, 10, 0, 0, 0, 10, 0, 3, 0, 15. Averaging the absolute values of the raw score deviations gives the average distance the raw scores are from the mean. Using the following defining equation, the average deviations of the grades of Students A and B, respectively, are computed to be 1.67 and 4.67.

Equation 6.1   Average Deviation $= \dfrac{\Sigma(|X - \bar{X}|)}{N}$

Although meaningful, the average deviation, like the range measures of dispersion, is not statistically versatile and, thus, has not played an important role in descriptive and inferential statistics.

Variance

Another set of operations that can be performed on the raw score deviations from the mean is to average the *squared* raw score deviations from the mean. This turns out to be a meaningful and useful measure of dispersion for a *population*. This parameter is called the **population variance** and is symbolized σ^2, (pronounced sigma-squared), σ being the lowercase Greek letter that corresponds to the English letter *s*.

While averaging the squared raw score deviations from the mean produces a useful parameter, the same operation performed on sample data does not produce a very useful statistic. Although it may adequately describe sample variability, it is not useful in statistical inference because it is a biased estimate of the population variance. You will recall from the discussion of the mean that a biased estimate of a parameter is one that on the average does not equal the parameter. A statistic that on the average does equal the population variance and, hence, is an *unbiased estimate* of the population parameter, σ^2, is called the sample variance. The **sample variance,** symbolized by s^2, is operationally defined as the sum of the squared raw score deviations from the mean divided by the degrees of freedom. The **degrees of freedom** refers to the number of scores in a sample that are free to vary and is symbolized *df*. A more precise meaning of degrees of freedom will be discussed in Chapter 11. Almost always, the *df* for any given sample is equal to the size of the sample minus 1. Thus, the defining equation for the sample variance, which is an *adjusted average of the squared deviations* from the mean (since 1 is being subtracted from N), is symbolized:

Equation 6.2
$$s^2 = \frac{\Sigma(X - \bar{X})^2}{N - 1}$$

Using Equation 6.2, the variance of Student A's grades is computed to be 5.45, whereas that of Student B's grades is computed to be 60.73. You should use Equation 6.2 to verify these computations.

Like the range statistics and the average deviation, the larger the sample variance the more spread out the distribution is. The sample variance, however, has certain advantages over the average deviation and range statistics as a measure of dispersion. First, the sample variance is an unbiased estimate of its corresponding population parameter. Second, unlike the range statistics, it takes into account every score in the distribution or data set. Third, it is statistically versatile. Unlike the average deviation and range statistics, it is used in statistical inference and to derive other descriptive statistics. Fourth, the defining equation for the sample variance can be algebraically manipulated to yield a formula that reduces computational errors.

Computing a Sample Variance from Raw Data or an Array. If you attempt to verity the sample variance computations for Students A and B using Equation 6.2, you probably will find the work to be tedious and prone to computational errors even if you use a calculator. Algebraic manipulation of Equation 6.2 leads to the following computational formula for the variance. Formula 6.1 does not require computing deviation scores and, therefore, is simpler to use than the defining equation and is less likely to lead to rounding errors.

Formula 6.1
$$s^2 = \frac{\Sigma X^2 - (\Sigma X)^2/N}{N - 1}$$

This computational formula directs you to subtract from the sum of the squared scores, ΣX^2, the squared sum of the scores divided by the sample size, $(\Sigma X)^2/N$, and then divide the difference obtained by the degrees of freedom, $N - 1$.

The variance, s^2, of the grades of each student, A and B, is recomputed in Table 6.1 using Formula 6.1.

PROGRESS ASSESSMENT 6.2

1. A sample of twelve students from a large mathematics class received the following grades on a midterm examination: 78, 80, 100, 60, 90, 95, 93, 92, 85, 65, 73, 70. Compute the sample variance using computational Formula 6.1.

TABLE 6.1
The Grades of Each of Two Students (A and B) on Twelve Quizzes and the Formula and Calculations Necessary for Computing the Sample Variance for Each Student's Grades

Student A		Student B	
Grade X	Squared grade X^2	Grade X	Squared grade X^2
75	5625	72	5184
71	5041	60	3600
72	5184	75	5625
75	5625	65	4225
77	5929	75	5625
75	5625	75	5625
79	6241	75	5625
78	6084	85	7225
74	5476	75	5625
73	5329	78	6084
76	5776	75	5625
75	5625	90	8100
900	67,560	900	68,168

$$s^2 = \frac{\Sigma X^2 - (\Sigma X)^2/N}{N - 1}$$

$$s^2 = \frac{67,560 - (900)^2/12}{11}$$
$$= 5.45$$

$$s^2 = \frac{68,168 - (900)^2/12}{11}$$
$$= 60.73$$

2. The following is the number of tornadoes in the United States for each of ten successive years from 1916 to 1925: 90, 121, 81, 64, 87, 105, 108, 102, 130, 119. Compute the sample variance using computational Formula 6.1.

Computing a Sample Variance from a Simple Frequency Distribution.

When working with data organized into a simple frequency distribution, computational Formula 6.1 for the sample variance translates into the following:

Formula 6.2
$$s^2 = \frac{\Sigma fX^2 - (\Sigma fX)^2/\Sigma f}{\Sigma f - 1}$$

The first set of symbols in the numerator on the right-hand side of Formula 6.2, ΣfX^2, directs you to multiply each squared score by its corresponding frequency and then sum these fX^2 values. The second set of symbols in the numerator, $(\Sigma fX)^2/\Sigma f$, directs you to multiply each score by its corresponding frequency, sum these fX values, square that sum, and divide the obtained product by the sum of the frequencies. The difference between the two values obtained by performing these operations is then divided by the degrees of freedom, $\Sigma f - 1$.

Formula 6.2 is used to obtain the variance of Student A's grades, which are organized into a simple frequency distribution in Table 6.2.

TABLE 6.2
A Simple Frequency Distribution of Student A's Grades on Twelve Quizzes and the Formula and Calculations Necessary for Computing the Sample Variance

Grade X	Frequency f	fX	X^2	fX^2
79	1	79	6241	6241
78	1	78	6084	6084
77	1	77	5929	5929
76	1	76	5776	5776
75	4	300	5625	22500
74	1	74	5476	5476
73	1	73	5329	5329
72	1	72	5184	5184
71	1	71	5041	5041
	12	900		67560

$$s^2 = \frac{\Sigma fX^2 - (\Sigma fX)^2/\Sigma f}{\Sigma f - 1}$$

$$s^2 = \frac{67,560 - (900)^2/12}{11} = 5.45$$

PROGRESS ASSESSMENT 6.3

The minimum daily temperature in New York City in January 1959 ranged from 14 to 38. The daily temperatures are given below. Compute the sample variance using computational Formula 6.2. Temperatures: 28, 38, 34, 26, 14, 14, 16, 21, 21, 20, 25, 25, 32, 30, 33, 24, 14, 14, 16, 33, 38, 25, 21, 21, 35, 20, 24, 18, 24, 38, 20.

Computing a Sample Variance from a Grouped Frequency Distribution. When working with data organized into a grouped frequency distribution, the variance of the distribution is computed with Formula 6.2 where X refers to midpoints of the class intervals. The variance for the grouped frequency distribution in Table 6.3 is computed using Formula 6.2.

PROGRESS ASSESSMENT 6.4

Compute the variance of the data in Table 6-A using Formula 6.2.

TABLE 6.3
A Grouped Frequency Distribution of the Number of Books Checked Out of the Campus Library by 400 College Students in Their Senior Year and the Formula and Calculations Necessary for Computing the Sample Variance

Class	Midpoint X'	Frequency f	fX'	X'^2	fX'^2
18–19	18.5	1	18.5	342.25	342.25
16–17	16.5	3	49.5	272.25	816.75
14–15	14.5	8	116.0	210.25	1682.00
12–13	12.5	15	187.5	156.25	2343.75
10–11	10.5	20	210.0	110.25	2205.00
8–9	8.5	75	637.5	72.25	5418.75
6–7	6.5	130	845.0	42.25	5492.50
4–5	4.5	113	508.5	20.25	2288.25
2–3	2.5	25	62.5	6.25	156.25
0–1	0.5	10	5.0	0.25	2.50
		400	2640.0		20748.00

$$s^2 = \frac{\Sigma fX^2 - (\Sigma fX)^2/\Sigma f}{\Sigma f - 1}$$

where X refers to X'

$$s^2 = \frac{20{,}748 - (2{,}640)^2/400}{399} = 8.33$$

TABLE 6-A
Grouped Frequency Distribution of Number of Hours Spent by Fifty Students Studying Statistics During the Ten Days Preceding the Final Examination

Hours of Studying Class	Frequency f
45–49	1
40–44	0
35–39	0
30–34	3
25–29	5
20–24	20
15–19	12
10–14	5
5–9	3
0–4	1

USING TRANSFORMED SCORES TO COMPUTE THE VARIANCE

Recall from Chapter 5 that transforming the midpoints in a grouped frequency distribution by subtracting some central midpoint and dividing the obtained difference by the width of the class interval permitted you to obtain the mean more easily and with less likelihood of error. The same transformation will also permit you to obtain the variance more easily with less likelihood of error. The variance, however, is influenced differently than the mean by that transformation. Thus, in order to use such transformed scores to obtain the variance of a distribution, you must first discover how the variance is affected by adding, subtracting, multiplying, and dividing each score in the distribution by a constant.

The Constant as a Key Factor

To see how changing the scores of a distribution by addition, subtraction, multiplication, or division by a constant affects the variance, you first need to compute the variance of some small set of data. For example, the variance of the scores 2, 4, and 6 is found to be 4. Now see what happens to this variance when you add a constant, such as 2, to each score. That is, compute the variance of (2 + 2), (4 + 2), and (6 + 2), or 4, 6, and 8, respectively. Compute the variance of 0, 2, and 4, the scores that result when the constant 2 is subtracted from 2, 4, and 6, respectively. When you discover the effect adding a constant to or subtracting a constant from a set of scores has on the variance of those scores, multiply or divide each score by a constant and discover the effect multiplication or division by a constant has on the variance. With multiplication or division you may have to try more than one constant before you discover that operation's influence on the variance. Making these discoveries on your own will help you understand and remember the procedure for obtaining the variance of a grouped frequency distribution using transformed scores.

PROGRESS ASSESSMENT 6.5

1. Find the sample variance of 4, 6, and 8, the numbers attained when the constant 2 is added to each score in the data set 2, 4, 6.

2. Find the sample variance of 0, 2, and 4, the numbers that result when 2 is subtracted from each of the numbers in the data set 2, 4, 6.

3. Find the sample variance of 4, 8, and 12, the numbers attained when each score in the data set 2, 4, 6, is multiplied by 2.

4. Now multiply by 3 each score in the data set in part 1 and compute the sample variance.

5. From the answers to parts 3 and 4, you should be able to determine what effect multiplying each score in a distribution by a constant has on the variance. If you cannot, continue to multiply by different constants, 5 and so on, until you discover the rule. Since division is multiplication by a reciprocal, state the variance of 1, 2, and 3, that is, the data set divided by the constant 2, without actually computing it.

Computation of the Variance

If you perform the suggested operations and compute the variance of the transformed scores, you discover that adding a constant to, or subtracting a constant from, a set of scores has no effect on the variance of those scores. On the other hand, multiplying or dividing each score in a distribution by a constant correspondingly affects the variance by the square of the constant, that is, if each score in a distribution with a variance equal to 20 is divided or multiplied by 2, then the variance of the $X/2$ or $2X$ scores is 20 divided or multiplied by 2^2, respectively. These discoveries not only enable you to compute the variance of grouped frequency distributions with ease and less likelihood of error but also aid in your understanding of standard scores discussed in Chapter 7 and the rationale of the analysis of variance examined in Chapter 14.

The variance of the data in Table 6.3 is recomputed in Table 6.4 as an example of how to use the method of transformed scores.

In the Table 6.4 calculations, 2.0827 is the computed variance of the scores transformed by subtracting the central midpoint 8.5 from every other

TABLE 6.4
A Grouped Frequency Distribution of the Number of Books Checked Out of the Campus Library by 400 College Students in Their Senior Year and the Formulas and Calculations Necessary for Computing the Sample Variance Using Transformed Scores

Class	Midpoint X'	$X' - 8.5$ X''	$X''/2$ X'''	Frequency f	fX'''	X''^2	fX''^2
18–19	18.5	10	5	1	5	25	25
16–17	16.5	8	4	3	12	16	48
14–15	14.5	6	3	8	24	9	72
12–13	12.5	4	2	15	30	4	60
10–11	10.5	2	1	20	20	1	20
8–9	8.5	0	0	75	0	0	0
6–7	6.5	−2	−1	130	−130	1	130
4–5	4.5	−4	−2	113	−226	4	452
2–3	2.5	−6	−3	25	−75	9	225
0–1	0.5	−8	−4	10	−40	16	160
				400	−380		1192

$$s'''^2 = \frac{\Sigma fX^2 - (\Sigma fX)^2/\Sigma f}{\Sigma f - 1} \quad \text{where } X \text{ refers to } X'''.$$

$$s'''^2 = \frac{1192 - (-380)^2/400}{399} = 2.0827$$

$$s^2 = s'''^2 (i^2)$$

$$s^2 = 2.0827 \, (4) = 8.33$$

midpoint and dividing the differences obtained by 2, the width of the class interval (i). To obtain the variance of the original distribution, you have to take into consideration how this transformation affects the variance of that distribution. Subtracting a central midpoint from each of the midpoints has no effect upon the variance. Dividing each resulting midpoint by the width of the class interval (i), however, affects the variance of the original distribution by the square of that constant. To obtain the variance of the original distribution, then, all you need to do is multiply the variance of the transformed scores by the class interval width squared (i^2). Thus, $2.0827 \times 4 = 8.33$, which is the value of s^2 obtained in Table 6.3.

PROGRESS ASSESSMENT 6.6

Use the method of transformed scores with computational Formula 6.2 to compute the variance of the grouped frequency distribution in Table 6-B.

TABLE 6-B
Grouped Frequency Distribution of the Number of Bronze Medals Won by Each of Forty-Seven Countries Participating in the Twenty-Third Summer Olympics in Los Angeles

Number of Medals Won Class	Frequency (countries) f
30–32	1
27–29	0
24–26	0
21–23	2
18–20	0
15–17	3
12–14	3
9–11	1
6–8	5
3–5	4
0–2	28

TYPES OF VARIANCE

In reading this chapter you may have noticed that the data, the grades of Students A and B, and the number of books checked out of the library by 400 college seniors differ in a number of ways. They differ not only in the way they have or have not been organized—for example, raw data or a simple frequency distribution for grades and a grouped frequency distribution for number of books—but also in what they represent. The grades represent many different scores for single individuals, whereas the number of books represent single scores for many individuals. Thus, the variances that were computed for these data sets represent two types of variance, **within-subject variance,** the variability of scores of a single individual or sample member, and **within-group variance,** the variability in the scores of a group of individuals or sample members

Distinctions between these and other types of variance become very important for understanding the logic of many procedures used in inferential statistics.

Two other types of variance frequently referred to in inferential statistics involve the variability in the means of the scores of individuals or groups of individuals. For example, scores of Students A and B and of other students in the class could be summarized by the mean. The means for Students A and B were 75. Other students may have attained quite different averages. The variability of the *means* of such individuals is referred to as **between-subject variance.** The scores of various groups can also be summarized by the mean. For example, the number of books checked out of the campus library by each class of seniors from a variety of colleges can be summarized by the mean. The variability in the means of such groups is referred to as **between-group variance.**

PROGRESS ASSESSMENT 6.7

For each of the following, specify whether the variance obtained on the measures would represent within-subject, between-subject, within-group, or between-group variance:

1. Golfing scores of an individual for nine games.
2. Mean maze running speed for four groups of rats.
3. GPA of ten students.
4. The on-target time of ten students on a pursuit rotor task.

STANDARD DEVIATION

Although variance measures are important and meaningful for statistical inference, they are not frequently used descriptive statistics. This is because the sample variance (s^2), an adjusted average of the squared deviation scores, is difficult to visualize for frequency polygons and other graphical representations of data. A widely used descriptive measure of dispersion, however, is the *square root* of the variance. This measure, which may be considered an adjusted-average raw score deviation is, as you might expect, symbolized *s* and is called the **standard deviation.** Thus, the computational formula for finding the *s* of raw data or an array is as follows:

Formula 6.3
$$s = \sqrt{\frac{\Sigma X^2 - (\Sigma X)^2/N}{N - 1}}$$

A similar computational formula for simple and grouped frequency distributions can be written for *s* by putting a radical sign over the right-hand side of Formula 6.2.

The standard deviation is the preferred measure of spread or dispersion when the mean is used as a measure of central tendency. It is a distance measure that is easy to visualize and depict in graphical representations of data. Figure 6.1, for example, presents the data from Table 6.3 as a frequency polygon in which the standard deviation is marked off along the X-axis by equidistant lines drawn perpendicularly from the graph to the X-axis. Each line represents a raw score whose distance from the mean is some multiple of the standard deviation.

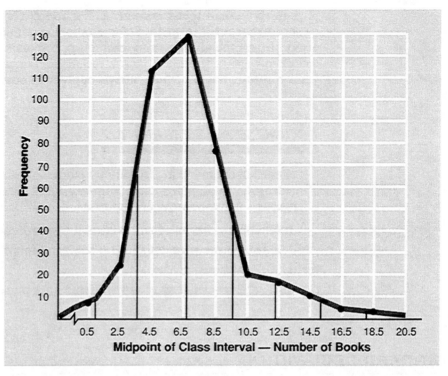

FIGURE 6.1 *Frequency polygon of the number of books checked out of the campus library by 400 college students in their senior year. The distance between the perpendicular lines from the polygon to the X-axis, as measured along the X-axis, equals the standard deviation.*

Figure 6.2, a line graph, depicts the average grade of Students A and B over each of the twelve quizzes, and Figure 6.3, a bar graph, depicts each student's average quiz score for the entire twelve quizzes. In each of these latter figures, the standard deviation is depicted by a line measured along the *Y*-axis. In Figure 6.2 the lines project through each of the data points, and the standard deviation, measured along the *Y*-axis, is the distance from the point to the end of the line in either the upward or downward direction. In Figure 6.3 the lines project through the top of the bars, and the standard deviation, measured along the *Y*-axis, is the distance from the top of the bar to the end of the line in either direction.

Other advantages of using the standard deviation as a measure of dispersion are that it takes into consideration every score in the distribution or data set; it has, therefore, better sampling stability; and it is derived from an unbiased estimate of a population parameter, even though it is not itself unbiased. The standard deviation is also important in understanding the meaning of regression examined in Chapter 8, and, as you will discover, it is statistically versatile, being used to derive other descriptive measures, such as standard scores described in Chapter 7 and measures of relationship discussed in Chapter 8.

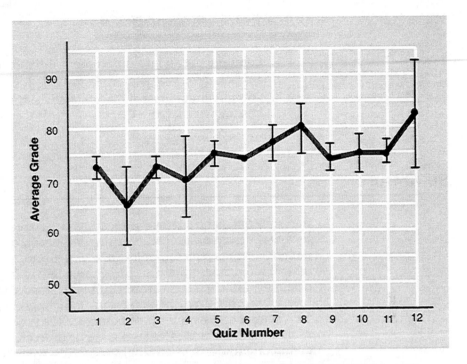

FIGURE 6.2 *A line graph depicting the average quiz scores of Students A and B over twelve quizzes. The distance from the data point in either the upward or downward direction to the end of the line projecting through the point, as measured along the Y-axis, equals the standard deviation.*

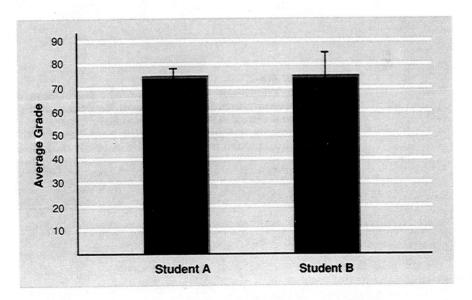

FIGURE 6.3 *A bar graph of the average grade of Student A and the average grade of Student B over twelve quizzes. The distance from the top of the bar to the end of the line in either direction, as measured along the Y-axis, equals the standard deviation.*

PROGRESS ASSESSMENT 6.8

1. Compute the standard deviation of the following numbers: 8, 9, 3, 2, 1, 3, 7, 5, 6, 9, 8, 9, 4, 5, 3, 6, 7, 9, 8, 4.
2. Compute the standard deviation of the simple frequency distribution shown in Table 6-C.

SUMMARY

Range statistics and deviations measures are presented as summary measures that describe the spread or dispersion of scores in a distribution or data set. The range, interquartile range, and the quartile deviation are said to have limited descriptive use. The same is said to be true for the average deviation, although this measure, unlike the range statistics, is influenced by every score in the distribution. Instructions are given for computing sample variance that is an unbiased estimate of the population variance. The sample variance is presented as a versatile descriptive statistic that plays an important role in statistical inference. However, the square root of the variance, the standard deviation—because it is easy to visualize and depict graphically, takes into consideration every score in a distribution, and is statistically versatile—is acknowledged to be the most frequently used measure of dispersion.

TABLE 6-C
Simple Frequency Distribution of the Number of Representatives in the House of Representatives Whose Political Affiliation Was Other than Democrat or Republican during Each Session of Congress from the 76th to the 100th Inclusive

Score (representatives) X	Frequency (sessions) f
6	1
5	0
4	2
3	0
2	5
1	7
0	10

KEY DEFINITIONS

absolute value of a score   The value of a score irrespective of its sign.

average deviation   An average of the absolute values of the raw score deviations from the mean.

between-group variance   The variance of the means of groups of individuals.

between-subject variance   The variance of the means of the individuals of a group.

degrees of freedom   The number of scores in a sample that are free to vary.

df   Symbol for degrees of freedom.

first quartile   A summary statistic that marks off the lower 25% of the scores of a distribution.

interquartile range   The distance between the first and third quartiles.

measure of dispersion   A summary statistic that describes how dispersed or spread out scores in a distribution are or how variable a distribution is.

population variance   Refers to the average of the squared raw score deviations from the population mean.

Q_1 Symbol for the first quartile, a summary statistic that marks off the lower 25% of the scores of a distribution.

Q_3 Symbol for the third quartile, a summary statistic that marks off the upper 25% of the scores of a distribution.

quartile deviation   Half of the interquartile range; also called the semi-interquartile range.

s Symbol for the standard deviation of a sample.

$s = \sqrt{[\Sigma X^2 - (\Sigma X)^2/N]/(N - 1)}$ Computational formula for the standard deviation.

s^2 Symbol for the sample variance.

$s^2 = [\Sigma X^2 - (\Sigma X)^2/N]/(N - 1)$ Computational formula for the sample variance that is an unbiased estimate of the population variance σ^2.

$s^2 = [\Sigma f X^2 - (\Sigma f X)^2/\Sigma f]/(\Sigma f - 1)$ Computational formula for the sample variance of frequency distributions.

sample variance   An adjusted average of the squared raw score deviations from the sample mean, that is, the sum of the raw score deviations from the sample mean divided by the degrees of freedom.

semi-interquartile range or **quartile deviation, $(Q_3 - Q_1)/2$**   Half of the interquartile range.

σ^2 (Pronounced ''sigma squared'') A symbol for the population variance.

standard deviation   An adjusted-average raw score deviation; the square root of the variance.

third quartile   A summary statistic that marks off the upper 25% of the scores of a distribution.

within-group variance   Variance of the scores within a group.

within-subject variance   Variance of an individual's scores.

REVIEW EXERCISES

1. The following is the average life span in years of some common laboratory animals: cat, 12; chimpanzee, 20; dog, 12; guinea pig, 4; Rhesus monkey, 15; white mouse, 3; pig, 10; rabbit, 5; white rat, 3.

   a. For these life-span data compute each of the following: (1) mean, (2) median, (3) mode, (4) range, (5) variance, and (6) standard deviation.

   b. Construct the most appropriate graph.

   c. Name the type of variance represented in part *a* (5).

2. The following data represent the number of hazardous waste sites in each of the 50 states in the U.S.A.: 8, 0, 5, 7, 34, 12, 6, 9, 32, 3, 0, 4, 14, 23, 6, 6, 9, 5, 5, 6, 21, 56, 36, 2, 12, 7, 2, 0, 12, 91, 4, 57, 6, 1, 27, 4, 4, 48, 8, 10, 1, 7, 21, 3, 2, 7, 19, 5, 26, 1.

   a. Construct a grouped frequency distribution with an upper real limit of the highest class equal to 99.5 and $i = 10$.

   b. For the frequency distribution constructed in part *a*, compute each of the following: (1) mean, (2) median, (3) mode, (4) range, (5) variance, and (6) standard deviation.

   c. Name the most appropriate measure of central tendency for the distribution in part *a*.

   d. Name the most appropriate measure of dispersion for the distribution in part *a*.

   e. Name the type of variance part *b* (5) represents.

   f. From an examination of the measures of central tendency, determine the direction of skew.

3. A poll was conducted in which fifty college students were questioned about the number of sporting events they attended during the academic year. The results of the poll are presented in the grouped frequency distribution shown in Table 6-D.

   a. Indicate which measures of central tendency cannot be computed, and give the reasons.

   b. Indicate which deviation measures of dispersion cannot be computed, and give the reasons.

   c. Point out the poor features of the grouped frequency distribution.

TABLE 6-D
Grouped Frequency Distribution of the Number of Sporting Events College Students Reported Attending during the Academic Year

Number of Events Class	Frequency f
45–54	1
35–44	2
25–34	7
15–24	8
5–14	20
<5	12

ANSWERS TO PROGRESS ASSESSMENTS

6.1   1. $8.5 - 4.5 = 4$

         2. $13.5 - 3.5 = 10$

6.2   1. 164.02

         2. 412.9

6.3   57.72

6.4   56.01

6.5   1. 4

         2. 4

         3. 16

         4. 36

         5. 1

6.6   50.01

6.7   1. within-subject

         2. between-group

         3. between subject

         4. within-group

6.8   1. 2.59

         2. 1.54

Measures of Relative Standing

*I*n Chapters 3 and 4 you found that you could readily extract more information from organized data than you could from the raw data themselves. You will now find that you can also assign a value to a raw score so that it yields more information than the raw score would in and of itself. You, in fact, did this when you constructed a relative or percent cumulative frequency distribution (Chapter 3). The percent cumulative frequency of a score or class interval, for example, assigns to the upper real limit of the score or class a percentage value that is more informative than the limit alone. It tells you, as you recall, the percentage of scores falling at or below that particular limit. The percent cumulative frequency can be obtained not only for the upper real limits of scores and classes but for any score in a data set.

This chapter provides a step-by-step procedure for assigning a value to a score that indicates the percentage of cases falling below the score. It also provides a step-by-step procedure for locating a score below which a specified percentage of cases fall. These procedures provide information that allows comparison of the relative position of scores within one or more distributions. This chapter also demonstrates how to convert raw score deviations to standard deviation units as a means of expressing relative standing.

PERCENTILE RANK

When the percent cumulative frequency of a score is obtained, its value indicates the percentile rank of that score. Thus, a **percentile rank** of a score is a value that indicates the percentage of cases falling at or below that score.

We are frequently more interested in knowing this kind of information than information yielded by the raw score alone. In fact, a raw score itself is seldom meaningful. Some of your professors, for example, have probably put only the number of points that you earned on an exam, such as 110, at the top of your exam paper. This raw score in itself is not very informative. It would be more informative if you also knew the total number of points that could have been earned. But you would probably want to know even more than that. You would be most interested in how you fared in comparison with the rest of the students who took the exam—in your relative position or standing within a specific group of individuals. Percentile rank is one measure of relative standing.

Estimating the Percentile Rank of a Score Graphically

You will recall from Chapter 4 that the percent cumulative frequency curve is generally used when you are interested in the position of an individual within a sample with respect to some sample characteristic. This, of course, is precisely what is meant by percentile rank. Thus, the percent cumulative frequency curve provides one method of estimating the percentile rank of a score.

In reviewing the construction of a percent cumulative frequency curve (Chapter 4), note again that the points on the graph are plotted directly above the upper real limits of the scores or classes, which are represented by numbers or graduations along the *X*-axis. The height of each point above the real limit is determined by the corresponding percent cumulative frequency of the limit, which is represented by a number along the *Y*-axis. To estimate the percentile rank of any score in the distribution, all you need to do is locate the score along the *X*-axis, draw a straight line from that point to the curve, and from that point where the line intersects the curve, draw another straight line to the *Y*-axis. In each case, the line must be perpendicular to the axis. To see how this is done, refer to Figure 7.1, in which the percentile rank of 110 is estimated to be 70 from the data in Table 7.1, which is a grouped frequency distribution of exam scores.

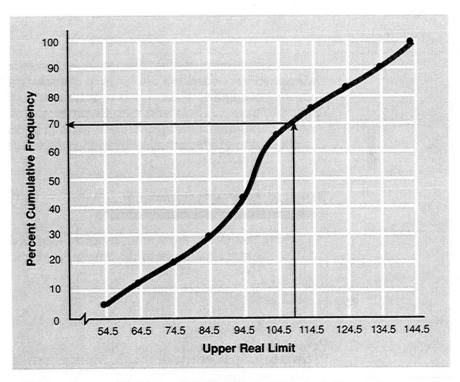

FIGURE 7.1 *A percent cumulative frequency curve for the data in Table 7.1 depicting the graphical method of obtaining percentile rank.*

TABLE 7.1

Grouped Frequency and Percent Cumulative Frequency Distributions of Exam Scores Used to Illustrate Graphical and Mathematical Estimations of Percentiles and Percentile Ranks

Class Interval	Frequency f	Percent Cumulative Frequency
135–144	15	100
125–134	17	92.5
115–124	18	84
105–114	20	75
95–104	45	65
85–94	26	42.5
75–84	18	29.5
65–74	16	20.5
55–64	15	12.5
45–54	10	5
	200	

This graphical method of estimating percentile rank is simple, quick, and relatively accurate if care is taken in constructing the cumulative frequency curve, and if the points at which the straight lines intersect the X- and Y-axes are easily identified. Even though this is usually not the case, it is recommended that you use this method in conjunction with and as a check on the mathematical derivation of percentile rank.

PROGRESS ASSESSMENT 7.1

Using the graphical method, estimate for the data depicted in Figure 7.1 the percentile rank of the following scores:

1. 97
2. 114.5
3. 56

Estimating Percentile Rank Mathematically

Although the mathematical derivation of percentile rank could be expressed in a concise formula, a formula will not be used to estimate the percentile rank of 110 in the frequency distribution in Table 7.1. Instead, a step-by-step procedure will be used in conjunction with a diagram (Figure 7.2) to give you an intuitive understanding of the mathematical derivation of percentile rank.

Figure 7.2 is an enlargement of a portion of the *X*-axis for the cumulative frequency curve of the data in Table 7.1. It depicts the class interval 105–114, which contains score 110, the number of scores below the lower real limit of that interval, and both the number of scores and the location of score 110 within that interval. Remember that for a percentile rank we are trying to determine the total number of scores that fall below the value 110. This total is then expressed as a percentage of the scores in the distribution.

The major problem in mathematically deriving a percentile rank is to estimate the number of scores that fall between the given score and the lower real limit of the interval containing the score—in the example, the number of scores (represented by ? in Figure 7.2) falling between 110 and 104.5. To do this we must make an assumption about the location of the scores within the class interval.

You will recall from Chapter 3 that when data are organized into a grouped frequency distribution, the identity of the scores within the interval is lost. The assumption made is that the scores within the interval are evenly distributed across that interval. This essentially means that the number of scores that fall between the lower real limit and any specified score will be proportional to the distance between the lower real limit and the score. For example, if the specified score is halfway between the lower and upper real limits, then half of the scores in the interval will fall between the lower real limit and the specified score. If a specified score is one-tenth of the way between the lower and upper real limits, then one-tenth of the scores in the interval will fall between the lower real limit and that score.

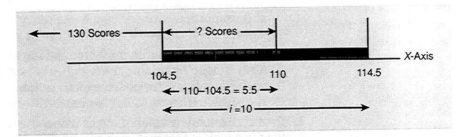

FIGURE 7.2 *A schematic representation of the mathematical estimation of percentile rank. It depicts an enlargement of the interval 105–114 along the X-axis of the cumulative frequency curve for the data of Table 7.1, the number of scores falling below the lower real limit of that interval, the number of scores (squares) and the location of 110 within that interval, the width of the class, and the distance from the lower real limit to the score 110. The number of scores falling between the lower real limit and 110, which is needed to determine the percentile rank of 110, is represented by the question mark (?).*

Once the number of scores between the lower real limit and the specified score is determined, it is added to the number of scores below the interval. That sum is then converted to a percentage in the same manner that you calculated cumulative percent frequency in Chapter 3, that is, by dividing it by the sum of the frequencies and multiplying the resulting quotient by 100.

A Step-by-Step Procedure for Deriving Percentile Rank. The preceding paragraph describes the mathematical procedure for obtaining an estimate of percentile rank. The following steps show how the procedure would be used to determine the percentile rank of 110 from the data in Table 7.1:

1. Locate the class interval containing the specified X-value, for example, 110. In Table 7.1 that class interval is 105–114.
2. Determine the number of scores falling below the specified X using the following procedure:
    a. Count the number of scores falling below the lower real limit (104.5) of that class; that is, find the cumulative frequency of the class below that containing 110. That number is 130.
    b. Compute the distance between the lower real limit (104.5) of the class interval containing the specified X (110) and the specified X itself. This is accomplished by subtracting the lower real limit from the specified X. In this case, $110 - 104.5 = 5.5$.
    c. Find what proportion this computed distance is to the width (i) of the class interval. This is accomplished by dividing the distance between the lower real limit and the specified X by i. For the current problem that would be $5.5/10 = 0.55$.
    d. Determine the number of scores falling within this calculated proportion of the interval. This is accomplished by multiplying this proportion of scores by the frequency (f) of the class interval, that is, $0.55 \times 20 = 11$ for the current problem.
    e. Calculate the total number of scores falling below the specified X. This is done by adding the number of scores that are contained in the specified interval to the total cumulative scores falling below the specified interval. In this case, $11 + 130 = 141$.
3. Convert the total number of scores below the specified X to a percentile rank. This is accomplished by dividing the total number of scores below the specified X by the sum of the frequencies (Σf) and multiplying the quotient obtained by 100. Thus, the percentile rank of 110 is $(141/200) \times 100 = 70.5 = 70$. Note that percentile rank is not accompanied by a percentage sign (%) and is always in whole numbers.

PROGRESS ASSESSMENT 7.2

For the data in Table 7.1, estimate, mathematically, the percentile ranks of the following scores and compare them with your graphical estimates in Progress Assessment 7.1:

1. 97
2. 114.5
3. 56

Application to Simple Frequency Distributions. The same procedure is used when estimating the percentile rank of scores organized into a simple frequency distribution, in which case the width (i) of a score equals 1. Similarly, the procedure described in the next section for grouped frequency distributions can also be applied to simple frequency distributions.

PROGRESS ASSESSMENT 7.3

The ages of 50 students enrolled in the Reserve Officers' Training Corps program at a large private college are shown in the simple frequency distribution in Table 7-A. What is the percentile rank of a student whose age is 20?

TABLE 7-A
Ages of Students Enrolled
in a Reserve Officers'
Training Corps Program
(N = 50)

Age X	Frequency f
22	2
21	9
20	7
19	14
18	16
17	2

QUANTILES: PERCENTILES, QUARTILES, AND DECILES

The raw score associated with a specified percentile rank is referred to as a percentile. Thus, a **percentile** is a point in a distribution of scores at or below which a specified percentage of the scores fall.

There may be many situations in which your primary concern is earning a score that would place you at some specified position within a group. Applicants to most colleges, universities, and graduate schools, for example, must reach a certain percentile on specific aptitude or achievement tests to qualify for admission.

Percentiles are symbolized P_k where k takes on values from 1 to 99 and refers to the percentile rank of the score. For example, P_{50}, the fiftieth percentile, is another symbol for the median, which as you recall from Chapter 5, is the point in a distribution of scores at or below which 50 percent of the scores fall. Similarly, P_{62}, the sixty-second percentile, is the point in a distribution at or below which 62 percent of the scores fall. The percentiles divide the area under a frequency polygon into 100 equal parts. The significance of the area under a frequency polygon will become apparent when you study the normal distribution (Chapter 9).

Certain percentiles are given special designations. For example, P_{25}, P_{50}, and P_{75} are also symbolized Q_1, Q_2, and Q_3, respectively. These, as you recall from Chapter 6, are called quartiles. As the name implies, the quartiles divide the area under a frequency polygon into four equal parts. The tenth through the ninetieth percentiles, that is, P_{10}, P_{20}, P_{30}, ... , P_{90}, are also designated D_1, D_2, D_3, . . . , D_9, respectively, and are called **deciles.** The deciles divide the area under a frequency polygon into ten equal parts. Collectively, percentiles, deciles, and quartiles are referred to as quantiles. **Quantiles** is the collective name for values that divide a frequency distribution into a specified number of groups with equal frequencies.

Estimating Quantiles Graphically

Estimating a quantile, that is, percentiles, deciles, or quartiles, from inspection of a percent cumulative frequency curve is also simple, quick, and relatively accurate. The first quartile in Figure 7.3 is estimated to be 79.5. You can see that this procedure is essentially opposite that of estimating percentile rank. Instead of beginning with a line drawn from the X-axis, we begin with a line drawn from the Y-axis to the curve. In Figure 7.3, we are interested in determining Q_1. We locate 25 along the Y-axis because Q_1 is an alternative way of expressing P_{25}, the point at or below which 25% of the cases fall. We then draw a straight line from this location on the Y-axis to the percent cumulative frequency curve. From the point where the line intersects the curve we draw a perpendicular line to the X-axis. The point where this line intersects the X-axis is our estimation of Q_1. Since the intersection appears to be in the middle of the class interval, 75–84, we estimate Q_1 to be X', that is, 79.5.

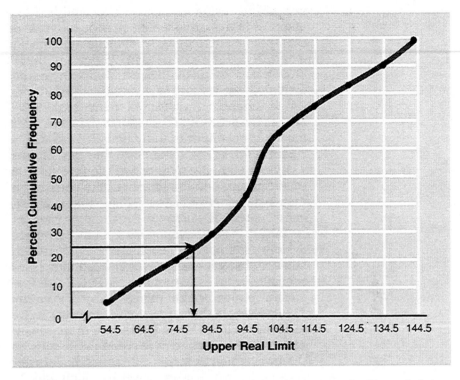

FIGURE 7.3 *A percent cumulative frequency curve for the data of Table 7.1 depicting the graphical method of estimating quantiles.*

PROGRESS ASSESSMENT 7.4

Estimate graphically from the cumulative frequency curve in Figure 7.3 the following quantiles.

1. D_3
2. P_{48}
3. Q_3

Estimating Quantiles Mathematically

The mathematical procedure used to estimate a quantile is also, to some extent, opposite the mathematical procedure used to estimate percentile rank. You will recall that the last thing you did in computing percentile rank was to convert a number of scores to a value indicating a percentage. The first thing you do in computing a quantile is convert a percentage into a number of scores. For example, if you are interested in obtaining Q_1 for the data in Table 7.1, the first thing you must do is determine how many scores will fall below Q_1. This is accomplished by first converting your quantile, in this case the first quartile (Q_1), to a percentile (P_k) and taking that specified percentage (k) of the total number of scores (Σf). In the example $Q_1 = P_{25}$ and k percent (25 percent) of the sum of the frequenices (200) is 0.25 × 200, which equals 50. Once you have done this you can determine the interval in which P_k occurs. Considering the data in Table 7.1, for example, P_{25} must fall in the interval 75–84 because there are 41 scores below the lower real limit of that class interval and 59 scores below the upper real limit of that interval. Thus, the 50 scores that fall below P_{25} must fall below some point within that interval.

Once you have determined the interval in which the specified percentile occurs, you can schematically represent your problem and procedure in a diagram like Figure 7.4. Looking at Figure 7.4 you can tell how many scores will fall between P_{25} and the lower real limit of the interval containing P_{25} because you know both the number of scores falling below the lower real limit and the number of scores falling below P_{25}. Hence, the number of scores falling between P_{25} and the lower real limit is the difference between these two numbers. Recall that the number of scores in this interval is proportional to the distance between the lower real limit and P_{25}. Knowing both the number of scores falling between P_{25} and the lower real limit, and the number of scores in the entire interval, you can easily determine the proportion of scores in the class interval that falls between the lower real limit and P_{25}. Once you have determined the proportion of scores that fall between the lower real limit and P_{25}, you can determine the distance between the lower real limit and P_{25}. Adding this distance to the lower real limit will, then, give you a value for P_{25}.

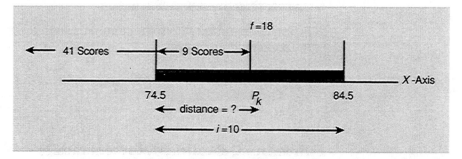

FIGURE 7.4 *A schematic representation of the mathematical estimation of a quantile. It depicts an enlargement of the interval 75–84 along the X-axis of the cumulative frequency curve for the data of Table 7.1, the number of scores falling below the lower real limit of that interval, the number of scores (squares) falling between the lower real limit and the quantile (P_k) to be estimated, the number of scores (squares) within the interval (f), and the class interval width (i). The distance between the lower real limit and P_k, which is needed to determine P_k, is represented by a question mark (?).*

The preceding paragraph explains in general terms the mathematical procedure for estimating quantiles. As we did with percentile rank, we now go through the procedure in a more detailed fashion. The steps for computing Q_1 for the data in Table 7.1 are as follows:

1. Determine the number of scores that fall below a specified quantile using the following procedure:

   a. Determine the percentile equivalent of your quantile. In the example, $Q_1 = P_{25}$.

   b. Take k percent of the sum of the frequencies. In the current example, $0.25 \times 200 = 50$.

2. Locate the class interval containing P_k using the following procedure:

   a. Add up the scores in the frequency column beginning with the lowest class until you find adjacent cumulative frequencies that bracket the number of scores that fall below P_k. (Note that if the frequencies add to exactly the number of scores that fall below P_k, then P_k will be the upper real limit of the class with that cumulative frequency.) In the example, the adjacent cumulative frequencies that bracket a cumulative frequency of 50 are 41 and 59.

   b. Select the class whose cumulative frequency is the highest of these two adjacent frequencies. In the example, this interval is 75–84. The P_k, then, is in this interval.

3. Determine P_k using the following procedure:

   a. Determine the number of scores that fall between P_k and the lower real limit of the interval containing P_k. This is accomplished by subtracting the number of scores that fall below the lower real limit of the interval containing P_k from the number of scores that fall below P_k. In this case, $50 - 41 = 9$.

   b. Convert the number of scores that fall between P_k and the lower real limit of the interval containing P_k to a proportion by dividing that number by the frequency of scores for the class interval. In the example, this proportion is $9/18 = 0.5$.

   c. Take this proportion of the class interval width (i), that is, $0.5 \times 10 = 5$ in the example.

   d. Calculate a value for P_k. This is done by adding the proportion of the class interval width (i) calculated in step 3c to the lower real limit of the class containing P_k. Thus, the value for P_k is $5 + 74.5 = 79.5$. Note that, unlike percentile rank, percentiles are rounded to the nearest whole number only if the variable measured is inherently a discrete variable, such as family size.

You will recognize this procedure as the one used to obtain the median in Chapter 5. As for the median, a precise formula could be written for obtaining quantiles in general.

PROGRESS ASSESSMENT 7.5

1. Compute (a) D_3 (b) P_{48} (c) Q_3 for the data in Table 7.1 and compare your results with your graphical estimates.
2. Compute (a) P_{50} (b) Q_1 (c) D_4 for the simple frequency distribution in Table 7-A, Progress Assessment 7.3.
3. Write a general formula for computing quantiles.

USING PERCENTILES AND PERCENTILE RANKS

Percentiles and percentile ranks are also useful if you are interested in comparing a sample member on two or more characteristics. For example, a teacher may want to know if a student's academic performance as measured by an achievement test is commensurate with his or her ability as measured by an aptitude test, or a pediatrician may want to know if a child's growth rate is comparable with respect to height and weight.

In both situations comparing raw scores directly may be inappropriate and misleading. In the former case, for example, the teacher may want to compare the student's scores on achievement and aptitude tests on which a raw score of 50 on one test could mean something quite different than a raw score of 50 on the other. In the latter case the pediatrician would be comparing inches and pounds where measures of 60 would obviously mean something quite different.

Determining the percentile rank of the individual's score in both distributions allows meaningful comparison. For example, if on the achievement test the student's percentile rank was 68, whereas on the aptitude test it was 84, the teacher would know that the student's performance is not commensurate with his or her ability. Similarly, if a child's height was at the 80th percentile for children of the same age but only at the 40th percentile for weight, the pediatrician may look more closely at the child's eating habits in an attempt to determine why height and weight are not progressing comparably.

PROGRESS ASSESSMENT 7.6

Two measures were taken on each of forty fifth-grade boys. One measure was the number of toys the boy claimed to own; the other measure was the number of friends that he claimed to have. Frequency distributions for these two measures are given in Table 7-B.

TABLE 7-B
The Number of Toys and the Number of Friends of Fifth-Grade Boys ($N = 40$)

Toys Class	Frequency f	Friends X	Frequency f
27–29	2	9	1
24–26	6	8	0
21–23	3	7	5
18–20	3	6	5
15–17	6	5	7
12–14	7	4	8
9–11	8	3	8
6–8	4	2	5
3–5	0	1	0
0–2	1	0	1

1. John had twenty-two toys and four friends. What was his percentile rank in each distribution?

2. How many friends must John have to attain the same percentile rank for friends as he has for toys?

3. Charles has five friends. How many toys must he own to attain the same relative standing for toys as he has for friends?

STANDARD OR z-SCORES

The mean, as you recall, is the measure of central tendency used most often. Thus, another way of making meaningful comparisons of scores in two different distributions is to use some common or standard unit of measurement to express an individual's distance from the mean in each distribution of scores. This is precisely what a standard score does. A **standard score** indicates how far a raw score is from the mean in standard deviation units. A standard score is symbolized by **z** and is also referred to as a **z-score**. It is operationally defined in Equation 7.1 as the quotient obtained when a raw score deviation from the mean ($X - \bar{X}$) is divided by the standard deviation (s). The z-score is another measure of relative standing.

Equation 7.1
$$z = \frac{X - \bar{X}}{s}$$

Transformation of a Raw Score to a Standard Score

The operations performed in transforming a raw score to a standard score are much like the operations you used in Chapters 5 and 6 when transforming scores to compute the mean and variance. You selected a midpoint of a class near the center of the distribution, subtracted it from every other midpoint, and then divided the differences obtained by the width measurement, i. In transforming a raw score to a z-score you select the mean instead of an arbitrary central midpoint, subtract the mean from the score you wish to transform, and divide the obtained difference by the width measurement, s.

Consider the following problem. Suppose that for the students in your statistics class the distribution of the first exam scores has a mean equal to 50 and a standard deviation equal to 4, and you have a score of 60. What would your score on the second exam have to be to maintain your relative standing if the mean and standard deviation of the second exam are 78 and 6, respectively?

This problem requires that you first transform a raw score into a standard score. This initial transformation of a raw score utilizes Equation 7.1. Sixty is substituted for x, 50 for $\bar{X}$, and 4 for s. Solving the equation for z would yield a standard score of $+2.5$:

$$z = \frac{60 - 50}{4} = \frac{10}{4} = +2.5$$

A plus ($+$) or minus ($-$) sign generally precedes the standard score to indicate its position relative to the mean. A plus standard score indicates that the raw score is above the mean; a minus standard score indicates that the raw score is below the mean. Thus, your score on the first exam places you 2.5 standard deviation units above the mean.

Transformation of a z-Score to a Raw Score

To maintain a class standing of 2.5 standard deviation units above the mean, your score on the second exam would also have to be 2.5 standard deviation units above the mean of that distribution. To determine what that score must be requires that you transform a standard score of $+2.5$ into a raw score in the distribution of the second exam scores. This requires substituting the appropriate values for z, s, and $\bar{X}$ in Equation 7.1 and solving for X. An algebraic manipulation of Equation 7.1 gives the following formula for X:

Formula 7.1 $X = z\,s + \bar{X}$

Substituting $+2.5$ for z, 6 for s, and 78 for $\bar{X}$ in Formula 7.1 yields a raw score equal to 93:

$$X = +2.5(6) + 78 = 93$$

Thus, your score on the second exam has to be 93 to maintain your class standing.

PROGRESS ASSESSMENT 7.7

1. In one distribution you have a score that is 2.3 standard deviations below the mean. What score in a second distribution must you have to maintain the same relative standing if the second distribution has an $\bar{X} = 33$ and $s = 2$?

2. One distribution has an $\bar{X} = 50$ and $s^2 = 16$; another distribution has $\bar{X} = 29$ and $s = 3$. What score would you have to have in the first distribution if you had a score of 32 in the second distribution and you wanted to have the same relative standing in both distributions?

An Important z-Score Characteristic

You learned in Chapter 5 that the mean is the point in a distribution about which the sum of the deviations equals zero. This means that the sum, and hence the mean, of z-scores also equals zero. This characteristic of z-scores makes them useful not only as a measure of relative standing but also as a means of determining whether or not a relationship exists between samples or sample characteristics. Also, since Equation 7.1 can be used to convert a distribution with any mean and standard deviation to a distribution with a mean and standard deviation of 0 and 1, respectively, z-scores enable us to measure the degree of the relationship between samples or sample characteristics. This is the topic of the next chapter.

PROGRESS ASSESSMENT 7.8

Demonstrate that the sum of the z-scores equals zero, that is, $z = 0$, for each of the following data sets:

1. Data set: 12, 17, 22
2. Data set: 25, 14, 10, 19, 22, 16, 20

SUMMARY

In this chapter you are introduced to frequently used measures of relative standing: percentile, percentile rank, and standard or z-score. You are given instructions on how to graphically and mathematically estimate percentile and percentile rank and how to use these estimates to compare either different individuals or individuals with themselves on two or more characteristics. The chapter also demonstrates how to convert raw scores to standard scores and vice versa. These standard scores are useful not only as measures of relative standing but also as a means for establishing and measuring the relationship between samples and sample characteristics.

KEY DEFINITIONS

decile   A quantile designation for values that divide the area under a frequency polygon into ten equal parts.

percentile   A quantile designation for values that divide the area under a frequency polygon into one hundred equal parts and a point in a distribution at or below which a specified percentage of the cases fall.

percentile rank   The percentile rank of a score is a value indicating the percentage of cases falling at or below that score.

P_k Symbol for percentile where k takes on values from 1 to 99.

quantiles   The collective name for values such as deciles, percentiles, and quartiles that divide a frequency distribution into a specified number of groups with equal frequencies.

standard or z-score   The distance of a raw score from the mean in standard deviation units.

$X = zs + \overline{X}$ Formula for transforming a z-score to a raw score.

z Symbol for a standard score or z-score.

z-score   The distance of a raw score from the mean in standard deviation units.

$z = (X - \overline{X})/s$ Defining equation for a standard score or z-score.

REVIEW EXERCISES

1. Grades on Abnormal Psychology midterm and final comprehensive examinations were as follows:

   Midterm: 60, 55, 78, 83, 67, 79, 76, 75, 81, 84, 83, 90, 93, 95, 98, 92, 75, 76, 78, 77, 79, 61, 49, 54, 87, 85, 78, 77, 81, 83, 76, 84, 90, 92, 76, 79, 84, 85, 87, 79, 64, 73, 88, 71, 83, 72, 77, 81, 90, 92.
   Final: 71, 40, 83, 91, 77, 92, 36, 71, 86, 85, 71, 70, 47, 57, 61, 88, 75, 90, 59, 63, 79, 81, 78, 77, 73, 75, 77, 79, 83, 87, 71, 68, 79, 83, 85, 89, 91, 81, 79, 80, 77, 67, 69, 70, 70, 73, 72, 70, 71, 84.

   a. Construct stem-and-leaf diagrams for the midterm and final examination scores.

   b. Construct a grouped frequency distribution for midterm exam grades with a lower apparent limit of the lowest class equal to 45 and $i = 5$.

   c. Construct a grouped frequency distribution for final exam grades with lower apparent limit of the highest class equal to 90 and $k = 10$.

   d. Using the graphical method of determining percentiles, determine the median and the interquartile range for the midterm exam scores.

   e. Using the graphical method of determining percentile ranks, determine the percentile rank of a final exam score of 73.

2. For each of the distributions in Review Exercise 1 compute the following:
   a. mean
   b. median
   c. mode
   d. variance
   e. standard deviation
   f. quartile deviation
   g. the percentile rank of 85
3. Considering the distributions in Exercise 1, what score on the final examination would
   a. have the same percentile rank as 70 on the midterm?
   b. be at the 79 percentile?
   c. have a standard score of 1.3?
   d. have the same z-score equivalent as 64 on the midterm?

ANSWERS TO PROGRESS ASSESSMENTS

7.1   **1.** 48
    2. 75
    3. 6

7.2   **1.** 48
    2. 75
    3. 6

7.3 71

7.4   **1.** 85
    2. 97
    3. 114.5

7.5   **1. a.** 84.88
      b. 96.94
      c. 114.5
    2. a. 19
      b. 18.16
      c. 18.64
    3. $P_k = LRL_p + i([n_{bp} - n_{LRL}]/f)$

7.6   **1.** toys = 76; friends = 45.
    2. 6
    3. 17

7.7   **1.** 28.4
    2. 54

7.8   **1.** $(-1) + (0) + (1) = 0$
    2. $(1.38) + (-0.79) + (-1.58) + (0.20) + (0.79) + (-0.39) + (0.39) = 0$

Measures of Relationship

A basic question in statistics asks if there is a relationship between sample characteristics. One attempt to answer this question involves manipulating one characteristic and assessing the effect of the manipulation on the other characteristic (see Chapter 2). However, many characteristics, such as an individual's height, shoe size, or weight, are generally not subject to such manipulation. How then can you establish whether or not a relationship exists between dependent measures such as weight and height?

In the previous chapter you saw how you could use the z-score as a measure of relative standing. In this chapter you will learn how to use the concepts of standard score and relative standing to establish if there is a relationship between two sample characteristics. And, once you have established that there is such a relationship, you will learn how to predict the value of one characteristic to be expected when a particular value of the other characteristic is known.

CORRELATION

If each element of a sample is measured on two characteristics, such as height and weight for a sample of six-year-old boys, the relationship between the two characteristics, generally referred to as the **correlation,** can be depicted graphically by a scatter plot as shown in Figure 8.1. You will recall from Chapter 4 that each point in a scatter plot represents an individual's score on each of the two characteristics. The underscored point in Figure 8.1, for example, represents a child whose height is 39 inches (X-axis) and whose weight is 49 pounts (Y-axis). Inspection of Figure 8.1 suggests that as height increases weight also increases.

When high scores on one variable tend to be associated with high scores on another variable, as they are for height and weight in Figure 8.1, the relationship between the variables is said to be positive. If, on the other hand, the scores on one variable tend to decrease as scores on the other variable increase, as those in Figure 8.2, the relationship is said to be negative.

Now compare the relationship between height and weight depicted in Figure 8.1 with the relationship between height and shoe size depicted in Figure 8.3. Although both are positive, height seems to provide better or more accurate information about weight than it does for shoe size since the weights at the given heights are not as dispersed as the shoe sizes.

THE PEARSON CORRELATION COEFFICIENT, *r*

How much more accurate is the information height provides about weight than the information it provides about shoe size? To determine this, you will need a **correlation coefficient,** an index that indicates the degree

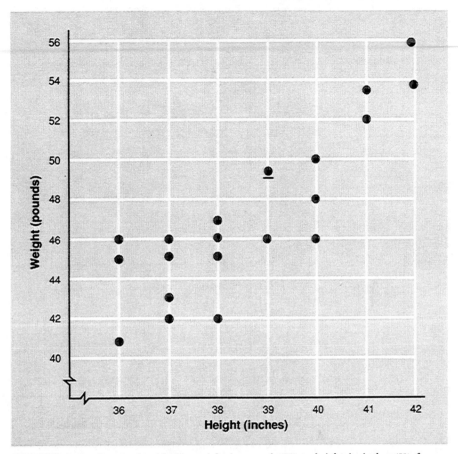

FIGURE 8.1 *Scatter plot relating weight in pounds (Y) to height in inches (X) for a sample of six-year-old boys.*

of the relationship between two variables or sample characteristics. Such an index requires that the measures taken on the two characteristics be comparable. This is where your knowledge of standard score and relative standing becomes very useful.

You will recall that by using z-scores you can determine whether or not an individual occupies the same position in two quite different distributions, such as height and weight. These positions are called the individual's relative standing in each of the two distributions. If each individual in a sample occupies the same position in two distributions, that is, has the same relative standing on each of the two characteristics, then information on one characteristic, such as height, provides very accurate information on the other characteristic, weight. In fact, if that is

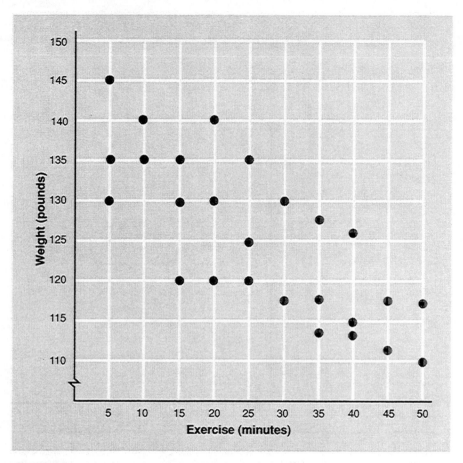

FIGURE 8.2 *Scatter plot relating weight in pounds (Y) to the number of minutes per day spent exercising (X) for a sample of young women.*

the case for height and weight, you can tell exactly what an individual's weight is if you know his height. In such a case, the relationship between the two characteristics, height and weight, is a perfect positive relationship. The more the individual's relative standings (z-scores) on the two characteristics differ or deviate from one another, the less accurate is the information that one characteristic provides about the other.

These deviation scores, symbolized $z_x - z_y$, provide the basis for an index that indicates the degree of relationship between two sample characteristics. Since the average of these deviation scores is necessarily zero (because the mean of z-scores equals zero), the relationship may be indexed by finding the sum of the squared deviations and dividing by the sample size minus one ($N - 1$) as you did when computing the variance (see Chapter 6, Equation 6.2). If you then take one-half of this value and subtract it from 1, you have an index, **r**, that can take on values only between -1 and $+1$. This index, which is defined by Equation 8.1 and is called the

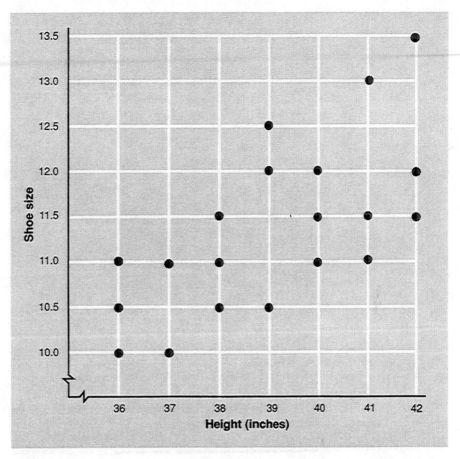

FIGURE 8.3 *Scatter plot relating shoe size of six-year-old boys (Y) to height in inches (X).*

Pearson correlation coefficient, is a measure of the degree of relationship of two sample characteristics measured along interval or ratio scales. This index was devised by a British scientist, Karl Pearson, in 1895.

Equation 8.1 $r = 1 - \frac{1}{2} [\Sigma(z_x - z_y)^2/(N - 1)]$

The sign of r, that is, $+$ or $-$, indicates the direction (positive or negative) of the relationship. When no sign precedes the value of r, it is taken to be positive. A positive sign indicates that high values on one characteristic tend to be associated with high values on the other characteristic. A negative sign indicates that high values on one characteristic tend to be associated with low values on the other. Coefficients that are of equal value but of opposite sign indicate equally strong relationships that are opposite in direction. A coefficient equal to zero indicates the absence of a relationship. Figure 8.4 depicts two characteristics, height and IQ, that have little or no relationship.

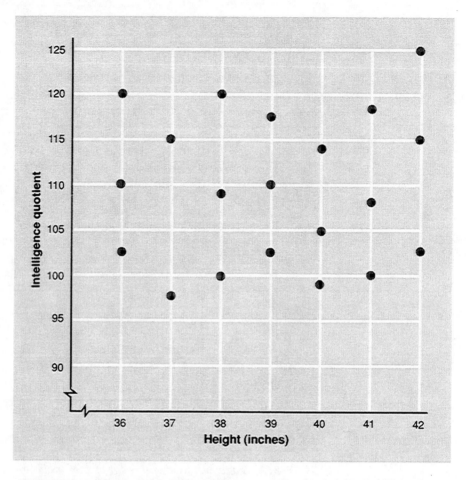

FIGURE 8.4 *Scatter plot indicating little or no relationship between intelligence quotient (Y) and height (X) for a sample of six-year-old boys.*

PROGRESS ASSESSMENT 8.1

From your everyday experiences and common knowledge, state whether or not you would expect a relationship to be positive, negative, or zero, that is, nonexistent, for the variables in each of the following items:

1. Number of cigarettes smoked per day and overall state of health.
2. Caloric intake and weight.
3. Head circumference and intelligence.
4. Saturated fat intake and cholesterol level.
5. Thermostat setting and heat bill.
6. Time spent studying and grade-point average.

Computing r

Since standard scores can be converted back into raw scores, a computational formula for the Pearson correlation coefficient can be written in raw score symbols as follows:

Formula 8.1
$$r = \frac{N\Sigma XY - (\Sigma X)(\Sigma Y)}{\sqrt{[N\Sigma X^2 - (\Sigma X)^2][N\Sigma Y^2 - (\Sigma Y)^2]}}$$

The data depicted in Figure 8.1 is shown in Table 8.1. The Pearson correlation coefficent is computed for these data at the bottom of the table using Formula 8.1.

TABLE 8.1
The Height (X) in Inches and Weight (Y) in Pounds for Each of a Sample (N = 20) of Six-Year-Old Boys and Calculations for r

Case	Height (X)	Weight (Y)	X^2	Y^2	XY
1	42	56	1764	3136	2352
2	42	53	1764	2809	2226
3	41	52	1681	2704	2132
4	41	50	1681	2500	2050
5	40	50	1600	2500	2000
6	40	48	1600	2304	1920
7	40	46	1600	2116	1840
8	39	49	1521	2401	1911
9	39	46	1521	2116	1794
10	38	47	1444	2209	1786
11	38	46	1444	2116	1748
12	38	45	1444	2025	1710
13	38	42	1444	1764	1596
14	37	46	1369	2116	1702
15	37	45	1369	2025	1665
16	37	43	1369	1849	1591
17	37	42	1369	1764	1554
18	36	46	1296	2116	1656
19	36	45	1296	2025	1620
20	36	41	1296	1681	1476
	772	938	29872	44276	36329

$$r = \frac{N(\Sigma XY) - (\Sigma X)(\Sigma Y)}{\sqrt{[N\Sigma X^2 - (\Sigma X)^2][N\Sigma Y^2 - (\Sigma Y)^2]}} = \frac{20(36329) - (772)(938)}{\sqrt{[20(29872) - 772^2][20(44276) - 938^2]}}$$

$$r = 0.85$$

PROGRESS ASSESSMENT 8.2

The gestation period in days (the number of days from conception to birth) and the expected life span in years (the average number of years from birth to death) are presented in Table 8-A for a variety of common animals. Determine the degree of relationship between these two variables by computing the Pearson correlation coefficient, *r*.

TABLE 8-A
The Gestation Period in Days (*X*) and the Life Span in Years (*Y*) for a Variety of Common Animals

Animal	Gestation (*X*)	Life Span (*Y*)
Black bear	219	18
Chipmunk	31	6
Domestic cat	63	12
Domestic dog	61	12
Guinea pig	68	4
Horse	330	20
Mouse	20	3
Pig	112	10
Rabbit	31	5
Rat	21	3

Statistical Significance of *r*

Once you have obtained a value for *r*, you must decide whether or not you should accept *r* as indicating a true relationship between the two variables. It is possible that *r* measured a chance relationship. That is, it is possible that if you repeated your sampling and measuring procedures, a relationship between the two variables would not be evident.

How do you make such a decision? You follow a set of rules referred to as a statistical test. The logic of the test requires that you assume a relationship between the variables *does not exist* in the population, that is, you assume ϱ (pronounced rho) = 0 where ϱ is the parameter equivalent of the statistic *r*. Such an assumption about a statistical population is called a **statistical hypothesis.**

You then determine what the probability of obtaining your *r* would be if your hypothesis is correct. If the probability is too low to lend support to your statistical hypothesis, you reject your hypothesis and consider your *r* to indicate a true relationship. If the probability is high enough to support your statistical hypothesis, then you would *not* consider your *r* to indicate a true relationship. The probability level that is the dividing line between what is considered a high or low probability is called the **level**

of significance. Although the level of significance is your choice, the convention has been to set it at 0.05, or 5 percent. If the probability of obtaining your *r* is 5 percent or less, then you should consider it too low to warrant support of your statistical hypothesis that $\varrho = 0$.

Fortunately, you do not have to compute these probabilities. For most statistical tests the probabilities of obtaining certain values for the statistic have been tabulated so that all you have to do is compare your obtained statistic with some table value to determine if you should or should not reject your hypothesis. The table in which to find the probability of obtaining your *r*-value is Table 2 in the Appendix at the back of the text. You can look up the *r*-value in Table 2 that is associated with a 5 percent probability or significance level of 0.05 for a sample that has $N - 2$ degrees of freedom, where *N* equals the number of paired observations or the sample size. If your |r| is equal to or greater than the value in the table, then it is referred to as having **statistical significance,** a condition in which the probability of occurrence is too low to warrant support of a statistical hypothesis. You would, therefore, reject your statistical hypothesis and conclude that the *r*-value that you obtained represents a true relationship.

PROGRESS ASSESSMENT 8.3

1. Determine if the correlation coefficient between height and weight in Table 8.1 is statistically significant.
2. Determine if the relationship between gestation and life span in Progress Assessment 8.2 is statistically significant.

r Compared to r^2

The correlation coefficient, *r*, indicates the strength of the relationship between two measured characteristics. Given similar sample sizes and similar variability in the measures on different sets of characteristics as those depicted in Figures 8.1 and 8.3, an *r* of 0.85 for the relationship between height and weight reflects a stronger relationship between the two characteristics than the *r* of 0.63 for height and shoe size.

The correlation coefficient, *r*, should never be interpreted as a proportion or percent. Its square, however, r^2, which is called the **coefficient of determination,** is considered to be the proportion or percentage of variance in one characteristic predictable from the other. For example, Table 8.1 indicates that the children's height varied from 36 to 42 inches. Thus, some of their differences in weight can be attributed to their different heights. However, some of their differences in weight can also be attributed to their eating habits among other things. How much of the variability in weight, then, is attributable to their different heights? This is what the coefficient of determination tells you. For the weights and heights in Table

8.1, the correlation coefficient, r, is 0.85. The coefficient of determination, r^2, is, then, 0.72. Thus, approximately 72 percent of the varability in weight of the children can be accounted for by the differences in their heights.

As you might guess, the percentage of variability in one characteristic that is not predictable from the other is equal to $1 - r^2$ and is called the **coefficient of nondetermination.** Therefore, 28 percent of the children's differences in weight is attributable to things other than height, such as eating habits.

PROGRESS ASSESSMENT 8.4

1. Determine the percentage of variance in the animals' life spans in Progress Assessment 8.2 that is predictable from gestation period.
2. Determine the percentage of variance in the animals' life spans in Progress Assessment 8.2 that is not predictable from gestation period.

Caution in Interpreting r

Although r may indicate a true relationship between two sample characteristics, it may be a mistake to conclude that it is a cause-and-effect relationship. Two characteristics can be correlated when they are similarly related to a third characteristic. For example, there may be a high correlation between nervousness and hair loss, but this does not imply that nervousness causes hair loss. Both nervousness and hair loss could be the result of an individual's diet. This, of course, does not mean that when there is a correlation between two characteristics or events a cause-and-effect relationship does not exist. A cause-and-effect relationship necessarily implies a correlation between the events or characteristics, but never does a correlation between characteristics or events imply a cause-and-effect relationship.

OTHER COEFFICIENTS OF CORRELATION

The Pearson correlation coefficient, r, is used to indicate the degree of relationship between two characteristics when the measures of the characteristics constitute interval or ratio scales. If one or both of the characteristics of interest are measured along nominal or ordinal scales, then other coefficients are used to obtain an index of the degree of the relationship.

Factors Determining the Appropriate Correlation Coefficient

When one characteristic is **dichotomous**—that is, can be only one thing or another such as home owner or not a home owner—and is assigned values on a nominal scale, while the other characteristic is measured on an interval or ratio scale, the **point biserial correlation coefficient, r_{pb},** is used to index the relationship. For example, r_{pb} would be a measure of the strength of the relationship between home ownership and income level.

When both X and Y characteristics are dichotomous, and when the numbers assigned to the characteristics constitute nominal scales, the **phi coefficient, r_{ϕ},** is used to index the degree of relationship. For example, the relationship between gender (X) and marital status (Y) would be indexed by the phi coefficient. In such a case the values 0 and 1 could designate the categories (X,Y) to which an individual belongs—for example, 0,1 for a married male; 1,1 for a single male; 0,0 for a married female; and 1,0 for a single female.

When the measures on both characteristics constitute ordinal scales, the **Spearman rank-order correlation coefficient, r_s,** is the appropriate index. No formula has been derived to obtain an index of the relationship between two characteristics when the measures of one characteristic are on an ordinal scale and the measures of the other characteristic are along an interval or ratio scale. However, the interval or ratio scale can be converted to an ordinal scale, and r_s can be computed.

The Pearson correlation coefficient formula can be used to obtain a value for any one of these coefficients. However, separate, more simplified formulas for computing each of these coefficients can be derived from Formula 8.1. One of these simplified formulas is used to obtain a value for r_s in the next section.

PROGRESS ASSESSMENT 8.5

For each pair of variables in the following list, name the correlation coefficient that would be most appropriate for indexing the relationship.

1. Amount of dietary cholesterol and yearly medical expense.
2. Ratings on beauty and ratings on talent.
3. Home owner and political affiliation (Republican or Democrat).
4. Air temperature and number of pieces of clothing worn.
5. Gender and yearly income.
6. Class rank and grade point average.

Spearman Rank-Order Correlation Coefficient

The Spearman rank-order correlation coefficient is obtained for the data of Figure 8.1 that is presented in Table 8.2 using a simplified formula derived from the computational formula for the Pearson correlation coefficient. This formula is expressed:

Formula 8.2 $r_s = 1 - \dfrac{6\Sigma d^2}{N(N^2 - 1)}$

TABLE 8.2
The Height (X) in Inches, Weight (Y) in Pounds, and Ranks (R) of Each Member of a Sample ($N = 20$) of Six-Year-Old Boys and Calculations for r_s

Case	Height X	Rank R_x	Weight Y	Rank R_y	d $R_x - R_y$	d^2 $(R_x - R_y)^2$
1	42	19.5	56	20.0	−0.5	0.25
2	42	19.5	53	19.0	0.5	0.25
3	41	17.5	52	18.0	−0.5	0.25
4	41	17.5	50	16.5	1.0	1.00
5	40	15.0	50	16.5	−1.5	2.25
6	40	15.0	48	14.0	1.0	1.00
7	40	15.0	46	10.0	5.0	25.00
8	39	12.5	49	15.0	−2.5	6.25
9	39	12.5	46	10.0	2.5	6.25
10	38	9.5	47	13.0	−3.5	12.25
11	38	9.5	46	10.0	−0.5	0.25
12	38	9.5	45	6.0	3.5	12.25
13	38	9.5	42	2.5	7.0	49.00
14	37	5.5	46	10.0	−4.5	16.25
15	37	5.5	45	6.0	−0.5	0.25
16	37	5.5	43	4.0	1.5	2.25
17	37	5.5	42	2.5	3.0	9.00
18	36	2.0	46	10.0	−8.0	64.00
19	36	2.0	45	6.0	−4.0	16.00
20	36	2.0	41	1.0	1.0	1.00
						229.00

$$r_s = 1 - \frac{6\Sigma d^2}{N(N^2 - 1)}$$

$$= 1 - \frac{6(229.00)}{[20(20^2 - 1)]}$$

$$= 0.83$$

In this formula, 6 is a constant, N refers to the number of paired observations, and d is the difference in the ranks of the paired observations.

In order to obtain r_s, the height and weight scores in Table 8.2 must be converted to an ordinal scale. This is accomplished by ranking the height and weight scores independently from 1 to 20. In Table 8.2, for example, the rank of 1 is given to the lowest weight and a rank of 20 to the highest. Tied values are given an average rank. For example, the three 36-inch height scores are given an average rank of 2, that is, the mean of ranks 1, 2, and 3. Note that the value for r_s does not equal the r-value obtained for the same data in Table 8.1. The r would, however, be the same value as the obtained r_s if Formula 8.1 were applied to the ranked weights and heights.

The procedure and rationale for determining the significance of r_s is similar to that for determining the significance of r except that Table 3 in the Appendix at the back of the text is used instead of Table 2. Note that in Table 3 the sample size (N) is used instead of the degrees of freedom (df) for locating the value of r_s that is statistically significant.

PROGRESS ASSESSMENT 8.6

1. A teacher ranked a small group of nursery school children on neatness in personal appearance and neatness in school work to see if there was a relationship. The ranks for each of ten children are shown in Table 8-B with a rank of 1 indicating the lowest degree of neatness. Obtain a value for the Spearman rank-order correlation coefficient.

TABLE 8-B
The Ranks for a Small Group ($N = 10$) of Nursery School Children on Neatness in Personal Appearance and Neatness in School Work

Child	Appearance	School Work
Mary	1	3
Alice	2	1
Seth	3	5
Mark	4	2
Ann	5	6
Henry	6	4
James	7	9
Beth	8	8
Nancy	9	7
Chris	10	10

2. In Table 8-C are men's, women's and children's average ratings to the nearest whole number for the top ten syndicated TV programs. Determine if the r_s index of the relationship between the women's and children's ratings is larger or smaller than the r_s index of the relationship between men's and children's ratings.

TABLE 8-C
Men's, Women's, and Children's Average Ratings of the Top Ten Syndicated Television Programs

Program	Men	Women	Children
1	12	16	7
2	6	10	3
3	6	7	3
4	5	7	4
5	6	6	3
6	4	6	1
7	4	5	7
8	2	6	1
9	3	6	0
10	5	5	3

3. Using Table 3 in the Appendix, determine if the relationship between neatness in appearance and neatness in school work in part 1 of this Progress Assessment is statistically significant.

4. Determine if the relationships between (a) women's and children's TV ratings and (b) men's and children's TV ratings in part 2 of this Progress Assessment are statistically significant.

THE VALUE OF CORRELATION IN PREDICTION

Even though correlation does not necessarily imply a cause-and-effect relationship, information about the strength of the relationship should be useful in estimating the value of one characteristic when the value of the other characteristic is known. If there were no relationship between height and weight for six-year-old boys, your best estimate of the weight of a six-year-old, regardless of his height, would be the mean weight of that age group. This, you will recall from Chapter 5, is because the mean of a distribution is a point around which most scores tend to cluster. On the other hand, a relationship between height and weight should permit you to estimate a more accurate weight for a boy of a specified height. Instead of estimating the weight of a boy of a specified height to be the mean weight of the entire age group, your best estimate would be the mean weight of boys of the specified height.

If the relationship between height and weight was a perfect positive relationship, that is, if $r = 1.0$, then the line connecting the mean weights of boys of different heights would be straight. The line connecting the mean values of one characteristic for several fixed values of another characteristic is called the **regression line.** The equation for the regression line is used to predict the value of one characteristic for a known or given value of another characteristic with which it is related.

Even if the relationship between two characteristics is not a perfect relationship, that is, $-1 < r < +1$, a straight line, also called a regression line, can be constructed that would be useful in making predictions.

The Regression Line

If you wish to predict how much a six-year old boy would weigh if he were 48 inches tall, you must be able to generate the equation for the best-fitting straight line through the points in the scatter plot. This equation is called the **regression equation:**

Equation 8.2 $$Y' = mX + b$$

In this equation Y' is a predicted value, m is the slope of the line, and b is the point where the line crosses the Y-axis, the Y-intercept.

The equation for the best-fitting straight line would be one that gives the most satisfactory estimates of m and b. The equation that makes the squares of your errors in prediction as small as possible is generally believed to yield the most satisfactory estimates of m and b. If your predicted Y-value (Y') for a child's weight was 49 pounds when his actual weight (Y) was 50 pounds, your prediction would be off by 1 pound. An error in prediction, then, can be symbolized $Y - Y'$, and the sum of the squares of your errors can be written $\Sigma(Y - Y')^2$. Thus, the equation that makes $\Sigma(Y - Y')^2$ as small as possible is the equation for the best-fitting straight line.

There are a number of procedures for generating the most satisfactory estimates of m and b. The easiest procedure involves summating two sets of equations. Each of your N-paired observations (X,Y), set up in the general form $Y = mX + b$, provides the first set. Summing this first set of equations yields Equation 8.3:

$$Y_1 = mX_1 + b$$
$$Y_2 = mX_2 + b$$
$$Y_3 = mX_3 + b$$
$$\cdots\cdots\cdots\cdots\cdots$$
$$Y_n = mX_n + b$$

Equation 8.3 $\Sigma Y = m\Sigma X + Nb$

The second set of equations is obtained by multiplying each equation in the above set by its X-value. Summing this set of equations yields Equation 8.4:

$$X_1 Y_1 = mX_1 X_1 + bX_1$$
$$X_2 Y_2 = mX_2 X_2 + bX_2$$
$$X_3 Y_3 = mX_3 X_3 + bX_3$$
$$\ldots \ldots \ldots \ldots \ldots \ldots \ldots$$
$$X_n Y_n = mX_n X_n + bX_n$$

Equation 8.4 $\Sigma XY = m\Sigma X^2 + b\Sigma X$

Equations 8.3 and 8.4 are then solved simultaneously by first multiplying each equation by the b coefficient of the other equation as follows:

$$(N)(\Sigma XY) = (N)m\Sigma X^2 + (N)b\Sigma X$$
$$(\Sigma X)(\Sigma Y) = m(\Sigma X)(\Sigma X) + Nb\,(\Sigma X)$$

The coefficient of b in Equation 8.3 is N and the coefficient of b in Equation 8.4 is ΣX.

One equation is then subtracted from the other to yield the following: $N(\Sigma XY) - (\Sigma X)(\Sigma Y) = Nm\Sigma X^2 - m(\Sigma X)(\Sigma X)$. Factoring the right-hand side of this equation to equal $m(N\Sigma X^2 - (\Sigma X)(\Sigma X)] = m[N\Sigma X^2 - (\Sigma X)^2]$ and dividing each side by $N\Sigma X^2 - (\Sigma X)^2$ yields the following equation for m:

Equation 8.5 $m = \dfrac{N\Sigma XY - (\Sigma X)(\Sigma Y)}{N\Sigma X^2 - (\Sigma X)^2}$

Rewriting Equation 8.3 to solve for b gives the following equation:

Equation 8.6 $b = \dfrac{-m(\Sigma X)}{N} + \dfrac{(\Sigma Y)}{N}$

Once a value for m is obtained, it can be substituted in Equation 8.6 to obtain a value for b.

You are encouraged to learn the procedure to generate Equations 8.3 and 8.4 rather than attempting to memorize Equations 8.5 and 8.6. Table 8.3 utilizes a small portion of the data of Figure 8.1 to provide a numerical illustration of this procedure.

The values of the slope and Y-intercept computed in Table 8.3 yield the following regression equation: $Y' = 2.34X - 43.65$.

The best-fitting straight line for the data in Table 8.3 is shown in Figure 8.5. To draw the best-fitting straight line, you simply substitute two different values for X and solve for Y'. In the example, we substituted heights of 37 and 42 inches for X and obtained values for Y equal to 42.9 and 54.6 pounds, respectively. A straight line is then drawn between the two points

TABLE 8.3
The Height (X) in Inches and Weight (Y) in Pounds of Each of a Sample ($N = 6$) of Six-Year-Old Boys and a Numerical Illustration of the Procedure Used to Generate the Regression Equation.

Height X	Weight Y	First Set of Equations $Y = mX + b$	Second Set of Equations $XY = mX^2 + bX$
36	41	$41 = 36m + b$	$1476 = 1296m + 36b$
37	45	$45 = 37m + b$	$1665 = 1369m + 37b$
38	42	$42 = 38m + b$	$1596 = 1\,'44m + 38b$
39	49	$49 = 39m + b$	$1911 = 1521m + 39b$
40	48	$48 = 40m + b$	$1920 = 1600m + 40b$
42	56	$56 = 42m + b$	$2352 = 1764m + 42b$
		$281 = 232m + 6b$	$10920 = 8994m + 232b$

Each of these summation equations is multiplied by the b coefficient of the other equation as follows:

$$(6)10920 = (6)8994m + (6)232b$$
$$(232)281 = (232)232m + (232)6b$$

Multiplying through by the coefficients of b and subtraction gives:

$$65520 = 53964m + 1392b$$
$$- \underline{(65192 = 53824m + 1392b)}$$
$$328 = 140m$$

Dividing both sides of the equation by 140 gives $2.34 = m$.

A value for b is then obtained by substituting the value for m in the sum of the first set of equations as follows:

$$281 = 232(2.34) + 6b$$
$$281 - (232)(2.34) = 6b$$
$$281 - 542.88 = 6b$$
$$- 261.88 = 6b$$
$$- 43.65 = b$$

(+'s in Figure 8.5) representing these (X, Y) pairs in the scatter plot. The regression equation for this line, since it minimizes $\Sigma(Y - Y')^2$, the square of the distances of the points from the line, is often referred to as the **least squares regression equation.**

PROGRESS ASSESSMENT 8.7

Find the least squares regression equation for the data in Progress Assessment 8.2.

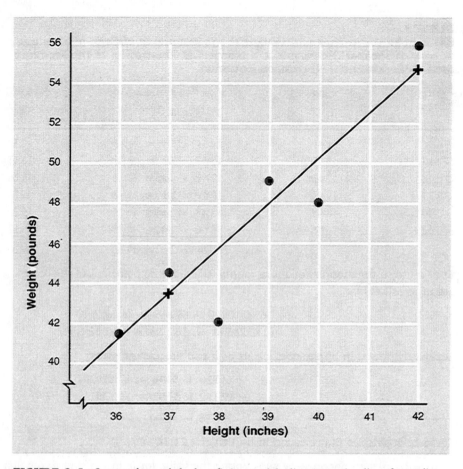

FIGURE 8.5 *Scatter plot and the best-fitting straight line (regression line) for predicting weight in pounds (Y) from height in inches (X) for a sample of six-year-old boys.*

Predicting Y from X

Once the least squares regression equation has been generated, prediction becomes a simple procedure. Merely substitute the known or given value of X into the regression equation and solve for Y'. For example, for the sample represented in Table 8.3 where $Y' = 2.34X - 43.65$, to predict what a boy's weight would be if his height were 48 inches, substitute 48 for X and solve for Y' as follows: $Y' = 2.34(48) - 43.65 = 68.67$. The boy's weight would be 69 pounds (68.67 rounded to the nearest whole number).

PROGRESS ASSESSMENT 8.8

Predict the life span (Progress Assessment 8.2) of an animal that has a gestation period of 45 days.

The Standard Error of Prediction

Although the least squares regression equation was developed to minimize errors in prediction, it does not necessarily eliminate errors. Thus, it would be advantageous to be able to estimate how much error is associated with a prediction. The smaller the standard deviation of the error scores, that is, $s_{Y-Y'}$, the more accurate will be the prediction. Thus, the standard deviation of the error scores is also called the **standard error of prediction, $s_{Y'}$**.

Fortunately, you do not have to compute the standard deviation of the error scores directly to obtain the standard error of prediction. The following is an alternative computational formula for the standard error of prediction.

Formula 8.3 $s_{Y'} = s_Y \sqrt{1 - r^2}$

PROGRESS ASSESSMENT 8.9

Determine the standard error of your prediction in Progress Assessment 8.8.

The Meaning of Regression

Regression differs from correlation in that, whereas correlation is concerned with the joint variation of two sample characteristics, regression is concerned with the variation in one sample characteristic when the other is held fixed at each of several levels. Consider the data set of Figure 8.1. For any given height there are various weights, that is, a distribution of weights. Each of these distributions has a mean. **Regression** refers to the tendency for the predicted value of weight for a given height to approach more closely its mean value than any other value. The smaller the value of r, the greater will be this tendency. This can best be understood by using the following alternative form of the regression equation:

Equation 8.7 $Y' = r(\frac{S_y}{S_x}) X - \bar{X}] + \bar{Y}$

Assuming homogeneity of variance, that is, $s_x = s_y$, an algebraic manipulation of Equation 8.7 yields the following:

Equation 8.8 $z_{y'} = r z_x$

You will recall that the mean of the z-scores equals zero (Chapter 7). With Equation 8.8 it can be shown that the smaller the value of r, the more closely $z_{y'}$ should approach zero, that is, the mean of the standard y-scores. Consider a height that is two standard deviations above the mean ($z_x = 2$) and r-values of 1, 0.75, 0.5, 0.25, and 0. The predicted weight values (Y') will be 2, 1.5, 1, 0.5, and 0 standard deviation units ($z_{y'}$) above the mean, respectively. Thus, you can see the importance of *r* in the accuracy of your prediction. If there is a perfect correlation, there is no regression towards the mean and you can predict *Y* exactly for any given *X*. If there is no correlation between characteristics ($r = 0$), then there is total regression toward the mean, and the mean of *Y* becomes the best, albeit not a very accurate, prediction for any given *X*. For values between 0 and ±1, the prediction from the least squares regression equation yields a more accurate estimate than the mean would be. The larger the *r*, the more accurate will be the prediction of *Y* from *X*.

SUMMARY

This chapter describes how the concepts of standard score and relative standing can be used to derive meaningful measures of the relationship between sample characteristics. A formula for computing the Pearson correlation coefficient, *r*, which indexes the relationship between characteristics measured along interval or ratio scales, is presented along with a procedure for determining the statistical significance of *r*. The meaning of *r* is also discussed in relation to coefficients of determination and nondetermination. Three other indices of relationship—the Spearman rank order correlation coefficient, the point-biserial coefficient, and the phi coefficient—which can be computed with the Pearson *r* formula, are discussed along with factors determining their use. The meaning of regression is examined, and a procedure is given for deriving the regression equation, which is used to predict the value of one characteristic for a known or given value of the other characteristic. A formula for estimating the standard error of prediction is also presented.

KEY DEFINITIONS

coefficient of determination   Percentage or proportion of variance in one characteristic predictable from the other characteristic.

coefficient of nondetermination   Percentage or proportion of variance in one characteristic that is not predictable from the other characteristic.

correlation   The relationship between two variables or sample characteristics.

correlation coefficient   An index of the degree of relationship between two variables or sample characteristics.

dichotomous   A term referring to the fact that a variable can take on only one value or another.

least squares regression equation   The regression equation that minimizes the square of the distance of the points from the line.

level of significance   The probability level that is the dividing line between what is considered to be a high or low probability.

$1 - r^2$ Mathematical expression of the coefficient of nondetermination.

Pearson correlation coefficient or **r**   An index of the relationship between two variables measured along interval or ratio scales.

phi coefficient or **r_ϕ**   An index of the relationship between two dichotomous variables measured along nominal scales.

point-biserial coefficient or **r_{pb}**   An index of the relationship between a variable measured along an interval or ratio scale and a dichotomous variable measured along a nominal scale.

r   Symbol for the Pearson correlation coefficient.

regression   The tendency for the predicted value of a variable to approach its mean value.

regression equation   The equation for the best-fitting straight line through the points in a scatter plot.

regression line   The line connecting the mean values of one characteristic for several fixed values of another characteristic.

$r = [N\Sigma XY - (\Sigma X)(\Sigma Y)]/\sqrt{[N\Sigma X^2 - (\Sigma X)^2][N\Sigma Y^2 - (\Sigma Y)^2]}$ Computational formula for the Pearson correlation coefficient.

ϱ   (pronounced ''rho'') A symbol for the relationship between two population characteristics; the parameter equivalent of the statistic r.

r_{pb}   Symbol for the point-biserial correlation coefficient.

r_ϕ   Symbol for the phi-coefficient.

r_s   Symbol for the Spearman rank-order correlation coefficient.

$r_s = 1 - 6\Sigma d^2/N(N^2 - 1)$ Computational formula for the Spearman correlation coefficient.

r^2   The coefficient of determination.

Spearman rank-order correlation coefficient or **r_s**   An index of the relationship between two variables measured along ordinal scales.

standard error of prediction or **$s_{Y'}$**   The standard deviation of errors in prediction.

statistical hypothesis   An assumption about a statistical population that one seeks to reject or fail to reject on the basis of information obtained from sample data.

statistical significance   A condition in which the probability of occurrence is too low to warrant support of a statistical hypothesis.

$s_{Y'}$ Symbol for the standard error of prediction.

$s_{Y'} = s_Y \sqrt{1 - r^2}$ Computational formula for obtaining the standard error of prediction.

$Y' = mX + b$ The regression equation.

REVIEW EXERCISES

1. The scores in Table 8-D represent the number of hours (X) spent preparing for a final biology exam by twelve biology majors and the grade (Y) achieved by each of them on the exam.

TABLE 8-D
Hours (X) Spent Studying
and the Grade (Y) Achieved
by 12 Biology Majors

Major	X	Y
1	20	99
2	20	90
3	18	92
4	17	87
5	16	90
6	12	80
7	12	85
8	12	75
9	10	87
10	10	80
11	8	70
12	5	60

 a. Construct a scatter plot for the hours of preparation and exam grades.
 b. What is the direction of the relationship, if any?
 c. For the number of hours of preparation (X-scores), (1) form a simple frequency distribution, (2) find the mean, (3) compute the variance, and (4) determine standard deviation.
 d. For biology grades (Y-scores), (1) form an array, (2) find the mean, (3) compute the variance, (4) determine the standard deviation of the scores.
 e. (1) Compute the appropriate correlation coefficient for the relationship between number of hours of preparation and biology grade and (2) determine if the correlation coefficient is significant.
 f. Does your value of the correlation coefficient support your answer to part *b*?
 g. Determine the equation for the best-fitting straight line.
 h. Predict the probable score for a student who would have spent fifteen hours preparing for the exam.
 i. What is the standard error of your estimate?
 j. What is the coefficient of (1) determination and (2) nondetermination?

2. Using the data from Table 8-D, complete the following:

    a. Rank the X and Y scores.

    b. Compute the Spearman rank-order correlation coefficient using the computational formula for r_s.

    c. Compute r_s by using the computational formula for the Pearson correlation coefficient on the ranks.

    d. Does your answer to part c agree with your answer to part b?

    e. Is your answer to part c, Review Exercise 2, the same as your answer to part e, Review Exercise 1?

3. For the data in Table 8-D:

    a. What effect would adding the constant 2 to each of the X-scores and the constant 3 to each of the Y-scores have on the Pearson correlation coefficient?

    b. Explain your answer to part a.

ANSWERS TO PROGRESS ASSESSMENTS

8.1
1. negative
2. positive
3. zero
4. positive
5. positive
6. positive

8.2 0.89

8.3
1. significant
2. significant

8.4
1. 79.2%
2. 20.8%

8.5
1. r
2. r_s
3. r_ϕ
4. r
5. r_{pb}
6. r_s

8.6
1. $r_s = 0.84$
2. smaller
3. significant
4. **a.** not significant
   b. not significant

8.7 $Y' = 0.054X + 4.14$

8.8 6.6 years

8.9 2.81

Probability and Decision Making

A major way we attempt to understand the world around us involves empirical research where data are collected, evaluated, and interpreted. To interpret data in relation to understanding the world, we must make certain decisions about this empirical information. Because we cannot observe and measure every event in the world, we rely on measuring some small aspect of it, and then we make an inference about the world in general. This process requires an understanding of the following concepts: the phenomenon to be investigated such that a testable research hypothesis can be generated; the procedures involved in collecting and organizing data (see Chapters 1–4); the methods used to analyze and interpret the data using inferential statistics whereby a reasonable guess from a sample (a small aspect of the world) is made about a population (the world in general); and the ability to relate this statistical interpretation to the original hypothesis.

Although these concepts are listed as "steps" in a process of evaluating data and ideas, a good investigator must at all times be aware of the interrelationship among them. For example, failure to think about how data will be analyzed before it is collected often leads to collecting information that is not interpretable. Likewise, simply looking at how the data are to be interpreted may lead to collecting analyzable data that have very little to do with the hypothesis or idea under investigation.

This chapter covers topics associated with statistically analyzing data in such a way that they can be related to a particular hypothesis. These topics include defining probability; discussing methods used to calculate probability, such as intuition, mathematical formulas, theoretical and empirical frequency distributions, and condensed versions of distributions expressed in table format; formulating both research and statistical hypotheses; using rules or conventions to evaluate these hypotheses; and discussing the types of mistakes that can be made whenever decisions about statistical hypotheses are based on probabilities.

DEFINING PROBABILITY

Anyone who has watched a weather forecaster on television has heard the term probability. In general, **probability** is a percentage or proportion indicating the likelihood of occurrence of some specified event (or events). Frequently meterologists will express probability as a percentage such as a 33 percent chance of rain. The meterologist is telling you that based on the information available, the event of interest, for example, rain tomorrow, has a probability of occurrence equal to 33 percent. As you know, percentages can also be expressed as proportions and thus a 33% chance of rain can also be stated as a probability of rain equal to 0.33 or 33/100, that is, 33 chances out of 100. Although in this text we will occasionally express probability as a percentage, you should be able to convert it to a decimal or a fraction reduced to its lowest terms. When expressed as a proportion, probability values range from 0.0 (meaning no likelihood of occurrence) to 1.00 (meaning that the event is certain to happen).

Probability can be defined at least three ways: (1) *subjectively* (personal approach), (2) *empirically* (relative frequency approach) and, (3) *classically* (theoretical approach). Although several factors influence the approach one takes with probability, very often the type of decision one is attempting to make has the greatest influence on the approach used. The following definitions and examples should help you understand these different approaches and demonstrate that the different views are not incompatible.

Subjective Definition

We have all made decisions based on our feelings or hunches that certain events will or will not occur. According to the **subjective view of probability,** probability is a measure of the strength of one's belief that an event will or will not happen. For example, suppose you decide not to take time away from studying for an announced economics exam to review your history assignments even though your roommate has a strong feeling that a history pop-quiz will be given the next day, which happens to be the tenth day of the term. (In general, you have come to mistrust your roommate's intuition as it is usually wrong.) The decision *not* to study history may have the following consequences: (1) You may do poorly on the history pop-quiz if it is given. (2) You may improve your exam score by devoting all your study time to economics. Thus, based solely on a subjective view that your roommate is wrong, you decide to use your extra time to study economics instead of reviewing history.

Although we frequently use the subjective view of probability in our daily lives, it is difficult to incorporate it as a procedure in empirical research because of the difficulty in measuring personal beliefs. In making decisions about research, investigators rely on the empirical and classical views of probability.

Empirical Definition

According to the **empirical view of probability,** probability is based on previous observations of whether or not the event occurred. In this case, probability is the ratio of number of times the event occurred divided by the number of observations. As the number of observations increases towards infinity, the true probability is assumed to be obtained.

Suppose, for example, records exist indicating whether or not a pop-quiz was given by your history instructor on any particular day in each of four terms over the last twenty-five years. You look at these records and observe that on four of the last 100 class meetings held on the tenth day of a term, this instructor gave a pop-quiz. Based on the 100 times this course was taught, you determine the probability of having a pop-quiz to be 0.04, that is, four occurrences of the pop-quiz divided by 100 observations (4/100 = 0.04). Based on this calculated probability, you must now decide whether extra effort should be put into reviewing your assignments in preparation for a pop-quiz that seems rather unlikely to occur. A reasonable decision might be that a pop-quiz will *not* be given as the chances of having a quiz are only 4 out of 100. The empirical evidence suggests that your opinion about not having a pop-quiz is correct and your roommate's opinion is incorrect.

As this example indicates, the empirical view requires that the number of observations be large enough for probability to be measured. Since records of pop-quizzes are probably not available to you, you will have to rely on a subjective view of probability when deciding whether or not to study for a pop-quiz. In contrast, meterologists have access to an extremely large number of observations of past weather conditions. These observations allow them to calculate the probability of rain for a given set of weather conditions based on the number of times it rained given similar weather conditions. There are many times in research where empirical distributions involving a large number of observations have not yet been obtained, and thus another view of probability, the classical view, is used in conjunction with the empirical view to determine the probability of such events.

Classical Definition

The **classical view of probability** defines probability on the basis of a ratio where the number of times a given event can occur is divided by the total number of all possible events that are equally likely to occur. This view is based on logical analyses and mathematical models. For example, when you flip a coin there are only two possibilities, heads or tails. Logic (in contrast to empirical observations) dictates that the probability of obtaining a head on any flip of this coin must equal 0.5. On any one flip, only one head can show up, and there are only two possible events, either a head or a tail. Expressed as a formula, the probability (p) of obtaining a head (H) on any one flip is, $p(H) = 1/2 = 0.5$. In general the probability of an event can be determined on the basis of the following formula:

Formula 9.1

$$p(A) = \frac{n_A}{n_{total}}$$

In Formula 9.1, A refers to any event, n_A refers to the number of A events, and n_{total} refers to all possible equally likely events.

Given certain conditions, probability estimates based on the empirical view are found to be very close to the probability estimates based on the classical view. Estimates based on the classical view of probability have proven to be useful to empirical researchers who observe samples and then make inferences about unobserved populations.

PROGRESS ASSESSMENT 9.1

Determine whether probabilities are defined subjectively, empirically, or classically in the following situations:

1. Calculating the odds of winning a particular state's lottery.
2. Picking the actual numbers you believe will win a state's lottery.
3. Predicting the winner of a political campaign based on an unbiased sample of registered voters.

CALCULATING PROBABILITIES

When using the subjective definition of probability in the history pop-quiz example, probability was determined on the basis of intuition. Your opinion was that a pop-quiz would not be given. When using the empirical definition or the classical definition of probabiltity, probability is determined on the basis of a mathematical expression, a ratio. Our use of statistics in the remainder of this text is based on theoretical and empirical definitions of probability where the likelihood of occurrence for a particular value of a statistic is determined on the basis of mathematical calculations. When probability is used in this fashion in the empirical sciences, it is usually calculated on the basis of a **theoretical frequency distribution,** which is a hypothetical frequency distribution based on logical analyses and mathematical models, or on the basis of a condensed version of a theoretical frequency distribution presented as a table.

Theoretical Distributions

You will recall from Chapters 3 and 4 that the number of times particular observed events occur can be organized as frequency distributions in table or graph format. The frequency distributions referred to in Chapters 3 and 4 are classified as **empirical frequency distributions** because they are distributions based on collected data. In contrast, *theoretical frequency distributions* are based on logical analyses and mathematical models, not on actual collected data.

Theoretical frequency distributions can be depicted graphically. Because they are based on an infinite number of points, the line connecting these points results in a smooth curve rather than the straight-line segments in a empirical frequency distribution. When expressed as a graph, relative frequency is represented on the *Y*-axis, and the events of interest are represented on the *X*-axis. Recall from Chapter 3 that relative frequency refers to expressing the frequency of a specific event as a percent of the total possible frequency. Because relative frequency is *always* represented

on the Y-axis of a theoretical frequency distribution and is expressed as
a percentage, the words ''relative frequency'' and the actual percentages
are often omitted as labels.

Normal Distribution

A distribution that has proven extremely useful in empirical research is
the normal distribution seen in Figure 9.1. The **normal distribution** is
a theoretical distribution of a continuous variable based on an infinite number of scores. The graphic representation of the normal distribution is called
the **normal curve.** Following are characteristics of the normal distribution and its graphic representation:

1. The normal distribution is bell-shaped and symmetrical.
2. The mean, median, and mode are located at the same point.
3. Because of its symmetry, the graph can be folded in half producing
   two identical portions. Thus, all characteristics of the right half of the
   curve are exactly the same for the left half.
4. Relative frequency is represented on the Y-axis, and the events of interest are expressed in standard z-scores on the X-axis.
5. Because it is a theoretical distribution, the tails of the curve get closer
   to the X-axis as they approach their theoretical infinity but never touch
   the X-axis. Generally, when working with the normal curve, it has
   become a convention to consider the curve as extending from − 3.0

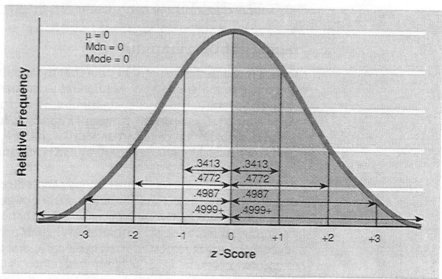

FIGURE 9.1 *Normal distribution showing examples of the relationship of the distance
between the mean and a z-score and the proportion of the area of the curve marked off
by this distance (* ⟵ *).*

z-scores to +3.0 z-scores. You will recall from Chapter 7 that z-score units are nothing more than transformations of any particular X score based on its distance from the mean (a negative value indicates distance to the left of the mean and a positive value indicates distance to the right) and expressed as a standard deviation unit, that is $z = (X - \mu)/\sigma$ (parameters μ and σ are used because we are dealing with theoretical distributions representing populations).

6. Relative frequency in the normal curve is directly related to the percent area of the curve. Calculating the relative frequency between any two z-values is a direct calculation of the percent area of the curve between these values. The proportion of the area of the curve in a specified region is then easily calculated by expressing percent area of the curve in decimal form. For example, if the relative frequency between two specified z-scores is 34.13, then the percent area of the curve marked off by these two z-scores is 34.13 percent, and the proportion of the area of the curve within this region is 0.3413.

7. When using the normal curve to determine the probability of specified events, probability is equal to the proportion of the area of the curve defined by the specified events. The proportion of the area of the curve, like probability, can range only between the values of zero and one. Look at the shaded region in Figure 9.1 covering all values above or to the right of the mean. You should recognize that the proportion of the area of the curve that falls in this region is 0.5000 (0.4999 + rounded to the nearest 1/10,000). This proportion is indicated in the lower portion of Figure 9.1. Thus, the probability of randomly selecting an event above the mean in this distribution is also 0.5. Because of the symmetry of the curve, the same is true for randomly selecting an event below the mean.

8. There is a constant relationship between the area under the curve and the distance along the X-axis as measured in z-score units. The following describes a few examples of this relationship as marked in Figure 9.1:

   a. Note the relationship of the distance between the mean and the standard scores of −3.0, −2.0, −1.0, +1.0, +2.0, and +3.0 and the proportion of the area of the curve marked off by these standard scores. The decimals in Figure 9.1 indicate the proportion of the area of the curve falling between the mean and a specified standard score as marked by specific arrows. For example, the proportion of the area of the curve that falls between μ and a z of −2.0 is 0.4772. Remember that the curve is symmetrical; distances to the left mark off identical proportions as the same distances to the right.

   b. As another example, note that the proportion of the area of the curve that falls between −1.0 and +1.0 z-scores is equal to 0.6826. Inspection of Figure 9.1 indicates that 0.3413 of the area of the curve falls between $z = -1.0$ and μ and that 0.3413 also falls between $z = +1.0$ and μ. Therefore, the sum of the two, 0.6826 (0.3413 + 0.3413), gives the total proportion of the curve that falls between $z = +1.0$ and $z = -1.0$.

c. Let us calculate the proportion of the curve that falls *above* a z-score of $+1.0$ as our final example of how to use the normal curve and some basic algebraic principles to determine proportions of specified areas of the curve. First note in Figure 9.1 that selecting a z-score of $+1.0$ divides the *right half* of the curve into two segments. One segment falls between $z = +1.0$ and the mean, and the other segment falls above $z = +1.0$. Note also in Figure 9.1 that the total proportion of the curve above the mean that makes up these two segments is 0.5 and that the proportion between $+1.0$ and the mean is 0.3413. Remember that we are determining the proportion of the area above a $+1.0$ z-score. Given that the total proportion above the mean equals 0.5, the difference between this total proportion and one segment gives the proportion of the area of the other segment. This difference is determined by subtracting the proportion between μ and $z = +1.0$ (0.3413) from the total proportion above μ (0.5). This difference of 0.1587 (0.5 − 0.3413) gives us the proportion of the area of the curve above a z-score of $+1.0$. As you will see in the Progress Assessment 9.2, the normal distribution characteristics listed as 6, 7, and 8 allow you to calculate the probability of randomly obtaining specified events from a distribution assumed to be normal.

PROGRESS ASSESSMENT 9.2

Use Figure 9.1 to answer the following:

1. Determine the proportion of the area of the curve between μ and $z = +2.0$.
2. Determine the relative frequency between μ and $z = +2.0$.
3. Determine the percent area of the curve that falls between μ and $z = +2.0$.
4. Determine the probability of randomly selecting a member of this distribution that falls between the μ and a $+2.0$ z-score.
5. Determine the probability of randomly selecting a member of this distribution that has a standard score *above* $z = +1.0$.
6. Determine the standard scores that mark off the central 68.26 percent of the distribution.

Empirical Distributions

As you will recall, empirical distributions are based on actual observations collected as data, whereas theoretical distributions are based on logical analyses and mathematical models. The theoretical normal distribution has proven to be useful because it is similar in shape to the empirical frequency distribution of so many events studied by researchers. Because of these similarities, the normal distribution can be used to estimate the probability of an empirical event whose frequency distribution is assumed to be normal. For example, intelligence test scores are assumed to be normally distributed, and as a result the normal distribution can be used to determine the likelihood of randomly selecting someone whose IQ is at or above a particular value. Figure 9.2 shows an empirical distribution of IQ's obtained by testing a *population* of 10,000 adults living in the United States and Canada. Compare Figures 9.1 and 9.2 with respect to their shape and their *X*- and *Y*-axes. The shape of each is very similar and the mean divides each distribution in half. In the case of the empirical distribution in Figure 9.2, the IQ scores obtained are plotted on the *X*-axis and the obtained frequencies are on the *Y*-axis. In this example the mean (μ) equals 100 and the standard deviation (σ) equals 15. In contrast, the *X*-axis on the theoretical distribution in Figure 9.1 represents standard *z*-scores whose mean is 0 and standard deviation is 1. (Recall from Chapter 7 why the mean and standard deviation of standard score distributions are always equal to 0 and 1, respectively.) Plotted on the *Y*-axis is relative frequency, which is used to determine the percent area of the curve marked off by two values along the *X*-axis.

Normal Curve Problems

Because of the characteristics of the normal distribution described above, calculating the probability of specified events assumed to be normally

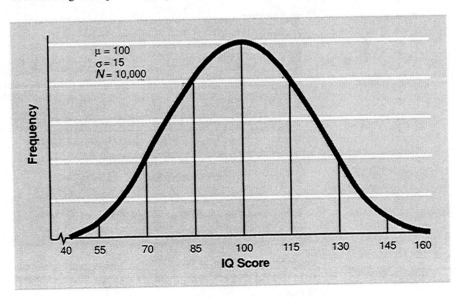

FIGURE 9.2 *Frequency polygon of hypothethical IQ scores obtained from a population of 10,000 adults living in the United States and Canada.*

distributed becomes a relatively easy procedure involving the following three steps. As an example of how these steps are used, reference is made to Figures 9.1 and 9.3 to determine the probability of randomly selecting an IQ score that falls between 115 and 130, inclusively.

1. Draw a diagram of the area of the curve to be determined similar to Figure 9.3. Note that both raw scores and z-scores are on the X-axis. In this problem the area marked off by the score 115 and 130 is shaded in and labeled appropriately.

2. Determine the z-score transformations of the raw scores using the formula $z = (X - \mu)/\sigma$ since the distribution in Figure 9.3 represents a population. In the example the z-score transformations of IQ scores of 115 and 130 are $+1.0$ [$(115 - 100)/15$] and $+2.0$ [$(130 - 100)/15$], respectively. Marking these z-scores on the drawing in Figure 9.3, you can see that calculating the area marked off by $+1.0$ and $+2.0$ z-scores determines the solution to the problem.

3. Examination of Figure 9.1 reveals that a proportion of 0.3413 falls between μ and $z = +1.0$. Similarly it can be seen that a proportion of 0.4772 falls between μ and $z = +2.0$. The subtraction of these two

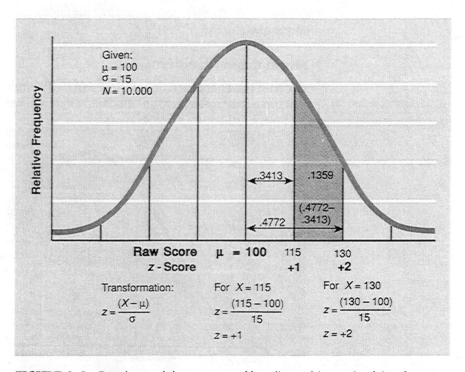

FIGURE 9.3 *Drawing needed to answer problem discussed in text involving the normal curve. Includes transformation formula and known information needed to solve problem.*

known proportions gives us the proportion of the total area of the curve between these two z-scores. This proportion also represents the probability of selecting an event between these z-scores. Thus, the probability of randomly selecting an adult who scored between 115 and 130, inclusive, from the population of 10,000 individuals who took the IQ test is 0.1359 (0.4772 - 0.3413).

The preceding steps are not only useful for determining probabilities of specified events, but are also useful in solving other types of problems encountered in research. For example, recall that the percent area of a curve of a frequency distribution is proportional to the relative frequency of the frequency distribution. Knowing that the frequency polygon in Figure 9.2 is based on a sample containing 10,000 individuals, you can easily determine the number of people with IQ scores that range between the +1.0 and +2.0 z-score units. In the preceding three steps, we determined the proportion of the area under this portion of the curve to be 0.1359. Converting this proportion to a percentage, the relative frequency is found to be 13.59. In other words, 13.59% of the 10,000 individuals had scores that fall in the region marked off by +1.0 and +2.0 z-scores. You will recall from Chapter 3 that relative frequency is a frequency of a specific score or set of scores expressed as a percent of the total number of events in the distribution. In the example, we can determine that 1359 individuals (13.59% of 10,000, that is, 0.1359 × 10,000) scored between +1.0 and +2.0 z-scores, that is, between IQ scores of 115 and 130, inclusive, in this distribution.

PROGRESS ASSESSMENT 9.3

Using Figure 9.2 where μ = 100, σ = 15, and N = 10,000, and assuming a normal distribution, solve problems 1–3 in the following manner: (a) translate the problem into a drawing of a curve that includes the given values in the problem and indicates the area that represents the solution to the problem; (b) if necessary, convert raw score units into standard z-score units and mark them on your diagram; and (c) use Figure 9.1 to fill in the proportion of the area of the curve in your diagram, and determine the correct answer to the problem by performing appropriate arithmetic functions to areas labeled on your diagram, such as adding areas of the curve, if solution requires combining different areas. Also carefully label your answers and express them in appropriate numerical form. If the solution requires percent area of curve, report percentages. In contrast, if probabilites are required, then express your answers in decimal form. Of course, if specific frequencies are called for, simply obtain the appropriate percent of the total frequency of scores contained in the distribution.

1. Determine the number of individuals with IQ score of 70 or less.
2. What is the probability of randomly selecting an individual whose IQ score is above 130 or below 55?
3. What is the relative frequency of individuals who obtained an IQ score at or above 115?

Normal Distribution Table

You probably noticed that the problems given earlier were easily solved because the z-scores of interest, such as + 1.0 or + 2.0, were clearly marked on the normal curve in Figure 9.1. What would you have done had you been interested in z-scores such as 1.10, 2.13, or 3.05? Clearly Figure 9.1 would not be of much help. You would need a diagram comparable to Figure 9.1 where the specific z-scores that are of interest to you are also marked.

As you might imagine, a diagram which marks the relationsip between the area of the normal curve and all possible z-scores is not feasible. Alternatively, a **normal distribution table** (also called the **normal curve table**), which summarizes the relationship between z-scores and proportion of the area of the normal curve, turns out to be an efficient way of presenting this important information. Table 4, at the back of the text, is an example of the normal distribution table.

Figure 9.1 indicates that a proportion of 0.3413 of the area of the curve falls between 0.0 and 1.0 z-score units. Although we know that 34.13 percent of the area of the curve falls in this region, you cannot precisely determine specific areas under the curve simply by visual inspection. The results of the mathematical calculations that allow us to precisely determine these areas, however, are presented in Appendix Table 4 in the back of the text. Note that there are three columns: Column 1, a z-score column; Column 2, a column indicating the proportion of the area of the curve between the mean and the z-score; and Column 3, a column indicating the area that extends beyond the specific z-score. Note also that area in Appendix Table 4 is expressed in decimal form as a proportion of the total area.

Look under the z-score column for $z = 1.0$ in Appendix Table 4. By looking across at the second column, you can determine that the proportion of the area that falls between the mean and $z = 1.0$ is 0.3413, as is also indicated in Figure 9.1. This information can then be used to determine that the probability of randomly selecting some event from this distribution that has a z-score somewhere between 0.0 and 1.0, inclusive, is equal to 0.3413. Remember that area of the curve is proportional to relative frequency, which is in turn proportional to the probability of occurrence of events defined in that area of the curve. By looking across at the third column, you can determine that 15.87 percent of the area of the curve falls above a z-score of 1.0, that is, 0.1587 converted to a percentage. Thus, the probability of randomly selecting an event that has a z-score above 1.0 is 0.1587. Take the time now to understand the relationship between Appendix Table 4 and the normal curve.

Knowing how to use the normal distribution table and the z-score formula also allows you to determine raw scores that mark off different areas of the curve. For example, using the information from Figure 9.2 where $N = 10,000$, $\sigma = 15$, and $\mu = 100$, we can determine the IQ score that marks off the upper 2.5 percent of the distribution. Figure 9.4 is a rough diagram of this problem where ? refers to the raw score we are trying to determine.

As Figure 9.4 indicates, we need a z-score that tells us where the upper 2.5 percent area of the curve is located. The normal distribution table will give us this value. Go to Appendix Table 4 and find the z-score that has 0.0250 proportion (that is, 2.5 percent expressed as a decimal) of the area above it. Look down the third column (remember we are looking for the area *above* the z-score that marks off the proportion 0.0250). In our example the z-score that does this is 1.96. (Be sure *you* have located this z-score in the table by looking down the third column!) Substituting the given

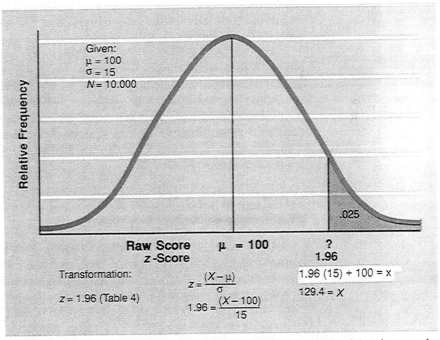

FIGURE 9.4 *Drawing needed to solve problem discussed in text involving the normal curve table.*

values into the formula $X = z(\sigma) + \mu$, initially discussed in Chapter 7, you can determine the raw score that marks off the upper 2.5 percent of this distribution. It is 129.4, that is, $[(1.96 \times 15) + 100]$.

The ability to use the normal curve and its table in this fashion is extremely useful to people who use statistics to make decisions. For example, a school psychologist interested in interviewing individuals whose IQ score is so high that it places them in the upper 2.5% of this distribution would know enough to interview only individuals who have IQ scores above 129. (Note that because IQ scores are measured in units, they were rounded off to the nearest whole unit.)

Another feature of the normal distribution table in the appendix of this text is that values for any given z under the second and third columns always sum up to 0.5. This is true because these two columns together refer to half of the area of the curve.

Note also that no negative numbers are given. Remember that the normal curve is symmetrical. Thus, the area marked off by a negative z-score is equal to the area marked off by a corresponding positive z-score. Examine Figure 9.1, and note that a proportion of 0.4772 of the area of the curve falls between the mean and $z = -2.0$. Find the z-score value of 2.0 in Appendix Table 4. Across from this value is listed the number 0.4772. This indicates that 0.4772 of the area of the curve falls between the mean and a z-score equal to $+2.0$ and that 0.4772 falls between the mean and a z-score equal to -2.0. Thus, the sign of a z-score simply indicates that the events of interest fall either above (a positive z-score) or below (a negative z-score) the mean.

In this example the probability of randomly obtaining an event whose z-score transformation falls between 0.0 and -2.0 is equal to 0.4772. As can be seen in Figure 9.1, z-scores less than -2.0 fall in the lower left portion of the normal curve and are thus located in Appendix Table 4 as being beyond the specified z-score of -2.0. Also notice that the probability of randomly obtaining an event in a normal distribution that has a z-score transformation of -2.0 or *less* is 0.0228, the value in the third column across from the z-score of 2.00.

PROGRESS ASSESSMENT 9.4

Solve problems 1–5 by completing the four steps that follow. Assume that the data referred to in the problems are from populations that are normally distributed. (a) Draw a diagram indicating the area of the normal curve that represents the solution to the problem. (b) Convert raw score units into standard score units and mark them on your diagram. (c) Use the normal distribution table, Appendix Table 4, to fill in the appropriate areas on your diagram expressed as proportions indicating probability levels. (d) Determine the correct answer to the problem by performing appropriate arithmetic functions, for example, adding area if appropriate. Clearly and completely label your answer. In solving the problems, assume that a group of psychologists interviews all incoming freshman students ($N = 4000$) at a large university and measures test anxiety for each student. In the method used, scores of test anxiety can range between 20 (low test anxiety) and 150 (high test anxiety). The mean of this distribution is 85 and the standard deviation is 20.

1. Determine the percentage of freshman who have anxiety scores above 140.

2. Determine the probability of randomly selecting a freshman whose anxiety scores is 140 or less.

3. Determine the number of freshman who have a test score below 38.

4. Determine which anxiety scores mark off the upper and lower 2.5 percent of the distribution.

5. What scores are so extreme at both ends that the probability of randomly selecting scores from these ends is equal to 0.05?

FORMING AND EVALUATING RESEARCH AND STATISTICAL HYPOTHESES

The major purpose for using inferential statistics in the remainder of this book is to make decisions about the truthfulness of certain hypotheses based on the probability of certain events happening by chance. Statistics used to evaluate hypotheses in this fashion are referred to as **test statistics.** Just as you used the normal distribution table to calculate probabilities associated with normal distributions, you will learn to calculate probabilities using specific test statistic tables that are based on theoretical frequency distributions of the specific test statistic.

Note that calculating probabilities using test statistics does not guarantee certainty when making decisions. Consider again the example at the beginning of this chapter. You are reasonably certain that a history pop-quiz will not be given based on data indicating a 0.04 likelihood of having a quiz (empirical view). There is no guarantee that a quiz will or will not be given. So, what do you do? Do you spend some of your study time on history even though you know for certain the economics exam will be given, or do you spend all of your time studying economics? Eventually you will make a decision, probably based on a variety of personal factors such as how well you are doing in both courses, which course you enjoy more, or the difficulty of the course.

In contrast to personal decisions about one's daily life, evaluating research hypotheses requires a more formal set of procedures. Use of these procedures requires an understanding of the following:

1. Research hypotheses.

2. Translation of research hypotheses into statistical hypotheses.

3. Statistical tests that involve: (a) decision rules and (b) test statistics used to calculate the likelihood of measured events happening by chance.

4. The principles determining how calculated probabilities are used to evaluate statistical hypotheses.

5. The principles determining how statistical hypotheses are used to evaluate research hypotheses.

An understanding of the types of errors that can occur whenever hypotheses are evaluated is also needed to appreciate the limitations of making decisions based on inferential statistics.

Research Hypothesis

In Chapter 2 you learned that a **research hypothesis** is a statement describing the relationship between certain events that can be empirically tested. When the experimental approach is used, the hypothesis states how changes in the independent variable cause changes in the dependent variable. When the correlational approach is used, the hypothesis states whether certain events are or are not related to each other in a systematic fashion. With both approaches you start with a general idea that is stated as a research hypothesis.

For example, a developmental psychobiologist may be interested in the effect of a specific drug on central nervous system development. To empirically evaluate the drug's effect, a more specific research hypothesis is needed. A good understanding of the research literature is extremely helpful in formulating a testable research hypothesis. Suppose previous research indicates that in a variety of species, including rats, this drug, when given to adults, modifies the size of nerve cells in the hippocampus, a specific area of the brain. Because of an interest in how the brain develops in rats and the research facilities available, a researcher decides to examine the effect of this drug on the developing rat brain. Assume no published reports exist about the effect of this new drug on the developing rat brain. Thus, the research hypothesis might be that this new drug affects the size of nerve cells in the hippocampus of eighteen-day-old rats. (In order to keep the example brief, one age level will be considered. An investigator would probably be interested in evaluating this drug with several age groups and several dosages.)

Several points need to be made about this specific research hypothesis. First, the statement refers to the effect of the drug in general, that is, if this statement is true then the drug would cause this effect in all eighteen-day-old rats. Likewise, if it is not true, then the drug should have no effect on hippocampal cells of any eighteen-day-old rat. Thus, a research hypothesis is stated about a population. Second, the hypothesis states only that the drug has an effect. It does not state the direction of the effect, whether it increases or decreases cell size. Third, in order to empirically evaluate the research hypothesis it must be translated into a testable statistical hypothesis.

Translating a Research Hypothesis into a Testable Statistical Hypothesis

A testable **statistical hypothesis** is a mathematical statement about one or more characteristics of a given population. Its formation involves the translation of a specific research hypothesis into a set of mutually exclusive and exhaustive mathematical statements about the distribution of a population's characteristic or statements about a population parameter. *Mutually exclusive* refers to the fact that only one statement or the other can be true at any one point in time. *Exhaustive* refers to the fact that all possible values of the characteristics of interest are included within the two statements.

The translation of a research hypothesis into a testable statistical hypothesis requires two steps. First, the research hypothesis, as the investigator *believes* it to be true, is translated into a mathematical statement, called the **alternative hypotheses (H_1)**. With the experimental approach the parameter most often used is the mean, μ. With the correlation approach the parameter most often used is rho, ϱ. The second step requires the negation of H_1. The negation of H_1 is called the **null hypothesis (H_0)**. The null hypothesis is a testable statistical hypothesis.

If the researcher in the example believes that the drug truly affects nerve cell size, it is logical to assume that the mean size of nerve cells in a population of rats that receives the drug (μ_{drug}) will *not be equal to* the mean size of nerve cells in a population of rats that does not receive the drug ($\mu_{no\ drug}$). Mathematically, the alternative hypothesis in this example is H_1: $\mu_{drug} \neq \mu_{no\ drug}$. Because the negation of H_1 determines the null hypothesis, H_0 is stated in this example as H_0: $\mu_{drug} = \mu_{no\ drug}$. The negation in this example involves a double negative. If the means are not equal to each other, the negation of this statement is that the means *are* equal to each other. Take the time to understand this example, as this mathematical format for stating statistical hypotheses will be used throughout the remainder of this text. Once the research hypothesis is translated into a testable statistical hypothesis, data can be collected to evaluate the statistical hypothesis.

Although the alternative hypothesis is conceptualized as what the investigator believes to be true, when formally stated, it follows the null hypothesis. The statistical hypotheses for the example should be formally presented as follows:

$$H_{(0)}:\ \mu_{drug} = \mu_{no\ drug}$$

$$H_{(1)}:\ \mu_{drug} \neq \mu_{no\ drug}$$

PROGRESS ASSESSMENT 9.5

Translate the following research hypotheses into statistical hypotheses. Assume that measurements of the events discussed can be obtained and are stated in a way that the investigator believes them to be true.

1. The research hypothesis is that subjects allowed to watch a violent television show will demonstrate different amounts of aggression than those who do not watch the same violent show.

2. The research hypothesis is that cigarette smoking and heart disease are correlated.

3. The research hypothesis is that people who are given supplemental doses of two grams of Vitamin C daily will not have the same number of colds as people who are not given the supplemental doses.

Applying a Statistical Test

After forming your research and statistical hypotheses, you must determine how your data are to be collected. As mentioned in Chapter 2, you must keep in mind a variety of practical concerns (time, money, and equipment), methodological concerns (appropriate operational definitions and capability of statistically analyzing data), and ethical concerns (such as whether or not subjects will be treated appropriately). Assuming you have correctly collected your data with these concerns in mind, you must then decide if your null hypothesis is not supported by your data. Making this decision requires the use of a statistical test. You may recall from Chapter 8 that a **statistical test** is a set of procedures used to evaluate a statistical hypothesis. Applying a statistical test is relatively simple. It requires that a decision rule be formed and a test statistic be calculated.

Decision Rule. A **decision rule** refers to the specific values of a test statistic that you have determined to be necessary for rejecting or failing to reject a null hypothesis. The decision rule most frequently used in the behavioral sciences is that the H_0 should be rejected if the probability of obtaining your calculated test statistic on the basis of chance is *less than or equal to* 0.05. The probability level associated with a specific decision rule is referred to as the **alpha level** or **level of significance.**

The symbol "α" (pronounced "alpha") is used to represent the level of significance. With an alpha level of 0.05, you have decided that you can be reasonably certain that the null hypothesis is incorrect if the likehood of your results occurring by chance is 0.05 or less. You reject the null hypothesis whenever you determine your results to be an improbable event. Results that have likelihood of occurring 5 times out of 100 or less are considered to be an improbable event.

Test Statistic. In order to apply this decision rule, you must have the ability to determine the probability of the events described in relation to the null hypothesis as happening by chance. You can calculate such probabilities by using an appropriate test statistic such as z. Test statistics allow you to determine the probability of obtaining your observed results simply on the basis of chance. If it is the case that your observed results are highly unlikely with respect to chance, that is, the probability of the event happening by chance is less than or equal to 0.05, you conclude that something other than chance is responsible for your results. The specific test statistic used is determined by such factors as the methods used to collect the data, the scale of measurement that describes the type of data collected, assumptions about parameters of the population from which the samples were selected, the types of samples selected, and number of variables and groups used to collect the data. Each of these factors will be discussed in the remaining chapters of the text as a variety of test statistics are examined.

Using Calculated Probabilities to Evaluate and Interpret Statistical Hypotheses

Although a decision rules does not involve a series of elaborate statements, it requires careful thought so that it will be understood and applied appropriately. Let us go back to the example of a pop-quiz to demonstrate how a decision rule might be applied in an informal setting. Assume that you doubt your roommate's intuition. You believe that you should not take time from studying for the announced economics exam to study for a pop-quiz in history. In this example we are not really evaluating research or statistical hypotheses but rather are trying to explain how a decision rule is applied. For the purpose of an example, let us proceed through evaluating your belief that you should not study for a pop-quiz based on general decision rule procedures using empirical probabilities.

Since the pseudo-research hypothesis in the example is that you should not take study time for an announced economics exam to prepare for possible pop-quiz, you must translate this pseudo-research hypothesis into a statistical hypothesis. The first step associated with translating this hypothesis requires that you state your alternative hypothesis, that is, what you believe to be true. Thus, your alternative hypothesis (H_1) is that a pop-quiz will *not* be given. The negation of the H_1 determines your null hypothesis (H_0), which in this case is that a pop-quiz *will* be given. As is required when applying decision rule procedures, you now have two mutually exclusive mathematical statements: H_0 (a pop-quiz will be given) and H_1 (a pop-quiz will not be given).

A critical question you are now faced with is which of the statements or hypotheses to reject, fail to reject, or accept. The logic of decision rules, as you will apply them with statistical tests, requires you to test H_0 and decide whether to reject or fail to reject it. Note that on the basis of one evaluation you would rarely accept the H_0. You either fail to reject H_0 or you reject H_0. If you fail to reject H_0, it means there is no evidence to support your research hypothesis. If you reject H_0, logic dictates that you accept H_1. When you have two mutually exclusive and exhaustive mathematical statements, if one is not acceptable then the other must be acceptable. Rejecting H_0 means that you have evidence to support your research hypothesis. In order to reject or fail to reject H_0, you must perform a statistical test.

Prior to collecting information about the likelihood of having a pop-quiz, you must form a decision rule stating the conditions for rejecting your null hypothesis. It is extremely important that the decision rule be formulated before data are collected. After the data have been collected, you want to evaluate your hypothesis, not formulate it. You will recall that the decision rule most frequently used is that H_0 (in this example, a pop-quiz will be given) will be rejected only if the probability of H_0 is 0.05 or less. If the probability of H_0 is greater than 5 chances out of 100, you must *fail* to reject H_0.

After you have formulated your hypotheses and your decision rule, it is appropriate to gather information to evaluate the null hypothesis. One way might be to go to the library where your teacher has records of the pop-quiz schedules over the last twenty-five years. Assume the records indicate that a pop-quiz has been given on the tenth class meeting of the term only 4 times out of the last 100 meetings. Thus you empirically determine that the probability of having a quiz is 0.04. Since alpha is equal to 0.05 in the decision rule and the calculated probability of having a pop-quiz is 0.04, the H_0 that a pop-quiz will be given is rejected, and therefore the H_1 that a pop-quiz will not be given is accepted.

Based on this evaluation of H_0, you conclude that the evidence (from the quiz file information in the library) indicates that your economics study time should not be reduced to prepare for a pop-quiz in history.

PUTTING IT ALL TOGETHER

The procedures involved in evaluating hypotheses using test statistics can be summarized in the following five steps:

1. Determine a research hypothesis based on your beliefs about the events of interest.

2. Form a statistical hypothesis by translating the research hypothesis into a set of mutually exclusive and exhaustive mathematical statements about some characteristics, usually the mean, or rho, of the population distribution by taking the following actions:

   a. Write your research hypothesis as you believe it to be true with respect to the distribution characteristic; this becomes the alternative hypothesis, (H_1).

   b. Negate H_1 and state this negation as the null hypothesis (H_0).

3. Perform a statistical test by doing the following:

   a. Formulate a decision rule that allows you to reject H_0 at a given level of significance (called the alpha level). For empirical behavioral research alpha is usually set at 0.05. In the following chapters you will use specific tables to determine the numerical values associated with your decision rule.

   b. Collect your data and calculate the probability of obtaining the results by chance using an appropriate test statistic. In the remaining chapters, you will learn procedures to calculate test statistics in order to determine such probabilities. These procedures are similar to those you use to calculate probabilities with the normal curve and its table.

4. Make a decision whether or not to reject the null hypothesis. If your calculated probability is less than or equal to 0.05, you reject the null hypothesis. If the calculated probability is greater than 0.05, you fail to reject the null hypothesis.

5. Translate your decision about the statistical hypothesis into a statement supporting or failing to support your research hypothesis.

PROGRESS ASSESSMENT 9.6

For each of the following problems translate the research hypothesis, which is stated as the investigator believes it to be true, into a testable statistical hypothesis. Then determine whether or not to reject the null hypothesis based on the probabilities listed. Alpha is set at 0.05.

1. A teacher believes that students will learn different amounts of material depending upon whether Textbook A or Textbook B is used in the course. Textbook A is assigned to half of the class and Textbook B to the other half. Students are randomly selected for each half. During the term students are treated identically except for the specific textbook. At the end of the term the teacher calculates the mean score for each half and determines the probability of obtaining these means to be equal to 0.06.

2. The same project is repeated in another class except that the teacher, instead of using two different textbooks, gives two different types of homework (Homework A—multiple choice questions and Homework B—fill-in-the-blank questions). At the end of the term, the teacher calculates the means for each group and determines the chance probability of obtaining these results is 0.01.

3. A researcher believes that time spent reading newspapers is related to academic performance. After determining the average number of hours spent reading the daily newspaper and the grade-point average of 2000 high-school seniors, the researcher calculates the probability of such results happening by chance to be 0.03.

CONSEQUENCES OF DECISION MAKING

You will recall that the decision rule is stated with respect to testing the null hypothesis. Because of this we will discuss making correct or incorrect decisions in relation to the truth or falsity of the null hypothesis that a pop-quiz in history will be given. The correctness or incorrectness of your decision depends, in part, upon the alpha level selected. Thus, if you are going to decide whether or not to study for your quiz on the basis of evaluating a statistical hypothesis, you must formulate a decision rule based on a particular alpha level.

If alpha is set at 0.05, then it means you are willing to reject the idea that a history quiz will be given if evidence indicates the likelihood of having a quiz is less than or equal to 5 chances out of 100. Another way of looking at this decision rule is to say that you are willing to be wrong 5 times out of 100 when you decide to reject the null hypothesis.

On the other hand, you might set alpha to 0.01 because you feel that failing the history quiz by neglecting to prepare for it is a serious consequence. Possibly it is your major, and you want to be more certain than just 95 times out of 100 that your evidence is indicating that a quiz will *not* be given. By setting alpha to 0.01, you are redefining what constitutes an improbable true null hypothesis. What you are saying is that only when the chances are less than 1 out of 100 that the null hypothesis is true will you reject the null hypothesis. In this case, you are willing to be wrong only 1 out of 100 times.

A True Null Hypothesis

For the purpose of example, let us assume that the history teacher has decided that a pop-quiz will be given. Although you do not know this yet, the null hypothesis (that a quiz will be given) in reality is true.

Incorrect Decision about a True H_0: Alpha Error.   If you decide that a quiz will not be given on the basis of your empirical information and the teacher gives you a quiz, then you obviously have made an error. Such an error is called an alpha or Type I error. An **alpha error** or **Type I** is the incorrect rejection of a true null hypothesis. The probability of making such an erro is equal to the alpha level of your decision rule. If you set alpha at 0.05 and your empirical information indicates that the chances of a pop-quiz are 4 out of 100, you reject the null hypothesis and do not study for the quiz. Consequently you do poorly on the history quiz as a result of making an alpha error. Note that whenever you reject a null hypothesis, you may be making an alpha error.

Correct Decision about a True H_0.   If on the other hand you had set alpha at 0.01 and the empirical information indicates that the chance of a pop-quiz is 4 out of 100, then you would not reject the null hypothesis that a quiz is to be given. Consequently, you study for the history quiz and achieve a better grade. Although you use some of your economic's study time to prepare for history, it is worthwhile because of your history quiz score. This is an example of correctly failing to reject a true null hypothesis. The probability of correctly concluding not to reject a true null hypothesis is equal to $1 - \alpha$. Given alpha equal to 0.01, the probability of correctly concluding not to reject the null hypothesis is 0.99 ($1.0 - 0.01 = 0.99$).

A False Null Hypothesis

Let us assume a different scenario where the history teacher has decided not to give a pop-quiz. Thus, your null hypothesis that a pop-quiz will be given is in reality false.

Incorrect Decision about a False H_0: Beta Error.   Suppose that you decide to set alpha at 0.01 rather than 0.05. Given this current scenario and a calculated likelihood of having a quiz equal to 0.04 (based on the library information you obtained about your history teacher's quizzes), you fail to reject your null hypothesis since 0.04 is not less than 0.01. In this case, you make a beta or Type II error. The **beta** or **Type II error** is defined as a situation where a *false* null hypothesis is *not* rejected. The probability of making a Type II error is equal to beta, symbolized as β. In this example, you study for a quiz that turns out not be be given. Consequently your economics grade suffers, while your history grade does not change. Your null hypothesis stating that a quiz is to be given is false, and your evaluation of this hypothesis does not allow you to reject this false null hypothesis. Thus, a Type II or beta error is made. Whenever you *fail* to reject a null hypothesis, you may make a β error.

Correct Decision about a False H_0.   Suppose again that your history teacher decides not to give a pop-quiz. The null hypothesis that a quiz is to be given is, therefore, false. If alpha is set at 0.05 and the empirical information obtained from the library indicates the likelihood of having a pop-quiz is 0.04, the logic of the statistical test requires that you *reject* the null hypothesis that a pop-quiz is to be given. In this scenario you correctly devote all of your study time to economics rather than use some of it to prepare for the history quiz. The probability of correctly rejecting a false null hypothesis is defined as the **power** of a statistical test and is equal to $1.0 - \beta$. Calculating β and power is discussed in Chapter 11.

Table 9.1 summarizes our discussion of evaluating true and false null hypotheses in relation to the example of a possible pop-quiz in history. You should learn the contents of Table 9.1 because they represent the types of errors and correct decisions made in evaluating any null hypothesis.

TABLE 9.1
Summary of Errors and Correct Decisions That Can Be Made When Performing Statistical Tests. *Note:* Your decision and its consequences are listed in relation to the possible state of affairs. Also, either H_0 is true *or* it is not true and that either you do not reject H_0 *or* you reject it. In this example the null and alternative hypotheses are written as:

H_0: History quiz will be given;

H_1: History quiz will *not* be given.

| | Your Decision (consequences) | |
True State of Affairs (reality)	H_0 Not Rejected (study history)	H_0 Rejected (do not study history)
H_0 *true* (history quiz)	*Correct decision* (do well in history and economics grade OK)	*Type I or alpha error* (history grade suffers and economics grade excellent)
H_0 *false* (no history quiz)	*Type II or beta error* (economics grade OK with no effect on history grade)	*Correct decision* (economics grade excellent with no effect on history grade)

PROGRESS ASSESSMENT 9.7

Create a table evaluating true and false null hypotheses similar to Table 9.1. Use the example discussed in the text about the effects of a drug on the average size of nerves cells in the hippocampus of rats where:

$$H_0: \mu_{drug} = \mu_{no\ drug}$$
$$H_1: \mu_{drug} \neq \mu_{no\ drug}$$

SUMMARY

This chapter covers important concepts that introduce the procedures used to make decisions about research and statistical hypotheses. Making decisions based on inferential statistics requires you to understand the definition of probability as defined from a subjective, empirical, and classical view. The use of the normal distribution and its table to calculate probabilities is also discussed in relation to populations. Emphasis is given to the theoretical normal distribution and its characteristics because of its similarity to many empirical distributions. The methods used to translate an empirical research hypothesis into a statistical hypothesis are discussed. Emphasis is placed on evaluating the null hypothesis at a given level of significance on the basis of a decision rule and on the probability of obtaining calculated results with the use of a test statistic. The potential errors, alpha (Type I) and beta (Type II), which can be made when evaluating null hypotheses, as well as potential correct decisions, and the symbols used to represent the probability of such decisions, are discussed in relation to theory and specific examples. This foundation leads directly into the use of procedures to calculate probabilities in inferential statistics based on theoretical distributions of specific test statistics.

KEY DEFINITIONS

α (pronounced "alpha") The symbol used to represent alpha level, that is, the probability of making an alpha error.

alpha error or **Type I error** An error an investigator makes when a true null hypothesis is rejected.

alpha level or **level of significance** The probability level used in a decision rule.

alternative hypothesis or H_1 A mathematical statement about a population characteristic based on what an investigator believes to be true as described in the investigator's research hypothesis.

β (pronounced "beta") The symbol used to represent the probability of making a Type II error.

beta error or **Type II error** An error an investigator makes when a false null hypothesis is not rejected.

classical view of probability A definition of probability based on logical analyses and mathematical models where probability is defined as a ratio based on the number of times a given event can occur divided by the total number of all possible events that are equally likely to occur.

decision rule The specific values of a test statistic that are necessary to reject or not to reject a null hypothesis for a given level of significance.

empirical view of probability A definition of probability based on a large number of previous observations indicating whether or not the event has occurred. Probability is given as a ratio based on the number of times an event has occurred divided by the number of observations.

empirical frequency distributions Frequency distributions based on collected data.

H_0 The symbol used to represent the null hypothesis.

H_1 The symbol used to represent the alternative hypothesis.

normal curve   The graphic representation of the normal distribution.

normal distribution   A specific theoretical frequency distribution of a continuous variable based on an infinite number of scores, which is characterized by its bell shape and symmetry. It is used frequently by investigators to estimate the probability of occurrence of empirical events.

normal distribution table or **normal curve table**   A listing of the relationship between z-scores and percent area of the normal curve based on the normal distribution.

null hypothesis or H_0 A mathematical statement about a population characteristic based on what an investigator believes to be false as described in the investigator's research hypothesis. It is the negation of the alternative hypothesis.

$p(A) = n_A/n_{total}$ A computational formula for determining the probability of an event (A).

power   The probability of correctly rejecting a false null hypothesis.

probability   A percentage or proportion indicating the likelihood of occurrence of some specified event (or events).

research hypothesis   A statement, describing the relationship between certain events, that can be empirically tested. An experimental research hypothesis describes how changes in an independent variable cause changes in a dependent variable. A correlational research hypothesis states whether events are or are not related to each other in a systematic fashion.

subjective view of probability   A definition of probability based on a measure of the strength of one's belief that an event will or will not occur.

statistical hypothesis   A mathematical statement about one or more characteristics of a given population.

statistical test   A set of procedures used to evaluate a statistical hypothesis.

theoretical frequency distribution   A hypothetical frequency distribution based on logical analyses and mathematical models.

test statistics   Statistics that are used to determine the probability of certain events described in relation to a null hypothesis as happening on the basis of chance.

REVIEW EXERCISES

1. A psychologist interested in determining the amount of time it takes air-traffic controllers to report being bored while watching a radar screen with few changes occurring studies 2000 volunteers. The frequency distribution shown

in Table 9-A is hypothetical data representing the amount of time (minutes) elapsed before air-traffic controllers report being bored after watching radar screens that have only one change systematically occurring at five-minute intervals. In this example assume that the 2000 subjects represent the total population of air-traffic controllers willing to volunteer for this project.

TABLE 9-A
Grouped Frequency Distribution
of Amount of Time (Minutes)
Elapsed Before Air-Traffic Controllers
Report Being Bored Watching Radar
Screen, $N = 2000$.

Class Interval	Frequency f
141–150	7
131–140	19
121–130	42
111–120	92
101–110	156
91–100	232
81–90	293
71–80	318
61–70	293
51–60	232
41–50	156
31–40	92
21–30	42
11–20	19
1–10	7

    a. When appropriate, use the method of transformed scores to calculate the mean, median, and mode.

    b. Based on your calculations in part *a*, is this distribution a normal distribution? Explain your answer.

    c. Using midpoints on the *X*-axis, construct a relative frequency polygon.

    d. Examine your relative frequency polygon and determine if it represents a normal distribution. Explain your answer.

    e. Using the method of transformed scores, calculate sigma.

    f. Using your values of the mean and of sigma, calculate z-scores for each midpoint and plot a relative frequency polygon of these z-scores.

    g. Compare the frequency polygons you construct for parts *c* and *f* and explain why their shapes stay the same.

2. Using the frequency distribution in Table 9-A, calculate the following:

    a. the 90th percentile

    b. the percentile rank of 55

3. Using the normal distribution table and your values of the mean and sigma for the distribution in part 1, determine the following with the use of a diagram:

    a. the 90th percentile of this distribution

    b. the percentile rank of the score 55

    c. why the answers to parts 2*a* and 3*a* and 2*b* and 3*b* are similar to each other

    d. the scores that mark off the upper and lower 2.5% of the distribution

    e. the probability of randomly selecting a score below 39 or above 119, inclusive

4. As a follow-up to this initial study, the investigator decides to examine the belief that the amount of coffee consumed on a daily basis is related to the time when subjects report being bored by the radar-screen task described above. The investigator asks the air-traffic controllers how much coffee they drink each day and correlates this with time to report being bored.

    a. Transform this research hypothesis into testable statistical hypothesis by forming an alternative and null hypothesis.

    b. What would you conclude about the null hypothesis if the calculated probability for the obtained correlation is 0.1 and alpha = 0.05?

    c. Given your conclusion, what is the name of the error you may be making?

5. This same investigator believes that college students would not perform the same as air-traffic controllers if given the same task. In a replication of the investigation described in part 1, half the subjects are college students and the other half are air-traffic controllers.

    a. Transform this research hypothesis into an appropriate statistical hypothesis involving a null and alternative hypothesis.

    b. What would you conclude about the null hypothesis if the calculated probability for the obtained results of this study is 0.03 and alpha = 0.05?

    c. Given your conclusion, what is the name of the error you may be making?

ANSWERS TO PROGRESS ASSESSMENTS

9.1   **1.** classical

        2. subjective

        3. empirical

9.2   **1.** 0.4772

        2. 47.72

        3. 47.72%

        4. 0.4772

        5. 0.1587

        6. -1.0 and $+1.0$ z-scores

9.3   **1.** A total of 228 individuals had IQ scores less than or equal to 70.

   2. The probability of randomly selecting an individual with an IQ score above 130 or below 55 is 0.0241.

   3. The relative frequency of individuals that obtained an IQ at or above 115 is 15.87.

9.4 **1.** The percentage of freshman who have anxiety scores above 140 is 0.3 percent.

   2. The probability of randomly selecting a freshman with an anxiety score less than 140 is 0.9970.

   3. The number of freshman that have an anxiety score below 38 is 38.

   4. The scores that mark off the upper and lower 2.5% of the distribution are 45.80 and 124.2.

   5. The scores that are so extreme that the probability of selecting them by chance is 0.05 or less are scores equal to or greater than 124.2 and scores equal to or less than 45.8.

9.5 **1.** $H_0: \mu_{violent} = \mu_{nonviolent}; H_1: \mu_{violent} \neq \mu_{nonviolent}$

   2. $H_0: \varrho = 0.0; H_1: \varrho \neq 0.0$

   3. $H_0: \mu_c = \mu_{no\ c}; H_1: \mu_c \neq \mu_{no\ c}.$

9.6 **1.** $H_0: \mu_A = \mu_B; H_1: \mu_A \neq \mu_B;$ fail to reject null hypothesis as probability of 0.06 is greater than the alpha level of 0.05.

   2. $H_0: \mu_A = \mu_B; H_1: \mu_A \neq \mu_B;$ reject null hypothesis as calculated probability of 0.01 is less than the alpha level of 0.05.

   3. $H_0: \varrho = 0.0; H_1: \varrho \neq 0.0;$ reject null hypothesis as calculated probability of 0.03 is less than the alpha level of 0.05.

9.7 See Table 9-B.

TABLE 9.B
Summary of Errors and Correct Decisions That Can Be Made When Performing Statistical Tests. *Note:* **Your decision and its consequences are listed in relation to the possible state of affairs. In this example:**

$$H_0: \mu_{drug} = \mu_{no\ drug}$$
$$H_1: \mu_{drug} \neq \mu_{no\ drug}$$

True state of affairs (reality)	Your Decision (consequences)	
	H_0 not rejected (drug considered ineffective)	H_0 rejected (drug considered effective)
H_0 true ($\mu_{drug} = \mu_{no\ drug}$)	*Correct decision* (ineffective drug not used in further research)	*Type I or alpha error* (ineffective drug used in further research)
H_0 false ($\mu_{drug} \neq \mu_{no\ drug}$)	*Type II or beta error* (effective drug not used in further research)	*Correct decision* (effective drug used in further research)

CHAPTER 10

Sampling Distributions, Inferential Statistics, and Hypothesis Evaluation

*I*n this chapter you will learn more about theoretical distributions. Theoretical distributions, called sampling distributions, are used by investigators who deal with empirical information to test hypotheses about population parameters. A **sampling distribution** is a theoretical distribution of a particular statistic (such as $\bar{X}$) for an infinite number of random samples of a specified size. The procedure used to evaluate a statistical hypothesis about a population parameter on the basis of a sampling distribution is identical to that used with the normal distribution described in Chapter 9. Although in the remainder of this text a number of sampling distributions will be discussed, this chapter focuses on the *sampling distribution of the mean*. As different sampling distributions are discussed in subsequent chapters, note the similarity in the logic used to evaluate statistical hypotheses.

SAMPLING DISTRIBUTIONS

Empirical scientists, such as psychologists, biologists, and sociologists, study many different phenomena. For example, some psychologists are interested in determining factors that can cause irrational fears which prevent individuals from leaving their home. Likewise, psychologists are interested in determining treatments that can be used to alleviate such irrational fears once they have developed. When studying such phenomena, psychologists hope to understand these events for people in general, not just those subjects who have participated in a particular study. In this example people in general are referred to as a population, whereas subjects participating in a study are referred to as a sample.

Because investigators rarely are able to measure an entire population, they must rely on studying representative samples to make inferences about a population. In order to make such inferences, investigators use inferential statistics involving sampling distributions.

SAMPLING DISTRIBUTION OF THE MEAN

As mentioned in the introduction to this chapter, sampling distributions can be obtained for any statistic. The following sections focus on the **sampling distribution of the mean ($\bar{X}$),** which is a theoretical distribution of an infinite number of means from random samples of a specified size.

You will recall from Chapters 5 and 6 that the mean and standard deviation are useful measures to obtain when working with populations and samples. These measures are also important when working with sampling distributions. To distinguish between measures that describe sampling distributions and those that describe samples and populations, per se, different names are given to the mean and standard deviation of a sampling distribution. The mean of a sampling distribution is called the **expected value.** The standard deviation of sampling distribution is called the **standard error.** The symbol $\mu_{\bar{X}}$ represents the expected value of the sampling distribution of the mean and the symbol $\sigma_{\bar{X}}$ represents its standard error.

Because sampling distributions theoretically involve an infinite number of samples, they are based on mathematical models. To understand these models it is helpful to go through examples of empirical distributions formed from a given number of samples selected from a finite population. Empirical distributions that are based on finite numbers and constructed for illustrative purposes can be used to demonstrate principles derived from theoretical sampling distributions.

Empirical Distributions of Sample Means

An empirical distribution of sample means can be obtained by randomly selecting a sample of a given size from a particular population, calculating the mean of the sample, placing the sample members back into the population, and then repeating this process until a large number of samples have been selected. After calculating the mean of each of the selected samples, a relative frequency polygon can be constructed where the specific values of the means are placed on the X-axis and the relative frequencies of these values are placed on the Y-axis.

Presented as a frequency polygon in Figure 10.1 are hypothetical population data of beak depth (distance between the top and bottom of the base of the beak) of a species of ground finch collected on one of the Galápagos Islands by a comparative psychologist interested in the effects of competition for food on the evolution of beak size. Assume that currently there is only one species of finch on the island and that the psychologist is able to measure the beak depth of each bird in the population. As indicated in Figure 10.1, μ of this population is equal to 20 and σ is equal to 2.4.

Figures 10.2 and 10.3 are examples of empirical distributions of means based on sample sizes 16 and 144, respectively. In Figures 10.2 and 10.3 the graphed data, mean beak depth, are from an arbitrary 2000 samples of ground finch randomly selected from the hypothetical population depicted in Figure 10.1. Sample sizes of 16 and 144 are also selected arbitrarily for illustrative purposes.

Expected Value. The expected value, that is, the mean of a sampling distribution, is defined as the mean of any distribution is defined. You will recall from Chapter 5 that the mean is the point in a distribution about which the sum of the deviations equals zero. For a sampling distribution, this defining equation is expressed as follows:

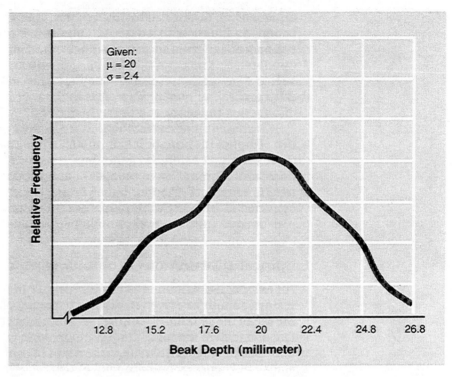

FIGURE 10.1 *Hypothetical frequency polygon of beak depth recorded for a population of ground finch on one of the Galapagos islands. Note that the shape of this polygon is not exactly that of the normal curve.*

Equation 10.1 $$\Sigma(\overline{X} - \mu_{\overline{x}}) = 0$$

In Equation 10.1, $\overline{X}$ represents the means of the samples and μ_X represents the expected value of the sampling distribution.

Because we are dealing with an empirical distribution of sample means, deviations are obtained by subtracting the expected value of the distribution, that is, the average sample mean, from *each* of the sample means.

The procedure used to calculate this expected value requires that the sum of the measured values ($\overline{X}$'s in this example) be divided by the total number of sample means, **k** (2000 in this example). Assume that the sum of the 2000 sample means graphed in Figure 10.2 is equal to 40,000, the expected value of this sampling distribution of the mean is then equal to 20 (40,000/2000).

Standard Error of the Mean.   The standard error of the sampling distribution of the mean is defined as the square root of the average squared

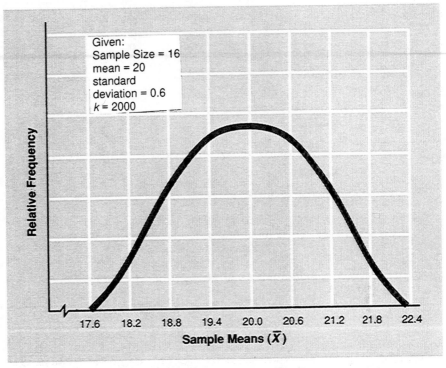

Given:
Sample Size = 16
mean = 20
standard
deviation = 0.6
k = 2000

FIGURE 10.2 *Hypothetical frequency polygon of a sampling distribution of sample means of beak depth obtained for 2000 samples of size 16 from the current population of ground finch on one of the Galápagos islands.*

deviations of the sample means from the expected value. The defining equation for the standard error, is as follows:

Equation 10.2
$$\sigma_{\bar{X}} = \sqrt{\frac{\Sigma(\bar{X} - \mu_{\bar{X}})^2}{k}}$$

In theory, **k** equals the number of all possible random samples of a specified size.

   If the 2000 samples represent all possible random samples of size 16 that could be selected from the hypothetical ground finch population, then the distribution in Figure 10.2 represents the sampling distribution of the mean for samples of size 16.

   The formula that can be used to calculate the standard error of this sampling distribution of the mean is as follows:

Formula 10.1
$$\sigma_{\bar{X}} = \sqrt{\frac{\Sigma(\bar{X}^2) - (\Sigma\bar{X})^2/k}{k}}$$

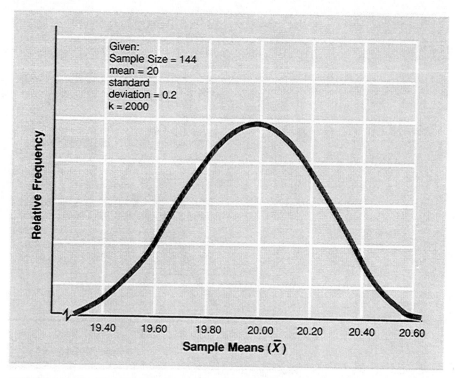

FIGURE 10.3 *Hypothetical frequency polygon of a sampling distribution of sample means of beak depth obtained for 2000 samples of size 144 obtained from the current population of ground finch on one of the Galápagos islands.*

Note also that if the investigator in the hypothetical example actually creates such a sampling distribution, then values for $\Sigma(\bar{X}^2)$ and $(\Sigma\bar{X})^2$ are available. For the purpose of illustration, assume that $\Sigma(\bar{X}^2)$ equals 25,500 and that $(\Sigma\bar{X})$ equals 6972. Substituting these values in Formula 10.1 indicates that $\sigma_{\bar{X}}$ equals 0.6, $\sqrt{[25,000 - 6972^2/2000]/2000}$.

Comparing the Empirical Distributions of the Sample Means.   The distributions in Figure 10.2 and 10.3 were created from the same population on the basis of selecting a large number of samples of two different sizes, 16 and 144. The effect of sample size is rather dramatic. As can be seen in these figures, the shape of the distribution greatly changes and approaches that of the normal distribution as sample size increases from 16 (Figure 10.2) to 144 (Figure 10.3). This change in shape is due to the fact that as sample size increases the sample means cluster closer to the expected value. Thus, as a consequence of increasing sample size, the standard error is reduced.

PROGRESS ASSESSMENT 10.1

The information listed in the accompanying table represents all (k = 25) possible random samples (N = 2) of condor eggs and their corresponding means that could be selected from an original population of 5 females that laid 1, 2, 3, 4, and 5 eggs each.

TABLE 10-A
All Possible Random Samples (N = 2) of Condor Eggs Laid and Corresponding Means with the Following Numbers of Eggs Laid by Each Member of the Original Population: 1, 2, 3, 4, 5.

Possible Samples (N = 2)					Corresponding Means for Samples (N = 2)				
1,1	2,1	3,1	4,1	5,1	1.0	1.5	2.0	2.5	3.0
1,2	2,2	3,2	4,2	5,2	1.5	2.0	2.5	3.0	3.5
1,3	2,3	3,3	4,3	5,3	2.0	2.5	3.0	3.5	4.0
1,4	2,4	3,4	4,4	5,4	2.5	3.0	3.5	4.0	4.5
1,5	2,5	3,5	4,5	5,5	3.0	3.5	4.0	4.5	5.0

1. Calculate μ for the original population.
2. Calculate σ for the original population.
3. Create a simple frequency distribution for the sample means. (Make it neat and organized, as you will use this distribution to calculate answers to parts 4–6.)
4. Create a relative frequency polygon for the sample means in your frequency distribution.
5. Calculate the expected value of the sampling distribution of the means from your simple frequency distribution.
6. Calculate the standard error of the sampling distribution of the means from your simple frequency distribution.

THE CENTRAL LIMIT THEOREM

Constructing sampling distributions, calculating standard errors, and calculating expected values as described in the preceding section is a very tedious and time-consuming process, if at all possible. Fortunately, the sampling distribution created from the means of an infinite number of random samples can be described on the basis of a mathematical theorem known as the central limit theorem. According to the **central limit theorem,** as sample size increases, the sampling distribution of the mean approaches the normal distribution regardless of the shape of the distribution of the original population. For very large samples, the expected value of the sampling distribution, $\mu_{\bar{x}}$, equals the mean of the original population, $\mu_{\bar{x}} = \mu$. This distribution has a standard error, $\sigma_{\bar{x}}$, equal to the standard deviation of the original population divided by the square root of the sample size, $\sigma_{\bar{x}} = \sigma/\sqrt{N}$.

Comparison of Figures 10.1, 10.2, and 10.3 illustrates the relationship between the mean of a population and the expected value of a sampling distribution as stated in the central limit theorem. The mean of the population in Figure 10.1 equals 20 as do the expected values of the distributions of the mean in Figures 10.2 and 10.3. This comparison also reveals the relationship between the standard error of a sampling distribution and the standard deviation of the original population as stated in the central limit theorem. The standard deviation of the population in Figure 10.1 is 2.4, and 2.4 divided by the square root of sample size, 4 ($\sqrt{16}$) in Figure 10.2 and 12 ($\sqrt{144}$) in Figure 10.3, yields standard errors of 0.6 and 0.2, respectively. Note that the standard error of the mean decreases with increases in sample size. Note also that as sample size increases, the shape of the sampling distribution of the mean approaches that of the normal curve regardless of the shape of the original population. Thus, use of the central limit theorem allows you to calculate or estimate the expected value and standard error of any sampling distribution of the mean if values for μ and σ of the original population are known or estimated.

PROGRESS ASSESSMENT 10.2

1. In parts 1 and 2 of Progress Assessment 10.1 you should have obtained values of $\mu = 3$ and $\sigma = 1.41$. For the sampling distribution you created in part 4 of Progress Assessment 10.1, based on sample size 2, use the central limit theorem to determine

   a. $\mu_{\bar{x}}$.

   b. $\sigma_{\bar{x}}$.

2. Compare the answers for $\mu_{\bar{x}}$ and $\sigma_{\bar{x}}$ that you obtained in part 1 of this Progress Assessment with the values that you should have obtained in parts 5 and 6 of Progress Assessment 10.1 where $\mu_{\bar{x}} = 3$ and $\sigma_{\bar{x}} = 1$. The answers should be the same. Explain why.

HYPOTHESIS EVALUATION

Understanding the normal curve, the central limit theorem, and basic approaches used to develop research hypotheses allows you to investigate a variety of questions posed by empirical scientists. You will recall from Chapter 9 the five steps which are used to evaluate hypotheses:

1. Form a research hypothesis.
2. Form a testable statistical hypothesis.
3. Perform a statistical test.
4. Decide whether or not to reject H_0.
5. State whether or not your decision supports your research hypothesis.

EVALUATING A HYPOTHESIS WHEN μ AND σ ARE KNOWN

Suppose in the Galápagos Islands example that the comparative psychologist unearths a large number of ground finch skeletons. A random sample of these skeletons ($N = 144$) has an average beak depth of 19.5 millimeters. The comparative psychologist hypothesizes that these are skeletal remains of a species of ground finch that became extinct as a result of competition for food with the current species. Let us see how the five steps concerning inferential statistics are used to evaluate this hypothesis.

Translating a Research Hypothesis into a Testable Statistical Hypothesis

Before you can formulate a testable statistical hypothesis, you must have a clear understanding of the research hypothesis. The research hypothesis in the example is that the skeletal remains are from a different species of ground finch than that represented by the current population. The comparative psychologist formed this hypothesis on the basis of his sample data ($N = 144$), which yielded an average beak depth (19.5 millimeters) smaller than the average beak depth for the population depicted in Figure 10.1. Note in Figure 10.1 that the X-axis represents specific X-values of beak depth for each individual member of the current population. The population characteristics, by themselves, cannot help the investigator determine if the skeletal remains of the sample belong to the current species or to a different species.

In contrast to Figure 10.1, the values plotted on the X-axis in Figure 10.3 represent sample means ($\bar{X}$'s). Assume that the distribution in Figure 10.3 actually represents the sampling distribution of the mean for random samples of size 144 for the population depicted in Figure 10.1. Because the investigator's hypothesis is based on a comparison of means, the sampling distribution of the mean must be used to determine the likelihood (probability) of obtaining such a sample mean if the expected value of the sampling distribution equals 20 millimeters. Thus, the null and alternative hypotheses are formed on the basis of the parameter, $\mu_{\bar{X}}$, the expected value of the sampling distribution of the means. The logic used to write the null (H_0) and alternative (H_1) hypotheses is the same as that described in Chapter 9.

The research hypothesis is used to formulate H_1. Since the research hypothesis is that the skeletal remains are *not* from members of the current species population for which the average beak depth (μ) equals 20 millimeters, H_1 is that the μ of the population for the skeletal sample does not equal 20. Since $\mu_{\bar{X}} = \mu$, H_1 can be formally stated as H_1: $\mu_{\bar{X}} \neq 20$. The negation of H_1 produces H_0. Thus H_0, the statistical hypothesis to be evaluated, can be formally stated as H_0: $\mu_{\bar{X}} = 20$.

Performing a Statistical Test

To perform a statistical test a decision rule is formed on the basis of an identified test statistic and a given alpha level. The test statistic must then be calculated to determine the likelihood of the measured results of the investigation.

Identification of Test Statistic.

The first step in forming a decision rule requires identification of an appropriate test statistic. Examination of the statistical hypotheses reveals that the test statistic selected must allow you to evaluate a distribution with $\mu_{\bar{X}}$ as an expected value. Such a distribution is, of course, the sampling distribution of the mean. According to the central limit theorem, when sample size is relatively large, the sampling distribution of the mean approaches the shape of the normal distribution. Given the sample size is 144, the sampling distribution of the mean would be normal. Recall from Chapter 9 that z-scores allow statistical hypotheses to be evaluated for normal distributions. For this reason z is identified as the test statistic in this example.

Selecting Alpha and Its Effect on Statistical Tests.

Given the test statistic has been selected, a second step involved in forming a decision rule is setting alpha or significance level. You will recall from Chapter 8 that the alpha or significance level frequently used in the behavioral sciences is equal to 0.05 or 5 percent. In this text most examples will involve this conventional alpha level. Because alpha must be modified under certain conditions, however, we will examine the effects of changing alpha to 0.01 in the examples described below.

As was pointed out in Chapter 9, a null hypothesis will be rejected if the evidence obtained is not likely to be due to chance. An alpha of 0.05 defines an unlikely event as one that has a probability equal to or less than 0.05. In this book we form nondirectional statistical hypotheses. **Nondirectional statistical hypotheses** are those used when the investigator has no reason to predict that the statistic will be either above or below the parameter stated in the null hypothesis. Nondirectional statistical hypotheses are evaluated on the basis of two-tailed statistical tests.

A **two-tailed statistical test** requires that the null hypothesis be rejected if your statistic is located at either extreme end of the hypothesized sampling distribution.

Figures 10.4 and 10.5 are two examples of normal distributions when alpha is set at 0.05 and 0.01, respectively. The shaded areas of the curves, referred to as critical regions, are used to determine whether or not the null hypothesis (H_0) should be rejected with a two-tailed test. **Critical regions** are those areas of a distribution that include values which are not likely to be due to chance. As can be seen in Figures 10.4 and 10.5, the critical regions divide alpha equally between both ends of the distribution. Because you want alpha to equal 0.05, you must select critical regions with a total proportion of the area equal to 0.05. If the evidence obtained indicates that your observations come from these regions, then the null hypothesis is rejected. The specific values that mark off the critical regions of a sampling distribution are called **critical values.** For the normal distribution critical values are usually expressed as z-scores.

In Figure 10.4 where alpha equals 0.05, the critical values for this sampling distribution are means which have z-scores equal to $+1.96$ and -1.96. These z-scores are obtained by examining Table 4, the normal curve table, in the appendix at the back of the text. In Column 3 of this table, the area beyond z represents one-half the alpha level, in this case, 0.025.

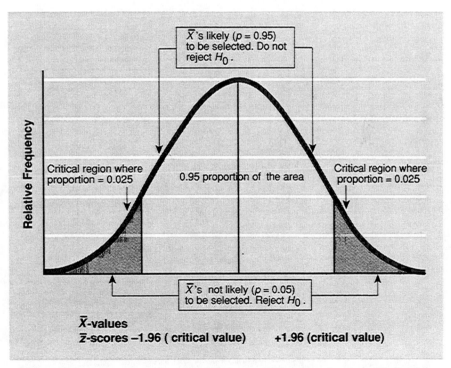

FIGURE 10.4 *Theoretical sampling distribution of the mean showing critical regions and critical values necessary to reject H_0 when alpha = 0.05.*

The corresponding z-score in Column 1 is 1.96 for the area above the mean and -1.96 for the area below the mean. When alpha is equal to 0.01, the critical z-values are $z = -2.58$ and $z = +2.58$, as the proportion of the area to be marked off on *both* sides is 0.005.

Note in Figures 10.4 and 10.5 how the critical regions move toward the ends of the distribution as alpha is changed from 0.05 to 0.01. This happens because a change from 0.05 to 0.01 means that only when the probability of the observed event is 0.01 or less will H_0 be rejected. In other words, the risk factor of being wrong when H_0 is rejected at the 1 percent level is smaller than when H_0 is rejected at the 5 percent level.

Stating the Decision Rule. Examination of Figure 10.4 reveals a general decision rule for a two-tailed test when alpha = 0.05. A **general decision rule** specifies the conditions under which H_0 is rejected. In the example, the general decision rule is that if the obtained sample mean has a probability of 0.025 or less of being selected from either end of the distribution, then H_0 is rejected.

When applying a general decision rule involving probabilities, researchers frequently translate it into a specific decision rule. A **specific**

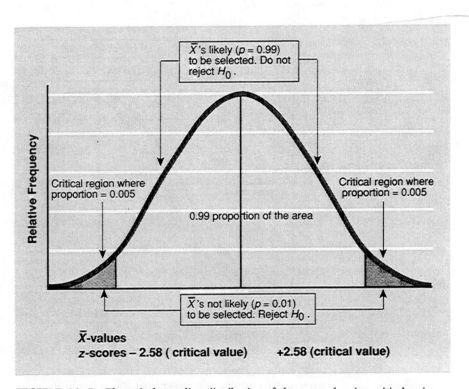

FIGURE 10.5 *Theoretical sampling distribution of the mean showing critical regions and critical values necessary to reject H_0 when alpha = 0.01.*

decision rule is a statement involving values of the identified test statistic that indicate when H_0 is to be rejected at a given alpha level.

In Figure 10.4, note that if the obtained sample mean comes from the critical regions of this distribution, then the null hypothesis is rejected. Note also that when alpha equals 0.05, the z-scores that mark off the critical regions for a normal distribution are always $+1.96$ and -1.96. If the z that is calculated (z_{calc}) on the basis of your observations is equal to or beyond these values, then your observed sample mean must fall within theses critical regions, which indicates that the null hypothesis is to be rejected. Thus, the **specific decision rule for z when alpha is equal to 0.05** is written as follows:

$$\text{If } |z_{calc}| \geq 1.96, \text{ reject } H_0.$$

By using the absolute value of z_{calc}, both positive and negative values of z are accounted for in this rule.

Understanding how general and specific decision rules are formed is important because they are applicable to all statistical tests.

Calculating the Test Statistic. The final step involved in performing a statistical test is that the test statistic be calculated to determine its likelihood or probability of occurring on the basis of chance. Because we are using a two-tailed test, we must determine the probability of selecting a sample mean ($\bar{X}$) that deviates from $\mu_{\bar{x}}$ (20) by as much or more than the obtained $\bar{X}$ (20.5), that is, by 0.5 or more ($19.5 \geq \bar{X} \geq 20.5$)

The approach used to determine this probability is exactly the same as that used in Chapter 9 using the normal curve. Remember that the central limit theorem states that as sample size increases, the sampling distribution of the mean resembles the normal distribution. Thus, determining the probability in the example is a normal curve problem requiring a diagram, a list of the information given, the z-score formula, and an understanding of the normal curve table.

Figure 10.3 is redrawn in Figure 10.6 to include information given in the problem (left side) and the z-score formula (right side) necessary to determine the probability of selecting a sample of size 144 whose mean deviates from the true mean (20) by as much or more than 0.5 in either direction ($19.5 \geq \bar{X} \geq 20.5$).

Two points should be made about Figure 10.6. First, this sampling distribution is assumed to be a normal distribution with an expected value equal to 20 and a standard error equal to 0.2 ($\sigma/\sqrt{N} = 2.4/\sqrt{144}$). Second, since a two-tailed test is used, the areas that fall above $\bar{X} = 20.5$ and below $\bar{X} = 19.5$ are shaded because we want to determine the probability of selecting a sample mean that deviates from the true mean by 0.5 or more. Once these areas of the curve are identified, we can then apply the standard z-score formula to determine the distance from the expected value ($\mu_{\bar{x}}$).

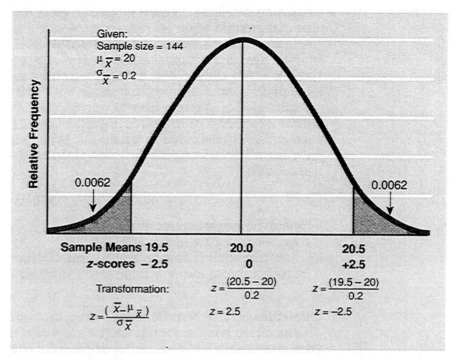

FIGURE 10.6 *Drawing needed to determine probability of selecting a sample of size 144 whose mean deviates from the true mean ($\mu_{\bar{X}}$) by 0.5 or more in either direction for a two-tailed statistical test.*

In Chapter 7 you learned that converting a specific value of a measured characteristic to a z-score requires subtracting the mean of a distribution from the specific value and dividing this difference by the standard deviation of the distribution. Because we are dealing with a sampling distribution of the mean, the specific measure of the characteristic of interest is the sample mean. The mean of the distribution is the expected value of the sampling distribution ($\mu_{\bar{X}} = 20$) and the standard deviation is the standard error of the sampling distribution, $\sigma_{\bar{X}} = 0.2$. When working with a sampling distribution of the mean based on a large sample size, the z-formula to be used is as follows:

Formula 10.2 $z = (\bar{X} - \mu_{\bar{X}})/\sigma_{\bar{X}}$

In the tails of the distribution of Figure 10.6, the calculations indicate that $\bar{X} = 20.5$ produces a z-score equal to 2.5 [$(20.5 - 20)/0.2$] and $\bar{X} = 19.5$ produces a z-score equal to -2.5 [$(19.5 - 20)/0.2$]. Using the normal curve table (Appendix, Table 4) the proportion of the area of the curve above the z-score of 2.5 is 0.0062, and the proportion of the area of the curve below a z-score of -2.5 is also 0.0062. Thus, the probability of randomly selecting a sample that has a mean that deviates from the true mean ($\mu_{\bar{X}} = 20$) by as much as 0.5 or more is 0.0124 (0.0062 + 0.0062).

Making Decisions about the Null and Research Hypotheses

Decisions must now be made about the null and research hypotheses. Initially a decision must be made to reject or fail to reject the null hypothesis. Then, on the basis of that decision, a decision about the research hypothesis is made.

Since 0.0124 is less than 0.05, the null hypothesis is rejected on the basis of the general probability decision rule. In relation to a specific decision rule, H_0 is rejected because the $|z_{calc}|$ which equals 2.5 is greater than 1.96.

In terms of the research hypothesis, the statistical analysis suggests that the skeletal remains do not come from a population of finches similar to the current species. This decision is made because the outcome of the statistical test indicates that the likelihood of obtaining a sample whose mean differs in either direction from the population mean by 0.5 is 0.0124. Such an event is considered unlikely given that its probability of occurrence is less than the stated alpha level of 0.05.

Reporting Results

In general, when reporting the outcome of a statistical test you are required to (1) describe what the outcome means with respect to the research hypothesis, (2) name the test statistic, (3) give an indication of the degrees of freedom or, as in the case of z, sample size, usually set off in parenthesis, (4) give the calculated value of the test statistic, and (5) indicate the probability, **p**, for obtaining the calculated value on the basis of chance. In a formal research report the results of the statistical test performed on the data collected in the Galápagos Islands example would read as follows:

> The statistical analysis supports the belief that the sample of skeletal remains with a mean ($\overline{X}$) beak depth of 20.5 is significantly different from the mean beak depth of the current population of ground finches, $z(144) = 2.5, p = 0.0124$.

Note that the use of the word *significantly* refers to the fact that the null hypothesis is rejected. Significance is used to describe results only when the probability of obtaining such results are less than the stated alpha level. In this case, alpha equals 0.05. Had the null hypothesis not been rejected, the results would have been considered to be statistically nonsignificant, and the p value listed would have been some value greater than the chosen alpha level of 0.05. Do not use the term *significant* as a synonym for *important* in the context of statistical tests.

PUTTING IT ALL TOGETHER

The preceding sections discussed the steps used to make decisions about hypotheses using inferential statistics. The steps are similar regardless of the test statistic and are used throughout the remainder of this text. The steps as they apply to the z-statistic and the hypothetical example of 144 beak depth values are summarized as follows:

1. State the research hypothesis.
2. Translate the research hypothesis into a set of mutually exclusive and exhaustive mathematical statements by (a) forming an alternative hypothesis (H_1) that is in agreement with the research hypothesis and by (b) negating H_1 to form the null hypothesis (H_0). In the example:

$$H_0: \mu_{\bar{X}} = 20 \text{ millimeters.}$$
$$H_1: \mu_{\bar{X}} \neq 20 \text{ millimeters.}$$

3. Perform a statistical test in the following manner:
   a. Identify a test statistic. In the example the test statistic is z.
   b. Select alpha. In the example, as is usually the case, alpha = 0.05.
   c. State a decision rule based on the selected alpha level. In the example, the rule is reject H_0 if the mean of the sample has a probability of 0.05 or less of being randomly selected from either end of the sampling distribution where sample size equals 144 and $\mu_{\bar{X}}$ = 20. More specifically, the rule can also be stated as follows: If $|z_{calc}| \geq 1.96$, then reject H_0.
   d. Calculate the test statistic. The value of a test statistic is obtained on the basis of a specified formula. In the example the formula is $z = (\bar{X} - \mu_{\bar{X}})/\sigma_{\bar{X}}$. For the two-tailed test in the example, z-score transformations produced z scores of $+2.5$ and -2.5.
   e. Determine the probability that the value of the test statistic would be obtained on the basis of chance. Using the normal distribution table, the probability of obtaining $\bar{X}$ that deviates from the true mean by as much as 0.5 is 0.0124.
4. Make a decision about the null hypothesis. In the example since 0.0124 is less than 0.05, the null hypothesis is rejected on the basis of the general decision rule. Likewise, the null hypothesis is rejected on the basis of the specific decision rule as $|z_{calc}|$ = 2.5 greater than 1.96.
5. Make a decision about your research hypothesis. On the basis of your decision about your null hypothesis, determine whether or not your results do or do not support your research hypothesis. In the example, the research hypothesis that the skeletal remains do not come from the current finch population is supported because H_0 is rejected.
6. Report the results of your statistical test in relation to your evaluation of the null hypothesis and whether or not this evaluation supports the research hypothesis. The report of this test may be stated as: The sample mean of 20.5 millimeters differs significantly from the population mean of 20.0 millimeters, $z(144) = 2.5$, $p = 0.0124$.

PROGRESS ASSESSMENT 10.3

Apply the following steps to parts 1 and 2 of this Progress Assessment.

a. State the research hypothesis.

b. State the null and alternative hypotheses.

c. Perform a statistical test by doing the following:

(1) Identify the test statistic.

(2) Select alpha.

(3) State a general decision rule and a specific decision rule.

(4) Calculate the probability of randomly selecting a sample mean that deviates from the true mean ($\mu_{\bar{X}}$ or μ) by as much or more in either direction as does the observed sample mean ($\bar{X}$) by using a diagram, z-transformation, and the normal curve table.

d. Evaluate the null hypothesis on the basis of general and specific decision rules.

e. Make a decision about your research hypothesis.

f. State your conclusion about the research hypothesis as you would in a formal research report.

1. Assume a sample size of 36 is used to determine if the skeletal remains in the Galápagos Islands example come from a population different from the population that has a mean (μ) beak depth equal to 20 millimeters and $\sigma = 2.4$ millimeters. Assume also that $\bar{X}$ of this sample equals 20.5.

2. A dean of admissions claims that the new recruitment efforts produced a freshman class of 400 students with a mean SAT score ($\bar{X} = 960$) different from all other previous classes. University records indicate that the average (μ) SAT score for all freshman ever admitted, excluding the current year's class, is 950. The σ of this distribution of SAT scores is 100.

RANDOM SAMPLES AND SAMPLE SIZE

The logic of inferential statistics discussed in this chapter is based on the assumption that a random sample has been selected. This is rarely accomplished. Instead researchers attempt to obtain samples that are obtained in an unbiased fashion, such as the randomization procedure discussed in Chapter 2. Until proven otherwise, samples chosen without observable biases are assumed representative of random samples needed to use inferential statistics.

Two specific points need to be made about the importance of sample size in inferential statistics. First, according to the central limit theorem as sample size gets larger, the shape of the sampling distribution gets closer and closer to the normal distribution. Generally a sample size of thirty or more produces a sampling distribution similar in shape to the normal distribution. Second, the power of a statistical test increases as sample size increases. Look at the graphs in Figure 10.2 and Figure 10.3 and you can see that as sample size increases, the standard error decreases. When $\sigma_{\bar{X}}$ is small, any given mean is more likely to be more standard units (z-scores) away from the expected value of the sampling distribution than when $\sigma_{\bar{X}}$ is large. As a result, a sample mean is more likely to fall in the critical region necessary to reject H_0 if the sample is not from the specified population. Thus, the chance of rejecting H_0, and hence the power of the test, increases. The question you are now faced with is how large a sample should you use in your investigation. This issue will be discussed in the next chapter.

PROGRESS ASSESSMENT 10.4

1. The following exercise should help you understand the relationship between sample size, $\sigma_{\bar{X}}$, and the effect a decrease in $\sigma_{\bar{X}}$ has on increasing the likelihood of obtaining an $\bar{X}$ that falls further from $\mu_{\bar{X}}$ (thus increasing power). Given deviations $(\bar{X} - \mu_{\bar{X}})$ equal to 15 in both directions away from the mean, that is, an $\bar{X} = 115$ and an $\bar{X} = 85$, $\mu_{\bar{X}} = 100$ and, σ equal to 30, compute for the following sample sizes (1) $\sigma_{\bar{X}}$, (2) $\pm$ z-scores, (3) p, the combined area at or above the $+z$-score and at or below the $-z$-score expressed as a probability.

   a. $N = 4$
   b. $N = 9$
   c. $N = 25$
   d. $N = 36$
   e. $N = 100$

2. Considering your answers in part 1 of this Progress Assessment, describe the relationship between an increase in sample size and

   a. the distance in standard deviation units between the obtained mean and the expected value of the sampling distribution.
   b. the likelihood of rejecting a false H_0 for a given sample mean.

SUMMARY

The material in this chapter provides the foundation for the use of inferential statistics. The concept of sampling distribution and its relationship to the original population from which the sampling distribution is created are described. The central limit theorem is briefly discussed in relation to determining the standard error and expected value of a sampling distribution based on a given sample size, when σ and μ of the original population are known. The principles involved in using the z-statistic to evaluate specific research hypotheses are also covered. In all of the examples where hypotheses are evaluated, σ and μ are known and samples sizes are ≥ 30. Given these conditions, the sampling distributions (which are hypothesized to represent distributions from which data are collected) are assumed to be normally distributed. Probabilities are therefore determined with the use of the normal distribution table. The six-step procedure that is used to evaluate a research hypothesis on the basis of a statistical test is elaborated in relation to a general and a specific decision rule for H_0. The influence of sample size on the power of a statistical test is discussed.

KEY DEFINITIONS

central limit theorem   A mathematical theorem that describes the sampling distribution of sample means. According to this theorem, if sample size is large ($N \geq 30$), the sampling distribution of the mean approaches a normal distribution with $\mu_{\bar{X}} = \mu$ and $\sigma_{\bar{X}} = \sigma/\sqrt{N}$.

critical regions   Areas of a sampling distribution that include values which are not likely to be due to chance.

critical values   Specific values that mark off the critical regions of a sampling distribution.

expected value   The mean of a sampling distribution.

general decision rule   A rule that specifies the conditions under which H_0 is rejected.

k   The symbol used to represent the number of samples.

$\mu_{\bar{X}}$ The symbol used to represent the expected value of the sampling distribution of the mean.

$\mu_{\bar{X}} = \mu$ An equality stated in the central limit theorem used to determine the expected value of a sampling distribution of the mean when μ is known.

nondirectional statistical hypotheses   Statistical hypotheses used when the investigator has no reason to predict that the statistic will be either above or below the parameter given in the null hypothesis.

p   The symbol used to indicate the probability of obtaining a calculated statistic on the basis of chance.

sampling distribution   A theoretical distribution of a particular statistic for an infinite number of random samples of a given size from a population of an infinite size.

sampling distribution of the mean, $\bar{X}$ A theoretical distribution of an infinite number of means from random samples of a specified size.

$\sigma_{\bar{X}}$ The symbol used to represent the standard error of the sampling distribution of the mean.

$\sigma_{\bar{X}} = \sqrt{\Sigma(\bar{X} - \mu_{\bar{X}})^2/k}$ The defining equation of the standard error of a sampling distribution of the mean.

$\sigma_{\bar{X}} = \sqrt{[\Sigma(\bar{X}^2) - (\Sigma\bar{X})^2/k]/k}$ A formula used to calculate the standard error of a sampling distribution of the mean.

$\sigma_{\bar{X}} = \sigma/\sqrt{N}$ An equality stated in the central limit theorem used to calculate the standard error of a sampling distribution of the mean when σ and sample size are known.

$\Sigma(\bar{X} - \mu_{\bar{X}}) = 0$ The defining equation of the expected value of the sampling distribution of the mean.

specific decision rule   A statement involving values of an identified test statistic that indicates when H_0 is to be rejected at a given alpha level.

specific decision rule for z when alpha equals 0.05   If $|z_{calc}| \geq 1.96$, reject the null hypothesis.

standard error   The standard deviation of a sampling distribution.

two-tailed statistical test   A statistical test that requires H_0 be rejected if the test statistic is located at either extreme end of the theoretical sampling distribution.

$z = (\bar{X} - \mu_{\bar{X}})/\sigma_{\bar{X}}$ The formula for the z-statistic used when working with a sampling distribution of the mean.

REVIEW EXERCISES

1. Using a diagram, the appropriate z-formula, Table 4 in the Appendix, information based on an original population with $\mu = 90$, $\sigma = 30$, and a sampling distribution of the mean created from samples of size 36 determine
   a. the $\bar{X}$ below which 80 percent of the sample means fall in the sampling distribution.
   b. the values of $\bar{X}$ that mark off the upper and lower 0.005 proportion of the area of the sampling distribution.
   c. the $\bar{X}$ below which 99.5 percent of the cases fall.
2. In the text of this chapter we rejected the H_0: $\mu_{\bar{X}} = 20$ millimeters for a sample of skeletal remains when the observed $\bar{X} = 19.5$ and a sample size $= 144$.
   a. Describe the type of error that can be made when the null hypothesis is rejected in this case.
   b. What are the specific consequences, as related to this example, of such an error?

3. In Progress Assessment 10.3, part 1, where we assumed a set of observations based on $N = 36$, the null hypothesis that $\mu_{\bar{X}} = 20$ millimeters was not rejected.

    a. Describe the type of error that can be made when the null hypothesis is not rejected in this example.

    b. What are the specific consequences, as related to this example, of such an error?

ANSWERS TO PROGRESS ASSESSMENTS

10.1   **1.** 3

        2. 1.41

        3. See Table 10-B.

TABLE 10-B
Simple Frequency Distribution of All Possible Random Sample ($N = 2$) Means Obtained from a Population Where Number of Condor Eggs Laid was: 1, 2, 3, 4, and 5

Means (X)	Frequency f
5.0	1
4.5	2
4.0	3
3.5	4
3.0	5
2.5	4
2.0	3
1.5	2
1.0	1

        4. See Figure 10-A.

        5. 3

        6. 1

10.2   **1. a.** 3

          b. 1

        2. According to the central limit theorem, $\mu_{\bar{X}} = \mu$ and $\sigma_{\bar{X}} = \sigma/\sqrt{N}$ will always be obtained for any sampling distribution of the mean.

10.3   **1. a.** The excavated sample is not from the current population.

          b. $H_0: \mu_{\bar{X}} = 20$ or $\mu = 20$, $H_1: \mu_{\bar{X}} \neq 20$ or $\mu \neq 20$.

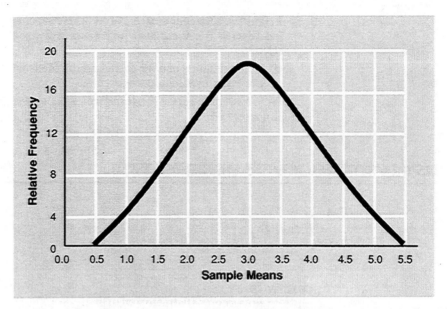

FIGURE 10-A *Relative frequency polygon of sampling distribution of the mean for all possible random samples of size 2 for Progress Assessment 10.1.*

    c. (1) z-statistic (2) 0.05 (3) If the probability is 0.05 or less of randomly selecting a sample mean that differs as much or more in either direction from the true mean (μ or $\mu_{\bar{x}}$) as does the observed sample mean, then reject H_0 or if $|z_{calc}| \geq 1.96$ then reject H_0 (4) $p = 0.2112$.

    d. Since $0.2112 \geq 0.05$, fail to reject H_0, or since $|z_{calc}| = 1.25$ is less than 1.96, fail to reject H_0.

    e. The results of the test do not support the research hypothesis.

    f. As no statistically significant differences are obtained, one cannot tell if the sample of skeletal remains with $\bar{X} = 20.5$ millimeters comes from a population which has $\mu = 20$ millimeters, $z(36) = 1.25$, $p = 0.2112$.

2. a. The average SAT score of this year's freshman class is different from that of the past classes.

    b. $H_0: \mu = 950$ or $\mu_{\bar{x}} = 950$; $H_1: \mu \neq 950$ or $\mu_{\bar{x}} \neq 950$.

    c. (1) z-statistic (2) 0.05 (3) If the probability is 0.05 or less of randomly obtaining a sample mean that differs as much or more in either direction from the true mean (μ or $\mu_{\bar{x}}$) as does the observed sample mean ($\bar{X}$), then reject the null hypothesis, or, if $|z_{calc}| \geq 1.96$ then reject H_0. (c) $p = 0.0456$.

    d. Reject H_0 since $0.0456 < 0.05$ or reject H_0 as $|z_{calc}| = 2$ is greater than 1.96.

    e. Results support the dean's hypothesis.

    f. Statistical analysis suggests that the mean SAT = 970 of this year's freshman class is significantly different from $\mu = 950$ of all students admitted in the past, $z(400) = 2$, $p = 0.0456$.

10.4   1. **a.** (1) 15 (2) $+1.0, -1.0$ (3) 0.3174
      b. (1) 10 (2) $+1.5, -1.5$ (3) 0.1336
      c. (1) 6 (2) $+2.5, -2.5$ (3) 0.0124
      d. (1) 5 (2) $+3.0, -3.0$ (3) 0.0026
      e. (1) 3 (2) $+5.0, -5.0$ (3) < 0.00004

    2. a. As sample size increases, a given mean is likely to be more standard deviation units away from the expected value of its sampling distribution.

      b. As sample size increases, the likelihood of rejecting a false H_0 for the given mean increases.

Evaluating Hypotheses and Estimating Parameters Using the *t*-Distribution: The One-Sample *t*-Test

R esearchers use inferential statistics primarily for two reasons. One is to estimate points or intervals. **Point estimation** is a procedure whereby a single value for a population parameter is estimated from sample data. You will recall from Chapter 5 that the sample mean, $\bar{X}$, is an unbiased estimate of the population parameter, μ. The sample mean is, in this case, a point estimate. In this chapter we obtain point estimates of the standard error of the mean, $\sigma_{\bar{X}}$, which you encountered in the previous chapter. **Interval estimation** is a procedure by which information obtained from a sample is used to determine intervals likely to contain the value of a specified parameter. In this chapter we obtain interval estimates for the population parameter, μ.

A second reason inferential statistics are used is to test hypotheses. **Hypothesis testing,** as pointed out in the previous chapter, is a procedure by which information obtained from a sample can be used to evaluate null and alternative hypotheses about a specific population.

A variety of parametric statistics is used for estimation and hypothesis testing. **Parametric statistics** are statistics based on theoretical distributions whose use requires that certain assumptions be true. These assumptions are about the parameters of the population from which the sample is obtained. The assumptions for parametric statistical tests vary slightly from test to test and, thus, are reiterated and elaborated as necessary for each test discussed throughout the remaining chapters. In this chapter we discuss a specific parametric statistic, the t-statistic. The *t-statistic* is a statistic used to test hypotheses about the expected value of a sampling distribution and to determine intervals that are likely to contain the expected value.

In discussing the t-statistic we examine its assumptions, characteristics, and how it is used to evaluate hypotheses. When examining the use of the t-statistic in testing hypotheses, we discuss the power of statistical tests, that is, the probability of correctly rejecting a false H_0, and the resources investigators use to increase the power of the t-test.

THE ONE-SAMPLE t-STATISTIC:
AN APPROXIMATION OF z

You encountered hypothesis testing procedures in Chapters 9 and 10 where the normal curve, the sampling distribution of the mean, and the z-statistic were used to evaluate hypotheses involving a single sample when μ and σ were known. Although the concepts discussed in those chapters provide the foundation for evaluating hypotheses on the basis of statistical reasoning, investigators usually do not know the parameters μ and σ. As a result, z defined as $(\bar{X} - \mu_{\bar{X}})/\sigma_{\bar{X}}$ is rarely used in empirical applications. More often, investigators hypothesize a value for μ as stated in the null hypothesis, estimate $\sigma_{\bar{X}}$ on the basis of the statistic s and sample size, and then, use the one-sample t-statistic. The **one-sample t-statistic** is a test statistic used to evaluate statistical hypotheses when μ is hypothesized and $\sigma_{\bar{X}}$ is estimated. The one-sample t-statistic is also used to estimate a range of values for μ based on $\bar{X}$ when μ is *not* hypothesized and $\sigma_{\bar{X}}$ is estimated.

Theoretical Distributions and Assumptions

You will recall the previous discussion in Chapters 9 and 10 of two different theoretical distributions, the normal distribution and the sampling distribution of the sample mean. Remember that theoretical distributions are formed on the basis of mathematical models involving specific assumptions. For example, if we assume that the mean is calculated for all possible random samples of size 30 or greater from an infinite population, then the central limit theorem can be used to describe the sampling distribution of the sample means as a normal distribution with an expected value equal to μ and standard error equal to $\sigma/\sqrt{N}$. Note that, in this case, you must have values of μ and σ to evaluate statistical hypotheses.

If investigators have access to every member of a population, then they can compute μ and σ. Because populations are usually very large, this rarely happens. Instead, data are collected from samples and are used to estimate population parameters. When parameters such as $\sigma_{\bar{X}}$ are estimated, then a statistic other than the z-statistic is generally used. The statistic that is most often used to test hypotheses about μ when $\sigma_{\bar{X}}$ is estimated is the t-statistic. The distribution of the t-statistic, like the normal distribution and the sampling distribution of the mean, is a theoretical distribution based on mathematical models involving several assumptions. These assumptions are also referred to as necessary conditions for using parametric statistics. In order to use the t-statistic correctly at least four conditions must be fulfilled:

1. The sample used by the investigator must be a random sample which is assumed to be unbiased. This means that sample selection has occurred with no systematic bias.

2. The *measurement* for each **sample element,** that is, each member of the sample, must be independent of the measurement obtained for any other sample element. In other words, the score assigned to any one member of the sample must not influence the score that is assigned to any other member of the sample.

3. The random sample must be selected from a population for which the characteristic of interest, for example, test score, is normally distributed. In practice, as opposed to theory, this third condition is not always rigorously examined. Unless the investigator has evidence to indicate that the population is extremely skewed, most populations are assumed to be normally distributed. Even when the population is not normally distributed, as long as it is relatively symmetrical, the probabilities obtained for a t-statistic are close to the values that would

be obtained for the z-statistic when sample size is relatively large. Unless otherwise indicated in this chapter, assume that samples have been randomly selected from populations in which the characteristic of interest is normally distributed. How you determine whether or not the characteristic of interest is normally distributed in the population from which a random sample is selected will be discussed in Chapter 17.

4. The measurements obtained for members of the sample should be along an interval or ratio scale. The t-statistic is generally not used with data measured along nominal or ordinal scales.

If these conditions are met, the one-sample t-statistic can be used to test hypotheses about μ or estimate values of μ when data are collected from a single sample.

PROGRESS ASSESSMENT 11.1

For each of the following determine which, if any, of the assumptions needed to use the t-statistic are *not* met.

1. A sample of college students is selected by obtaining the names of all students currently enrolled in an elective freshman English course at a particular university. Scores from a standardized vocabulary test are obtained for all students in the English course and compared to vocabulary test scores obtained for all students at the university.

2. Pairs of students are given an assignment in a general psychology class for which each member in the pair is given the same grade. The instructor then obtains the grades for each and every student and compares the current class grades with those collected in the past.

3. A sample of incoming freshman is randomly selected from the entire incoming freshman class and their SAT scores are obtained and compared to scores for all the freshman students at the university.

Computing the One-Sample t-Statistic

The t-statistic used to evaluate hypotheses about a single sample is very similar to the z-statistic. It is determined by subtracting a *hypothesized* value of the population mean (symbolized μ_0 from the sample mean $(\bar{X})$ which is then divided by the *estimate* $(s_{\bar{X}})$ of the standard error of the mean $(\sigma_{\bar{X}})$. The formula for t is given as follows:

Formula 11.1

$$t = \frac{(\bar{X} - \mu_0)}{s_{\bar{X}}}$$

Note the similarity to the z-formula where $z = (\bar{X} - \mu_{\bar{x}})/\sigma_{\bar{x}}$. In this case, the distance in standard deviation units between a sample mean ($\bar{X}$) and the expected value ($\mu_{\bar{x}}$) is determined by dividing the difference between the sample mean and the expected value ($\bar{X} - \mu_{\bar{x}}$) by the standard error of the mean ($\sigma_{\bar{x}}$).

In comparison, the expected value (μ_0) in the t-formula has the subscript 0. Because μ is not known, investigators hypothesize values for μ. The specific value of the hypothesized μ is given in the null hypothesis (H_0) which also includes the subscript 0.

The t-statistic also differs from the z-statistic in a more significant way. Because σ is not known, the value for the standard error of the sampling distribution cannot be directly determined by $\sigma/\sqrt{N}$. Instead s, the estimate of σ discussed in Chapter 6, is used to *estimate* the standard error, symbolized as $s_{\bar{x}}$. The value of $s_{\bar{x}}$ is obtained by dividing s by the square root of N. Expressed as a formula, the estimate of the standard error of the sample means is as follows:

Formula 11.2
$$s_{\bar{X}} = \frac{s}{\sqrt{N}}$$

Except for the estimate of σ and hypothesized μ in the t-statistic formula, there is little difference between the t-formula and the z-formula used with the sampling distribution of the mean.

PROGRESS ASSESSMENT 11.2

A psychologist obtains the number of hours of sleep reported by sixteen subjects randomly selected from a population of normal adults that are hypothesized to sleep an average (μ_0) of eight hours each day. Given values of $\bar{X} = 9$ and $s = 3.6$, calculate a value for t.

The t-Distribution

You will recall that the sampling distribution of the mean for sample sizes equal to or greater than 30 can be described on the basis of the z-statistic. With sample sizes 30 and above, the shape of the sampling distribution of the mean varies only slightly and closely approximates the shape of the normal curve. In contrast, when the sampling distribution of the mean is based on sample sizes less than 30, the sampling distribution of the mean varies greatly and does not closely approximate the normal distribution. With sample sizes less than 30, there is a distinct distribution for each sample size which becomes less and less normal as sample size decreases. These distinct distributions represent a family of distributions which, because they can be described on the basis of the t-statistic, are referred to as t-distributions.

The **t-distribution,** then, is actually a family of theoretical sampling distributions. The shape of each specific t-distribution changes as a function of sample size. Because s is used in determining $s_{\bar{X}}$ (the estimate of $\sigma_{\bar{X}}$) for the t-statistic, the shape of the t-distribution is defined in relation to degrees of freedom associated with calculating s.

Degrees of Freedom. Recall from Chapter 6 that degrees of freedom, symbolized *df,* can be defined as the number of events involved in a specific calculation that are free to vary or, in other words, can take on any possible value. One way of looking at degrees of freedom is to think of them as the total number of events that are not affected by any mathematical requirement. For example, pick three values for the events *a, b,* and *c.* In this case *df* equals 3 since there are three events, *a, b,* and *c,* and no mathematical requirement. If we now ask you to determine values for these events in the formula $a + b + c$, having the one mathematical requirement that their sum equal zero, then *df* in this example equals 2. In this example of $a + b + c = 0$, you can select any numerical value for any two variables. Once these two values are selected, however, the third event must be given a value that adheres to the mathematical requirement that the sum be equal to 0. If $a = 10$ and $b = 15$, then *c must* equal -25. The third event in this example is *not* free to vary.

We could go through an infinite number of cases changing the values of *a* and *b.* However, in all cases, once *a* and *b* are assigned values, *c* cannot vary. If we change the situation and list two mathematical requirements, that the sum of the three must equal zero and that one of the variables must equal five, then the number of degrees of freedom is equal to one. There are three events, *a, b,* and *c,* and two mathematical requirements. The requirements are that the events must sum to zero and one of the events must equal five. Therefore, $df = 1$ $(3 - 2)$. Given the above explanation, *df* can then be calculated in any situation by subtracting the number of mathematical requirements from the total number of events being examined.

When calculating $s_{\bar{X}}$, the value of s is determined on the basis of the defining equation $s = \sqrt{\sum (X - \bar{X})^2 / N - 1}$. Calculations from this equation are determined on the basis of the number of sample elements, *N.* The only mathematical requirement placed on the measures of the *N*-sample elements is that $\Sigma(X - \bar{X}) = 0$. Thus, there is only one mathematical requirement placed on the one-sample t-statistic formula. Degrees of freedom for the one-sample t-distribution are therefore defined as $N - 1$. Alternatively when estimating standard deviation (or variance), *df* can be specifically defined as the number of deviations $(X - \bar{X})$ minus the number of points about which the deviations are taken. The estimate of any one sample standard-deviation *df* will therefore always equal $N - 1$ since the mean of a sample is the one point about which the *N*-deviations $(X - \bar{X})$ are taken.

The Shape of t-Distributions and the Table of Critical Values.

In Figure 11.1, three t-distributions have been drawn with df = 2, 26, and 120. Note that each distribution is symmetrical, has a mean equal to 0, and becomes flatter as sample size decreases. You can also see that the critical regions for alpha = 0.05, marked in each distribution, move further and further away from the mean as sample size gets smaller. Because these critical regions change as a function of the specific t-distribution, forming a decision rule for a one-sample t-test can be done more efficiently with the use of a table of critical values than with a table listing all possible t-scores that mark off areas of the t-distribution.

In contrast to the general decision rule procedure described in Chapter 10 for the z-statistic, it is not necessary to calculate the probability of randomly obtaining a t-statistic that differs from the mean of sampling distribution of t as much or more than the observed t. Rather, a specific decision rule is formed using a table of critical t-values. Table 5, in the Appendix at the back of the book, lists critical values that mark off the t-distribution for specific df when alpha equals 0.05 and 0.01. For example, for sample

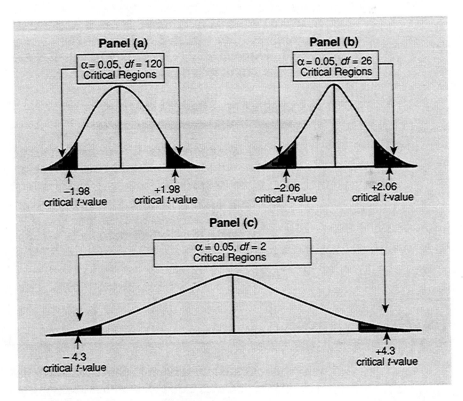

FIGURE 11.1   *Three t-distributions showing critical regions and critical values where α = 0.05 and df equal 120, 26, or 2.*

size 27 the critical value of the one-sample t-test with alpha = 0.05 and df = 26 is 2.06. Note that the alpha level (0.05 in this example) listed at the top of Table 5 and that df (26 in this example as 27 − 1 = 26) listed as the first column in Table 5 are used to select the appropriate critical values. Examination of Figure 11.1, Panel (b), where df = 26, also reveals that 2.06 is the value that marks off the critical regions of this t-distribution when alpha is equal to 0.05. Based on the logic described in Chapter 10, the decision rule for evaluating H_0 when df = 26 and α = 0.05 can therefore be written as follows:

$$\text{If } |t_{calc}| \geq 2.06, \text{ then reject } H_0.$$

Using Decision Rules. A decision rule involving critical values indicates the minimum absolute value of the statistic that can be considered significant at the designated alpha level. As can be seen in Figure 11.1, the decision rule allows you to determine if your calculated t falls inside or outside of the critical regions used to reject H_0 for a specific t-distribution at a given alpha level. Application of specific decision rules does not allow for determination of exact probabilities. Therefore, when reporting outcomes of statistical tests involving specific decision rules, investigators simply report probability values (p) as ≤ or > the designated alpha level, for example, $t(26)$ = 3.00, $p \leq 0.05$ or $t(26)$ = 1.5, $p > 0.05$ for alpha set at 0.05. If the probability is equal to or less than the designated alpha level, H_0 is rejected; otherwise H_0 is not rejected.

PROGRESS ASSESSMENT 11.3

1. Using Appendix Table 5 located in the back of the book, write the decision rule that should be used for the one-sample t-test when df = 16 and α = 0.05.
2. Using Appendix Table 5, formally report the outcome of the following t-calculations for sample size N = 17 as it would be done in the literature including the value of t, df, and a probability level, p.

   a. t_{calc} = 2.13
   b. t_{calc} = 2.09

HYPOTHESIS TESTING

With the conditions described above we can now use the t-test to evaluate statistical hypotheses based on research involving one sample. The procedure for evaluating hypotheses involves the steps discussed in Chapters 9 and 10. These steps, which you should now know from memory, are as follows:

1. Form a research hypothesis.
2. Form statistical hypotheses.
3. Perform a statistical test with the use of a specific decision rule and calculated statistic.
4. Evaluate the null hypothesis.
5. Make a decision about your research hypothesis.
6. Formally report statistical results in relation to the research hypothesis.

Forming Research and Statistical Hypotheses

Our discussion on forming research hypotheses in the previous chapters was necessarily brief. However, you should know that the ability to form good research hypotheses depends on an understanding of the topic to be investigated. Only then can you generate questions that can be examined on the basis of research and statistical analysis. As you take more courses and read more research reports, you will be exposed to various hypotheses that have been examined and gain a better understanding of how to form hypotheses that can be evaluated with statistical tests.

To get an idea of how research involving statistical analysis proceeds, let us examine some questions that a new director of a university's learning skills center might ask to determine specific programs that need improvement.

Purpose of the Research. Before data and statistical procedures are used to evaluate hypotheses, the purpose of the research must be determined. In this example, assume that the director first decides to determine whether or not students at this university devote enough time to studying. Based on his training as an educational psychologist, the director believes that students should spend about 2.5 hours of study time for every one-credit-hour of class time. Thus, a student taking four 3-credit-hour courses should be studying about 30 hours ($4 \times 3 \times 2.5$) per week.

As a starting point, the director begins by informally asking faculty if they believe that students taking 12 credit hours study an average of 30 hours per week. Some faculty believe students study more than 30 hours and others believe they study less than 30 hours. Few of the faculty believe that 30 is the average number of hours studied. On the basis of this initial information, the director believes that a μ_0 of 30 hours *does not represent* the average study time of students taking 12 credit hours at this school. Because the information for this belief is based on informal discussions with some faculty, the director decides to test this belief more formally by collecting data.

Formal Statements of Research and Statistical Hypotheses. The director's research interest is to determine whether or not the average study time for students taking 12 credits is 30 hours per week. Because a value has been hypothesized for μ, an answer to the director's question about student study time can be best obtained by using inferential statistics to evaluate hypotheses.

Whenever values of parameters are hypothesized, a statistical test is required to determine if these hypothesized values are representative of the population from which the sample data were collected. In our example, the director's research hypothesis is that the average study time for all students taking 12 credits at this university is *not* 30 hours. Translating this research hypothesis into a statistical hypothesis gives $H_1: \mu_0 \neq 30$. The negation of H_1 gives the null hypothesis as $H_0: \mu_0 = 30$.

Measurement of the Characteristic of Interest

The director can precisely determine the μ of the population of students if the actual number of hours each student spends studying is available. Simply add up these numbers and divide by the total number of students. However, assume that 25,000 students attend this university. It would be practically impossible for the director to obtain these numbers. Each student would have to be directly observed and the numbers of hours spent studying recorded. A more feasible method is one that requires the director to collect data from a representative group of the student population and make inferences about the population parameters on the basis of sample data. Collecting data requires the director to develop an operational definition of the characteristic of interest, study time.

You will recall that operational definitions are used to describe concepts in terms of how they are measured. The director operationally defines study time as the number of hours that students report they study each week. The students are asked to keep a daily journal of the time spent studying to the nearest 0.25 hour and submit it on the first day of finals. Final exam week is excluded as it is considered not to be representative of a typical week during the semester. From these journals, the director calculates the average weekly number of hours each student reports studying. These are the data analyzed.

You will recall from Chapter 2 the characteristics of nominal, ordinal, interval, and ratio scales. Before investigators collect data, they must identify the measurement scale they will use. The type of statistical analysis to be performed on the data is determined, in part, on the basis of the scale of measurement. Because, in the example, the operational definition of number of hours studied is a value representing elapsed time (a scale that has an absolute zero) the scale of measurement is a ratio scale. If the scale of measurement used to collect the data is interval or ratio, then a parametric test statistic is appropriate.

Once the characteristic of interest is operationally defined and the scale of measurement identified, a test statistic is chosen.

Choosing a Test Statistic

As you will see in the remaining chapters, a factor that influences the type of test statistic selected by an investigator is also determined, in part, on the basis of number of samples used. The specific question that is asked by an investigator directly determines the number of samples to be used. Because the director in the example is interested in determining whether a representative sample selected from the student population will provide evidence to reject the null hypothesis, only one sample is used. When one sample is used and the parameters μ and σ are unknown, the parametric test that is used to evaluate the hypothesis about μ is the one-sample t-test.

Use of the t-test requires that a sample be selected randomly. The director asks the registrar if a list of students taking twelve credits can be generated on the basis of random selection. According to the registrar, obtaining such a list poses no problem. The registrar, however, needs to know how many names should be on the list. Determining the number of subjects to use in an investigation is just as important as how they are to be selected.

Sample Size and Power

Now that most of the preliminary planning is completed, the investigator must collect the data from a sample of an appropriate size. Up to this point, the discussion of sample size in this text has been general. Values of sample size have been arbitrarily assigned in the examples given. When conducting research, *you* have to decide the size of the sample to be used. Calculating sample size requires a more detailed explanation of some of the concepts that were discussed in previous chapters. One of the most important of these concepts is the power of the test.

We noted in Chapter 10 that as sample size increases, the power of a statistical test increases. You will recall that power is defined as the probability of correctly rejecting a false null hypothesis and is equal to $1 - \beta$, where β is the probability of making a Type II error. Usually, investigators hope to reject the null hypothesis. Failure to reject the null hypothesis may be due to (1) the fact that in reality the null hypothesis is true or (2) the data collected failed to allow the investigator to detect a false null hypothesis.

If H_0 is not rejected, you cannot unequivocally interpret the results of your experiment in relation to your research hypothesis. Because the truthfulness of H_0 cannot be altered by the investigator, steps are taken to use procedures which provide as high a level of power as is economically feasible.

Once a particular test statistic is selected, several factors can influence the power of the test including

1. the alpha level, the probability of a Type I error set by the investigator;

2. the difference between the true value of population mean, μ, and the hypothesized value of the population mean μ_0, symbolized $\mu - \mu_0$;

3. the variability in the original population represented by σ;

4. sample size, N.

All four of these factors are interrelated with power. Changes in any one of these factors will lead to a change in power. In order to calculate the value of any one of these five factors, including power, four of them must be assigned values. Since we are attempting to calculate sample size, N, let us examine how values are assigned to the other four factors: α, power, $\mu - \mu_0$, and σ.

The Value of Alpha. Recall that alpha is the probability of making a Type I error, which is the error made when the null hypothesis is incorrectly rejected. Usually alpha is equal to 0.05; however, there are times when it is set to 0.01. If the only event changed is alpha, then as alpha is decreased, for example, from 0.05 to 0.01, power is decreased.

β and the Power of a Statistical Test. How much power an investigator chooses is dependent not only on the probability of making a Type I error, α, but also on the probability of making a Type II error, β. Since the logic of evaluating hypotheses with statistical tests is based on testing the null hypothesis in hopes of rejecting it, Type I errors are usually considered to be more serious than Type II errors. As a result, investigators rarely increase α above 0.05 and β is some value greater than 0.05. We must therefore determine a value for β in order to determine power that is equal to $1 - \beta$.

In the examples used in this text β equals 0.2, a recommended minimal value. Thus, power, $1 - \beta$, equals 0.8. By setting alpha equal to 0.05 and beta equal to 0.2, we are suggesting that a Type I error is more serious than a Type II error because we are allowing a Type II error to be four times as likely as a Type I error. This can be seen in the ratio of the probability of a Type II error (0.2) to the probability of a Type I error (0.05), that is, $0.2/0.05 = 4.0$.

Given the above conditions, power is equal to 0.8 ($1 - 0.2$), a minimal level suggested as a convention for the value of power (see Kirk, 1982). This recommendation of power = 0.8 should not be taken as a hard and fast rule for all research. The discussion of power and the conditions under which it should be changed, however, would take us beyond the scope of this text. At this point, it is important for you to know that (1) as β increases, the power of a statistical test decreases since power is equal to $1 - \beta$ and (2) the recommendation is to set power at 0.8.

Effect Size Based on ($\mu - \mu_0$) and σ. Both the magnitude of $\mu - \mu_0$ and σ affect the power of the test. Since we cannot know for certain what the actual difference between the true mean (μ) and hypothesized mean (μ_0) is, Cohen (1988) has suggested that the ratio ($\mu - \mu_0$)/σ be used to obtain a relative measure called effect size. **Effect size** is the minimal difference between the true mean and the hypothesized mean expressed in standard deviation units that an investigator wishes to detect when evaluating statistical hypotheses.

Estimating values of effect size can be accomplished by using (1) values for μ, μ_0, and σ obtained from published research, (2) personal beliefs (for example, the director interested in the study habits of students may believe that a difference of at least 0.5 standard deviation units between the hypothesized 30 hours and the actual amount of time students study is necessary before any action is taken), or (3) special conventions such as those suggested by Cohen.

These three methods are listed on the basis of a priority by which effect size is to be estimated. Investigators need to know the published reports and have a good understanding of the area being investigated in order to use the first two methods. Since this text is written for individuals entering research, we will rely on the third method of special conventions (the method to be used when the other two cannot be used) to demonstrate how sample size should be determined in relation to the power of a statistical test.

Cohen has suggested conventions of effect size where $(\mu - \mu_0)/\sigma$ equals values of 0.2, 0.5, or 0.8 as recommendations for small, medium, or large effect sizes, respectively. Investigators using these conventions simply have to decide whether they are interested in detecting small, medium, or large effect sizes. For example, the director of the learning skills center may only be interested in taking action if the students at the university deviate from the hypothesized 30 hours by at least a medium difference.

Whether to look for a small, medium, or large effect size depends on a number of factors. For problems in this text, we tell you the effect size. When you are doing research in a classroom setting, your instructor should provide this information. As you become familiar with the research literature, you will learn to estimate effect size from published research. At this stage, it is important for you to know that power is directly related to effect size; that is, the larger the *true* effect size the greater the power.

In summary, evaluating hypotheses on the basis of statistical tests requires you to think about a variety of factors including α, $1 - \beta$, and effect size or $(\mu - \mu_0)/\sigma$. Once you have considered these factors, calculating N for the one-sample t-test is done with the use of Table 11.1. For tests other than the one-sample t and values for power other than 0.8, interested readers are referred to Cohen (1988).

Estimation of Sample Size. Given values of $\alpha = 0.05$ and $\beta = 0.2$ and assuming the director of the learning skills center in the example wants to detect a medium effect size, Table 11.1 can be used to estimate sample size. Examine Table 11.1 and note that effect size can be used to estimate the size of N needed for a two-tailed statistical test when power is equal to 0.8 and alpha = 0.05 or 0.01. In the example, a sample size equal to 33 is needed.

Why the Fuss over Sample Size?   Now you have determined that 33 subjects are needed. Why use the detailed procedures described in the previous sections to determine a value for N? Why not just pick as large a number as possible for N given an investigator's available resources? The answer is that this method for estimating sample size can keep an investigator from wasting time and effort on projects involving statistical tests which are highly unlikely to lead to interpretable results. For example, suppose previous research indicates that the effect size the learning skills director should expect to find is small. In this case, where power = 0.8 and alpha = 0.05, Table 11.1 indicates that the director would need 199 students. The director may not have the resources to examine 199 students and might decide to examine the question of average study time using some other approach that does not involve a one-sample t-test.

Alternatively, the director might decide to use as many students as available resources allow, let us say 15. Alpha must remain at the standard convention level of 0.05 and the true effect size is still small. If only 15 students are used, then the likelihood of correctly rejecting the null hypothesis is substantially decreased. The bottom line of this scenario in which $N = 15$ is that the null hypothesis is not likely to be rejected even when in reality it is false.

You should now understand why estimating sample size is something that a good investigator should routinely do before a research project is started.

PROGRESS ASSESSMENT 11.4

Using Table 11.1 determine the minimal sample size needed to detect a large effect size with power = 0.8 for alpha equal to

1. 0.05
2. 0.01

TABLE 11.1
**Approximate N Required to Achieve Power = 0.8
When $\alpha = 0.05$ or 0.01 for a Two-Tailed Test Using
the One-Sample t-Test**

| | Effect Size | | |
Alpha Level	Small	Medium	Large
0.05	199	33	14
0.01	294	49	20

Values obtained on the basis of procedures discussed in Cohen (1988) and final values rounded up to the next integer.

Obtaining Subjects

You will recall in the example that the operational definition of study time is number of hours spent studying that students report in daily journals. Although keeping a journal does not require much effort, the director of the learning skills center needs to provide some type of incentive to obtain subjects. Assume, as an incentive, $20 is to be given to each student at the end of the term when the journal is given to the director.

Before the director actually contacts students, the research proposal must be reviewed by an Institutional Review Committee that functions to protect subjects' welfare. If the committee approves the proposal, the investigator then obtains from the registrar a random sample of 33 students taking 12 credits. In all likelihood some of the 33 students will not complete the project. If a large number of students drop out, the results obtained may not generalize to the population because the sample may no longer represent a random sample. If this happens, it can be argued that something other than chance has affected how the sample was selected. In such a case, it may be that the sample is determined, in part, on the basis of willingness to work and accept responsibility. For our example, assume that all 33 students submit their journals at the end of the term.

Performing the Statistical Test

Now that we have identified the one-sample t-statistic as the test statistic, a specific decision rule can be formulated to evaluate H_0 that $\mu_0 = 30$ at the 5 percent level of significance.

Determining the Decision Rule. Turn to the table of critical t-values, Table 5 in the Appendix, at the back of the text and look under the column labeled df. Because the t-distributions do not change rapidly after 30 df, critical values listed for many df between 30 and infinity are often omitted. When the actual df is not listed in a table of critical values, the general convention followed is to use the closest df below the actual df. When df exceeds 120, a general convention is to use the normal curve's critical values, which are 1.96 when alpha equals 0.05 and 2.58 when alpha equals 0.01.

In the example where $df = 32$ (33 − 1), we must use $df = 30$ in Table 5 as the number 32 is not listed and 30 is the next lower df. Across from $df = 30$, under the column headed $\alpha = 0.05$, notice that the value is equal to 2.04. Based on the logic that is described in Chapter 10 involving the formation of decision rules, the null hypothesis should be rejected in this example if the absolute value of the calculated t-statistic is greater than or equal to 2.04. This rule is written as follows. Reject H_0 if $|t_{calc}| \geq 2.04$.

Calculating the t-Statistic. Recall that the t-statistic is calculated on the basis of Formula 11.1 where $t = (\bar{X} - \mu_0)/s_{\bar{X}}$. Assume that the data presented in Table 11.2 represents the average number of weekly hours spent studying for each subject. Note that at the bottom of this table five calculation steps are performed to obtain a value of t for the example involving student study time.

Once values for ΣX and ΣX^2 are obtained as is done in Step 1, a value for the mean, $\bar{X}$, is obtained. The calculations at Step 2 indicate that $\bar{X}$ equals 24.84. Because s is used to calculate $s_{\bar{X}}$, proceeding with the third set of calculations reveals that s is equal to 6.92. The 1.21 value for $s_{\bar{X}}$ is obtained in Step 4 by dividing s by $\sqrt{N}$. In the fifth and final step t is calculated to be -4.26 [$(24.84 - 30)/1.21$] and its absolute value is 4.26.

TABLE 11.2
Average Number of Weekly Hours Studied (X) for Each Student Participating in Study Habits Project, $N = 33$. Also listed are values needed to calculate the one-sample t-statistic.

X	X	X	X	X	X
30.00	18.50	20.25	40.50	31.75	19.00
25.25	32.00	33.75	34.25	16.50	17.50
20.00	22.50	39.25	14.50	15.00	30.50
24.50	25.00	26.25	15.50	18.50	27.00
23.25	32.50	20.00	25.50	19.25	30.00
27.50	21.50	22.50			

Calculation Steps:

1. $\Sigma X = 819.75$ $\Sigma X^2 = 21894.31$

2. $\bar{X} = \dfrac{\Sigma X}{N} = \dfrac{819.75}{33} = 24.84$

3. $s = \sqrt{s^2} = \sqrt{\dfrac{\Sigma X^2 - \dfrac{(\Sigma X)^2}{N}}{N-1}} = \sqrt{\dfrac{21894.31 - \dfrac{(819.75)^2}{33}}{32}} = 6.92$

3. $s_{\bar{X}} = \dfrac{s}{\sqrt{N}} = \dfrac{6.92}{\sqrt{33}} = 1.21$

4. $t = \dfrac{\bar{X} - \mu_0}{s_{\bar{X}}} = \dfrac{24.84 - 30}{1.21} = -4.26$

PROGRESS ASSESSMENT 11.5

1. Write the decision rule for evaluating statistical hypotheses with sample size equal to 8 and $\alpha = 0.05$.
2. Calculate t for the following data set: 2, 3, 3, 6, 5, 5, 7, 9 where $\mu_0 = 3.2$.

Evaluating Statistical and Research Hypotheses

Because the absolute value of the calculated t (4.26) is greater than 2.04 (the critical value in the decision rule), the null hypothesis that $\mu = 30$ hours is rejected. The director of the learning skills center in the example concludes that the sample of students does not come from a population where the average (μ) study time is 30 hours per week, $t(32) = -4.26$, $p \leq 0.05$.

Note that had the null hypothesis not been rejected, the director may decide to pursue areas other than amount of study time, such as problem solving, note taking, and so forth. Alternatively, the director may even start all over with a different operational definition of study time or may decide to calculate the average (parameter) study time of all students. Unfortunately, the logic involved in statistical hypothesis testing only allows for concluding that the null hypothesis is false whenever the null hypothesis is rejected. Failing to reject the null hypothesis cannot be used as unequivocal evidence to argue that the null hypothesis is true.

PROGRESS ASSESSMENT 11.6

1. Based on your calculations in Progress Assessment 11.5, evaluate the statistical hypotheses that $H_0: \mu = 3.2$ and $H_1: \mu \neq 3.2$.

2. Suppose a psychology student does not believe that students enrolled at a particular university sleep an average of 8 hours a night as is commonly hypothesized. A random sample of sixteen students is surveyed by this psychology student and the number of hours students report sleeping each night are: 4, 4, 5, 5, 6, 6, 7, 8, 8, 8, 8, 8, 9, 9, 10, 10. Based on the following six steps determine whether or not the sample selected should be considered representative of a population with $\mu = 8$ hours.

   a. State the research hypothesis.

   b. State the statistical hypotheses.

   c. Perform a statistical test by
      (1) stating a specific decision rule, and
      (2) calculating the specific t-value.

   d. Evaluate the null hypothesis on the basis of the specific decision rule.

   e. Make a decision about your research hypothesis.

   f. State your conclusions about the research hypothesis as you would in a formal research report.

INTERVAL ESTIMATION

As mentioned in the introduction to this chapter, in addition to hypothesis testing, parametric statistics are also used to establish confidence intervals. **Confidence intervals (CI)** are intervals that have a certain probability of containing the true value of the population parameter. The procedure used to establish confidence intervals is an interval estimation procedure. This procedure is very similar to a hypothesis testing procedure except that it provides more information.

With the hypothesis testing procedure, the specific value of a parameter evaluated is only the one stated in the null hypothesis. In the previous example, the null hypothesis that students at a particular university study on average 30 hours each week is rejected on the basis of the collected data in Table 11.2. Thus, the only claim that can be made is that students taking 12 credits at the university do not study, on average, 30 hours per week. An alternative value for μ cannot be estimated on the basis of this test of the statistical hypothesis. Rather than testing a specific hypothesis, investigators often want to determine, with a specified degree of confidence, a range of values (confidence interval) likely to contain the value of a parameter such as μ.

Establishing Confidence Intervals

Confidence intervals are usually determined when an investigator is not likely to have a hypothesized value for μ and wants to obtain a range of possible values for μ. Suppose the learning skills center's director has no research hypothesis to test. It may be of interest to determine the number of hours students study by establishing a confidence interval that identifies an interval of values likely to contain the actual mean number of weekly hours studied by all students at this university.

You will recall from the section about hypothesis testing that the purpose for collecting the data in Table 11.2 was to determine if all students taking 12 credit hours study an average of 30 hours. Because a value for μ was hypothesized, a statistical test was used to reach a conclusion about the student's average study time. In contrast, when the purpose for collecting the data is to estimate a range of values of a parameter such as μ, an interval estimation procedure is used. Thus, the specific purpose of the investigator's research directly determines whether statistics are used to test statistical hypotheses about parameters or to estimate probable values of the parameters.

The interval estimation procedure is based on many of the same principles as those used for testing statistical hypotheses. For example, the conditions that must be met for using the t-statistic to establish confidence intervals are the same as those listed previously for using the t-statistic to evaluate statistical hypotheses.

The 95 Percent Confidence Interval. Figure 11.2 is a drawing of a *t*-distribution for *df* = 30. We choose this distribution because it is the distribution needed to determine confidence intervals for the example involving student study time (*N* = 33) with the use of Appendix Table 5 where the closest lower *df* = 30.

As can be seen in Figure 11.2, this interval has a range of values that can be defined on the basis of two values: the value + 2.04 in the right side of the figure and the value − 2.04 in the left side. These values are determined by going to the table of critical *t*-values, Table 5 in the Appendix, using *df* = 30 (as 32 is not listed in the table), and alpha = 0.05. In the 0.05 column, where *df* = 30, is the absolute value of the *t*-scores that marks off the upper and lower 0.025 area of the curve. You will recall from the discussion of the normal curve in Chapter 10 that if 0.05 of the area falls outside these two values, then 0.95 (1 − 0.05) of the area must fall within this region as indicated in Figure 11.2. Therefore, the probability of obtaining a *t*-score that falls within this region is equal to 0.95. If these two *t*-score values, + 2.04 and − 2.04, are converted to corresponding estimates of μ, these estimates define the **95 percent confidence interval,** the interval of scores that has a 95 percent chance of containing the true value of μ.

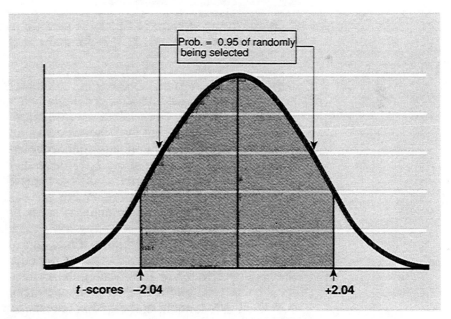

FIGURE 11.2 *Sampling distribution of one-sample t-statistic where df = 30. Shaded area represents t-scores having a probability = 0.95 of randomly being selected.*

Confidence interval limits are the two critical t-score values expressed in relation to a sample mean and $s_{\bar{X}}$ that define the smallest (**lower limit**) and largest (**upper limit**) estimates of μ.

The calculations needed to convert these two t-scores to confidence interval limits requires a few algebraic manipulations of Formula 11.1, the one sample t-statistic formula. These manipulations yield the following formulas for the upper and lower limits of the 95 percent confidence interval, respectively.

Formula 11.3   upper limit of 95% CI $= \bar{X} + t_{\text{table}}(s_{\bar{X}})$

Formula 11.4   lower limit of 95% CI $= \bar{X} - t_{\text{table}}(s_{\bar{X}})$

In Formulas 11.3 and 11.4, t_{table} is the critical value of t for a given df where alpha is set at 0.05.

In the example where the director of the learning skills center calculated $\bar{X} = 24.84$ hours and $s_{\bar{X}} = 1.21$ (see Table 11.1), the upper limit of the 95 percent confidence interval is equal to 27.31 [24.84 + 2.04(1.21)] and the lower limit is equal to 22.37[24.84 − 2.04(1.21)]. Formally expressed, the 95 percent confidence interval is given as 95% CI: $22.37 \leq \mu \leq 27.31$.

PROGRESS ASSESSMENT 11.7

Establish the 95 percent CI for the mean of a population from which a sample of size $N = 25$, $\bar{X} = 30$, and $s = 8$ is selected.

Confidence Intervals in General.   Although most investigators use 95 percent confidence intervals, occasionally a 99 percent confidence interval is determined. The procedures are similar to that of the 95 percent confidence interval except that t is the critical value at alpha equal to 0.01 for appropriate df. In general, any confidence interval can be established by substituting the appropriate t_{table} value in Formulas 11.3 and 11.4 where t_{table} is determined on the basis of the specific confidence interval to be determined for a given alpha and df.

In the example examining students' study habits, the 99 percent confidence interval is obtained on the basis of the calculations where t_{table} for alpha $= 0.01$ is 2.75. Substituting this t_{table} in Formulas 11.3 and 11.4 [24.84 ± 2.75 (1.21)] indicates that the 99 percent confidence interval based on the data collected by the learning skills director is $21.51 \leq \mu \leq 28.17$. The director can state with 99 percent confidence that the interval 21.51 to 28.17, inclusive, contains the value for the mean number of hours studied each week by students at the university taking 12 credit hours.

There is a price to pay for using one or the other of these confidence intervals. By increasing the confidence that the interval contains μ, specificity of your estimate is sacrificed. With the 95 percent confidence interval, the estimate of μ ranges from 22.37 to 27.31, whereas with the 99 percent confidence interval, the estimate is a larger range of values extending from 21.51 to 28.17. This example indicates that the more confidence you want in your estimate the less specific you can be about the estimate of your parameter. Which confidence level you select depends on a variety of factors, many of which depend on reasons unique to the question being asked by the investigator. We therefore recommend that you follow the general convention of obtaining a 95 percent confidence interval unless specifically directed to do otherwise.

PROGRESS ASSESSMENT 11.8

For the data and values provided in part 2 of Progress Assessment 11.6, determine

1. the 95 percent confidence interval.
2. the 99 percent confidence interval.

Interpreting Confidence Intervals

Based on the information provided in the previous sections, the director of the learning skills center is likely to summarize the results of this study by stating with 95 percent confidence that the interval 22.37 to 27.31 estimates the mean (μ) weekly study time of students at the university.

This research finding can be used by the director in a variety of ways. A student who sees the director might want to know the average amount of study time for students at this school. The 95 percent confidence interval can be used to answer this question. The director may also, on the basis of the confidence interval, decide that students should spend more time studying. The director may then look at programs that are used to increase study time.

Note that care must be taken in interpreting confidence intervals. As is the case when statistics are used in hypothesis testing procedures, it is also the case that errors can be made when creating confidence intervals. The 95 percent confidence interval does not guarantee that any one of the estimates of μ is actually the true value of μ. Rather, these procedures allow you to state that when samples are randomly selected a large number of times, the 95 percent confidence interval has a probability $= 0.95$ of containing the true value of μ. Accordingly, the probability that the interval does not contain the true value of μ is equal to 0.05. If the director in the example repeated the described research project a large number of times, for example, 100 times using 100 different randomly selected samples, it is expected that for 5 out of 100 samples the confidence interval generated would *not* contain the true value of μ.

SUMMARY

In this chapter the *t*-statistic is discussed as the appropriate statistic for hypothesis testing and interval estimation procedures when investigations involve only one sample and μ and σ are *not* known. A table of critical *t*-values based on the family of *t*-distributions (defined on the basis of their degrees of freedom) is used to form specific decision rules for evaluating statistical hypotheses with the one-sample *t*-test. A discussion of the power of a statistical test and estimating sample size to maintain a specific power is presented. The table of critical *t*-values is also used in this chapter to establish confidence intervals in situations where an investigator wants to estimate a range of values for the parameter μ.

KEY DEFINITIONS

CI   A symbol used to represent confidence interval.

confidence interval   An interval that has a certain probability of containing the true value of the population parameter.

confidence interval limits   The critical *t*-score values expressed in relation to a sample mean and $s_{\bar{x}}$ that define the smallest and largest estimated values of μ.

effect size   The minimal difference between the true mean (μ) and the hypothesized mean (μ_0) expressed in standard deviation units, ($\mu - \mu_0)/\sigma$, that an investigator wishes to detect when evaluating statistical hypotheses.

hypothesis testing   A procedure used to evaluate the null and alternative hypotheses about a specific population involving information obtained from a sample or samples.

interval estimation   A procedure used to determine intervals likely to contain (usually with a probability of 0.95) the value of a specified parameter.

lower limit of a confidence interval   The smallest value in a confidence interval used to estimate μ.

μ_0   The symbol used for the *hypothesized* value of a population mean.

$N - 1$ Degrees of freedom for the one-sample *t*-statistic where N equals sample size.

95 percent confidence interval   A range of values that has a probability of 0.95 of containing μ.

one-sample *t*-statistic   A test statistic used when $\sigma_{\bar{x}}$ is estimated from the data of a sample to evaluate a statistical hypothesis when μ is hypothesized or to estimate a range of values for μ when μ is not hypothesized.

parametric statistics   A variety of test statistics based on theoretical distributions whose use requires that certain assumptions, including assumptions about the parameters of the populations from which the observed sample or samples were obtained, be true.

point estimation   A procedure whereby a single value for a population parameter is estimated from sample data.

sample element   A term used to refer to a member of a sample.

$s_{\overline{X}}$ The symbol used to represent the estimate of the standard error of the mean.

$s_{\overline{X}} = s/\sqrt{N}$ The formula used to obtain a value for the estimate of the standard error of the mean where s is an estimate of the population standard deviation and N = sample size.

t-distribution   A family of theoretical sampling distributions. The shape of each specific t-distribution changes as a function of sample size.

t-statistic   A statistic used to test hypotheses about the expected value of a sampling distribution and to determine intervals that are likely to contain the expected value.

$t = (\overline{X} - \mu_0)/s_{\overline{X}}$ The formula for the one-sample t-statistic.

upper limit of the confidence interval   The largest value in a confidence interval used to estimate μ.

$\overline{X} - t_{\text{table}}(s_{\overline{X}})$ The formula used to calculate the lower limit of a confidence interval.

$\overline{X} + t_{\text{table}}(s_{\overline{X}})$ The formula used to calculate the upper limit of a confidence inverval.

REVIEW EXERCISES

For each of the following numbered problems determine

a. the purpose for collecting the data described in the problem.
b. if hypothesis testing procedures, interval estimation procedures, or neither are needed to complete the purpose described in part *a*.
c. the operational definition of the event measured.
d. the scale of measurement used to obtain the data.
e. the statistic and its formula that is to be used.
f. the specific decision rule, if appropriate.
g. the appropriate calculated test-statistic, CI, or probability values.

h. an evaluation of H_0, if appropriate.

i. what the evaluation of the H_0 means or how the CI should be interpreted, if appropriate.

1. In the general population the average (μ) capacity of short-term memory is seven items or bits of information. A psychology instructor believes that seven items is not the average for students at a particular college. The results of the short-term memory test given to a random sample of sixteen students yields a mean ($\bar{X}$) equal to eight items correctly recalled and an $s = 1.92$. Do the results support the psychologist's belief?

2. Given an average IQ score equal to 100 and standard deviation equal to 15 for all people who take a particular IQ test, what is the probability of randomly selecting a sample of size 36 that deviates from a mean of 100 in either direction by 3 or more IQ points? (*Hint:* A diagram is helpful).

3. College students enrolled in an experimental psychology class are asked to estimate with 95 percent confidence the average amount of caffeine consumed daily by students at the university as measured by number of ounces of coffee drunk each day. A survey obtained with a random sample of 100 students reveals a mean daily consumption of 30 ounces of coffee. The standard deviation is calculated to be 16.

ANSWERS TO PROGRESS ASSESSMENTS

11.1   **1.** not a random sample

        2. not random and measures are not independent

        3. conditions met

11.2 $t = 1.11$

11.3   **1.** If $|t_{calc}| \geq 2.12$, then reject H_0.

        2. a. $t(16) = 2.13, p \leq 0.05$

           b. $t(16) = 2.09, p > 0.05$

11.4   **1.** 14

        2. 20

11.5   **1.** If $|t_{calc}| \geq 2.36$, then reject H_0.

        2. $t = 2.20$

11.6   **1.** Fail to reject H_0 that $\mu = 3.2$ as $|t_{calc}| = 2.20$ is less than 2.36.

        2. a. The investigator does not believe that students at the university sleep an average of 8 hours each night.

           b. $H_0: \mu = 8, H_1: \mu \neq 8$

           c. (1) Reject H_0 if $|t_{calc}| \geq 2.13$.

               (2) $t = -1.65$

           d. Fail to reject H_0 as $|t_{calc}|$ equal to 1.65 is less than 2.13.

     e. The results cannot be used to support the research hypothesis.

     f. There is no evidence to suggest that students at this university do not sleep an average of 8 hours a night. $t(15) = -1.65, p > 0.05$.

11.7   95% CI: $26.70 \leq \mu \leq 33.30$

11.8   **1.** 95% CI: $6.15 \leq \mu \leq 8.23$

        2. 99% CI: $5.74 \leq \mu \leq 8.64$

CHAPTER 12

Tests for Treatment Effects on Two Independent Samples

*I*n Chapter 10 we discussed the use of the *z*-statistic to test hypotheses involving a single sample when μ and σ are known. In Chapter 11 this developed into a discussion of the use of the one-sample *t*-statistic in hypothesis testing when μ is hypothesized and σ is estimated. This chapter extends the discussion of the *t*-test by introducing the **t-test for two random independent samples,** a parametric test used to determine if there is a significant difference between the means of two random independent samples. As is the case for many parametric tests, when certain conditions or assumptions are not met, a nonparametric test can be used.

Nonparametric statistical tests are used when no assumptions are made about the specific shape of the population distribution or distributions from which the sample or samples are selected. Furthermore, population parameters are *not* hypothesized; rather, the null hypothesis states that two or more population distributions do not differ. The **Mann-Whitney *U*-test** is one nonparametric test that is used when conditions for the *t*-test for two random independent samples are not met.

NECESSARY CONDITIONS FOR USING THE *t*-STATISTIC WITH TWO INDEPENDENT SAMPLES

The *t*-statistic, as discussed in this chapter, is a statistic that can be used to analyze data collected from two random independent samples. Recall from Chapter 2 that the independent variable in an experiment is manipulated in order to determine if it affects a dependent variable. The minimal manipulation an investigator can make involves only two levels of an independent variable. For example, the independent variable can be manipulated on the basis of its presence or absence or on the basis of various levels such as high or low. Such requirements require the use of two samples.

In addition to direct manipulation of an independent variable, investigators also use two samples selected from two populations known to differ on the basis of some inherent attribute, such as sex or age, to evaluate whether or not the two populations differ with respect to some dependent measure, such as problem-solving ability or political attitude.

Whether or not direct manipulation of an independent variable is involved, the goal of the investigation involving two random independent samples is to evaluate whether or not the two populations, represented by the samples, differ with respect to some dependent measure. The *t*-statistic for two random independent samples is used to meet this goal.

Use of the parametric *t*-statistic to analyze data from two random independent samples requires that the following five conditions be met:

1. *The samples must be obtained on the basis of random selection or on the basis of random assignment.* Most often in experimentation random assignment is used. You are familiar with the procedures first discussed in Chapter 2 for producing randomized samples by using random as-

signment. Using procedures that prevent any systematic bias in the selection of subjects, an investigator can randomly assign available subjects to the two samples. By figuratively placing the names of all available subjects into a hat, an investigator can pick the first half of the names and assign them to one sample and the remaining half to the other sample. This technique ensures that subjects are assigned randomly.

Incidentally, this procedure also produces two samples with equal N's. In this example, the size of sample one, designated as N_1, is equal to the size of sample two, designated as N_2. Note that the use of the t-statistic does *not* require equal N's. Also, labels 1 and 2 are arbitrarily assigned to samples, populations, and symbols in this chapter simply for the purpose of identification in the discussions.

2. *Any one measured observation must be independent of any other measured observation.* In other words, the value of the dependent measure that is obtained under one level of the independent variable must not in any way influence the value of the dependent measure that is obtained under that level or the other level of the independent variable. In Chapter 2 you learned that independent samples are samples for which assignment of a subject to one particular sample has no effect on how any other member of the pool of subjects is selected for another sample. Independent samples are obtained when an investigator uses random assignment or randomly selects samples from a single population or from two groups assumed to be representative of two different populations, such as freshmen and sophomores, males and females, and so forth.

3. *The subjects must be selected from a population in which the dependent measure is normally distributed.* As when using the one-sample t-statistic, this normality condition is not always rigorously examined. Because the probabilities obtained using the t-statistic with normal and nonnormal distributions are very similar except when distributions are extremely skewed, investigators generally assume population distributions are normal or nonnormal on the basis of visual examination of the data organized as a frequency distribution. Unless otherwise indicated, assume that the condition of normality is met in the examples in this text.

4. *The scale of measurement that is used to obtain the dependent measure should be an interval or ratio scale.* If the scale of measurement is nominal or ordinal, the t-test for independent samples is generally not used to perform statistical tests.

5. *The variances of the dependent measure of the populations from which the samples are selected should be equal.* This condition or assumption is known as the assumption of homogeneity of variance, expressed as $\sigma_1^2 = \sigma_2^2$, where subscripts refer to the populations represented by samples 1 and 2. In practice this assumption is generally assumed to be true. However, it can be easily tested using a statistic known as F.

TESTING THE HYPOTHESIS THAT $\sigma_1^2 = \sigma_2^2$

The **F-statistic** is a parametric statistic that can be used to determine whether the variances of two populations are the same (homogeneous) or different (heterogeneous) based on observations obtained from random independent samples of each population. Although a more complete discussion of the F-statistic is presented in Chapter 14, this chapter briefly examines this F-statistic as it is used to test the assumption of homogeneity of variance of two random independent samples.

Hypothesis-testing procedures used to evaluate hypotheses about the parameter σ^2 involve a series of steps similar to that used to evaluate hypotheses about μ. The first step when testing for homogeneity of variance is to state the null and alternative hypotheses. For testing homogeneity of variance H_0 is always stated as $\sigma_1^2 = \sigma_2^2$ and H_1 as $\sigma_1^2 \neq \sigma_2^2$. Second, a statistical test involving a specific decision rule and the calculation of the F-statistic is then performed to evaluate H_0. Third, on the basis of this evaluation a decision is made to reject or fail to reject H_0. Fourth, if H_0 is rejected, then heterogeneity of variance is assumed and the t-statistic is not used.

As previously mentioned, the test statistic to be used to evaluate the hypothesis of homogeneity of variance is the F-statistic. Two conditions must be met to use the F-statistic for testing homogeneity of variance: (1) the data must be measured along an interval or ratio scale, and (2) samples must be randomly and independently selected from populations where the characteristic of interest is normally distributed. Given that an investigator has direct control over all but the normality condition, careful planning should allow the F-statistic to be used to test the condition of homogeneity of variance of two random independent samples. If the conditions are met, the F-statistic is calculated as follows:

Formula 12.1 $\qquad\qquad F = s_{\text{larger}}^2 / s_{\text{smaller}}^2$

For Formula 12.1, s^2 is calculated for both samples, and the larger variance is used as the numerator and the smaller variance as the denominator.

Before specifying a decision rule, think about the F-ratio of $s_{\text{larger}}^2 / s_{\text{smaller}}^2$. If the variances of the two samples are similar or equal to each other, then the ratio will produce a value close to or equal to 1. If the variances are quite different from each other, then you can expect this ratio to produce a value greater than 1. The larger the difference between the two variances, the larger the value of F. Although this explanation should give you an intuitive understanding of the F-statistic, a specific decision rule is needed to evaluate the null hypothesis that the population variances are equal to each other.

Turn to Appendix Table 6, which lists the critical F-values needed to reject H_0 when alpha equals 0.05 or 0.01. In addition to a designated alpha level, use of this table requires that degrees of freedom (df) for the numerator and denominator be determined. Recall from Chapter 11 that *df* refers to the number of observed events that are free to take on any value when mathematical restrictions are imposed on the calculations. The *df* for each of the variance estimates is $N - 1$, where N refers to sample size of a specific sample, since the only mathematical restriction placed on these estimates is that the deviations from the mean $(X - \bar{X})$ for each s^2 sum to zero. Calculating *df* for each s^2 as $N - 1$ allows you to use Appendix Table 6 to determine specific critical values of *F*.

Suppose, for example, that $N = 25$ for the sample with the larger s^2 and $N = 23$ for the sample with the smaller s^2. Go across the top of Table 6 to $df = 24$ and find where this column intersects with the row designated on the side of Table 6 where $df = 22$. This column and row intersect at the value 2.03. This value is used to form the specific decision rule to evaluate H_0. For this example the decision rule can be written as follows:

$$\text{If } F_{calc} \geq 2.03, \text{ reject } H_0.$$

After a specific decision rule is formed, the investigator must then calculate *F* and determine whether or not to reject the null hypothesis of homogeneity of variance, $\sigma_1^2 = \sigma_2^2$. If the null hypothesis is rejected, the investigator concludes that the variances are not equal, that is, the variances are heterogeneous. The consequence of such a conclusion is that a test other than the *t*-test should be used to proceed with the hypothesis-testing procedures. If the null hypothesis is not rejected on the basis of this test of homogeneity of variance, then the investigator has no reason to stop hypotheses-testing procedures using the *t*-statistic with data collected from two random independent samples.

PROGRESS ASSESSMENT 12.1

List the steps used to evaluate a homogeneity of variance hypothesis and test the hypothesis where $s_1^2 = 40$, $N_1 = 10$, $s_2^2 = 10$, and $N_2 = 16$.

THE *t*-STATISTIC FOR TWO RANDOM INDEPENDENT SAMPLES AND ITS DISTRIBUTION

As Chapters 10 and 11 indicated, the use of statistics to test hypotheses about the means of populations or any other parameters requires the use of sampling distributions, expected values, standard errors, and critical values obtained at a designated alpha level.

Sampling Distribution of the Difference between Two Means

When data are collected from two random independent samples, the *t*-statistic and its theoretical sampling distribution are used to evaluate statistical hypotheses about the means. This distribution is known as the sampling distribution of the difference between two means. The **sampling distribution of the difference between two means** is a theoretical distribution based on the difference between the means of all possible pairs of random samples of given sizes selected from a population.

Expected Value of the Sampling Distribution

The expected value of this theoretical distribution, symbolized as μ_{diff}, is equal to the difference between the population means from which the samples are randomly selected. The following is the defining equation for μ_{diff}:

Equation 12.1 $$\mu_{\text{diff}} = \mu_1 - \mu_2$$

Standard Error of the Sampling Distribution

The standard error of this theoretical distribution, symbolized as σ_{diff}, is defined in the following equation:

Equation 12.2 $$\sigma_{\text{diff}} = \sqrt{\frac{\sigma_1^2}{N_1} + \frac{\sigma_2^2}{N_2}}$$

In Equation 12.2, N_1 refers to the size of one sample and N_2 refers to the size of the other sample.

Application of the *t*-statistic

The above calculations for μ_{diff} and σ_{diff} can be obtained if the values of μ_1, μ_2, σ_1, and σ_2 are known. Investigators, however, rarely know the values of these parameters. Instead, they hypothesize and estimate parameters in order to perform statistical tests involving two random independent samples.

The expected value of the sampling distribution of the difference between two means is hypothesized and stated in the null hypothesis. The standard error of this distribution is estimated on the basis of pooling (combining) the data collected from each of the two random independent samples. The *t*-statistic is then calculated by subtracting the hypothesized expected value, μ_{diff}, from the statistic, $\bar{X}_1 - \bar{X}_2$, and dividing this difference by the *estimate* of the standard error of the sampling distribution of the difference between two means, s_{diff}. The defining equation for the *t*-statistic is as follows:

Equation 12.3 $$t = \frac{(\bar{X}_1 - \bar{X}_2) - \mu_{\text{diff}}}{s_{\text{diff}}}$$

Translating Equation 12.3 into a computation formula requires an understanding of μ_{diff} and s_{diff} as discussed in the next two sections.

A Hypothesized Value for μ_{diff}

Before discussing the hypothesized value of μ_{diff} given in H_0, let us review the process by which H_1 and H_0 are formed. You first form H_1 on the basis of what is believed to be true and then form H_0 by negating H_1. When two samples are used, investigators usually believe that the two populations represented by the samples are somehow different with respect to the mean value of the dependent measure. This difference may be due to the manipulation of the independent variable in an experiment or some inherent attribute of the two different populations investigated, for example, age differences if two groups such as teenagers and senior citizens are selected.

Investigators in the behavioral sciences rarely have enough information to know whether the independent variable or inherent population attribute has the effect of specifically increasing or decreasing the dependent measure. Therefore, investigators generally hypothesize that the population means are not equal to each other. This is symbolized in an alternative statistical hypothesis as $H_1: \mu_1 \neq \mu_2$, which is equivalent to $H_1: \mu_1 - \mu_2 \neq 0$. As in the past, H_0 is formed by negating H_1, which translates to $H_0: \mu_1 = \mu_2$ or its equivalent $H_0: \mu_1 - \mu_2 = 0$. Because μ_{diff} is equal to $\mu_1 - \mu_2$, the value most frequently hypothesized for μ_{diff} is 0. Since μ_{diff} is always hypothesized to equal 0 in the examples used in this text, the formula for t is written without specifically listing the value of 0 for μ_{diff}. Rewriting Equation 12.3 without the hypothesized value of μ_{diff} gives the following formula:

Formula 12.2
$$t = \frac{(\bar{X}_1 - \bar{X}_2)}{s_{\text{diff}}}$$

Estimation of σ_{diff}

Since you already know how to calculate $\bar{X}_1$ and $\bar{X}_2$, the only calculation that needs further explanation is s_{diff}, the estimate of the standard error of the sampling distribution of the difference between two means, σ_{diff}.

Equation 12.2 indicates that the standard error of the sampling distribution of the difference between two sample means, σ_{diff}, is equal to $\sqrt{\sigma_1^2/N_1 + \sigma_2^2/N_2}$. Recall that the use of the t-statistic with two samples requires that the variances of the populations from which the samples are selected are equal to each other. In other words, σ_1^2 equals σ_2^2. In essence, the procedure used to estimate σ_1^2 should also estimate σ_2^2 since theoretically the samples are drawn from the same population or from populations with equal variances. Similarly, the procedure used to estimate σ_2^2 should also provide an estimate of σ_1^2. Each sample therefore provides an independent unbiased estimate of the population variance. When you have two unbiased estimates of a population variance, the best estimate would be a pooled estimate. The pooled estimate provides a more accurate estimate than information from either sample alone.

The pooled estimate of the population variance obtained from two random independent samples, symbolized as s_p^2, is obtained by multiplying each sample variance by its respective *df*, summing these products, and dividing this sum by the combined *df* ($N_1 - 1 + N_2 - 1$). This pooled estimate of the population variance is more easily seen in the following formula:

Formula 12.3 $$s_p^2 = \frac{(N_1 - 1)s_1^2 + (N_2 - 1)s_2^2}{(N_1 - 1) + (N_2 - 1)}$$

The value obtained for s_p^2 is then used in *estimating* σ_{diff}. Since σ_{diff} is equal to $\sqrt{\sigma_1^2/N_1 + \sigma_2^2/N_2}$, substituting s_p^2 for the estimates of σ_1^2 and σ_2^2 gives the following formula for s_{diff}:

Formula 12.4 $$s_{\text{diff}} = \sqrt{\frac{s_p^2}{N_1} + \frac{s_p^2}{N_2}}$$

The value of s_{diff} is then substituted into the formula: $t = \overline{X}_1 - \overline{X}_2/s_{\text{diff}}$, to obtain a value for t.

PROGRESS ASSESSMENT 12.2

Given values of $s_1^2 = 3.6$, $\overline{X}_1 = 10$, $s_2^2 = 4.9$, and $\overline{X}_2 = 6$, where $N_1 = 25$ and $N_2 = 16$, determine

1. s_p^2.
2. s_{diff}.
3. t.

Determination of a Decision Rule: Using a Table of Critical Values

Once the t-statistic for two random independent samples is selected as the test statistic, decision rules based on critical t-values can be formulated to evaluate a specific null hypothesis.

The t-distribution, as you know, is a family of distributions defined on the basis of its *df*. By using the appropriate *df*, Appendix Table 5 can be used to determine critical values for the t-statistic to assess the difference between the means of two random independent samples. Degrees of freedom for the t-statistic for two random independent samples is defined in the usual manner as the number of events that are free to take on any value when estimating parameters from statistics. Since both s_1^2, used to estimate σ_1^2, and s_2^2, used to estimate σ_2^2, are used in the t-

formula, *df* is calculated by obtaining the sum of the *df* associated with each variance estimate. Thus, the *df* for the *t*-statistic used with two random independent samples is $N_1 - 1 + N_2 - 1$, which is expressed as $N_1 + N_2 - 2$.

If two random independent samples of size 10 are used by an investigator, then *df* equals 18 based on the calculation of 10 + 10 − 2. Examination of Table 5 reveals a critical *t*-value of 2.10 when *df* = 18 and alpha = 0.05. The specific decision rule for evaluating a null hypothesis involving two random independent samples where each *N* = 10 is therefore written as follows:

$$\text{If } |t_{calc}| \geq 2.10, \text{ reject } H_0.$$

How to Put It All Together

Let us now demonstrate the procedures used to evaluate statistical hypotheses with a *t*-statistic for two random independent samples. Data are presented in Table 12.1 from a hypothetical experiment performed to determine if a mnemonic device (memory aid) affects the ability to remember a list of words. The data represent dependent measures collected from two random independent samples selected from a large general psychology class.

For one of the samples, each subject is asked to read repeatedly a list of twenty words to the experimenter throughout a four-minute interval. This sample is referred to as the rote memorization group and is arbitrarily designated as Group 1. Each subject in the other sample is given themes from a common nursery rhyme to create a different story involving the list of twenty words. Each subject in this group is given two minutes to create such a story and then is given two minutes to tell the story to the experimenter. This group of subjects is referred to as the mnemonic device group and is designated as Group 2.

Both groups are then asked to write the list of twenty words. For each subject, the number of correctly written items is recorded.

Translating the Research Hypothesis into a Statistical Hypothesis and Forming the Null Hypothesis.   Because the investigator believes that a mnemonic device will affect retention for the list of words, the H_1 is written as $\mu_1 - \mu_2 \neq 0$ or $\mu_{diff} \neq 0$. In other words, the investigator believes that the average number of items correctly recalled in the rote memorization population is different from the average number of items correctly recalled in the mnemonic device population. The negation of H_1 reveals that the null hypothesis is written as H_0: $\mu_1 - \mu_2 = 0$ or $\mu_{diff} = 0$.

Performing the Statistical Test.   Because a value for the parameter, μ_{diff}, is hypothesized and because two random independent samples are used to collect data along a ratio scale, a *t*-test for two random independent samples is selected to evaluate the null hypothesis that $\mu_{diff} = 0$. Use

TABLE 12.1
Number of Items Recalled Immediately after Practicing a List of Twenty Words for Groups Using Rote Memorization Procedures or a Mnemonic Device

Rote Group		Mnemonic Group	
X_1	X_1^2	X_2	X_2^2
9	81	14	196
10	100	16	256
14	196	15	225
13	169	18	324
16	256	20	400
14	196	19	361
15	225	18	324
11	121	15	225
102	1344	135	2311

Step 1:
$$s^2 = \frac{\Sigma X^2 - \dfrac{(\Sigma X)^2}{N}}{N - 1}$$

$$s_1^2 = \frac{1344 - \dfrac{(102)^2}{8}}{7} \qquad s_2^2 = \frac{2311 - \dfrac{(135)^2}{8}}{7}$$

$$= 6.21 \qquad\qquad = 4.70$$

$$\bar{X}_1 = \frac{102}{8} = 12.75 \qquad \bar{X}_2 = \frac{135}{8} = 16.88$$

Step 2:
$$s_p^2 = \frac{(N_1 - 1)s_1^2 + (N_2 - 1)s_2^2}{N_1 - 1 + N_2 - 1}$$

$$\frac{(7)(6.21) + (7)(4.7)}{8 - 1 + 8 - 1} = 5.45$$

Step 3:
$$s_{\text{diff}} = \sqrt{\frac{s_p^2}{N_1} + \frac{s_p^2}{N_2}}$$

$$= \sqrt{\frac{5.45}{8} + \frac{5.45}{8}} = 1.17$$

Step 4:
$$t = \frac{\bar{X}_1 - \bar{X}_2}{s_{\text{diff}}} = \frac{12.75 - 16.88}{1.17} = -3.53$$

of the *t*-test for two random independent samples also requires the test of the hypothesis that $\sigma_1^2 = \sigma_2^2$ does not indicate heterogeneity of variance.

The decision rule used with a *t*-test for two random independent samples is formed by obtaining a critical value of *t* from Appendix Table 6, where α equals 0.05 and *df*, in this case, equals 14. Because this critical value equals 2.14, the specific decision rule for the example is written as follows:

$$\text{If } |t_{\text{calc}}| \geq 2.14, \text{ reject } H_0.$$

The final step in performing the statistical test requires that a value for *t* be calculated with the data presented in Table 12.1. The four steps needed to calculate the value of *t* for these data are shown at the bottom of the table.

In Step 1, values for each sample's $\overline{X}$ and s^2 are obtained in the usual manner. The s^2 values are used to calculate s_p^2 using Formula 12.3 in Step 2. The value for s_p^2 is used in Step 3 to calculate s_{diff} using Formula 12.4. Finally, a value equal to -3.53 is calculated for *t* in Step 4 using Formula 12.2.

Evaluating the Null Hypothesis and the Research Hypothesis. Because the absolute value of t_{calc}, 3.53, is greater than 2.14, the critical value in the decision rule, the null hypothesis is rejected. The results of this analysis indicate that the mean number, 16.88, of items recalled by the mnemonic group is significantly different from the mean number, 12.75, of items recalled by the rote memorization group, $t(14) = -3.53$, $p < 0.05$. These results support the investigator's research hypothesis. They suggest that use of a mnemonic device, such as a story based on a familiar nursery rhyme, improves retention in comparison to rote memorization.

PROGRESS ASSESSMENT 12.3

A personnel director believes that employees working the evening shift differ from employees working the day shift in level of job satisfaction. A random sample of ten subjects is selected from each shift and given an extensive questionnaire measuring job satisfaction. Scores for this questionnaire can range between 0 and 60, where 60 represents high job satisfaction. The scores are considered to be measured along an interval scale and are as follows:

Day-shift scores (Group 1): 56, 22, 30, 40, 42, 45, 50, 58, 56, 50.

Evening shift scores (Group 2): 40, 48, 56, 41, 55, 38, 45, 53, 43, 58.

1. Using the steps associated with testing the hypothesis that $\sigma_1^2 = \sigma_2^2$, determine if the two samples come from populations with equal variances and whether a *t*-test can be used to test the director's belief about job satisfaction.

    2. Based on the five steps associated with testing the hypothesis about μ_{diff}, determine if the day and evening shifts differ with respect to job satisfaction.

A NONPARAMETRIC TEST FOR TWO INDEPENDENT SAMPLES: THE MANN-WHITNEY *U*-TEST

In the beginning of this chapter, the conditions necessary for using the *t*-test for two random independent samples are discussed. If these conditions are met, the *t*-test is used because it has a greater power than nonparametric statistical tests used to analyze data collected from two random independent samples.

There are at least three situations, however, when use of the *t*-test for two random independent samples may not be appropriate: (1) the condition of homogeneity of variance is not met, (2) the condition of normality is not met, or (3) the scale of measurement is not at least an interval scale. Given any of these three situations, nonparametric statistical tests are generally used.

You will recall that in performing nonparametric statistical tests, population parameters are *not* hypothesized in H_0 and H_1, and no assumptions are made about the form of the population distributions represented by the samples of interest. The statistical hypothesis evaluated with a nonparametric statistical test is that the population distributions are not different.

A nonparametric test comparable to the *t*-test for two random independent samples is the Mann-Whitney *U*-test.

Conditions for Using the Mann-Whitney *U*-Test

The conditions necessary for using the Mann-Whitney *U* are (1) the samples are random independent samples and (2) data are collected along a scale having at least ordinal characteristics. You will recall from Chapter 2 that data measured along interval or ratio scales can be converted to an ordinal scale. Data measured along a nominal scale is, therefore, the only type of data that cannot be analyzed with a Mann-Whitney *U*-test.

Use of the Mann-Whitney *U*-Test

The data presented in Table 12.2 represent computer keyboard typing scores, collected from nineteen fourth-graders randomly assigned to one of two groups. The groups are differentiated on the basis of two different computer software tutorials that are used to teach students keyboard layout on a computer. Subjects in each group use the specific software program one hour per day for two weeks before taking the typing test.

TABLE 12.2
Typing Scores of Nineteen Fourth-Grade Students Randomly Assigned to Work with One of Two Computer Tutorials Designed to Teach Keyboard Layout

	Tutorial 1		Tutorial 2	
	X_1	X_1^2	X_2	X_2^2
	90	8100	92	8464
	80	6400	50	2500
	85	7225	70	4900
	80	6400	82	6721
	96	9216	79	6241
	80	6400	74	5476
	84	7056	76	5776
	90	8100	76	5776
	86	7396	78	6084
	771	66293	88	7744
			765	59685

$$s_1^2 = \frac{66293 - \frac{(771)^2}{9}}{9 - 1}$$

$$= 30.5$$

$$s_2^2 = \frac{59685 - \frac{(765)^2}{10}}{10 - 1}$$

$$= 129.17$$

$$F = \frac{s_{larger}^2}{s_{smaller}^2} = \frac{129.17}{30.5} = 4.24$$

Decision Rule: Reject H_0 if $F_{calc} \geq 3.39$

Conclusion: Condition of homogeneity of variance not fulfilled; *t*-test cannot be used

---

The students' teacher wants to determine if typing scores are affected by one tutorial more than by the other tutorial. Because an *F*-test, performed as shown at the bottom of Table 12.2, reveals that variances for the two groups are not homogeneous, the *t*-test is not used to evaluate the teacher's hypothesis. Instead, the Mann-Whitney *U*-test is performed.

Translating the Research Hypothesis into a Statistical Hypothesis. Whenever nonparametric statistics are used, the statistical hypotheses are statements about the population distributions rather than statements about parameters. Because the teacher believes that the effectiveness of the two tutorials differ, the alternative hypothesis is written H_1: *The population distribution of the two software groups' typing scores are different.* Negation of H_1 produces H_0: *The population distributions for both software groups' typing scores are not different.*

Performing the Statistical Test. After it is decided that the Mann-Whitney U-test is to be used, a specific decision rule must be formed.

Critical U-values for alpha equal to 0.05 and 0.01 are presented in Appendix Table 7. In this table sample sizes are used to locate critical values. Find the size of sample 1, N_1, in the top row of the table and determine where this column intersects with the row associated with the size of sample 2, N_2. The value listed at this intersection is the critical value for U. In order to reject the null hypothesis, the calculated value of U must be *equal to or less than* the value listed in the table. For the data presented in Table 12.2, where $N_1 = 9$ and $N_2 = 10$, the critical value obtained in Table 7 with alpha $= 0.05$ is 20. The specific decision rule for this example is written as follows:

$$\text{If } U_{\text{calc}} \leq 20, \text{ reject } H_0.$$

In order to perform the Mann-Whitney U-test, the data from both samples, whether collected along a ratio, an interval, or an ordinal scale, must be ranked collectively. So that the scores can be easily ranked, the data in Table 12.2 are organized in descending order in Table 12.3. A rank of 1 is given to the lowest observed score, which is 50, in Table 12.3. The next higher score is given a rank of 2. All scores are then ranked in this sequence. In the case of ties, an average of the ranks is given to the specific scores. For example, 76 occurs twice, and therefore, these two scores are given a rank of 4.5 $[(4 + 5)/2]$ since they are the fourth and fifth scores to be ranked. Once the data are ranked and the ranks are summed, the Mann-Whitney U-statistic can be calculated with the following formulas, where R_1 and R_2 refer to the sums of the ranks for sample 1 and sample 2, respectively.

Formula 12.5
$$U_1 = N_1N_2 + \frac{N_1(N_1 + 1)}{2} - R_1$$

and

$$U_2 = N_1N_2 + \frac{N_2(N_2 + 1)}{2} - R_2$$

The *smaller* of the two U-values is used to evaluate the null hypothesis. In the example in Table 12.3, the value of $U_1 = 17$ is compared to the critical value in the decision rule.

Evaluating the Statistical and the Research Hypothesis. Since the smaller U, 17, is *less* than the critical value, 20, the null hypothesis is rejected. The investigator concludes that the two tutorials differ in effectiveness in teaching keyboard skills to fourth-graders, $U(9, 10) = 17, p < 0.05$.

TABLE 12.3
Data from Table 12.2 Where Raw Scores Are Placed in Descending Order within Each Group for the Purpose of Ranking Scores

	Tutorial 1		Tutorial 2	
X_1	Rank		X_2	Rank
96	19		92	18
90	16.5		88	15
90	16.5		82	11
86	14		79	7
85	13		78	6
84	12		76	4.5
80	9		76	4.5
80	9		74	3
80	9		70	2
	118 = R_1		50	1
				72 = R_2

$U_1 =$

$$N_1 N_2 + \frac{N_1(N_1 + 1)}{2} - R_1 =$$

$$9(10) + \frac{9(10)}{2} - 118 =$$

$U_1 = 17$

$U_2 =$

$$N_1 N_2 + \frac{N_2(N_2 + 1)}{2} - R_2 =$$

$$9(10) + \frac{10(11)}{2} - 72 =$$

$U_2 = 73$

Decision Rule: Reject H_0 if $U_{\text{smaller}} \leq 20$

Conclusion: Reject H_0 since U_1, the smaller U, is less than the critical value of 20. Tutorials produce different performance.

PROGRESS ASSESSMENT 12.4

A social psychologist believes that presenting a one-sided message has a different effect on a listener's rating of a speaker's presentation ability than presenting a two-sided message. Seventeen college students are randomly assigned to two groups: Group 1 ($N = 9$) hears a one-sided message about the benefits of jogging on the cardiovascular system, and Group 2 ($N = 8$) hears a two-sided message about the benefits of jogging on the cardiovascular system and the potential harm on the knees.

After hearing the specific message, each subject is asked to judge the speaker's communication ability on a scale of 1 (extremely poor) to 11 (extremely good) where 6 represents average ability. The following are the rating scores for each group:

Group 1 (one-sided message): 8, 8, 8, 5, 5, 5, 3, 3, 2.

Group 2 (two-sided message): 11, 11, 10, 9, 7, 6, 4, 4.

1. Using the most appropriate test statistic and the five steps associated with hypothesis testing, determine whether the data can be used as evidence to support the psychologist's belief.

2. Explain why you selected your specific test statistic.

What the Mann-Whitney U-Test Measures

The Mann-Whitney U-test measures the degree to which two sets of ranks overlap. If the two samples come from populations in which the distributions of the characteristic of interest do not differ, then there should be considerable amount of overlap between the two sets of ranks; that is, the sums of the ranks for the two sets should be nearly the same value. If the samples come from populations in which the distributions of scores are extremely different, then there should be little overlap and the sums of the ranks for the two sets should be quite different. For example, if there is no overlap at all, the sum of the ranks for one set of scores will be the smallest possible obtainable sum, and the sum of the ranks for the other set of scores will be the largest possible obtainable sum. The smaller U-value in such a case would be zero. The smaller U-value can be considered as an index of the degree of overlap. The smaller U-value can be obtained by applying Formula 12.5 or by assessing the degree of overlap more directly.

Compare each X_2-raw score with every X_1-raw score in Table 12.3. If the X_2-score is smaller than the X_1-score, assign a zero value for that score. If the X_2-score is equal to the X_1-score, assign a 0.5 value, and if it is larger than the X_1-score, assign a value of 1. Obtain a total of these assigned values for each X_2-score and sum these X_2-totals. For example, since the highest X_2-score, 92, is larger than 8 of the X_1-scores, the total for 92 is 8. Because 88 is larger than 6 of the X_1-scores, its total is 6. The total for 82 is 3 as it is larger than only three of the X_1-scores. The X_2-scores from 79 down to 50 are all smaller than all X_1-scores: their totals equal 0. Adding these totals $(8 + 6 + 3 + 0)$ gives a value of 17, the same value obtained for the smaller U using Formula 12.5.

PROGRESS ASSESSMENT 12.5

Compare each X_1-score with every X_2-score in Table 12.3 to determine the larger U-value for these two samples.

Further Notes on the Mann-Whitney *U*-Test

Tie scores often occur between the two groups, as opposed to the example in Table 12.3 where tie scores occur within groups. Although the effect of ties is usually negligible, a correction for ties can be included in the calculation for the Mann-Whitney *U*-statistic. It is also the case that if either sample size is greater than 20, the *z*-distribution is used to identify critical values needed to evaluate the null hypothesis. Furthermore, in Appendix Table 7 an asterisk (*) indicates that the null hypothesis cannot be evaluated for certain size samples with the procedure described in this text. If a Mann-Whitney *U*-test is to be performed for any of these cases, then texts such as Siegel and Castellan (1988) should be consulted.

SUMMARY

The conditions for which the *t*-test can be used to evaluate hypotheses dealing with the data collected from two random independent samples are discussed. More specifically, the *t*-statistic, its theoretical distribution, and computational formulas are presented. Nonparametric statistical procedures are introduced as alternatives to be used when the conditions for using parametric statistics are not met. Use of the Mann-Whitney *U*-test as an alternative for the *t*-test for two random independent samples is discussed.

KEY DEFINITIONS

F-statistic   A parametric statistic for determining whether the variances of two populations are homogeneous based on observations obtained from two random independent samples.

$F = s^2_{larger} / s^2_{smaller}$ Formula used to determine F where s^2 is calculated for both samples and the larger variance is used as the numerator and the smaller variance is used as the denominator.

Mann-Whitney *U*-test   A nonparametric test that is used when the conditions for the *t*-test for two independent samples are not met.

$N_1 + N_2 - 2$ Formula for calculating the *df* for the *t*-statistic used with two random independent samples.

nonparametric statistical tests   Tests used when population parameters are *not* hypothesized in H_0 and H_1 and no assumptions are made about the form of the population distributions from which the samples are selected. The statistical hypothesis evaluated with nonparametric statistical test is that the population distributions are not different.

Sampling distribution of the difference between two means A theoretical distribution based on the difference between the means of all possible pairs of random samples of given sizes selected from a population.

s_{diff} Symbol for the *estimate* of the standard error of the sampling distribution of the difference between two means.

$s_{diff} = \sqrt{s_p^2/N_1 + s_p^2/N_2}$ Formula for calculating an estimate of the standard error of the sampling distribution of the difference between two means.

s_p^2 Symbol for the pooled estimate of the population variance obtained from two random independent samples.

$s_p^2 = [(N_1 - 1)s_1^2 + (N_2 - 1)s_2^2]/[(N_1 - 1) + (N_2 - 1)]$ Formula for calculating a value of the pooled estimate of the population variance.

σ_{diff} Symbol for the standard error of the sampling distribution of the difference between means.

$\sigma_{diff} = \sqrt{\sigma_1^2/N_1 + \sigma_2^2/N_2}$ Defining equation for the standard error of the theoretical sampling distribution of the difference between means.

t-test for two random independent samples A parametric test used to determine if there is a significant difference between the means of two random independent samples.

$t = [(\overline{X}_1 - \overline{X}_2) - \mu_{diff}]/s_{diff}$ Equation for the t-statistic for two random independent samples where μ_{diff} is the hypothesized expected value stated in the null hypothesis.

$t = (\overline{X}_1 - \overline{X}_2)/s_{diff}$ Formula used for calculating a value for t for two random independent samples.

μ_{diff} The symbol for the expected value of the sampling distribution of the difference between means.

$\mu_{diff} = \mu_1 - \mu_2$ Defining equation of the expected value of the sampling distribution of the difference between means.

$U_1 = N_1N_2 + [N_1(N_1 + 1)]/2 - R_1$ and $U_2 = N_1N_2 + [N_2(N_2 + 1)]/2 - R_2$ Formulas for calculating a value for the Mann-Whitney U-statistic where the smaller of the two U-values is used to evaluate the null hypothesis.

REVIEW EXERCISES

For each of the projects described below do the following:

a. Determine the purpose of the project, for example, to estimate values for a population mean.

b. Determine the number and type of samples used in the project.

c. State the dependent measure or measures.

d. State the scale on which the dependent variable is measured, that is, nominal, ordinal, interval, or ratio.

e. Determine whether a correlation coefficient, r or r_s, and its test for significance, t-test for one sample, confidence interval, t-test for two samples, or Mann-Whitney U-test should be used to complete the project. Defend your choice.

f. Based on your answer in part e, complete the project below as if you were the investigator described in the project. (If appropriate, remember to use the five steps associated with hypothesis testing and to test for homogeneity of variance if you have two independent samples and the data are measured along an interval or ratio scale.

1. A physiological psychologist performs an experiment to examine the belief that a specific brain structure plays a role in rats' ability to learn. Sixteen rats are randomly assigned to two equal-size groups. The specific brain structure is surgically destroyed on both sides of the brain for rats assigned to Group 1. Group 2 is treated similarly in that each rat is subjected to an operation procedure except that the specific brain structure is not destroyed. Two weeks after recovering from the operation, all rats are given ten training trials in a relatively simple maze. Total number of errors made over the ten trials are recorded. Determine if destruction of the specific brain structure affects maze learning based on the following data:

Group 1 errors (Brain structure destroyed): 40, 39, 28, 34, 43, 49, 35, 30.

Group 2 errors (Brain structure not destroyed): 20, 25, 42, 41, 33, 27, 38, 30.

2. A cross-country coach asks a sports psychologist to evaluate a new weight-training program that the coach may institute as a standard program for all members of the team. Nine of the seventeen team members are randomly assigned to Group 1, the new weight-training program. The other eight members are randomly assigned to Group 2, which continues with a weight-training program that has been used in previous years. After four weeks of training, the team competes in a district meet involving 125 different runners. Following are data showing each team member's placement in the race where 1 indicates first place. Determine if the new weight-training program produced different performances than the old weight-training program.

Group 1 placement (New Weight Program): 91, 90, 80, 65, 60, 23, 20, 10, 5.

Group 2 placement (Previous Weight Program): 113, 111, 95, 74, 72, 70, 25, 15.

3. A school psychologist is interested in determining if there is a relationship between the number of hours spent studying and the number of hours spent reading for enjoyment, for example, reading mystery novels, newspapers, or magazines. The names of eight students are randomly selected from the school roster. The number of weekly hours (to the nearest one-half hour) spent studying and spent reading for enjoyment are obtained for each student. Based on the information presented in Table 12-A, determine if there is a relationship between these two events.

TABLE 12-A
The Number of Weekly Hours Spent Studying and
Reading for Enjoyment by Eight Students

Student	Hours Studying	Hours Enjoyment
1	15.0	6.0
2	10.0	5.0
3	8.5	4.5
4	6.0	2.0
5	5.0	1.0
6	4.0	0.5
7	6.0	1.5
8	12.0	5.5

4. A community psychologist wants to determine average number of yearly patient visits that are judged by family physicians to be related to behavioral problems and not physiological problems. The psychologist randomly obtains the names of eleven physicians from a directory that lists all general practitioners in the area. Each physician is asked to determine the number of patients examined in the past year for problems that the physician diagnoses as behavioral rather than physiological in origin. Based on the information that follows, estimate the average number of patient visits in this community that physicians believe to be the result of behavior-related problems.

Number of patients diagnosed with behavioral problems: 1233, 1115, 1450, 1510, 1620, 1845, 1327, 2122, 1694, 1775, 2006.

ANSWERS TO PROGRESS ASSESSMENTS

12.1　Statistical hypotheses: H_0: $\sigma_1^2 = \sigma_2^2$, H_1: $\sigma_1^2 \neq \sigma_2^2$.
Perform statistical test where decision rule is reject H_0 if $F_{calc} \geq 2.59$ and F-test produces a value of 4.
Evaluate H_0. Since 4 is greater than 2.59 reject H_0.
Interpretation: variances are heterogenous.

12.2　1. $s_p^2 = 4.1$
　　　2. $s_{diff} = 0.65$
　　　3. $t = (10 - 6)/0.65 = 6.15$

12.3　1. Statistical hypotheses: H_0: $\sigma_1^2 = \sigma_2^2$, H_1: $\sigma_1^2 \neq \sigma_2^2$.
Perform statistic test where decision rule is reject H_0 if $F_{calc} \geq 3.18$ and F-test produces a value of 2.58.
Evaluate H_0. Since 2.58 is less than 3.18, H_0 is not rejected.
Interpretation: there is no evidence to indicate that the variances are heterogenous and, thus, t-test for independent samples can be used.

2. Research hypothesis: investigator believes there is a difference between the day and evening shifts regarding job satisfaction.

Statistical hypotheses: H_0: $\mu_1 - \mu_2 = 0$, H_1: $\mu_1 - \mu_2 \neq 0$.

Perform statistical test where decision rule is reject H_0 if $|t_{calc}| \geq 2.10$ and the t-test for two random independent samples produces an absolute value of 0.64.

Evaluate H_0. Since $|-0.64|$ is less than 2.10, fail to reject H_0.

Interpretation: investigator has no evidence to indicate that day and evening shifts differ with respect to job satisfaction, $t(18) = -0.64$, $p > 0.05$.

12.4 Research hypothesis: investigator believes that a one-sided message affects listener's judgment about a speaker's ability differently than does a two-sided message.

Statistical hypotheses: H_0: The population distributions do not differ; H_1: The population distributions differ.

Perform statistical test where decision rule is reject H_0 if $U_{smaller} \leq 15$ and U_2 is the smaller U which has a value of 18.

Evaluate H_0. Fail to reject H_0 since 18 is greater than 15.

Interpretation: cannot determine from this analysis if one-sided message has a different effect than two sided-message on listener's judgment about speaker's presentation ability, $U(9, 8) = 18$, $p > 0.05$.

2. Mann-Whitney U-test is used because students' rankings of speakers' abilities are collected along an ordinal scale.

12.5 $10 + 9 + 9 + 8 + 8 + 8 + 7 + 7 + 7 = 73$.

Tests for Treatment Effects on Two Dependent Samples

*I*n the experimental designs of the previous chapter, samples selected from a population were random independent samples. The reason for using random independent samples is twofold. First, random independent samples are used to increase the probability that the samples are representative of populations from which they were drawn. Statistics of representative samples can be used to estimate population parameters. Also, the results of experiments involving such samples can be generalized to their respective populations. Second, random independent samples are used to increase the likelihood that the samples do not differ with respect to factors that influence the dependent variable before the introduction of the experimental treatment. By so doing, differences observed in the dependent variable during the experiment can be attributed to changes in the independent variable.

Random independent sampling, however, is not the only way investigators attempt to obtain samples that do not differ with respect to the characteristic of interest. Chapter 2 indicated that samples can also be selected in such a way that selection of the members for one sample directly determines which member will be selected for another sample. Samples selected in this manner are called *dependent samples*.

The elements of dependent samples are related on the dependent variable or on factors that are believed to influence the dependent variable. If, for example, age is an important factor in blood cholesterol level, then an experimenter interested in the effect of a particular drug on cholesterol level may randomly select same-age pairs of individuals from different age groups and randomly assign one member from each pair to receive the drug. The other member of the pair receives a placebo.

Since such assignment leads to dependent rather than independent samples and, therefore, does not meet the condition of independence required for a valid interpretation of the test statistics discussed in the previous chapter, different tests are needed to determine if the drug significantly affects blood cholesterol level.

This chapter focuses on the advantages of using dependent samples, ways of achieving dependence in sampling, and test statistics used to assess treatment effects in experiments using such samples.

ADVANTAGES OF USING DEPENDENT SAMPLES

Measures taken on the dependent variable are influenced by the independent variable, the sample member, and uncontrolled sources of variation introduced during the experiment. A difference between sample means, therefore, is attributed to a potential difference in treatment effects, a difference due to unique features of sample members, and a difference attributable to experimental error such as errors in measurement. The purpose of analysis is to determine if the observed difference in sample means reflects a difference in treatment effects.

In the previous chapter you found that you could determine if there is a difference in treatment effects by using the t-test to compare the observed difference in sample means $(\bar{X}_1 - \bar{X}_2)$ with an estimate of the standard error of a difference between means, s_{diff}. The estimate, s_{diff}, reflects chance variation, which is variation attributable to the unique features of sample members and experimental error. The larger the observed difference $(\bar{X}_1 - \bar{X}_2)$ compared to s_{diff}, the more likely you are to attribute the observed difference to treatment effects. The smaller s_{diff}, then, the more readily treatment effects will be detected, that is, the greater will be the power of the test.

The major advantage of using dependent samples in comparison with independent samples is that dependent samples permit an investigator to account for the variation attributable to the corresponding sample members and thereby reduce s_{diff}. Another advantage of using dependent samples is that dependence in sampling increases the probability that the samples are comparable with respect to the characteristic of interest before introduction of the independent variable.

WAYS OF ACHIEVING DEPENDENCE IN SAMPLING

There are several ways to achieve dependence in sampling. We will use the hypothetical cholesterol experiment to illustrate the ways in which samples can be related.

Matching

Matching refers to the procedure of forming samples in such a way that each sample member has a member in the other sample with which it is identical or highly similar on a characteristic that could potentially influence measures of the dependent variable.

By Mutual Category. Selecting and assigning subjects to groups on the basis of age as in the cholesterol example in the introduction to this chapter is one way to achieve dependence in sampling. Samples are related on the basis of a mutual category. A **mutual category** refers to a characteristic or set of characteristics that are shared by a class of individuals or elements and that have the potential to influence measures of the dependent variable in a experiment. In the cholesterol example, *age* is the mutual category. Subjects of the same age are more likely to have similar cholesterol levels than subjects of different ages. Forming samples so that a subject of any particular age in one sample has a corresponding member of the same age in the other sample makes the samples dependent. The cholesterol levels of the corresponding members of the two samples are, then, likely to be related.

By Genetic Factors.   Selecting subjects and forming groups on the basis of a mutual category is not the only way, and perhaps not even the best way, dependence in sampling can be achieved in the hypothetical cholesterol experiment. Since there is a heredity component in blood cholesterol level, individuals with a common or identical heredity are more likely to have similar blood cholesterol levels than individuals with a different heredity. Subjects could, therefore, be matched on genetic factors. **Genetic factors** are factors resulting from a common heredity that have the potential to influence measures of the dependent variable.

Sets of identical twins could be randomly selected from the population of twins. One randomly selected twin of a set is placed in the drug group; the other twin is placed in the placebo group. This random assignment is continued until all twins have been assigned to the two groups. Since the twin selected for the placebo group directly depends upon which pair-member is assigned to the drug group, the samples are dependent samples and the dependent measures are related on the basis of a common heredity.

By Premeasurement.   The experimenter interested in achieving dependence in sampling can also form dependent samples by actually premeasuring and matching individuals on the dependent variable. **Matching by premeasuring the dependent variable** is the procedure of assigning subjects to samples in such a way that for each sample member there is a member in other sample with the same or highly similar measure of the characteristic of interest.

In the hypothetical cholesterol experiment, for example, the blood cholesterol levels of a random sample of individuals are measured. Pairs of individuals with the same or a highly similar level are then selected and a random member of each pair is placed in the drug group. The other member of the pair is placed in the placebo group. The samples are dependent samples with cholesterol levels related on the basis of premeasurement.

Repeated Measures

There is yet another way of achieving dependence in sampling that is perhaps most suitable to the hypothetical cholesterol experiment. This way, called **repeated measures,** requires measuring the dependent variable for a sample member under each treatment condition.

For example, the experimenter measures the cholesterol level of each member of a random sample prior to administering the drug. The cholesterol level is again measured after the drug is administered. The predrug and postdrug cholesterol levels are then compared. The assumption is that each sample member's *position* in the group before and after the drug treatment will be the same. If sample member A has a higher predrug level than member B, member A should also have a higher postdrug level than member B regardless of whether the drug has a lowering or elevating effect on blood cholesterol level.

When the repeated measures are measures taken before and after the introduction of the independent variable as in this example, the experimental design is often referred to as a **before-after** or **pretest-posttest design.**

PROGRESS ASSESSMENT 13.1

For each of the following tell how dependency in sampling is achieved.

1. Students' attitudes toward drinking alcohol are measured before and after viewing a movie on the devastating emotional effects of alcoholism on family life.

2. To assess the effect of somatotrophin (growth hormone) on the development of motor behavior in male mice, two infant male mice are selected from each of eight litters. One mouse from each litter is given minute amounts of the growth hormone in a saline solution. The littermates are given the saline solution only.

3. A therapist wanting to determine which of the two therapies is most effective in the treatment of obesity selects ten pairs of obese individuals where the members of each pair are the same weight. A random member of each pair undergoes one therapeutic procedure; the remaining members undergo the other therapy.

STANDARD ERROR OF A DIFFERENCE BETWEEN THE MEANS OF DEPENDENT SAMPLES

The standard error of the sampling distribution of a difference between means of two random independent samples was estimated in Chapter 12 on the basis of pooling (combining) the data collected from the two samples. The computational formula for obtaining this estimate is as follows:

$$s_{\text{diff}} = \sqrt{\frac{s_p^2}{N_1} + \frac{s_p^2}{N_2}}$$

This estimate, we said, reflects chance variation in means, that is, variation attributed to unique features of sample members and experimental error. By using dependent samples we can compute and remove variation due to the unique features of sample members from pooled sample variance. The standard error of a difference between means obtained from this modified pooled variance should reflect only variation attributable to experimental error. The next three sections provide you with an understanding of and the procedures involved in making this modification.

Estimating Variation Due to Unique Features of Sample Members

Variation in the dependent measures due to the unique features of sample members is a measure of the tendency for scores of corresponding members of dependent samples to covary and, hence, is referred to as **covariance.** A measure of covariance is the adjusted average of the products of deviation scores for corresponding members of dependent samples. Covariance is symbolized s_{cov}^2. The defining equation for s_{cov}^2 is as follows:

Equation 13.1 $$s_{cov}^2 = \frac{\Sigma(X - \bar{X})(Y - \bar{Y})}{N - 1}$$

In this equation, X is a measure of the dependent variable for a member in sample 1, and Y is a measure of the dependent variable for the corresponding member of sample 2. The $\bar{X}$ and $\bar{Y}$ refer to the means of samples 1 and 2, respectively. The N refers to the number of pairs of scores. Dividing by $N - 1$ rather than by N is the adjustment on the average.

Algebraic manipulation of Equation 13.1 provides a computational formula for s_{cov}^2 that does not require computing deviation scores:

Formula 13.1 $$s_{cov}^2 = \frac{\Sigma XY - (\Sigma X)(\Sigma Y)/N}{N - 1}$$

In this formula, N also refers to the number of pairs of scores.

Computing Covariance: A Numerical Example

For the purpose of illustration, assume that you wish to study the effect of violent TV shows on the aggressive behavior of children. You believe that watching violence on TV will alter children's agressive behavior. You operationally define aggression and then record the number of agressive responses made by a group of six children during a half-hour observation period both before and after watching two hours of violent TV shows. Your null hypothesis is $\mu_{before} = \mu_{after}$ or $\mu_{diff} = 0$. Hypothetical data are presented in Table 13.1:

To compute the covariance, a product of each child's scores during the half-hour observation periods before and after viewing the TV shows is obtained. These products are shown in the XY-column. The X-, Y-, and XY-columns are summed and the obtained sums are substituted in Formula 13.1:

$$s_{cov}^2 = \frac{\Sigma XY - (\Sigma X)(\Sigma Y)/N}{N - 1} = \frac{688 - (55)(70)/6}{6 - 1}$$

$$= \frac{688 - 641.67}{5} = \frac{46.33}{5} = 9.27$$

TABLE 13.1
Number of Aggressive Behaviors Exhibited by Six Children before (X) and after (Y) Viewing Two Hours of Violent TV Shows, the Product (XY) of Each Child's Scores, and the Difference ($X - Y = D$) and Squared Difference (D^2) Scores

| Child | Aggressive Behaviors before TV Viewing | Aggressive Behaviors after TV Viewing | Product of Scores | Difference Score | Squared Difference Score |
	X	Y	XY	D	D^2
1	6	9	54	-3	9
2	4	8	32	-4	16
3	12	12	144	0	0
4	14	15	210	-1	1
5	9	12	108	-3	9
6	10	14	140	-4	16
	55	70	688	-15	51

Computing the Standard Error of a Difference between Means

Once the covariance is computed, you can subtract it from each pooled variance and compute a standard error of a difference between means of dependent samples as follows:

Formula 13.2 $$s_{\text{diff}} = \sqrt{\frac{(s_p^2 - s_{\text{cov}}^2)}{N_1} + \frac{(s_p^2 - s_{\text{cov}}^2)}{N_2}}$$

For the hypothetical data in Table 13.1, the standard error of a differnce between means is as follows:

$$s_{\text{diff}} = \sqrt{\frac{(10.62 - 9.27)}{6} + \frac{(10.62 - 9.27)}{6}}$$

$$= \sqrt{0.225 + 0.225} = \sqrt{0.45} = 0.67$$

In comparison to the standard error of a difference between means of independent samples, s_{diff} for dependent samples reflects only variation attributed to experimental error. This reduction in overall variation when used in the t-formula increases the power of the t-test.

Using Difference Scores

In the preceding sections you were shown how the use of dependent samples allows you to reduce the value of s_{diff} by subtracting covariance. When the covariance has been calculated, s_{diff} is generally computed using Formula 13.2. When the raw data are available, however, a simplified formula that does not require calculating s_{cov}^2 is generally used to obtain s_{diff} for dependent samples. This simplified formula, an algebraic equivalent of Formula 13.2, is as follows:

Formula 13.3 $$s_{\text{diff}} = \sqrt{\frac{s_D^2}{N}}$$

In Formula 13.3, s_D^2 is the variance of the difference scores for corresponding sample members and N is the number of difference scores.

To apply Formula 13.3 you must compute a difference score, **D**, for each pair of related measures by subtracting from each X-value in sample 1 the corresponding Y-value in sample 2. For the hypothetical aggression experiment, these difference scores are shown in the D-column in Table 13.1. The variance of these difference scores, s_D^2, is computed using variance Formula 6.1 where D is substituted for X in the formula as follows:

$$s_D^2 = \frac{\Sigma D^2 - (\Sigma D)^2/N}{N-1} = \frac{51 - (-15)^2/6}{6-1} = \frac{13.5}{5} = 2.7$$

Using Formula 13.3, the standard error of a difference between means of groups in the aggression experiment is as follows:

$$s_{\text{diff}} = \sqrt{\frac{2.7}{6}} = 0.67$$

PROGRESS ASSESSMENT 13.2

For dependent samples in the following hypothetical experiment compute

1. the covariance.

2. the standard error of a difference between means using Formula 13.2.

3. the standard error of a difference between means using Formula 13.3.

   Sale items in grocery stores are usually put at the end of an aisle rather being left in their usual location. A psychologist interested in consumer behavior wants to know if this is an effective means of displaying sale items. The cooperation of eight randomly selected grocery stores that are displaying the same unadvertised sale item is solicited and obtained. A random half of the stores are requested to put their sale item at one end of the aisle in which it is usually located for the first three days of the sale and at its usual location for the last three days of the sale; the remaining four stores leave the sale item at its usual location for the first three days and place it at one end of the aisle for the last three days. At the end of each three-day period, the number of sale items sold is tallied. The data for the eight stores are presented in Table 13-A.

TABLE 13-A
Number of Sale Items Sold by Eight
Different Grocery Stores When the Items Were
at Their Usual Location in the Store and When
They Were at the End of the Aisle

	Number of Sale Items Sold	
Store	Displayed at Usual Location	Displayed at End of Aisle
1	34	47
2	29	30
3	53	62
4	62	65
5	24	19
6	33	33
7	49	51
8	27	38

PARAMETRIC TEST OF A DIFFERENCE BETWEEN THE MEANS OF TWO DEPENDENT SAMPLES

The parametric test used to determine if there is a significant difference between the means of treatment populations from which two dependent samples are drawn is called the **dependent samples *t*-test.** As with the *t*-test for random independent samples, the *t*-test for dependent samples compares an observed difference in means with the standard error of the difference between means. The *t*-formula generally used is as follows:

Formula 13.4
$$t = \frac{\bar{D}}{\sqrt{\dfrac{s_D^2}{N}}}$$

In this formula, $\bar{D}$ is the mean of the difference scores that is equivalent to the difference between means ($\bar{X} - \bar{Y}$). If s_{cov}^2 has been calculated, *t* can also be obtained by dividing $\bar{X} - \bar{Y}$ by Formula 13.2.

Formula 13.4 is applied to the hypothetical aggression data in Table 13.1 as follows:

$$t = \frac{\bar{D}}{\sqrt{\frac{s_D^2}{N}}} = \frac{-2.5}{\sqrt{0.45}} = -3.73$$

The degrees of freedom associated with the dependent samples t-test is $N - 1$ where N refers to the number of pairs of scores.

The general decision rule is as follows:

If $|t_{calc}| \geq t_{table}$, reject H_0: $\mu_{diff} = 0$.

Comparing the calculated absolute value (3.73) of t with the t-value (2.57) in Appendix Table 5 at the 0.05 level of significance indicates that H_0 is rejected. This analysis of the hypothetical aggression data suggests that watching violent TV shows increases the aggressive behavior of children, $t(5) = -3.73$, $p < 0.05$.

PROGRESS ASSESSMENT 13.3

For the consumer behavior experiment of Progress Assessment 13.2:

1. Compute t.
2. Determine if the calculated t is significant at the 0.05 level of significance.

NONPARAMETRIC TEST OF TREATMENT EFFECTS ON TWO DEPENDENT SAMPLES

With the exception of the condition of independence, the conditions underlying the dependent samples t-test are the same as for the t-test for random independent samples discussed in Chapter 12. If the condition of randomness is not satisfied, no test is valid. If the condition of homogeneity of variance is not met, then a nonparametric test may be appropriate. The procedure for testing for homogeneity of variance, however, is not the same procedure used with independent samples. It involves a variation of the t-statistic not discussed in this text. A nonparametric test may also be appropriate if data are collected along an ordinal scale or if there is nonnormality of the population characteristic of interest.

The Wilcoxon Matched-Pairs Signed-Ranks Test

A nonparametric test of treatment effects on two dependent samples is the **Wilcoxon Matched-Pairs Signed-Ranks test.** This test requires:

1. obtaining a difference score, *D*, for corresponding or related measures as was done for the *t*-test for dependent samples.
2. ranking the absolute values of the difference scores, excluding zero, from the lowest to the highest with tied scores being given the average of the corresponding ranks.
3. affixing the sign of the difference score to its rank.
4. summing the positive and negative ranks independently.
5. assigning the smaller absolute value of the summed ranks to the Wilcoxon statistic, **T**.

Assume that the hypothetical aggression experiment is repeated with an additional eight children and the results in Table 13.2 are obtained. Assume also that a test for equality of variances causes you to reject the hypothesis of homogeneity of variance. The Wilcoxon Matched-Pairs Signed-Ranks test is, then, an appropriate test to evaluate the null hypothesis. The null hypothesis simply states that the population distributions before and after watching violent TV shows do not differ.

The Wilcoxon *T*-statistic is computed for the data in Table 13.2 as follows:

1. The difference scores, *D*, are obtained by subtracting the after-scores from the before-scores.
2. The *R*-column gives the rank of the *absolute value* of the *signed* D-scores. Note that the zero D-score is not ranked since it has neither plus nor minus status.
3. In the *S-R* (signed-rank) column, each rank is affixed with the sign (+, −) of its corresponding *D*-score.
4. The positive-signed ranks and negative-signed ranks are then summed independently.
5. The statistic, *T*, is the smaller absolute value of the two rank sums; in this case $T = |T_+| = 1.5$.

The Logic of the Test

If television violence has no effect on the aggressive behavior of children, you would expect that some children would display more aggressive behavior before watching violent TV shows than after. You would also expect other children to display less aggressive behavior before watching the TV shows than after. In other words you would *not* expect the absolute values of the summed signed ranks, T_+ and T_-, to be very different. The smaller the difference between the two rank sums, the more likely it is that the two distributions of scores come from populations that do not differ. If television violence has an effect on the aggressive behavior of children, you would expect a large difference in the absolute rank sums. One sum would be quite large while the other would be quite small. Appendix Table

TABLE 13.2
Number of Aggressive Behaviors Exhibited by Eight Children before
(X) and after (Y) Viewing Two Hours of Violence on TV. The
Difference ($D = X - Y$) between Each Child's Scores, the Rank (R) and
Signed-Ranks (S-R) of the Difference Scores, and the Absolute Sum of
the Signed-Ranks ($|T_+|$ and $|T_-|$) Are Also Shown.

Child	Aggressive Behaviors before TV Viewing X	Aggressive Behaviors after TV Viewing Y	Difference Score D	Difference Score Rank R	Difference Score Signed-Rank S-R
1	8	14	− 6	7	− 7
2	4	7	− 3	5.5	− 5.5
3	5	4	+ 1	1.5	+ 1.5
4	6	6	0		
5	4	5	− 1	1.5	− 1.5
6	5	7	− 2	3.5	− 3.5
7	6	9	− 3	5.5	− 5.5
8	2	4	− 2	3.5	− 3.5

$$|T_+| = 1.5$$
$$|T_-| = 26.5$$

8 provides values of the smaller of two absolute sums for a specified number of signed ranks that would be considered small enough to warrant rejecting the null hypothesis at the 5 and 1 percent significance levels.

The Decision Rule and Evaluation of H_0

The general decision rule for the Wilcoxon T statistic is stated as follows:

If $|T_-|$ or $|T_+| \leq T_{table}$, then reject H_0.

The value for T_{table} is determined by locating the T-value associated with the number of signed ranks (N) for the designated significance level in Appendix Table 8. For the aggression experiment in Table 13.2, there are seven signed ranks. The value shown in Appendix Table 8 in the 0.05 column that is associated with seven signed ranks is 2. An absolute rank sum of 2 or less, then, is needed to reject H_0 at the 5 percent level of significance. Since the value obtained for T in the hypothetical aggression experiment is 1.5, H_0 is rejected. The results indicate, therefore, that TV violence increases the aggressive behavior of children, $T(7) = 1.5$, $p < 0.05$.

PROGRESS ASSESSMENT 13.4

A physical education instructor is interested in which of two training programs (A and B) is the more effective in developing chest muscles in men. Seven pairs of identical male twins are selected for study. A random member of each pair is assigned to program A. The other twins are assigned to program B. The chest measurements for the twins after four months of training are shown in the accompanying table.

TABLE 13-B
Chest Measurements in Inches of Seven
Pairs of Identical Twins after Training
under Program A or B

Twins Pair	Chest Measurements (Inches)	
	Program A	Program B
1	48	49
2	50	49
3	46	49
4	42	47
5	38	45
6	44	48
7	40	46

1. Perform the Wilcoxon Matched-Pairs Signed-Ranks test.
2. Determine if T is significant at the 0.05 level of significance.
3. Do you reject or fail to reject H_0?
4. What does your decision about H_0 mean in terms of the physical education instructor's interest?

SUMMARY

This chapter introduces you to the use of dependent samples in research. Four ways of achieving dependence in sampling are discussed: (1) matching by a mutual category, (2) matching by genetic factors, (3) matching by premeasurement of the characteristic of interest, and (4) repeating measures. Reducing the standard error of a difference between means is claimed to be the major advantage of using dependent samples. You are shown that the estimate of the standard error of a difference between means can be reduced by subtracting the covariance of the dependent samples from the sample variances. This reduced estimate used as the denominator of the dependent samples t-test allows you to detect treatment differences more readily. A numerical example of the dependent samples *t*-test, the parametric test of a difference between the means of dependent samples, is given. The Wilcoxon Matched-Pairs Signed-Rank test is introduced as the nonparametric equivalent of the dependent samples *t*-test.

KEY DEFINITIONS

before-after or **pretest-posttest design**   Experimental design in which the dependent variable is measured for sample elements before and after introduction of the independent variable.

covariance   A measure of the tendency for scores of corresponding members of dependent samples to covary. The adjusted average of the products of deviation scores for corresponding members of dependent samples.

D   Symbol for the difference between scores of corresponding members of dependent samples.

$\bar{D}$ (pronounced "*D*-bar") Symbol for the mean of the difference scores for corresponding members of dependent samples.

dependent samples *t*-test   A parametric test to determine if there is a significant difference between the means of treatment populations from which two dependent samples are drawn.

genetic factors   Factors resulting from a common heredity that have the potential to influence measures of the dependent variable.

matching   A procedure of forming groups in such a way that each sample member has a member in the other sample with which it is identical or highly similar on a characteristic that could potentially influence measures of the dependent variable.

matching by premeasuring the dependent variable   The procedure of assigning subjects to samples in such a way that for each sample member there is a member in the other sample with the same or highly similar measure of the characteristic of interest.

mutual category   A characteristic or set of characteristics that are shared by individuals or elements and that have the potential to influence measures of the dependent variable.

repeated measures   The procedure of measuring the dependent variable for each sample member under each treatment condition.

s_{cov}^2   Symbol for the covariance of samples 1 and 2.

$s_{cov}^2 = \Sigma(X - \bar{X})(Y - \bar{Y})/(N - 1)$ Defining equation for the covariance.

$s_{cov}^2 = [\Sigma XY - (\Sigma X)(\Sigma Y)/N]/(N - 1)$ Computational formula for the covariance.

$s_{diff} = \sqrt{\dfrac{[(s_p^2 - s_{cov}^2)}{N_1} + \dfrac{(s_p^2 - s_{cov}^2)]}{N_2}}$ Estimate of the standard error of a difference between means of dependent samples.

$s_{\text{diff}} = \sqrt{s_D^2/N}$ Estimate of the standard error of a difference between means of dependent samples computed from difference scores for corresponding sample members.

$t = \overline{D}/\sqrt{s_D^2/N}$ Formula for the dependent samples t-test that uses difference scores to compute the standard error of the difference between means.

T The smaller absolute value of the sums of signed ranks computed in the Wilcoxon Matched-Pairs Signed-Ranks test.

Wilcoxon Matched-Pairs Signed-Ranks test A nonparametric test of treatment effects on two dependent samples.

REVIEW EXERCISES

For each of the following experimental designs:

   a. State the dependent and independent variables.

   b. State the scale on which the dependent variable is measured.

   c. Tell whether the dependent variable is continuous or discrete.

   d. State whether the samples are dependent or independent.

   e. State whether the samples are random or randomized samples.

   f. If the samples are dependent, calculate the most appropriate correlation coefficient; otherwise answer "NA" (nonapplicable).

   g. If the samples are dependent, tell how dependency was achieved; otherwise answer "NA."

   h. Calculate the mean and variance of each sample.

   i. If the samples are independent, perform the test for homogeneity of variance.

   j. Perform the most appropriate test to determine if there is a significant difference in treatment effects. If samples are dependent samples, this judgment is to be made on the basis of scale of measurement.

   k. State the null hypothesis in words (and symbols if applicable) tested in part j.

   l. State whether you reject or fail to reject H_0.

   m. Tell what your decision about H_0 means in terms of the research hypothesis.

   1. A developmental psychologist who is interested in how children process information hypothesizes that they will respond more quickly to pairs of similar stimuli than to pairs of dissimilar stimuli. Capital letters serve as stimuli. Pairs of similar stimuli consist of two identical letters such as UU whereas pairs of dissimilar stimuli consist of different letters such as LP. An equal number of similar and dissimilar pairs of letters are presented in a random order to nine randomly selected third-grade children. The presentation of the stimuli lasts one second and the child responds to the stimuli by pushing one of two buttons. Five of the children press the right button for similar stimuli and the left for dissimilar stimuli. For the remaining children, the button assignment is reversed. The amount of time in milliseconds it takes them to press the button is recorded. The children are given ten practice trials to ensure that they understand the task. The average time it takes each child to respond to similar and dissimilar stimuli is in Table 13-C.

TABLE 13.C
Amount of Time in Milliseconds It Takes Third-Grade Children to Respond to Similar and Dissimilar Letter Pairs (N = 9)

	Letter Pairs	
Child	Similar Pair	Dissimilar Pair
1	705	988
2	699	897
3	599	788
4	789	799
5	559	674
6	689	681
7	577	611
8	677	689
9	778	812

2. Incidental learning is studied in two groups of retarded children given different instructions. Ten pairs of individuals with identical mental ages are selected from special education classes from three counties in New Jersey. One member of each pair is randomly placed in one group. The remaining individuals form the second group. Each group is presented with a series of twenty-four pictures consisting of common animals, such as cat, dog, and horse, and things, such as tree, house, and car. One group is instructed to name each of the pictures (label instructions). The other group is instructed to put the pictures into groups of animals and things (category instructions). The investigator hypothesizes that categorizing information will facilitate recall. One hour after the subjects perform the task as instructed, they are asked to recall as many of the pictures as they can. The number of items recalled by each group is shown in Table 13-D.

3. Retroactive interference is a backward-acting interference. Things that you learn today can possibly interfere with the recall of things previously learned. To study the effect of retroactive interference on the recall of verbal material, a psychology teacher enlists the aid of sixteen volunteers from the general psychology class. The sixteen volunteers are randomly divided into two groups of equal size. Each group is given a list of eighteen paired associates to learn. The paired associates are three consonant nonsense syllables such as BKT-LMZ where the first syllable (BKT) is the stimulus syllable and the second (LMZ) is the response syllable. When the stimulus syllable is presented, the subject gives the response syllable. The subjects in both groups are presented the list until one perfect recitation is given. On the following day, the subjects in one group (experimental group) are given another list to learn in which the stimulus syllables are the same as in the first list but the response sylla-

TABLE 13-D
Number of Picture Items Recalled by Ten
Pairs of Retarded Children with Identical
Mental Ages after Given Label Instructions
or Category Instructions

Children	Type of Instructions	
Pair	Label	Category
1	13	14
2	14	15
3	12	14
4	8	12
5	7	11
6	10	10
7	11	11
8	9	10
9	7	12
10	5	10

bles are different. The second group (control group) is not given another list to learn. The next day each group is tested on the original list. The teacher expects that the experimental group will exhibit the effect of retroactive interference. The number of correct responses to the original list are:

Experimental: 9, 12, 12, 9, 8, 10, 11, 6

Control: 14, 12, 15, 13, 14, 12, 13, 13

ANSWERS TO PROGRESS ASSESSMENTS

13.1	1. repeated measures
	2. matching by genetics factors
	3. matching by premeasurement
13.2	1. 206.02
	2. 2.18
	3. 2.18
13.3	1. -1.95
	2. not significant
13.4	1. $T = 1.5$
	2. significant
	3. reject
	4. Program B is more effective.

CHAPTER 14

Completely Randomized Designs and the One-Way Analysis of Variance

*T*he experimental design discussed in Chapter 12 in which a different treatment level of an independent variable was administered to each of two random independent samples represents the simplest case of a class of designs called **completely randomized designs.** This class of designs is symbolized **CR-k** where **k** must be equal to or greater than two ($k \geq 2$) and represents the number of treatment levels of a single independent variable. This chapter focuses on designs in which $k > 2$.

Let us consider one instance of such a design. Suppose you wish to determine if different levels of food deprivation have different effects on the wheel-running activity of rats. Assume that your dependent variable is the number of wheel revolutions made by rats in a thirty-minute period after being deprived of food for some specified interval of time. Your single independent variable is hours of food deprivation. Suppose further that you choose to have a group that is not deprived of food (0 hours of deprivation) and groups that are deprived of food for 6, 12, 18, and 24 hours. You have, then, five treatment levels. Your experimental design is a CR-5 design where CR-5 indicates a completely randomized design that includes five treatment levels of the single independent variable, *hours of food deprivation.*

The statistical tests that you have learned thus far are not suitable to analyze an experiment like the hypothetical deprivation-activity experiment. This chapter introduces you to statistical tests used to analyze data from experiments with two or more levels of a single independent variable.

THE PARAMETRIC ONE-WAY ANALYSIS OF VARIANCE

Although the *t*-test was devised to test H_0: $\mu_1 = \mu_2$ when $k = 2$, a more generalized parametric test, called the **analysis of variance (ANOVA),** is used to test a hypothesis about means for any number of treatment levels ($k \geq 2$). Because the CR-k design involves only a single independent variable, the ANOVA used to analyze the data generated by a CR-k experiment is referred to as a **one-way ANOVA.**

Null Hypothesis for the One-Way ANOVA

The **null hypothesis for the parametric one-way ANOVA** is that means of the populations from which the samples were drawn are equal, that is, H_0: $\mu_1 = \mu_2 = \mu_3 = \ldots = \mu_k$. For the hypothetical deprivation-activity experiment, the null hypothesis is H_0: $\mu_1 = \mu_2 = \mu_3 = \mu_4 = \mu_5$. The alternative hypothesis, H_1, is that the means are not all equal. If any one mean is not equal to each and every other mean, then you reject H_0 and accept H_1. For example, if $\mu_1 \neq \mu_5$ and all other means are equal to each other and to μ_5 and μ_1, you reject H_0.

PROGRESS ASSESSMENT 14.1

For hypothetical experiments 1 and 2 complete the following steps:

- **a.** Identify the single independent variable.
- **b.** Symbolize the experimental design.
- **c.** State the null hypothesis in words.
- **d.** Symbolize the null hypothesis.
- **e.** State the alternative hypothesis.

1. In an experiment designed to determine if a person's affective state influences the number of word associations triggered by an affectively neutral stimulus, three groups of six college sophomores have their affective states altered by exposing them to an odor stimulus that has previously been established as pleasant, neutral, or unpleasant. Each subject is asked to make as many associations as possible in ten seconds to each of ten affectively neutral words while exposed to one of the three odors. The dependent measure is the subject's average number of word associations made to the ten affectively neutral stimulus words.

2. The effect of several weight-reduction programs is assessed using thirty-two adult females randomly selected from a large group of individuals who have gone to an obesity treatment center to lose weight. The thirty-two subjects are randomized with respect to programs. Six subjects are assigned to an exercise-only program in which they are to exercise one hour per day but are allowed to eat as much as they please. Seven subjects are told not to exercise and are placed on an eighteen-hundred-calorie-per-day dietetic regimen. Five subjects are required to exercise one hour per day while on an eighteen-hundred-calorie-per-day dietetic regimen. Eight subjests are assigned to an eating regimen on which they go without food one day per week. The remaining six subjects are used as controls and are not placed on any specific exercise or eating regimen.

The Questions ANOVA Answers

It may seem absurd to hypothesize that the means of the populations from which the samples were drawn are equal when, usually, the samples have been drawn from the same population. You might ask, how can they *not* be equal? When testing H_0, you are really asking if any one of your treatments has changed the sample characteristic of interest so much that the sample can no longer be considered as coming from the population from which it was originally selected. In essence, you are asking whether or not the sample must now be considered as coming from a population in which the characteristic of interest has been quantitatively altered.

Suppose, for example, that the number of wheel revolutions per thirty-minute period for a population of rats not deprived of food was normally distributed with $\mu = 90$, and suppose that depriving a sample of rats for twenty-four hours yielded an $\overline{X} = 120$ revolutions. The question that you want the test of H_0 to answer is whether or not rats deprived of food for twenty-four hours can still be considered as coming from a population whose wheel-running average per thirty-minute period is 90. In other words, you want to know if it is probable that a random sample from a population with $\mu = 90$ would have an $\overline{X} = 120$.

If you reject H_0, you conclude that the twenty-four hour deprivation treatment changed wheel-running activity to such a degree that rats so deprived can no longer be considered as coming from a population whose average wheel revolutions per thirty-minute period is 90. In other words, you conclude that it is not very probable that the original population would yield a sample with $\overline{X} = 120$. However, rejecting H_0 when the number of treatment levels is greater than two only tells you that one or more population means differ from each other. It does not tell you which means differ.

The ANOVA, then, is a test that tells you not only whether or not you should reject H_0 but also whether or not you should continue your statistical analysis. Later in this chapter you will be introduced to tests that allow you to determine which population means differ from each other when your ANOVA indicates that there is some inequality of means.

Why ANOVA Is Needed

You were told earlier that the ANOVA was devised to test a hypothesis about means when the number of treatment levels is equal to or greater than two. Now you may be wondering why the t-test could not be used to test the hypothesis $H_0: \mu_1 = \mu_2 = \mu_3 = \ldots = \mu_k$ by making comparisons between every pair of treatment means. If any pair of means differed significantly, would that not be grounds for rejecting $H_0: \mu_1 = \mu_2 = \mu_3 = \ldots = \mu_k$?

There are two reasons why it is undesirable to use the t-test when $k > 2$. First, it could be very time consuming. For example, if your experiment involves thirteen treatment levels, you will have to make seventy-eight such comparisons. Second, and more importantly, when you set your significance level at 0.05 for comparing any one pair of means with a t-test, you can expect to reject a true hypothesis and make an alpha error (see Chapter 9) 5 percent of the time or one in twenty comparisons. Thus, even if the means of the populations from which the samples were drawn did not differ, with thirteen treatment levels generating seventy-eight comparisons, you would be led to reject your *overall* $H_0: \mu_1 = \mu_2 = \mu_3 = \ldots = \mu_k$, since you could expect to reject a true hypothesis about a pair of means approximately four times in seventy-eight comparisons. In other words, the likelihood of rejecting an *overall* true H_0 with the t-test is almost a certainty when the number of comparisons to be made is very large.

The ANOVA, in contrast, takes into consideration the number of treatment levels and maintains the alpha error at 5 percent no matter how many possible comparisons the different treatment levels generate.

The Logic of ANOVA

You may be wondering why, if you are testing hypotheses about means, you analyze variance. The logic of ANOVA in this regard is simple and elegant.

Recall from Chapter 6 that there are both within-group and between-group sources of variation and that the within-group variance, s^2, is an unbiased estimate of the population variance, σ^2. Recall also that the between-group variance is based on the variance of the means and that the variance of the means $\sigma_{\bar{X}}^2$ bears a particular relationship to the population variance σ^2 (examined in Chapter 10). That relationship is $\sigma_{\bar{X}}^2 = \sigma^2/N$ where N refers to sample size. Since $s^2/N = s_{\bar{X}}^2$, then N times the variance of the means is also an unbiased estimate of the population variance, σ^2. This is referred to as the **between-group estimate of σ^2**. You test the null hypothesis about the means, that is H_0: $\mu_1 = \mu_2 = \mu_3 = \ldots = \mu_k$ by examining the ratio of the between-group estimate of σ^2 to the within-group estimate of σ^2. The **within-group estimate of σ^2** is the pooled sample variances. This ratio is the familiar **F-ratio** (see Chapter 12). If both of these statistics are estimating σ^2, then the F-ratio is approximately 1.0.

It is when these two statistics do not appear to be estimating the same σ^2 that you reject your H_0 about the means. These statistics do not appear to be estimating the same parameter when the between-group estimate is susbtantially larger than the within-group estimate. The between-group estimate will be substantially larger than the within-group estimate when your treatments differentially affect the characteristic of interest and thereby increase the variability of the means.

You can easily understand why differential treatment effects lead to a change in the between-group estimate and not in the within-group estimate of σ^2. Any specified treatment is assumed to have the same effect on all members of the sample. It either increases or decreases the measures taken on the sample members by a constant. As you discovered in Chapter 6, however, adding or subtracting a constant to the scores taken on a sample has no effect upon the sample variance. Therefore, regardless of whether or not your treatment levels are having different effects, the within-group estimate of σ^2 should not change as a result of your experimental treatment.

If your treatment levels are not having different effects on the characteristic of interest, then the same constant is added to or subtracted from all the means because, as indicated in Chapter 5, whatever you do to the sample scores by a constant you also do to the mean. Therefore, if the different treatment levels are not having different effects on the characteristic of interest, then the between-group variance also does not change as a result of the experimental treatment. Hence, the ratio of the between-group estimate to the within-group estimate, the F-ratio, should be close to 1.0 and you do not reject the H_0: $\mu_1 = \mu_2 = \mu_3 = \ldots = \mu_k$.

If, on the other hand, two or more of the treatment levels are having different effects, then the different treatments add or subtract different constants to their sample means. This, in effect, influences the means by a variable. Adding a variable to or subtracting one from the means increases the variance of the means and, hence, increases the F-ratio.

If the deviation from 1.0 of the F-ratio is greater than expected by chance, you reject H_0: $\mu_1 = \mu_2 = \mu_3 = \ldots = \mu_k$ and conclude that one or more of the treatments has altered the characteristic of interest to such a degree that the samples can no longer be considered as coming from populations with equal means.

You determine if the F-ratio is significant in the same way that you determined its significance when you tested the hypothesis of homogeneity of variance (in Chapter 12). In Appendix Table 6, you find the F associated with the degrees of freedom of the between-group estimate (numerator of F-ratio) and the *df* of within-group estimate (denominator of F-ratio) of σ^2. The decision rule is as follows:

$$\text{If } F_{\text{calc}} \geq F_{\text{table}}, \text{ reject } H_0.$$

An Illustration of the Logic of ANOVA

Suppose in the hypothetical deprivation-activity experiment referred to earlier in this chapter that the data in Table 14.1 represent the predeprivation number of wheel revolutions that are made by five groups of five rats each randomly selected from the same population. If you compute the within-group and between-group variances, you can expect that the F-ratio indicates that the means of the populations from which the samples were drawn do not differ significantly. This, as mentioned previously, is one purpose of random selection.

We will now compute between-group and within-group estimates of σ^2. As was indicated in Chapter 12, when you have two different unbiased within-group estimates of the population variance, the best estimate is a pooled estimate, s_p^2, a kind of average estimate. The same is true when you have more than two unbiased within-group estimates. The pooling or averaging of more than two estimates is a direct generalization from the pooling of two estimates. As indicated in Chapter 12, for two estimates the pooled estimate is

$$s_p^2 = \frac{(N_1 - 1)s_1^2 + (N_2 - 1)s_2^2}{N_1 + N_2 - 2}.$$

For more than two estimates the following generalization applies:

Formula 14.1
$$s_p^2 = \frac{(N - 1)s_1^2 + (N_2 - 1)s_2^2 + \ldots + (N_k - 1)s_k^2}{N_1 + N_2 + \ldots N_k - k}$$

The within-group estimate of σ^2 from the data in Table 14.1 is computed to be 28.6 using Formula 14.1 as follows:

$$s_p^2 = \frac{4(40) + 4(14.5) + 4(26.5) + 4(29.5) + 4(32.5)}{25 - 5}$$

$$= \frac{572}{20} = 28.6$$

The between-group estimate of σ^2 from the data in Table 14.1 is obtained by multiplying the variance of the means by the sample size ($N = 5$). The variance of the means is computed by substituting the sum of means ($\Sigma\bar{X}$) *and the sum of squared means* ($\Sigma\bar{X}^2$) for the ΣX and ΣX^2, respectively, in Formula 6.1 as follows:

$$s_{\bar{X}}^2 = \frac{40689 - \frac{(451)^2}{5}}{4} = 2.2$$

The between-group estimate of σ^2 is $5 \times 2.2 = 11.0$. The *F*-ratio is $11.0/28.6 = 0.38$. After comparing 0.38 with the *F*-value in Appendix Table 6 associated with 4 *df* for the numerator and 20 *df* for the denominator ($F_{table} = 2.87$), you do not reject H_0: $\mu_1 = \mu_2 = \mu_3 = \mu_4 = \mu_5$ as would have been expected since all five samples were selected from the same population and no treatment had been administered.

Suppose now that you impose your deprivation conditions on the rats and that deprivation has the effect of increasing the number of revolutions per thirty-minute period by five revolutions for every six hours that a rat is deprived. Superimposing the deprivation effects on the predeprivation levels of activity in Table 14.1 yields Table 14.2.

TABLE 14.1
Predeprivation Number of Wheel Revolutions Made by Five Groups of Rats to Be Deprived for 0, 6, 12, 18, or 24 Hours in the Hypothetical Deprivation-Activity Experiment and Summary Data for Computing the Within-Group and Between-Group Estimates of σ^2

	Number of Wheel Revolutions					
0 Hours	**6 Hours**	**12 Hours**	**18 Hours**	**24 Hours**		
86	86	90	96	96		
94	93	83	86	92		
82	91	97	89	88		
90	89	92	88	99		
98	96	88	81	85		
$\bar{X} = 90$	91	90	88	92		
$s^2 = 40.0$	14.5	26.5	29.5	32.5	$\Sigma\bar{X} = 451$	
$\bar{X}^2 = 8100$	8281	8100	7744	8464	$\Sigma\bar{X}^2 = 40689$	

TABLE 14.2
Postdeprivation Number of Wheel Revolutions Made by Five Groups of Rats Deprived for 0, 6, 12, 18, or 24 Hours in the Hypothetical Deprivation-Activity Experiment and Summary Statistics

0 Hours	6 Hours	12 Hours	18 Hours	24 Hours
86	91	100	111	116
94	98	93	101	112
82	96	107	104	108
90	94	102	103	119
98	101	98	96	105
$\bar{X}$ = 90	96	100	103	112
s^2 = 40.0	14.5	26.5	29.5	32.5

Comparing Table 14.2 with Table 14.1 you can see that increasing the number of wheel revolutions by five for each six hours that a rat is deprived has no effect upon the variance within groups and, therefore, no effect upon the within-group estimate of σ^2. The within-group estimate remains 28.6.

You can also see in comparing Table 14.2 with Table 14.1 that the increment in wheel revolutions as a result of deprivation does affect the means. It is also clear that the range of means in Table 14.2 is substantially larger than the range of means in Table 14.1. This indicates that the variance of the means has changed. Computing the variance of the means in the same manner as computed earlier yields a value of 67.2. Multiplying this value by the sample size (N = 5), that is, $Ns_{\bar{X}}^2$, yields a between-group estimate of σ^2 equal to 336.0. The F-ratio, then, is 336.0/28.6 = 11.75. Comparing this value with the table-value (2.87) in Appendix Table 6 associated with 4 (numerator) and 20 (denominator) df leads you to reject H_0: μ_1 = μ_2 = μ_3 = μ_4 = μ_5.

When you reject H_0 you accept H_1 which states that the means are not all equal. You conclude, therefore, that different levels of food deprivation differentially affect the mean number of wheel revolutions made by rats in a thirty-minute period. As you see, analyzing variance enables you to determine whether or not there is a difference in the means of the populations from which the samples were drawn and, consequently, whether or not the independent variable has had an effect on the dependent variable.

PROGRESS ASSESSMENT 14.2

Assume that in a *CR-3* experiment measures of the characteristic of interest *before* introduction of the independent variable yields within-group variance equal to between-group variance. Describe what happens to within-group and between-group variances if introduction of the independent variable has the effect of

1. decreasing the individual scores at each treatment level by 6.

2. increasing the individual scores at one treatment level by 4 and at the other two treatment levels by 10, and

3. decreasing the individual scores at one treatment level by 8 and not changing the scores at the other two treatment levels.

TERMINOLOGY, SYMBOLS, AND COMPUTATIONAL CONCEPTS

The defining equation for the variance shown in Chapter 6 (Equation 6.2), $s^2 = \Sigma(X - \bar{X})^2/(N - 1)$, tells you that the variance is the sum of the squared deviations from the mean divided by the **degrees of freedom.** In ANOVA similar terminology is applied to the components of this formula.

Terminology

In ANOVA, the sum of the squared deviations from the mean is referred to as the **sum of squares** and is symbolized **SS**. The SS used in obtaining the within-group estimate of σ^2 is referred to as the **within-group sum of squares** and is symbolized SS_{wg}. Similarly, the sum of squares used in obtaining a between-group estimate of σ^2 is called the **between-group sum of squares** and is symbolized SS_{bg}. In ANOVA, a third sum of squares referred to as the total sum of squares, symbolized SS_{tot}, is also obtained. The **total sum of squares** is defined as the sum of the squared deviations of all the obtained scores from the mean of all the scores. Its use will be explained shortly.

The symbol for degrees of freedom (df) is familiar to you, and so you should easily recognize df_{wg}, df_{bg}, and df_{tot} as symbols for the degrees of freedom associated with within-group variance, between-group variance, and total variance, respectively.

Variance in the ANOVA is called **mean square,** symbolized **MS,** and refers to the adjusted average of squared deviations from the mean. Thus, MS_{wg} symbolizes the **within-group mean square,** which is the adjusted average of the pooled within-group deviation scores. Similarly, MS_{bg} symbolizes the **between-group mean square,** which is the adjusted average of the deviations of the sample means from the mean of all the scores. The **F-ratio in the one-way ANOVA** is the ratio of the MS_{bg} to the MS_{wg}, the only two mean squares used in the one-way ANOVA.

Computational Symbols

In computing SS_{tot}, SS_{wg}, and SS_{bg}, you will find it convenient to obtain the values for three computational number symbols *(1)*, *(2)*, and *(3)* proposed by Winer (1962).

The symbol *(1)* = G^2/nk, where **G** symbolizes the sum of all the scores obtained in the experiment **(grand sum)**, **n** refers to the number of scores for a treatment level or group, *k* refers to the number of treatment levels or groups, and the product of *n* times *k* *(nk)* equals the total number of scores obtained in the experiment when the group sizes are equal. When group sizes are not equal, the denominator of *(1)* is generally symbolized **N_{tot}**, which indicates the total number of obtained scores. The symbol *(1)*, then, refers to the value obtained when the squared sum of all the scores is divided by the total number of scores.

The symbol *(2)* = ΣX^2 refers to the sum of all squared scores.

The symbol *(3)* = $\Sigma T_j^2/n$ where the subscript *j* denotes the treatment level, *n* refers to the number of scores under treatment level *j*, and *T_j* represents the sum of the scores for the specified treatment level, for example, T_1 = sum of treatment 1, T_2 = sum of treatment 2, and so on. Thus, *(3)* represents the numerical value obtained when the treatment level totals are squared, divided by their respective sample sizes, and summed.

Note that the denominator in each of these computational symbols refers to the number of scores that make up each squared value in the numerator. In other words *nk* or N_{tot} scores make up *G* in *(1)*, one score makes up each *X* that is squared in *(2)*, 1 being the understood denominator of ΣX^2, and *n* scores make up the T_j's in *(3)*.

Defining Equations and Computational Formulas

To give you a better understanding of SS_{tot}, SS_{wg}, and SS_{bg}, defining equations as well as computational formulas are presented. In the defining equations, $\overline{G}$ (pronounced "G-bar") refers to the **grand mean,** that is, the mean of all the scores, and $\overline{T}_j$ (pronounced "T_j-bar") refers to the mean of treatment group *j*.

Equations and Formulas for SS.

We begin with the defining equation and computational formula for SS_{tot} because they should be somewhat familiar to you. Actually, with the exception of a change in symbols from $\overline{X}$ to $\overline{G}$ and from ΣX to G, the defining equation and computational formula for SS_{tot} are the same as the respective numerator of the defining equation and computational formula for s^2 (discussed in Chapter 6). The SS_{tot}, which is the sum of the squared deviations of all the obtained scores from the grand mean, is symbolized as follows:

Equation 14.1 $$SS_{tot} = \Sigma(X - \overline{G})^2$$

It can be shown algebraically that Equation 14.1 is equivalent to the following computational formula for SS_{tot}:

Formula 14.2 $$SS_{tot} = (2) - (1) = \Sigma X^2 - \frac{G^2}{nk}$$

Formula 14.2 directs you to subtract from the sum of all the squared scores, ΣX^2, the squared sum of all the scores divided by the number of scores, G^2/nk. You should recognize theses symbols as the computational symbols explained earlier. Although we are now presenting the computational formulas in terms of numerical symbols (1), (2), and (3) and their respective **monomials** (single quantities), G^2/nk, ΣX^2, and $\Sigma T_j^2/n$, you will find later in this section and in subsequent sections that it is convenient to present the computational formulas for SS only in terms of the numerical symbols.

From the numerator of Formula 14.1 you should recognize the within-group sum of squares, SS_{wg}, as the sum of the sums of squares of the individual groups. Thus, the defining equation for SS_{wg} is as follows:

Equation 14.2 $$SS_{wg} = \Sigma SS_j = \Sigma[\Sigma(X - \bar{T}_j)^2]$$

You should also recognize $\Sigma(X - \bar{T}_j)^2$ as the numerator of Equation 6.1 introduced in Chapter 6, the defining equation for s^2, where $\bar{T}$ is substituted for the familiar $\bar{X}$. Therefore the computational formula for SS_{wg} is as follows:

Formula 14.3 $$SS_{wg} = (2) - (3) = \Sigma X^2 - \frac{\Sigma T_j^2}{n}$$

The between-group sum of squares is defined as the group size (n) times the sum of the squared deviations of the group means from the grand mean. This definition is symbolized as follows:

Equation 14.3 $$SS_{bg} = n[\Sigma(\bar{T}_j - \bar{G})^2]$$

In terms of the computation symbols explained in the preceding section, the defining equation can be shown to be algebraically equivalent to the following computational formula:

Formula 14.4 $$SS_{bg} = (3) - (1) = \frac{\Sigma T_j^2}{n} - \frac{G^2}{nk}$$

Formulas for df. Degrees of freedom, as indicated in Chapter 11, is defined as the number of deviations minus the number of independent points about which the deviations are taken. There is only one point ($\bar{G}$) about which the deviations are taken in computing SS_{tot}. Since there are nk deviations in computing SS_{tot}, the formula for computing the df_{tot} is as follows:

Formula 14.5 $$df_{tot} = nk - 1$$

For *CR-k* designs in which group sizes are unequal, Formula 14.5 becomes $df_{tot} = N_{tot} - 1.$

In computing SS_{wg} there are nk deviations taken about k-points, that is, the k treatment means $(\overline{T}_j)$. The df_{wg} formula is then:

Formula 14.6 $df_{wg} = nk - k = k(n - 1)$

For CR-k designs in which group sizes are unequal, Formula 14.6 becomes $df_{wg} = N_{tot} - k$. Alternatively the **within-group degrees of freedom** is equivalent to the sum of the degrees of freedom for the individual treatment groups.

There is also only one point $(\overline{G})$ about which the deviations are taken in computing SS_{bg}, and there are k deviations, one for each group mean. Thus, the **between-group degrees of freedom** is the number of group means minus one. The formula for computing df_{bg} is as follows:

Formula 14.7 $df_{bg} = k - 1$

Formulas for MS and F.   In ANOVA, the mean square is obtained by dividing a specific SS by its corresponding df as shown in the following formulas:

Formula 14.8 $MS_{wg} = \dfrac{SS_{wg}}{df_{wg}}$

Formula 14.9 $MS_{bg} = \dfrac{SS_{bg}}{df_{bg}}$

As mentioned above, the F-ratio in the one-way ANOVA is the ratio of the MS_{bg} to MS_{wg} as shown below:

Formula 14.10 $F = \dfrac{MS_{bg}}{MS_{wg}}$

The computational symbols and formulas used to calculate F for the one-way ANOVA are summarized in Table 14.3:

TABLE 14.3
Summary Table of Computational Symbols and Formulas for Computing Sum of Squares (SS), Degrees of Freedom (df), Mean Square (MS), and the F-ratio (F)

Computational Symbols	Source	SS	df	MS	F
$(1) = G^2/nk$	Between groups	$(3) - (1)$	$k - 1$	SS_{bg}/df_{bg}	MS_{bg}/MS_{wg}
$(2) = \Sigma X^2$	Within groups	$(2) - (3)$	$k(n - 1)$	SS_{wg}/df_{wg}	
$(3) = \Sigma T_j^2/n_j$	Total	$(2) - (1)$	$nk - 1$		

PROGRESS ASSESSMENT 14.3

The values for computational symbols (*1*), (*2*), and (*3*) given in the Table 14-A have been computed for the hypothetical experiment in Progress Assessment 14.1, part 2.

TABLE 14-A
Summary Table for ANOVA Performed on the Data of Experiment in Progress Assessment 14.1, Part 2

Computational Symbol Values	Source	SS	df	MS	F
(1) = 7350.78	Between groups	___	___	___	___
(2) = 9113.00	Within groups	___	___	___	
(3) = 8785.13	Total	___	___		

1. Demonstrate your understanding of the formulas for *SS*, *df*, *MS*, and *F* by completing the table.
2. Determine if the *F*-ratio is significant at the 0.01 level of significance.
3. Reach a conclusion about the null hypothesis.

Partitioning SS_{tot}

It can be illustrated graphically and shown algebraically that a deviation of a sample score from the grand mean ($\bar{G}$) consists of the deviation of the score from the group mean and the deviation of the group mean from the grand mean. Consider the diagram in Figure 14.1. The group mean equals 50 and the grand mean equals 45. The deviation ($X - \bar{G}$) of the score 52 from the grand mean is $52 - 45 = 7$. The deviation ($X - \bar{T}_j$) of the score 52 from the group mean is $52 - 50 = 2$, and the deviation ($\bar{T}_j - \bar{G}$) of the group mean from the grand mean is $50 - 45 = 5$. You can see that the sum of these two deviations, $X - \bar{T}_j = 2$ and $\bar{T}_j - \bar{G} = 5$, equals the deviation ($X - \bar{G}$) = 7 of the score from the grand mean, ($X - \bar{T}_j$) + ($\bar{T}_j - \bar{G}$) = ($X - \bar{G}$), that is, $2 + 5 = 7$.

Corresponding, it can be shown algebraically that the sum of the squared deviations of the scores from the grand mean is equal to the sum of the squared deviations of the scores from their group mean plus the sum of the squared deviations of the group means from the grand mean, that is, $SS_{tot} = SS_{wg} + SS_{bg}$.

$$SS_{wg} = (2) - (3) = \Sigma X^2 - \frac{\Sigma T_j^2}{n}$$

$$+\ SS_{bg} = (3) - (1) = \frac{\Sigma T_j^2}{n} - \frac{G^2}{nk}$$

$$=\ SS_{tot} = (2) - (1) = \Sigma X^2 - \frac{G^2}{nk}$$

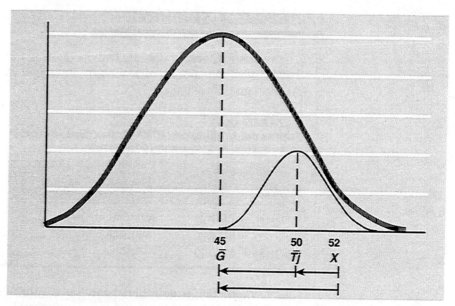

FIGURE 14.1 *Diagram illustrating that the deviation of a score (X) from the grand mean ($\bar{G}$) of k samples is equal to the sum of the deviation of the score (X) from its sample mean ($\bar{T}_j$) and the deviation of the sample mean ($\bar{T}_j$) from the grand mean ($\bar{G}$).*

Similarly, it can be shown algebraically that $df_{tot} = df_{wg} + df_{bg}$.

$$df_{wg} = k(n - 1) = nk - k$$
$$+\ df_{bg} = k - 1$$
$$= df_{tot} = (nk - k) + (k - 1) = nk - 1$$

Since $SS_{wg} + SS_{bg} = SS_{tot}$ and $df_{wg} + df_{bg} = df_{tot}$, SS_{tot} is used to check SS_{wg} and SS_{bg} computations, and df_{tot} is used to check df_{wg} and df_{bg} computations. Because the SS_{wg} and SS_{bg} make up the total sum of squares, computing SS_{wg} and SS_{bg} is referred to as *partitioning* the SS_{tot} into its component parts. In Chapter 16, you will see that the completely randomized design is the building block for a class of designs in which SS_{bg} can also be partitioned.

PROGRESS ASSESSMENT 14.4

Demonstrate your understanding of the relationships among SS_{bg}, SS_{wg}, and SS_{tot}, among df_{bg}, df_{wg}, and df_{tot}, among SS, df, and MS, and among MS_{bg}, MS_{wg}, and F by completing

1. Table 14-B.
2. Table 14-C.

TABLE 14-B
Partially Completed ANOVA Table

Source	SS	df	MS	F
Between groups	____	2	18.00	2.00
Within groups	____	____	____	
Total	____	11		

TABLE 14-C
Partially Completed ANOVA Table

Source	SS	df	MS	F
Between groups	_____	____	____	8.00
Within groups	_____	70	____	
Total	1836.00	74		

APPLYING ANOVA: A NUMERICAL EXAMPLE

We will now use the computational symbols and formulas in Table 14.3 to perform ANOVA on the data of Table 14.4. You should recognize these data as the hypothetical deprivation-activity data of Table 14.2. Table 14.4 differs from Table 14.2 in that it includes treatment (T_j) and grand (G) sums, and values for X^2 and T_j^2/n. These are included to help you understand how the values for the computational symbols are obtained.

TABLE 14.4
Postdeprivation Number of Wheel Revolutions (X) Made by Five Groups of Rats Deprived for 0, 6, 12, 18, or 24 Hours in the Hypothetical Deprivation-Activity Experiment and Summary Data Used to Calculate Values for Computational Symbols for ANOVA

	0 Hours		6 Hours		12 Hours		18 Hours		24 Hours	
	X	X^2	X	X^2	X	X^2	X	X^2	X	X^2
	86	7396	91	8281	100	10000	111	12321	116	13456
	94	8836	98	9604	93	8649	101	10201	112	12544
	82	6724	96	9216	107	11449	104	10816	108	11664
	90	8100	94	8836	102	10404	103	10609	119	14161
	98	9604	101	10201	98	9604	96	9216	105	11025
T_j	450		480		500		515		560	$G = 2505$
$T_j^2/n_j =$		40500		46080		50000		53045		62720

Computing Values for T_j and G

In performing ANOVA, the first thing to do is to compute values for T_j and G. It is less time consuming to compute values for T_j first because $\Sigma T_j = G$. You obtain a value for T_j by summing the X-values for the treatment level j. For example, if you let T_1, T_2, T_3, T_4, and T_5 correspond to the treatment groups that underwent 0, 6, 12, 18, and 24 hours of deprivation, respectively, then T_2 is obtained by summing 91, 98, 96, 94, and 101, which are the scores (X) in Table 14.4 of the rats undergoing treatment T_2 or 6 hours of deprivation. A value for G is then obtained by summing T_j as follows:

$$\Sigma T_j = G = 450 + 480 + 500 + 515 + 560 = 2505$$

Computing Values for Computational Symbols and *SS*

Having computed values for T_j and G, you should now compute values for the three computational symbols. Symbol (1) directs you to square G and divide the resulting value by the total number of scores, nk, that is $2505^2/25 = 251{,}001$. Computational symbol (2) directs you to square each X-value (these squared values constitute the X^2-columns in Table 14.4) and sum the squares. The sum of the X^2-values in Table 14.4 is 252,917. Computational symbol (3) directs you to square the sum of each treatment, divide each squared sum by its sample size, and add the resulting quotients as follows:

$$\Sigma \frac{T_j^2}{n} = \frac{T_1^2}{n} + \frac{T_2^2}{n} + \frac{T_3^2}{n} + \frac{T_4^2}{n} + \frac{T_5^2}{n}$$

$$= 40500 + 46080 + 50000 + 53045 + 62720$$

$$= 252{,}345$$

The values for symbols (1), (2), and (3) have been entered in Table 14.5.

The values of the computational symbols are then used to compute the values for SS_{bg}, SS_{wg}, and SS_{tot} in Table 14.5 as follows:

$$SS_{bg} = (3) - (1) = 252{,}345 - 251{,}001 = 1344$$

$$SS_{wg} = (2) - (3) = 252{,}917 - 252{,}345 = 572$$

$$SS_{tot} = (2) - (1) = 252{,}917 - 251{,}001 = 1916$$

Computing Values for *df*

The values for the degrees of freedom in Table 14.5 are obtained by using the *df*-formulas in Table 14.3 as follows:

$$df_{bg} = k - 1 = 5 - 1 = 4$$

$$df_{wg} = k(n - 1) = 5(5 - 1) = 20$$

$$df_{tot} = nk - 1 = 25 - 1 = 24$$

TABLE 14.5
Summary Table for ANOVA Performed on the Hypothetical
Deprivation-Activity Data of Table 14.4

Computational Symbol Values (a)	Source of Variation (b)	SS (c)	df (d)	MS (e)	F (f)
(1) = 251,001	Between groups	1344	4	336	11.75
(2) = 252,917	Within groups	572	20	28.6	
(3) = 252,345	Total	1916	24		

Computing Values for *MS* and *F*

Values for *MS* are obtained by dividing *SS* by its corresponding *df*:

$$MS_{bg} = \frac{SS_{bg}}{df_{bg}} = \frac{1344}{4} = 336$$

$$MS_{wg} = \frac{SS_{wg}}{df_{wg}} = \frac{572}{20} = 28.6$$

A value for *F* is then obtained by getting the ratio of the between-group estimate of σ^2 (MS_{bg}) to the within-group estimate of σ^2 (MS_{wg}) as follows:

$$F = \frac{MS_{bg}}{MS_{wg}} = \frac{336}{28.6} = 11.75$$

SUMMARIZING THE RESULTS OF ANOVA

If information obtained in ANOVA is to be used for further analysis, it is useful to organize the results in some working format. The most commonly used working format, however, is not the most suitable format for presenting your results in scientific reports. The following section describes the most widely used formats for summarizing and reporting the results of ANOVA.

Working Format

The values obtained for the computational symbols (*1*), (*2*), and (*3*) and *SS*, *df*, *MS*, and *F* are summarized in Table 14.5. The table is a convenient format for summarizing ANOVA. It allows you to see at a glance the computational values [column (a)] used in computing the between-group and within-group estimates [column (e)] of σ^2 and the overall outcome (*F*-ratio) of the analysis [column (f)]. You will also find the table useful if the ANOVA indicates you should continue your analysis, that is, if the number of treatment levels is greater than two ($k > 2$) and *F* is significant.

You can see that F is the same value as that obtained when we computed the two estimates of σ^2 using the familiar procedures of pooling the within-group variances and multiplying the variance of the means by the sample size. There are, however, advantages to using the computational symbols and formulas that we used in generating Table 14.5 rather than the more familiar s_p^2 and $Ns_{\bar{x}}^2$ procedures. For example, the newer formulas, unlike the more familiar ones, allow you to compute the between-group estimate of σ^2 when group sizes are unequal. Also, the computational symbols or the monomials they represent are used in performing ANOVA on data generated from experiments of more complex designs such as those you will encounter in Chapter 16.

Reporting Format

Although Table 14.5 is convenient for summarizing ANOVA, you typically do not present ANOVA in that format when writing up a scientific report. In the results section of a scientific report, you present summary measures such as means and standard deviations for your groups in a graph or table. You then indicate whether or not the ANOVA performed on the data yielded a significant effect of your independent variable and present the F-value with associated degrees of freedom in parentheses and the preset level of significance. We previously found the F-value (11.75) obtained in the ANOVA of the hypothetical deprivation-activity experiment to be significant. Thus, in a report on that experiment you could say that the ANOVA performed on the number of wheel revolutions made by rats in a a thirty-minute period yielded a significant effect of hours of food deprivation, $F(4, 20) = 11.75$, $p < 0.05$.

PROGRESS ASSESSMENT 14.5

The data in Table 14-D are those for the hypothetical experiment in Progress Assessment 14.1, part 1.

TABLE 14-D
Mean Number of Word Associations Made to Ten Affectively Neutral Word Stimuli in the Presence of Pleasant, Neutral, or Unpleasant Odors

Pleasant Odor	Neutral Odor	Unpleasant Odor
5.8	4.3	3.0
4.6	4.4	2.5
6.4	5.5	3.7
5.4	4.2	5.5
5.3	4.2	2.7
6.4	4.1	3.6

1. Perform an ANOVA on the data in Table 14-D and summarize your results in a working format.
2. Determine if your F-ratio is significant with $\alpha = 0.05$.
3. Symbolize H_0.
4. Reach a conclusion about H_0.
5. Report the results of your ANOVA as you would in a scientific report.

MEAN COMPARISONS FOLLOWING ANOVA

As mentioned previously, obtaining a significant F in ANOVA tells you that it is highly probable that the means of the populations from which your samples were drawn are not equal. If the number of treatment levels is greater than two, it does not tell you what means are likely to have differed from one another. Thus, your significant F directs you to further analyze your data. How you further analyze your data depends to a large extent on decisions you made or did not make in the planning stage of your experiment.

Planned Comparisons

If, in planning an experiment, you decide that there are certain mean comparisons that you should make, the comparisons are called **planned comparisons** and the tests you would use are called *a priori* **tests**. For example, if in planning the deprivation-activity experiment, you intended to compare each of the 6-, 12-, 18-, and 24-hour food-deprived groups with the 0-hour deprived control, or if you planned to compare each mean with every other mean, then these comparisons between two groups, **pairwise comparisons,** would be considered planned comparisons and would require *a priori* tests.

Unplanned Comparisons

If, on the other hand, during the planning stage of an experiment you have no specific comparisons in mind and a significant F leads you to explore the data to find out the source of the significant effect, then pairwise comparisons would be **unplanned comparisons** and would require *a posteriori* or *post hoc* **tests**.

Difference between *A Priori* and *A Posteriori* Tests

An important difference between *a priori* and *a posteriori* tests has to do with what values are used to determine if H_0 is rejected. If, for example, the F-test is used for planned comparisons, Appendix Table 6 is used to determine whether or not the H_0 for any specific pairwise comparison is rejected because each planned pairwise comparison is considered to be the basis on which alpha has been established. In essence, each comparison is considered to be a separate *CR-2* experiment. If the *F*-test is used for unplanned comparisons, then the individual comparisons are not considered as separate experiments, and Appendix Table 6 has to be adjusted to keep alpha at a fixed level as the number of possible comparisons increases (see the discussion on the need for a test like ANOVA at the beginning of this chapter).

An *A Priori* F-Test

In Chapter 2 we emphasized the need to give considerable thought as to how data should be analyzed and evaluated before attempting to collect data. In keeping with this emphasis we present an *a priori* *F*-test for making planned comparisons. Following is the formula for *F*:

Formula 14.11
$$F = \frac{(\bar{T}_j - \bar{T}_{j'})^2}{MS_{wg} \left(\frac{1}{n_j} + \frac{1}{n_{j'}} \right)}$$

where $\bar{T}_j$ and $\bar{T}_{j'}$ represent means of different groups in the experiment and n_j and $n_{j'}$ are the respective group sizes. The *df* associated with *F* are 1 and $k(n - 1)$ when *n*'s are equal and 1 and $N_{tot} - k$ when *n*'s are unequal. Formula 14.11 is used to compare the mean activity of the 6-hour deprived experimental group with the mean activity of the 0-hour deprived control group as follows:

$$F = \frac{(96 - 90)^2}{28.6(\frac{1}{5} + \frac{1}{5})} = \frac{36}{11.44} = 3.15$$

The calculated *F*, 3.15, is smaller than the *F*, 4.35, in Appendix Table 6 at the 0.05 level of significance with 1 and 20 *df*. You would, therefore, fail to reject H_0: $\mu_1 = \mu_2$ and conclude that six hours of food deprivation has no significant effect on the wheel-running activity of rats.

PROGRESS ASSESSMENT 14.6

The means for the five groups in the hypothetical weight-reduction experiment of Progress Assessment 14.1, part 2, are 13.33 (exercise only, $n = 6$), 18.57 (diet only, $n = 7$), 25.00 (diet plus exercise, $n = 5$), 16.25 (one-day fast, $n = 8$), and 3.33 (control, $n = 6$). Use the *a priori* *F*-test to compare the mean of each of the weight-reduction program groups with the mean of the control group and determine which mean differences are significant at the 0.01 level of significance. See Answers to Progress Assessments, 14.3, for values of *df* and *MS*.

Critical Values

When n's are equal and the number of pairwise comparisons to be made is large, it is too time consuming to perform a separate F-test for each comparison. In such cases it is preferable to obtain a **critical value (CV)**, the smallest absolute difference between $\bar{T}_j$ and $\bar{T}_{j'}$ that can be considered significant at the preset significance level.

Obtaining a critical value involves a procedure similar to that used in Chapter 11 to establish confidence intervals. You find in Appendix Table 6 for 1 and k ($n - 1$) degrees of freedom the value for F_{table} associated with the preset significance level and set that value equal to the right-hand side of Formula 14.11. You then multiply each side of the equation by the value of the denominator of the right-hand side of the equation (Formula 14.11) and take the square root of both sides. The value obtained is the critical value for a significant difference between $\bar{T}_j$ and $\bar{T}_{j'}$. The formula for a (CV) for $\bar{T}_j - \bar{T}_{j'}$ is as follows:

Formula 14.12 $\quad CV = \sqrt{F_{table}\,[MS_{wg}(\dfrac{1}{n_j} + \dfrac{1}{n_{j'}})]}$

If you plan to make all possible pairwise comparisons, you could set up a table of mean differences such as Table 14.6 where each value in the table is the absolute difference score for each pair of means. For example, the mean difference 9 in Table 14.6 is the absolute difference between $\bar{T}_4$ and $\bar{T}_5$:

$$9 = |\bar{T}_5 - \bar{T}_4| = |\bar{T}_4 - \bar{T}_5|$$

To determine the critical value for $|\bar{T}_j - \bar{T}_{j'}|$ in the table of mean differences at the 0.05 level of significance, enter Appendix Table 6 with 1 and 20 df to obtain $F_{table} = 4.35$. Substituting this value in Formula

TABLE 14.6
Absolute Values of Mean Differences ($|\bar{T}_j - \bar{T}_{j'}|$) for All Possible Pairwise Comparisons in the Hypothetical Deprivation-Activity Experiment

	$\bar{T}_2 = 96$	$\bar{T}_3 = 100$	$\bar{T}_4 = 103$	$\bar{T}_5 = 112$
$\bar{T}_1 = 90$	6	10*	13*	22*
$\bar{T}_2 = 96$		4	7	16*
$\bar{T}_3 = 100$			3	12*
$\bar{T}_4 = 103$				9*

* indicates $p \le 0.05$

14.12 along with MS_{wg} $(1/n_j + 1/n_{j'})$ and taking the square root of the product yields

$$CV = \sqrt{\frac{4.35(28.6)2}{5}} = 7.05.$$

Thus, all mean differences that are equal to or greater than 7.05 (indicated by an asterisk in Table 14.6) are significant at the 0.05 level of significance. As indicated, six of the ten pairwise comparisons are significant.

When the n's are unequal, an overall CV cannot be obtained. If such is the case, a separate F-test needs to be performed for each comparison.

PROGRESS ASSESSMENT 14.7

1. Establish a critical value at the 0.05 level of significance for all pairwise comparisons of the groups in Progress Assessment 14.5.

2. Set up a table of mean differences for the data in Progress Assessment 14.5 and indicate with an asterisk the differences that are significant at the 0.05 level of significance.

CONDITIONS UNDERLYING ANOVA

As with all statistical tests, the outcome of ANOVA can be correctly interpreted only if certain conditions have been satisfied. The conditions that must be satisfied for ANOVA to be correctly interpreted are identical to the conditions underlying the t-test for random independent samples. These conditions, you will recall, are as follows:

1. The samples must be randomly selected or must fullfull the conditions of randomness, such as randomized samples or samples that have been pretested for comparability.

2. The samples must be independent, that is, a subject's selection or assignment to a sample in no way affects how other subjects are selected or assigned to samples. Further, the dependent measures taken on the members of one sample must not be correlated with the dependent measures taken on members of other samples.

3. The measure of the dependent variable should be on an interval or ratio scale.

4. The samples must come from populations in which the characteristic of interest is normally distributed.

5. It is assumed that a specific level of the independent variable affects every member of the sample in the same way and, hence, does not

alter the sample variance. Thus, it is assumed that the variances of the characteristic of interest in the populations from which the samples were drawn are equal, that is, $\sigma_1^2 = \sigma_2^2 = \sigma_3^2 = \ldots \sigma_k^2$. This is the assumption of homogeneity of variance.

If any of these conditions is not satisfied, the distribution of the obtained F-value will be more variable than the theoretical **F-distribution** (Appendix Table 6) with which it is compared. This could result in rejecting a true H_0 (α-error) and concluding that the effect of your independent variable is significant at some preset level when it is not.

Procedures to Ensure That the Conditions of ANOVA Are Met

Ordinarily, you are aware of whether or not your samples are random independent samples. Although random selection may not be possible, you may be able to randomize the assignment of subjects or use other procedures that would ensure that the conditions of random independent samples have been met. Generally, then, the conditions of randomness and independence are rarely violated if you give these conditions consideration in the planning stage of your research and, of course, you select your dependent variable and the measuring instrument that you will use to measure it. Thus, the scale that you measure your dependent variable on is also under your direct control.

The conditions of normality and homogeneity of variance, however, are not under such direct control. Nevertheless, oftentimes they can be indirectly or statistically manipulated. For example, since heterogeneity of variance arises when different levels of the independent variable are differentially affecting posttreatment variances, selecting a dependent variable that has a large variance may prevent treatment-induced changes in variability from having appreciable effects. Normality can also be manipulated. Dependent variables that are not generally normally distributed can be transformed to dependent variables that are. Time scores, for example, that are often skewed can be transformed to reciprocal time scores, which are likely to be normally distributed.

Violations of the Conditions of ANOVA

When you do not have random independent samples, the one-way ANOVA does not lead to valid conclusions. This results when you do not give data collection sufficient consideration in the planning stage of your experiment. Nothing can be done. You have wasted time, effort, and money and have placed an unnecessary burden on your subjects. This is not necessarily the case if you fail to measure your dependent variable along an interval or ratio scale. Statistical tests appropriate for use with ordinal data are available. Also, violations of the conditions of normality and homogeneity of variance need not be so drastic or final. Generally, slight departures from normality and homogeneity of variance do not lead to an incorrect interpretation of ANOVA. Marked departures from normality and homogeneity of variance, however, do.

Marked departures from normality occur when the original population and posttreatment populations are extremely peaked or **leptokurtic,** extremely flat or **platykurtic,** or when different levels of the independent variable lead to different distributions of the characteristic of interest. There are tests that indicate whether or not there is departure from normality in large samples. Ordinarily, however, such tests are not carried out unless there is some reason to suspect a marked departure from normality. A marked departure from normality would most likely be detected by casting the scores in the form of a frequency distribution. For smaller samples, you must rely on your knowledge of the population characteristics or take solace in the finding that the F-distribution is insensitive to the distribution of the characteristic of interest if the distribution is common to all posttreatment populations. Fortunately, when there is marked departure from normality, there are alternative nonparametric tests that can lead to valid conclusions.

Nonparametric tests are also used when there is marked departure from homogeneity of variance. Marked departure from homogeneity of variance occurs when the variance of the original population is small in comparison to the variance of the posttreatment populations or when the different treatments lead to different amount of variability in the characteristic of interest. Again, fortunately, an F-test similar to the test for homogeneity of variance discussed in Chapter 12 allows you to determine if there is heterogeneity of variance when there are more than two levels of the independent variable. If heterogeneity of variance is detected, there is a nonparametric ANOVA by ranks that allows you to determine whether or not the independent variable is having an effect.

THE F_{max} TEST FOR DETECTING HETEROGENEITY OF VARIANCE

In most cases you will have no knowledge of the effect that different levels of the independent variable will have on the population variance. To determine if your independent variable has led to a serious departure from homogeneity of variance, you can test the null hypothesis, H_0: $\sigma_1^2 = \sigma_2^2 = \sigma_3^2 = \ldots = \sigma_k^2$, by getting the ratio of the largest variance to the smallest variance. This ratio is distributed as F_{max} for k treatment levels and $df = n - 1$ where $n - 1$ is the df for each within group variance. When the group sizes are unequal, $n - 1$ for the *largest sample* (not the largest variance) is used as the df.

Computation of F_{max}

The formula for F_{max} is as follows:

Formula 14.13 $\quad F_{max} = \dfrac{\text{largest variance}}{\text{smallest variance}} = \dfrac{s^2_{largest}}{s^2_{smallest}}$

An application of Formula 14.13 is illustrated using the data from Table 14.2. The variances of the five treatment groups in the hypothetical deprivation-activity experiment are 40.0, 14.5, 26.5, 29.5, and 32.5 for the 0-, 6-, 12-, 18-, and 24-hour deprived groups, respectively. Thus,

$$F_{max} = \frac{40.0}{14.5} = 2.76$$

From the F_{max} table (Appendix Table 9), at the 0.05 level of significance, when $k = 5$ and $n - 1 = 4$, $F_{max} = 25.2$. Since the F_{max} obtained for the deprivation-activity experiment is less than the table-value, you fail to reject H_0: $\sigma^2_1 = \sigma^2_2 = \sigma^2_3 = \sigma^2_4 = \sigma^2_5$. If the F_{max} test indicated that you were to reject the hypothesis of homogeneity of variance, then the parametric one-way ANOVA would not be an appropriate analysis.

A *CR-k* Design for Which the Parametric One-Way ANOVA Is Not Appropriate

A number of experiments have shown that when subjected to a situation in which their behavior has no effect on an environmental event, humans and animals have difficulty responding appropriately in subsequent, similar situations. This phenomenon is referred to as learned helplessness.

Suppose that, in one such experiment, four groups of college sophomores are subjected to different numbers (0, 10, 20, or 30) of unsolvable five-letter anagrams and are later given 30 unsolvable six-letter anagrams to solve in a one-hour period. The different numbers of unsolvable anagrams constitute different levels of the independent variable and the number of solvable anagrams solved in the one-hour period constitutes the dependent measure. Suppose further that the data in Table 14.7 represent the outcome of this experiment.

The F_{max} test performed on the data of Table 14.7 yields the following: $F_{max} = 95.6/1.4 = 68.3$. Comparing 68.3 with the value of F_{max} in Appendix Table 9 at the 0.05 level of significance where $k = 4$ and $n - 1 = 6$ leads you to reject the hypothesis of homogeneity of variance. Since there is marked heterogeneity of variance, the data cannot be properly evaluated using the parametric one-way ANOVA. However, a nonparametric test can be used to determine if your independent variable has an effect.

PROGRESS ASSESSMENT 14.8

1. Perform the F_{max} test on the data of Progress Assessment 14.5.
2. Determine if heterogeneity of variance is detected by the F_{max} test.

TABLE 14.7
The Number of Solvable Anagrams Solved in a One-Hour Period by Groups 1, 2, 3, and 4 after Being Subjected to 0, 10, 20, and 30 Unsolvable Anagrams, Respectively

	Group 1	Group 2	Group 3	Group 4
	28	29	27	24
	26	26	14	0
	29	18	14	5
	27	22	24	19
	28	25	19	7
	29	20	17	21
				10
$\bar{X} =$	27.8	23.3	19.1	12.3
s^2	1.4	16.7	28.6	95.6

A NONPARAMETRIC ONE-WAY ANOVA

The **Kruskal-Wallis one-way ANOVA by ranks** is a nonparametric test that is used to determine if k random independent samples come from different populations. As with the parametric one-way ANOVA discussed above, the Kruskal-Wallis test helps you to decide if the differences that you observe among your groups is due to sampling error or indicate real population differences. Like all nonparametric tests, however, it does not provide information about population parameters. Thus, the Kruskal-Wallis ANOVA does not test the hypothesis that all the means are equal. It simply tests the null hypothesis that the populations from which the samples were drawn do not differ.

Deciding When the Kruskal-Wallis Test Is Appropriate

The Kruskal-Wallis test is typically used when the dependent variable constitutes an ordinal scale or when the dependent variable is measured on an interval or ratio scale and the condition of normality or homogeneity of variance is not met. The Kruskal-Wallis ANOVA, however, is applied only to data that are ranked collectively. Thus, if the measure of your dependent variable is along an interval or ratio scale, or along an ordinal scale that is not ranked across groups, the measures must be ranked collectively. This is accomplished by ranking the measures from all group members from the lowest to the highest just as you did when performing the Mann-Whitney U-test (Chapter 12). The data of Table 14.7 are ranked collectively in Table 14.8.

TABLE 14.8
Ranked Data for the Number of Solvable Anagrams
Solved in One Hour by Groups 1, 2, 3, and 4 after
Being Subjected to 0, 10, 20, and 30 Unsolvable
Anagrams, Respectively

Group 1	Group 2	Group 3	Group 4
21.5	24	19.5	14.5
17.5	17.5	5.5	1
24	8	5.5	2
19.5	13	14.5	9.5
21.5	16	9.5	3
24	11	7	12
			4
$R_1 = 128.0$	$R_2 = 89.5$	$R_3 = 61.5$	$R_4 = 46.0$

Applying the Formula for the Kruskal-Wallis Statistic, *K-W*

The formula for the Kruskal-Wallis statistic, **K-W**, is as follows:

Formula 14.14 $K\text{-}W = \dfrac{12}{N_{tot}(N_{tot} + 1)}\left(\dfrac{\Sigma R_j^2}{n_j}\right) - 3(N_{tot} + 1)$

In Formula 14.14, N_{tot} is the total number of scores, n_j is the number of scores in the jth treatment level, R_j is the sum of the ranks for the jth treatment level, and 3 and 12 are constants.

Formula 14.14 is applied to the ranked data of Table 14.8 as follows:

$$K\text{-}W = \frac{12}{25(25 + 1)}\left(\frac{128.0^2}{6} + \frac{89.5^2}{6} + \frac{61.5^2}{6} + \frac{46.0^2}{7}\right) - 3(25 + 1)$$

$$= 0.018(4998.37) - 78 = 11.97$$

Stating a Decision Rule and Evaluating *H₀*

Following is the decision rule for a test of the null hypothesis:

$$\text{If } K\text{-}W_{calc} \geq K\text{-}W_{table}, \text{ reject } H_0.$$

For sample sizes greater than 5, the calculated value of *K-W* is compared to the critical value of *K-W* associated with $k\text{-}1$ df in Appendix Table 10 at the preset level of significance. Comparing the 11.97 calculated for *K-W* in the hypothetical anagram experiment of Table 14.8 with the critical value (7.81) of *K-W* for 3 df at the 0.05 significance level directs you to reject H_0: the populations from which the samples were drawn do not differ.

For sample sizes smaller than 5, special probability tables need to be computed. Siegel and Castellan (1988) present one such table for sample sizes 1 to 5 when $k = 3$.

Making Planned Comparisons Following the Kruskal-Wallis ANOVA

For planned comparisons following rejection of H_0 with the Kruskal-Wallis test, investigators often use the Mann-Whitney U-test.

PROGRESS ASSESSMENT 14.9

A psychology instructor wants to find out if the physical location in which students study for exams is a determining factor in the grade they achieve on the exam. Prior to the first exam the instructor surveys twenty-five freshmen enrolled in the Principles of Psychology course to find out where they plan to study for the upcoming exam. Nine say that they always study in the dormitory room and plan to study there for the upcoming exam. Eight say they plan to study in the library and eight say they plan to study in a classroom. The exam scores for the three groups are shown in Table 14-E.

TABLE 14-E
Exams Scores of Three Groups of Freshmen Who Studied in Either a Dormitory, the Library, or a Classroom

Exam Scores after Dormitory Study	Exam Scores after Library Study	Exam Scores after Classroom Study
78	86	92
63	83	86
87	89	79
72	86	88
70	85	90
65	81	93
59	87	82
71	86	79
73		

1. Perform the F_{max} test and determine if there is heterogeneity of variance at the 1% level of significance.
2. Rank the exam scores, assigning 1 to the lowest score, 2 to the next higher score, and so forth.
3. Perform the Kruskal-Wallis one-way ANOVA on the ranked scores.
4. State the null hypothesis that the Kruskal-Wallis ANOVA is testing.
5. On the basis of your obtained K-W, reach a conclusion about H_0.

SUMMARY

In this chapter you are introduced to an experimental design, the completely randomized design, in which there are two or more levels of a single independent variable. You are also provided with the analytical tools to determine if different levels of the independent variable differentially affect the dependent variable. These tools are referred to as analyses of variance. (ANOVA). Both the parametric and nonparametric ANOVA are presented. The special symbols and formulas associated with the parametric ANOVA are discussed at length and examples of their application are given. The hypothesis being tested by ANOVA, the need for a test like ANOVA, and the logic of ANOVA are also presented along with the tests for making planned comparisons following ANOVA. Consideration is given to the conditions under which the parametric and nonparametric tests would be most appropriately applied. Consideration is also given to the $F_{\max}$ test, which is used to test the hypothesis of homogeneity of variance, a condition required for the parametric ANOVA.

KEY DEFINITIONS

analysis of variance (ANOVA)   A parametric test used to test a hypothesis about means for any number of treatment levels ($k \geq 2$).

ANOVA   Acronym for analysis of variance.

a posteriori **test** or *post hoc* **test**   A test used to make unplanned comparisons of means, that is, comparisons that were not planned prior to collecting the data.

a priori **test**   A test used to make planned comparisons of means, that is, comparisons that are decided on in the planning stages of the experiment.

between-group degrees of freedom   The number of group means minus one.

between-group estimate of σ^2   Group size (n) times the variance of the means.   The between-group sum of squares divided by the between-group degrees of freedom.

between-group mean square   The adjusted average of the deviations of the sample means from the mean of all the scores.

between-group sum of squares   The sample size times the sum of the squared deviations of the sample means from the grand mean.

completely randomized designs   A class of experimental designs in which there are two or more treatment levels of a single independent variable.

critical value   The smallest absolute value of a mean difference that will lead to a rejection of the null hypothesis, $H_0: \mu_j = \mu_{j'}$.

CR-k   The symbol for a completely randomized design in which there are k-independent samples.

CV   The symbol for critical value.

CV $= \sqrt{F_{\text{table}}\,[MS_{\text{wg}}(1/n_j + 1/n_{j'})]}$ Critical value for the *a priori* F-test for making comparisons between means.

degrees of freedom   The number of deviations minus the number of points about which the deviations are taken.

***df*$_{\text{bg}}$**   The symbol for between-group degrees of freedom.

***df*$_{\text{bg}}$ $= k - 1$**   The formula for computing the between-group degrees of freedom.

***df*$_{\text{tot}}$**   The symbol for the total degrees of freedom.

***df*$_{\text{tot}}$ $= nk - 1$**   The formula for computing the total degrees of freedom when samples sizes are equal.

***df*$_{\text{tot}}$ $= N_{\text{tot}} - 1$**   The formula for computing the total degrees of freedom when samples sizes are unequal.

***df*$_{\text{wg}}$**   The symbol for the within-group degrees of freedom.

***df*$_{\text{wg}}$ $= k(n - 1)$**   The formula for computing the within-group degrees of freedom when sample sizes are equal.

***df*$_{\text{wg}}$ $= N_{\text{tot}} - k$**   The formula for computing the within-group degrees of freedom when the sample sizes are unequal.

***F*-distribution**   Theoretical distribution of the ratio of two variances.

F $= MS_{\text{bg}}/MS_{\text{wg}}$ Formula for obtaining F in the one-way ANOVA.

F $= (\bar{T}_j - \bar{T}_{j'})^2/MS_{\text{wg}}(1/n_j + 1/n_{j'})$ The formula for obtaining F in the *a priori* F-test.

***F*$_{\text{max}}$**   The ratio of the largest variance to the smallest variance when there are more than two levels of an independent variable.

***F*$_{\text{max}}$ $= s^2_{\text{largest}}/s^2_{\text{smallest}}$**   Formula used to compute F_{max}.

***F*-ratio** or ***F* in the one-way ANOVA**   Ratio of the between-group mean square to the within-group mean square.

G   The grand total; the symbol for the sum of all scores obtained in the experiment.

Ḡ   (pronounced "G-bar") The grand mean; the symbol for the mean of all the scores obtained in the experiment.

grand mean   Mean of all the scores obtained in the experiment.

grand sum   Sum of all the scores obtained in the experiment.

j   The subscript used to denote a specific $(j = 1, 2, 3, \ldots k)$ treatment or group.

k   The symbol used to denote the number of treatment levels or groups in a completely randomized design.

Kruskal-Wallis one-way ANOVA by ranks   A nonparametric test used to determine if k independent samples come from different populations, where $k \geq 2$.

K-W   The symbol for the statistic obtained in the Kruskal-Wallis one-way ANOVA by ranks.

K-W = $[12/N_{tot}(N_{tot} + 1)]\Sigma(R_j^2/n_j) - 3(N_{tot} + 1)$ The formula used to obtain the statistic for the Kruskal-Wallis one-way ANOVA by ranks.

leptokurtic   The term used to refer to a distribution that is extremely peaked in appearance.

mean square   Variance in the ANOVA; the adjusted average of squared deviations from the mean.

monomial   An expression consisting of one term.

MS   The symbol for mean square.

MS_{bg}   The symbol for the between-group mean square.

$MS_{bg} = SS_{bg}/df_{bg}$ The formula used to compute the between-group mean square.

MS_{wg}   The symbol for the within-group mean square.

$MS_{wg} = SS_{wg}/df_{wg}$ The formula used to compute the within-group mean square.

$\mu_1 = \mu_2 = \mu_3 = \ldots = \mu_k$ The symbolized null hypothesis for the parametric one-way ANOVA.

n   The symbol for the number of scores in a group.

n_j   The symbol for the number of scores in a specific ($j = 1, 2, 3 \ldots k$) group.

N_{tot}   Symbol for the total number of obtained scores when group sizes are not equal.

null hypothesis for the parametric one-way ANOVA   A statement that the means of the populations from which the samples were drawn are equal.

one-way ANOVA   The analysis of variance used to analyze the data generated by a *CR-k* experiment.

pairwise comparisons   Comparisons between any two groups in an experimental design involving two or more groups.

planned comparisons   The comparisons one decides to make in the planning stages of an experiment.

platykurtic   The term used to refer to a distribution that is extremely flat in appearance.

R_j   The symbol for the sum of the ranked scores of a specific ($j = 1, 2, 3, \ldots k$) treatment group.

$s_p^2 = \dfrac{(N_1 - 1)s_1^2 + (N_2 - 1)s_2^2 + \ldots + (N_k - 1)s_k^2}{N_1 + N_2 + \ldots N_k - k}$ The formula for computing the pooled variance of k independent samples.

SS The symbol for the sum of squares used in the parametric one-way ANOVA.

SS_{bg} The symbol for the between-group sum of squares.

$SS_{bg} = n[\Sigma(\bar{T}_j - \bar{G})^2]$ The defining equation for the between-group sum of squares.

$SS_{bg} = (3) - (1) = \Sigma T_j^2/n - G^2/nk$ The computational formula for the between-group sum of squares.

SS_{tot} The symbol for the total sum of squares.

$SS_{tot} = \Sigma(X - \bar{G})^2$ The defining equation for the total sum of squares.

$SS_{tot} = (2) - (1) = \Sigma X^2 - G^2/nk$ The computational formula for the total sum of squares.

SS_{wg} The symbol for the within-group sum of squares.

$SS_{wg} = \Sigma SS_j = \Sigma[\Sigma(X - \bar{T}_j)^2]$ The defining equation for the within-group sum of squares.

$SS_{wg} = (2) - (3) = \Sigma X^2 - \Sigma T_j^2/n$ The computational formula for the within-group sum of squares.

sum of squares The term given to the sum of the squared deviations from the mean in the parametric one-way ANOVA.

T_j The symbol for the sum of the scores for a specific ($j = 1, 2, 3, \ldots k$) treatment group.

$\bar{T}_j$ (pronounced "T_j-bar") The mean of the scores of a specific ($j = 1, 2, 3 \ldots k$) treatment group.

total sum of squares The sum of the squared deviations of all the obtained scores from the mean of all the scores.

unplanned comparisons Comparisons used to explore the data to find out the source of significance of the F in ANOVA.

within-group degrees of freedom The sum of the degrees of freedom for the individual treatment groups.

within-group estimate of σ^2 The within-group sum of squares divided by the within-group degrees of freedom.

within-group mean square The name given to the within-group estimate of σ^2.

within-group sum of squares The sum of the sums of squares of the individual treatment groups.

REVIEW EXERCISES

For experimental designs in Problems 1 and 2 do the following:

a. State the dependent and independent variables.

b. State the scale on which the dependent variable is measured: nominal, ordinal, interval, or ratio.

c. Tell whether the dependent variable is continuous or discrete.

d. Determine if the samples are biased, random, or randomized samples.

e. Symbolize the type of design.

f. Compute the mean and variance of each treatment group.

g. Perform the F_{max} test for homogeneity of variance.

h. State whether F_{max} is significant at the 0.05 level of significance.

i. On the basis of F_{max}, perform the most appropriate ANOVA and determine if the F or K-W is significant.

j. State the null hypothesis in words.

k. If the parametric ANOVA is performed, give the hypothesis in symbols.

l. Use the appropriate *a priori* test to compare each experimental group with the control group.

m. If the parametric ANOVA is performed, establish a critical value for all pairwise comparisons, set up a table of mean differences, and indicate which differences are significant at the 5 percent level of significance (indicate with an asterisk).

n. State the research hypothesis.

o. Tell whether or not the experimental results support the research hypothesis.

1. Modeling is a therapeutic technique used often with children. It is particularly effective in alleviating fear. Children who are afraid to engage in a particular activity may be less afraid if they see that others do not get hurt when they engage in that activity. A social learning theorist wants to see which of several models is the most effective in alleviating fear in seven- to nine-year-old boys. The theorist hypothesizes that boys will be most influenced by models their own age. Twenty-four boys, age seven to nine, with a severe dog phobia are randomly assigned to each of four equal-size treatment groups. Each of the groups is shown a half-hour movie about dogs. In three of the movies human individuals interact with dogs and do not get hurt. In one of these, seven- to nine-year-old boys are shown playing with dogs—chasing them, being chased by them, petting them, and so forth. In another, fourteen- to sixteen-year-old boys are engaged in similar activities with dogs. The last movie in which there is human interaction with dogs uses adult males as the model. In the fourth movie, the dogs engage in nonaggressive behavior but there is no interaction with humans. After viewing the movie, the children are individually taken to a courtyard where they are left alone with a dog. Several independent observers who are unaware of the type of movie that the child watched measure the closest distance (in feet) that the child comes to the dog with 0 feet indicating contact with the dog. Finding the measured distances of the independent observers to be in close agreement, the social learning theorist selects the median score for each child to analyze. The data are shown in Table 14-F.

2. Memory for a learned event can be interfered with by memories of similar events acquired earlier (proactive interference) or later (retroactive interference) than the memory of the event in question. An investigator believes that proactive interference will result in greater memory impairment for verbal learning than will retroactive interference. To determine which type of interference produces the greater memory impairment for word lists, the investigator has three groups of ten subjects each learn lists of twenty-five consonant-vowel-consonant nonsense syllables such as MOL, TAK, FEQ. The subjects who comprise the three groups are randomly assigned to the three treatment levels of the independent variable. The subjects of one group learn list A followed by list B and then are immediately tested for recall of list B (proactive interference group). The subjects of another group learn list B followed by list A and are then immediately tested for recall of list B (retroactive interference group). Members of the third group learn only list B and are tested for recall of list B (control group). Five members of the control group are asked to recall list B immediately after learning the list. The other five members are asked to recall list B after a time comparable to that taken by the retroactive interference group to learn list A. An analysis of the number of nonsense syllables recalled by the two halves of the control group indicates there is no significance difference in recall. The data of the two subgroups are, therefore, combined for subsequent analysis. The data are shown in Table 14-G.

3. A statistics professor wants to know if the type of final exam given makes a difference in how well students perform on the exam. One semester when there are twenty students in the class the professor decides to administer two different kinds of tests for the final. One test consists of twenty-five problems that the student has to solve. The second test has the same twenty-five problems in the form of multiple-choice questions. The professor randomly puts the two types of test in a pile and then passes them out to the students. Each correct answer is worth 4 points. The following are the scores earned by the two groups of students:

Problems: 89, 78, 89, 71, 91, 88, 79, 89, 93, 95

Multiple Choice: 78, 67, 74, 88, 78, 85, 75, 78, 82, 81

a. Compute the mean, median, and mode for each group.

b. Compute the range, variance, and standard deviation for each group.

c. Convert the mode in each distribution to a z-score.

d. Test for homogeneity of variance.

e. Perform the most appropriate test to determine if the two groups differ significantly at the 0.05 level of significance.

TABLE 14-F
Median Distance from Dog in Feet after Viewing Films of Seven- to Nine-Year-Old Models, Fourteen- to Sixteen-Year-Old Models, Adult Models, or No Models Interacting with Dogs

Models Age 7–9	Models Age 14–16	Adult Models	No Models
10.0	6.7	10.0	15.5
7.5	10.6	12.0	20.0
10.1	13.2	13.5	18.5
13.8	15.3	15.5	17.4
11.5	15.0	12.1	19.1
8.1	14.2	14.4	21.5

TABLE 14-G
Number of Nonsense Syllables Recalled

Proactive Interference Group	Retroactive Interference Group	Control Group
14	15	19
8	16	21
12	13	20
11	12	22
19	11	19
13	20	18
11	22	19
9	11	21
12	12	22
17	10	23

    f. State whether you reject or fail to reject H_0.

    g. Symbolize H_0.

    h. Perform an ANOVA on the two groups.

    i. Compare your results from the ANOVA with the two-sample test in part *e*; discover the relationship between the two statistics.

ANSWERS TO PROGRESS ASSESSMENTS

14.1   **1. a.** The single independent variable is the type of odor used to induce an affective state.

        b. *CR*-3

        c. The means of the populations from which the samples were drawn are equal.

        d. $H_0: \mu_1 = \mu_2 = \mu_3$

        e. H_1: The means of the populations from which the samples were drawn are not all equal.

    2. a. The single independent variable is the type of weight-reduction program.

        b. *CR*-5

        c. The means of the populations from which the samples were drawn are equal.

        d. $H_0: \mu_1 = \mu_2 = \mu_3 = \mu_4 = \mu_5$

        e. H_1: The means of the populations from which the samples were drawn are not all equal.

14.2   **1.** The within-group and between-group variances remain the same.

    2. The within-group variance remains the same and the between-group variance increases.

3. The within-group variance remains the same and the between-group variance increases.

14.3   1. See Table 14-H.

TABLE 14-H
Values for *SS, df, MS,* and *F* for Table 14-A

Source	SS	df	MS	F
Between groups	1434.35	4	358.59	29.54
Within groups	327.87	27	12.14	
Total	1762.22	31		

2. The *F*-ratio is significant at the 0.01 level.

3. Reject H_0.

14.4   1. See Table 14-I.

2. See Table 14-J.

14.5   1. See Table 14-K.

2. *F* is significant.

3. H_0: $\mu_1 = \mu_2 = \mu_3$

4. Reject H_0.

5. $F_{(2, 15)} = 10.71$, $p < 0.05$

14.6 $F_{(1, 27)} = 24.69$, $p < 0.01$ (exercise only vs. control); $F_{(1, 27)} = 61.77$, $p < 0.01$ (diet only vs. control); $F_{(1, 27)} = 105.53$, $p < 0.01$ (exercise plus diet vs. control); $F_{(1, 27)} = 47.16$, $p < 0.01$ (one-day fast vs. control).

14.7   1. $CV = 0.99$

2. See Table 14-L.

TABLE 14-I
Values for *SS, df, MS* and *F* for Table 14-B

Source	SS	df	MS	F
Between groups	36.00	2	18.00	2.00
Within groups	81.00	9	9.00	
Total	117.00	11		

TABLE 14-J
Values for *SS, df, MS,* and *F* for Table 14-C

Source	SS	df	MS	F
Between groups	576.00	4	144.00	8.00
Within groups	1260.00	70	18.00	
Total	1836.00	74		

TABLE 14-K
Summary Table for ANOVA Performed on Hypothetical Data in Table 14-D

Computational Symbol Values	Source	SS	df	MS	F
(1) = 369.92	Between groups	13.93	2	6.96	10.71
(2) = 393.60	Within groups	9.75	15	0.65	
(3) = 383.85	Total	23.68	17		

TABLE 14-L
Absolute Values of Mean Differences for the Data in Table 14-D in Progress Assessment 14.5

	$\bar{T}_{neutral}$	$\bar{T}_{unpleasant}$
$\bar{T}_{pleasant}$	1.20*	2.15*
$\bar{T}_{neutral}$		0.95

*indicates $p \leq 0.05$

14.8
1. $F_{max} = 4.32$
2. Heterogeneity is not detected.

14.9
1. Because $F_{max} = 11.60$ which is greater than the critical value, heterogeneity is detected.
2. See Table 14-M.
3. $K\text{-}W = 10.02$
4. The populations from which the samples were drawn do not differ.
5. Reject H_0.

TABLE 14-M
Ranks of Exam Scores in Table 14-E.

Exam Score after Dormitory Study	Exam Score after Library Study	Exam Score after Classroom Study
8	16.5	24
2	13	16.5
19.5	22	9.5
6	16.5	21
4	14	23
3	11	25
1	19.5	12
5	16.5	9.5
7		

Randomized Block and Repeated Measures Designs: Dependent Samples Analyses of Variance

ment levels of a single independent variable and does not require a subject to experience more than one level. Also, in comparison with factorial designs discussed in the next chapter, there is simplicity in the analysis and interpretation of results.

Negative features derive mainly from the bases on which blocks are formed. If the number of treatment levels is large, it may be impossible to form blocks on the basis of a common heredity or difficult to form them with minimal within-group variability on the basis of a mutual category. Also, if matching by premeasurement of the dependent variable is the basis on which blocks are formed to obtain *k*-matched subjects, a lot more individuals may need to be pretested or measured than will participate in the experiment.

PROGRESS ASSESSMENT 15.2

For Problems 1 and 2 do the following:

  a. Identify the single independent variable.
  b. Symbolize the design.
  c. Indicate the blocking factor.

  1. In the Thematic Apperception Test, an individual views pictures of a person or persons and makes up a story about the pictures. An investigator interested in factors that influence the fantasy content of the stories recruits three subjects from each of ten age groups ranging from five to fifty years old. Each member of an age group views the pictures under a different one of three lighting conditions. The stories are scored for their fantasy content.

  2. To investigate the effects of success and failure on an individual's attention to the social environment, a social psychologist has individuals who are strangers to each other arrive in a waiting room at the same time. The individuals spend ten minutes together and then each is taken to a separate room and questioned about the other people in the waiting room (for example, How many people were blond? How many had an article of red clothing?). The individuals are scored on their accuracy and divided into three groups in which the members of any one group have corresponding members in the other two groups with identical scores. Each member of a group is required to perform a task. The experimenter then manipulates the feelings of the individuals by telling them that they performed very well (success condition), very poorly (failure condition), or by telling them nothing (control condition). A confederate of the experimenter then enters the room, engages in some activity unrelated to the individuals and the experimenter, and leaves. The individuals who perform the task are later asked about the characteristics of the confederate. The number of characteristics remembered by the individuals is tallied.

REPEATED MEASURES (*RM-k*) DESIGN

Experimental designs that employ a single independent variable and assign each subject or sample member to *all* treatment levels are referred to as **repeated-measures designs.** This class of designs is symbolized ***RM-k*** where $k \geq 2$ and represents the number of treatment levels of a single independent variable. The term *repeated-measures* refers to the procedure of obtaining a measure of the dependent variable for each subject or sample element for each of the k-treatment levels. The order in which the subjects experience the different treatment levels is generally randomly assigned or established in such a way as to control for sequence effects. Assigning treatment levels to subjects in a way that controls for sequence effects is referred to as **counterbalance assignment.** One way to control for sequence effects is to ensure that each possible ordering of the k-treatment levels is assigned an equal number of times.

Just as the experimenter employing the *RB-k* design is not generally interested in a difference between blocks, the experimenter employing the *RM-k* design most often is not interested in differences between subjects. The major reason for using the *RM-k* design is to separate individual differences from experimental error to more easily detect treatment effects.

Experimental Examples of the *RM-k* Design

The *RM-k* designs differ in the order in which subjects experience the treatment levels and in the number (k) of treatment levels. The following experimental designs illustrate three different orderings.

Random Assignment. A drug company interested in the effectiveness of three different pain relievers in eliminating headaches recruits seven individuals who suffer frequently from intense headaches. Each recruit is given four different packets identified by letters *a, b, c,* and *d*. Each of three of the packets contain a different one of the pain-relieving drugs in pill form. The remaining packet contains a placebo, a pill resembling the pain pills but without the pain-relieving ingredient. The recruits are instructed to take the pills in a packet after the onset of four headaches that occur at least forty-eight hours apart. They are also instructed which packet, *a, b, c,* or *d*, to take after the first, second, third, and fourth headache. The order in which the packets are to be taken is randomized for each subject. Each recruit is asked to record the time it takes from taking the pills until the headache is gone.

In this *RM-4* design, random assignment of the order in which the pain reliever is taken is appropriate because the stipulated forty-eight hour spacing makes it unlikely that there would be any carryover effect of the drugs from one headache to another. When there is the possibility of such carryover effects, counterbalance assignment would be in order.

Counterbalance Assignment. An investigator of short-term memory is interested in whether or not the duration of tachistoscopic exposure of words is a potent variable in the short-term retention of word lists. A tachistoscope is an electronically or hand-operated apparatus that projects single-glance visual stimuli for a brief (0.01 to 0.1 seconds) period of time.

Six people are randomly selected from a pool of subjects to participate in an experiment. Each participant is given five consecutive trials under each of three exposure durations: 0.01, 0.05, and 0.1 second. A trial consists of the presentation of fifteen words at two-second intervals. Each of the six participants experiences the exposure durations in a different one of the six possible orders: 0.01, 0.05, 0.1; 0.01, 0.1, 0.05; 0.05, 0.01, 0.1; 0.05, 0.1, 0.01; 0.1, 0.05, 0.01; 0.1, 0.01, 0.05. The assignment of these arranged orders to subjects is on a random basis. Immediately after the last trial for an exposure duration, the participant is asked to recall in any order as many of the fifteen words as possible. The number of items recalled constitutes the data subjected to statistical analysis.

In this *RM*-3 design, counterbalance assignment is more appropriate than random assignment of durations because this assignment of treatment levels is designed to distribute practice effects as evenly as possible over the three durations.

Fixed-Order Assignment. At times it is impossible to counterbalance or randomly assign treatment levels. This occurs quite often in learning experiments where interest is in the subjects' performance assessed over trials, sessions, or intervals of time. In these cases the technique used is a **fixed-order assignment,** an ordering in which the subject experiences the treatment levels as determined by the intrinsic characteristics of the independent variable.

For example, a researcher devises an apparatus to measure learning in infant rats where a correct response by the rat pup results in reinforcement of the response. The apparatus consists of a small container that houses a small panel which the infant rat can easily depress by pushing its nose against it. Each depression of the panel results in a drop of milk (food reinforcement) being delivered to the rat's mouth. To determine if the apparatus is effective in the instrumental training of rat pups, the researcher computes and statistically analyzes the number of panel depressions for each five-minute period of a 30-minute training session. The six 5-minute periods constitute the treatment levels in this *RM*-6 design.

It should be obvious that a 5-minute period cannot be randomly assigned to subjects. A subject cannot experience the second 5-minute period before the first, or the fifth before the fourth. It should also be clear that the researcher's question cannot be answered with a *RB-k* design.

Positive and Negative Features of the *RM-k* Design

The positive and negative features of the *RM-k* design are similar to those of the *RB-k* design.

On the positive side, the *RM-k* design can employ any number of treatment levels and offers simplicity in the analysis and interpretation of the results. Also, like the *RB-k* design, in comparison with the *CR-k* design, the *RM-k* design is more powerful in that its use makes it more likely that a false null hypothesis will be rejected. An advantage that the *RM-k* design has over both the *CR-k* and the *RB-k* designs is economy in terms of subjects. The *CR-k* and *RB-k* designs will generally require *k* times as many subjects as the *RM-k* design.

On the negative side, requiring a subject to participate under all levels of the independent variable can be problematic. If the number of treatment levels is large and the treatment is taxing, a subject may not be able to undergo all treatment levels. Also, if the subject does experience all levels of the independent variable, there is always the possibility that sequence or practice effects will *confound* (that is, be inextricably mixed up with) treatment effects, making the results of the analysis difficult to interpret. This is particularly troublesome when the order in which the levels are to be experienced cannot be counterbalanced across subjects.

PROGRESS ASSESSMENT 15.3

For Problems 1 and 2 do the following:

a. Identify the independent variable
b. Symbolize the experimental design.
c. Determine the assignment (random, counterbalanced, or fixed-order) of subjects to the levels of the independent variable.

1. An electrical tool manufacturer engages a human engineering firm to determine which of four differently shaped handles would be best for a new power screwdriver the company is producing. Four prototype screwdrivers are assembled, each with a different handle. An engineer then has eight individuals use each of the screwdrivers three times to screw and unscrew fifty screws into a wooden plank. Three of twenty-four different possible orders are assigned randomly to each individual so that each subject uses all four screwdrivers once before using any one a second time. The amount of time to the nearest minute it takes to complete the job with each screwdriver is averaged for each individual.

2. To assess the effectiveness of three types of sounds produced by home smoke alarms to arouse sleeping persons, a consumer product testing agency tests each alarm with nine members of its research staff. Each smoke alarm is assigned a different number from 1 to

> 3. Each number is written on a separate piece of paper and placed in a box. Each member of the research staff to be tested selects without replacement each of the three slips of paper. The order in which the numbers are drawn from the box is the order in which the staff member experiences the three alarms. The amount of time to the nearest second that it takes for the alarm to awaken the staff member, as indicated by changes in brain waves, is the dependent variable.

THE PARAMETRIC DEPENDENT SAMPLES ANOVA

The analysis performed on the data from an experiment set up as either an *RB-k* or an *RM-k* design is called a **dependent samples ANOVA.** The statistical analyses of *RB-k* and *RM-k* designs differ only in the way the total variation is partitioned and in the interpretation of results.

The Process of Partitioning *SS* and *df*

As in the one-way ANOVA performed on completely randomized designs (*CR-k*), the total source of variation in the dependent samples ANOVA is partitioned into component sources of variation. In the analysis of an *RB-k* design, the total variation is partitioned into the variance of the means of blocks called the **between-block variance** and the variance of the scores within a block called the **within-block variance.** In the analysis of an *RM-k* design the total variation is partitioned into *between-subject* and *within-subject* sources (see Chapter 6).

In the *RB-k* and *RM-k* designs, within sources of variation are further partitioned into sources of variance attributable to treatment and sources of variance due to experimental error. Figure 15.1 illustrates the partitioning of *SS* and *df* for both the *RB-k* and the *RM-k* designs.

Terminology and Symbols

The terminology and symbols, such as sum of squares (*SS*), degrees of freedom (*df*), mean-square (*MS*) and *F*-ratio (*F*) that are used in the analysis applicable to the *CR-k* design discussed in Chapter 14 are common to ANOVA and consequently are also used in the analysis applicable to the *RB-k* and *RM-k* designs. In addition, the dependent samples ANOVA uses the same three computational number symbols and the corresponding monomials as the *CR-k* design: $(1) = G^2/nk$, $(2) = \Sigma X^2$ and $(3) = \Sigma T_j^2/n$.

The *RB-k* and *RM-k* designs also require a fourth computational symbol, one used in computing the variation attributed to blocks or subjects. Since in most psychological experiments the experimental units are referred

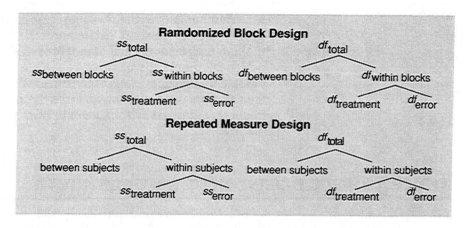

FIGURE 15.1   *Partitioning of SS and df for RB-k and RM-k designs.*

to as subjects, the letter used to designate the source of variance attributed to blocks or subjects is S. The fourth computation symbol, then, is $(4) = \Sigma S^2/k$ where S represents the sum of the k measures on any given block in the *RB-k* design or on any given subject in the *RM-k* design.

Application of ANOVA: A Numerical Example

For purposes of illustrating the dependent samples ANOVA, suppose a psychologist from the University of British Columbia is interested in whether children respond to an optical illusion similarly under different levels of illumination.

For the illusory stimuli, the psychologist selects a bar with a diagonal line extending from one side. (See Panel (a) in Figure 15.2). Each child is given a pencil and asked to indicate the point at which the line would protrude from the other end of the bar if the line were extended through it. If the protruding line is drawn with a ruler, it appears as if the two diagonal segments do not lie on the same line; this is called the Poggendorf illusion. The protruding line is generally seen as leaving the bar at a higher point than would occur if it were drawn with a ruler. (See Panel (b) in Figure 15.2). The dependent variable is the distance between the exiting point indicated by the children and the actual point of exit when the line segment is extended using a ruler.

Each child is tested three times under each of three levels of illumina-tio: bright, normal, dim. No feedback is given to the child on how far his or her line protruded from where a straight line should protrude. Since lack of feedback should obviate practice effects, the illumination order

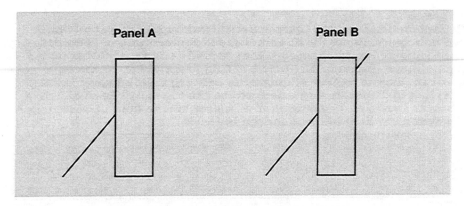

FIGURE 15.2 *Test items for the Poggendorf illusion.*

under which each child is tested is assigned randomly. An application of the related measures ANOVA to hypothetical data is illustrated in Table 15.1.

Section (i) presents the scores and squared scores for the hypothetical illusion experiment along with the treatment sums, G, and ΣX^2. It should be clear from the arrangement of values in (i) how the sums are obtained. In Section (ii) the procedures for obtaining values for the computational number symbols and their corresponding monomials are given. These values are then substituted for the number symbols in the computation formulas for SS presented in Section (iii). Section (iv) provides df formulas and the values of df for the hypothetical illusion experiment. Section (v) summarizes the ANOVA. The mean squares (MS) are obtained as in all ANOVA by dividing SS by the corresponding df. The F-ratio for the effect of treatment is obtained by dividing the MS for treatment by the MS for experimental error. Note that for both SS and df the between-subjects and within-subjects values sum to the corresponding total values. Also note that for both SS and df the treatment (illumination level) and experimental error values sum to the corresponding within-subjects values. The $df_{\text{treatment}}$ and df_{error} are used to obtain the critical value of F in Appendix Table 6 for evaluating H_0 at the preset level of significance.

The Decision Rule for Evaluating H_0

The hypothesis being tested by the dependent samples ANOVA performed on an $RB\text{-}k$ design is the same as that for the one-way ANOVA performed on $CR\text{-}k$ designs, namely, that the means of the populations from which the samples were drawn are equal with respect to the characteristic of interest. In the case of $RM\text{-}k$ designs where a single sample is usually drawn from a population, the hypothesis is that the means of the treatment populations are equal. In either case it is symbolized: H_0: $\mu_1 = \mu_2 = \mu_3 = \ldots \mu_k$

TABLE 15.1
Hypothetical Data and Computational Procedures (i), Computational Symbols and Values (ii), *SS* Formulas and Procedures (iii), *df* Formulas and Values (iv), and Related Measures ANOVA Summary Table (v) for the Illusion Experiment. Numerical Data (i) Represent a Three-Trial Mean Distance to Nearest Millimeter between Child's Indicated Point of Exit of the Protruding Line Segment and the Actual Point of Exit of a Line Drawn as the Completion of a Straight Line from the Entering Segment for Each of the Illumination Levels.

	Subject	Illumination Level						

	Subject	Dim		Normal		Bright		
		X	X^2	X	X^2	X	X^2	
	1	1	1	3	9	2	4	S_1 = 6
	2	2	4	4	16	5	25	S_2 = 11
	3	2	4	1	1	4	16	S_3 = 7
	4	4	16	4	16	6	36	S_4 = 14
(i)	5	3	9	5	25	6	36	S_5 = 14
	6	1	1	5	25	7	49	S_6 = 13
	7	0	0	2	4	3	9	S_7 = 5
	8	4	16	4	16	5	25	S_8 = 13
	9	5	25	4	16	7	49	S_9 = 16
	10	3	9	4	16	4	16	S_{10} = 11
		T_1 = 25		T_2 = 36		T_3 = 49		G = 110
		ΣX_1^2 = 85		ΣX_2^2 = 144		ΣX_3^2 = 265		ΣX^2 = 494

(continued)

(ii)

$$(1) = \frac{G^2}{nk} = \frac{110^2}{10(3)} = \frac{12,100}{30} = 403.33$$

$$(2) = \Sigma X^2 = 494$$

$$(3) = \frac{\Sigma T_j^2}{n} = \frac{(25^2 + 36^2 + 49^2)}{10} = \frac{4,322}{10} = 432.2$$

$$(4) = \frac{\Sigma S^2}{k} = \frac{(6^2 + 11^2 + 7^2 + 14^2 + 14^2 + 13^2 + 5^2 + 13^2 + 16^2 + 11^2)}{3} = \frac{1338}{3} = 446$$

(iii)

$$SS_{\text{between subj.}} = (4) - (1) = 446.00 - 403.33 = 42.67$$

$$SS_{\text{within subj.}} = (2) - (4) = 494.00 - 446.00 = 48.00$$

$$SS_{\text{treatment}} = (3) - (1) = 432.20 - 403.33 = 28.87$$

$$SS_{\text{error}} = (2) - (4) - (3) + (1) = 494.00 - 446.00 - 432.20 + 403.33 = 19.13$$

$$SS_{\text{total}} = (2) - (1) = 494.00 - 403.33 = 90.67$$

TABLE 15.1 **(Continued)**

$df_{\text{between subj.}} = n - 1 = 10 - 1 = 9$

$df_{\text{within subj.}} = n(k - 1) = 10(2) = 20$

(iv) $df_{\text{treatment}} = k - 1 = 3 - 1 = 2$

$df_{\text{error}} = (n - 1)(k - 1) = (10 - 1)(3 - 1) = 18$

$df_{\text{total}} = nk - 1 = 10(3) - 1 = 29$

	Source	SS	df	MS	F
	Between subjects	42.67	9	4.74	
(v)	Within subjects	48.00	20	2.4	
	Treatment (Level)	28.87	2	14.44	13.62
	Experimental error	19.13	18	1.06	
	Total	90.67	29		

Following is the decision rule for evaluating H_0:

$$\text{If } F_{\text{calc}} \geq F_{\text{table}}, \text{ reject } H_0.$$

Comparing F_{calc} (13.62) for the hypothetical Poggendorf illusion experiment in Table 15.1 with the critical value (3.55) of F for 2 and 18 df in Appendix Table 6 indicates that H_0 should be rejected.

Mean Comparisons Following ANOVA

As with the *CR-k* design, a significant F-value for an *RB-k* or *RM-k* design when $k > 2$ not only tells you that it is highly probable that the means of the treatment populations are not equal but also directs you to make further comparisons. The F-test used for planned comparisons following the ANOVA performed on the data of a *CR-k* design can also be used to make comparisons between treatment means of *RB-k* and *RM-k* designs. Since the sample sizes are necessarily equal in *RB-k* and *RM-k* designs, the formula for F shown in Chapter 14 (Formula 14.11) is expressed more simply as follows:

Formula 15.1 $$F = \frac{(\bar{T}_j - \bar{T}_{j'})^2}{2MS_{\text{error}}/n}$$

The df associated with F are 1 and df_{error}. Following is the decision rule for this comparison:

$$\text{If } F_{\text{calc}} \geq F_{\text{table}}, \text{ reject } H_0: \mu_j = \mu_{j'}.$$

Since in the hypothetical illusion experiment there is a significant effect of illumination level, Formula 15.1 is used in the following computations to make planned comparisons between the effects of dim and normal levels of illumination and between bright and normal levels of illumination:

$$F_{\text{dim vs. normal}} = \frac{(2.5 - 3.6)^2}{2(1.06)/10} = \frac{1.21}{0.212} = 5.71$$

$$F_{\text{bright vs. normal}} = \frac{(4.9 - 3.6)^2}{2(1.06)/10} = \frac{1.69}{0.212} = 7.97$$

A comparison of these calculated F's with the critical F-value from Appendix Table 6 for 1 and 18 df tells you that the illusional effects under both dim and bright illumination levels differ significantly from the illusional effect under normal lighting conditions. From the mean values it is clear that dim lighting produces less of an illusional effect and bright lighting produces more of an illusional effect than is seen under normal levels of illumination.

Interpretation of Results

As mentioned in the introduction to the dependent samples ANOVA, the analyses of $RB\text{-}k$ and $RM\text{-}k$ designs differ not only in the way the total source of variation is partitioned but also in the interpretation of results. The results of an experiment in which a blocking factor has been used generalize to a population of elements or subjects that have experienced only one of the k levels of the independent variable. The results of an experiment in which repeated measures are used, on the other hand, generalize to a population of elements or subjects that have experienced all k levels of the independent variable.

The Conditions Underlying the Dependent Samples ANOVA

The general conditions of random selection, normality and homogeneity of variance that must be satisfied for the correct interpretation of other parametric analyses of variance must also be met if the dependent samples ANOVA is to be correctly interpreted. Furthermore, the dependent measure should achieve interval or ratio scale status. If there is a serious departure from any of these conditions, the dependent samples ANOVA is not appropriate.

Since an equal distribution of variation across treatment levels is generally accomplished by the matching of subjects in the $RB\text{-}k$ design and by having the same subjects undergo all k levels of the independent variable in the $RM\text{-}k$ design, there is generally little reason to suspect heterogeneity of variance. Thus, a test for homogeneity of variance is rarely performed with dependent samples. Except for the condition of randomness that must be met, a nonparametric analysis should be performed only if there is a serious departure from the condition of normality or if the dependent measure does not meet the scale requirements.

PROGRESS ASSESSMENT 15.4

A student interested in psychophysics wishes to determine if the two-point threshold is the same for different parts of the body. The two-point threshold is the distance two tactile stimuli (such as the points of a drawing compass) must be apart to be felt as two separate touches. Six students selected from the experimental psychology course agree to participate in the experiment. Four parts of the body are selected for testing: upper lip, forehead, palm, and calf. Each student is tested five times on each part of the body. The order of testing is randomized for each subject. The median distance in millimeters for each body part for each student is shown in Table 15-A.

TABLE 15-A
Median Distance in Millimeters for Two-Point Threshold for Four Different Parts of the Body

Subject	Upper Lip	Forehead	Palm	Calf
1	10	22	12	52
2	6	14	15	48
3	8	18	12	45
4	7	19	14	47
5	9	18	10	46
6	8	17	9	50

1. Analyze the data in Table 15-A and put the results of the analysis in a summary table.
2. Determine if the F-ratio is significant at the 0.05 level of significance.
3. Symbolize the null hypothesis and state your decision with respect to H_0.
4. Tell what your decision about H_0 means in terms of the student's project.
5. Using the *a priori* F-test determine if the two most sensitive parts of the body differ in threshold.

A NONPARAMETRIC DEPENDENT SAMPLES ANOVA

A frequently used nonparametric analogue of the parametric dependent samples ANOVA that is used to test for differences among two or more treatment groups is the **Friedman-Ranks ANOVA.** The measure of the dependent variable taken on each subject or block must achieve at least ordinal status. Regardless of the scale of measurement, ordinal, interval, or ratio, the data analyzed by the Friedman-Ranks ANOVA, like those for most nonparametric tests discussed in this text, are always ranks.

Experimental Example

For purposes of understanding the Friedman-Ranks ANOVA assume that an experimenter wishes to test the hypothesis that human infants will spend more time looking at a normal-face oval pattern than at scrambled-face or nonface oval patterns. Twelve infants between the ages of three and six months are randomly selected from a pool of infants whose mothers have given the researcher permission to use their children a subjects in an attention-span experiment.

To test the hypothesis, the experimenter places each child in a chamber in which both eye movements and the images the eyes reflect can be monitored. There are three levels of the independent variable (1) an oval with a normal-face pattern, (2) an oval with a scrambled-face pattern (for example, eyes, nose, and mouth in wrong places), and (3) a plain oval pattern. Each child is presented with each of the ovals three times for one minute each time. The dependent variable is attention to the patterns and is operationally defined in terms of time spent looking at the patterns. The average time in seconds that the child spends looking at the different patterns is determined from the eye movements and reflected images and is the measure analyzed. Hypothetical data for this experiment are presented in Table 15.2.

Application of the Friedman-Ranks ANOVA

A grouped frequency distribution of the time measures from the three groups indicate a marked departure from normality and so the parametric dependent samples ANOVA may not be appropriate. The Friedman-Ranks ANOVA is then applied.

As mentioned previously and as the name implies, the Friedman-Ranks ANOVA requires that the measures taken on the dependent variable be ranked. The ranking procedure for the Friedman-Ranks ANOVA differs from the procedure used for the Kruskal-Wallis ANOVA by ranks. Each subject's scores in an *RM-k* design or each block's scores in an *RB-k* design are ranked independently of the other subjects or blocks. The smallest score for each subject or block is assigned the lowest rank, one; the next smallest is given the next lowest rank, two; and so on. Each score's rank (bold print) is adjacent to it in Table 15.2.

TABLE 15.2
The Average Time in Seconds Spent Looking at Each of Three Oval Face Patterns: Normal, Scrambled, Plain. The Rank (Boldface) of Each Infant's Times Is Adjacent to the Time Score.

	Normal		Scrambled		Plain	
Infant	Time score	Rank	Time score	Rank	Time score	Rank
1	38	**3**	26	**2**	20	**1**
2	43	**3**	16	**1**	17	**2**
3	20	**2**	21	**3**	16	**1**
4	30	**3**	22	**2**	21	**1**
5	32	**3**	27	**1**	28	**2**
6	18	**3**	17	**2**	16	**1**
7	22	**2**	23	**3**	21	**1**
8	16	**1**	22	**2**	23	**3**
9	30	**3**	25	**2**	24	**1**
10	19	**3**	18	**2**	16	**1**
11	24	**2**	26	**3**	19	**1**
12	25	**2**	26	**3**	16	**1**

The statistic **F-R** for the Friedman-Ranks ANOVA is computed with the following formula:

Formula 15.2
$$F\text{-}R = \frac{12}{nk(k+1)} \Sigma R_j^2 - 3n(k+1)$$

In this formula, n refers to the number of subjects or blocks, R_j is the sum of the ranks for the jth treatment, k symbolizes the number of treatments, and 12 and 3 are constants.

For the hypothetical data in Table 15.2

$$F\text{-}R = \frac{12}{(12)(3)(3+1)} (30^2 + 26^2 + 16^2) - (3)(12)(3+1)$$

$$= \frac{12}{144} (1832) - 144$$

$$= 152.67 - 144$$

$$= 8.67.$$

The Logic of the Friedman-Ranks ANOVA

The null hypothesis tested by the Friedman-Ranks ANOVA is that the treatment populations do not differ. If that hypothesis is true, then an infant's attention span in the hypothetical experiment would be independent of the pattern shown, and the distribution of ranks within infants should be random. If the distribution of ranks were random, you would expect the ranks, 1, 2, and 3 in the hypothetical infant-attention experiment to occur with nearly equal frequency under each of the pattern conditions. If this were the case, the sum of the ranks for the three pattern conditions would also be nearly equal. The Friedman-Ranks ANOVA is measuring the likelihood that the sums of the ranks for the different levels of the independent variable is a product of chance.

The Decision Rule and Evaluation of H_0

You decide whether or not the various levels of the independent variable have different effects on the dependent variable by evaluating the F-R statistic at the preset level of significance. You evaluate the significance of F-R by comparing the calculated value of F-R with the critical value of F-R for k-1 df in Appendix Table 10. The decision rule is as follows:

$$\text{If } F\text{-}R_{calc} \geq F\text{-}R_{table}, \text{ reject } H_0.$$

Rejecting H_0 means that you consider it to be unlikely that differences in the rank sums occurred by chance. You conclude that it is more likely due to the different levels of the independent variable.

The calculated value of F-R (8.67) for the hypothetical infant-attention experiment is larger than the critical value (5.99) of F-R with 2 df at the 0.05 level of significance. You conclude therefore that pattern is a statistically significant factor in the attention span of human infants, F-$R(2) = 8.67$, $p < 0.05$.

Planned Comparisons following the Friedman-Ranks ANOVA

Even though H_0 is rejected, the experimenter cannot conclude that the research hypothesis is supported. You will recall that the research hypothesis in the infant-attention experiment was that children would spend more time attending to a normal face pattern than to scrambled or nonface patterns. Rejecting the statistical H_0 in that case simply informs the experimenter that it is likely that children's attention span differs for different patterns. A significant F-R, like a significant F with a parametric ANOVA, directs the experimenter to make further comparisons when $k > 2$. For planned comparisons following the Friedman-Ranks ANOVA, the Wilcoxon Matched-Pairs Signed-Ranks test is generally used.

PROGRESS ASSESSMENT 15.5

A psychology student is assigned the problem of determining which of four flavors (lemon, coffee, chocolate, and garlic) can be identified most readily without smell. The student randomly selects seven individuals from a subject pool for the experimental psychology course. The subjects are seated at a table and are asked to pinch their nostrils before the substance to be tasted is brought close. The flavor is then placed in the subject's mouth. The subject is instructed to swish the liquid around, release the nostrils, inhale softly through the mouth and nose, and identify the flavor. Each subject is tested ten times with each flavor. The flavors are presented to each subject in a random order. The subjects rinse their mouths thoroughly after each taste trial. Table 15-B shows the percent correct identifications by each subject for the four flavors.

TABLE 15-B
Percentage of Correct Flavor Indentifications

Subject	Lemon	Coffee	Chocolate	Garlic
1	50	0	10	20
2	40	20	10	0
3	70	30	20	10
4	30	10	40	0
5	40	10	20	0
6	40	0	20	10
7	80	0	30	10

1. Symbolize the design.
2. Analyze the data in Table 15-B with the Friedman-Ranks ANOVA.
3. State the null hypothesis being tested.
4. Determine if H_0 is or is not rejected.
5. Perform the Wilcoxon Matched-Pairs Signed-Ranks test on the data of the two flavors with the two highest correct identifications.
6. What is the answer to the student's problem?

SUMMARY

In this chapter you are introduced to two experimental designs, the randomized block design and the repeated measures design. Both designs require that there be two or more levels of a single independent variable. Both designs require that measures of the dependent variable across the levels of the independent variable be related. You are shown that the designs differ in the way the measures on the dependent variable are related. In the randomized block design, measures on different subjects are related as a result of matching on the basis of a mutual category, a common heredity, or premeasurement of the dependent variable. In the repeated measures design, measures are related by comparing subjects with themselves under the different levels of the independent variable. This chapter then introduces the parametric dependent samples ANOVA that is used with both designs to determine if different levels of the independent variable differentially affect the dependent variable. You are reminded of the conditions underlying the parametric ANOVA and are introduced to the Friedman-Ranks ANOVA, a nonparametric test that can be used when certain conditions of the parametric ANOVA are not met.

KEY DEFINITIONS

block   A set of subjects matched on the basis of some preexperimental similarity.

blocking factor   The basis on which subjects are matched.

between-block variance   The variance of the means of blocks.

counterbalance assignment   Assignment of treatment levels to subjects in a way that controls for sequence effects.

dependent samples ANOVA   The analysis performed on the data from an experiment setup as either an *RB-k* or an *RM-k* design.

$F = (\bar{T}_j - \bar{T}_{j'})^2/(2MS_{\text{error}}/n)$ A simplified version of the *a priori* F-test used to make planned comparisons following the dependent samples ANOVA.

fixed-order assignment   Order in which treatment levels are experienced as determined by the intrinsic characteristics of the independent variable.

Friedman-Ranks ANOVA   A nonparametric analogue of the parametric dependent samples ANOVA that is used to test for differences among two or more treatment groups.

$F\text{-}R$ The symbol for the statistic computed in the Friedman-Ranks ANOVA.

$F\text{-}R = \{12/[nk(k + 1)]\}\ \Sigma(R_j^2) - 3n(k + 1)$ Formula for the statistic computed in the Friedman-Ranks ANOVA.

randomized block design   An experimental design employing two or more levels of a single independent variable and a blocking factor.

RB-k   Symbol for a randomized block design.

repeated measure design   An experimental design employing two or more levels of a single independent variable in which each subject or sample element experiences all of the treatment levels.

RM-k   Symbol for a repeated measures design.

$\Sigma S^2/k$ Computational monomial used to compute the sums of squares associated with blocks or subjects in *RB-k* and *RM-k* designs.

within-block variance   Variance of the scores within a block

REVIEW EXERCISES

For the experimental designs in Problems 1, 2, and 3 do the following:

a. State the dependent and independent variables.

b. State the scale on which the dependent variable is measured.

c. Tell whether the dependent variable is continuous or discrete.

d. Symbolize the type of design.

e. If the design involves dependent samples, state the basis on which the measures are related, that is, blocking or repeated measures; if the design does not involve dependent samples, indicate by NA (nonapplicable).

f. If the design is a randomized block design, state the basis on which blocks are formed—mutual category, genetics, or premeasurement; if the design is a repeated measures design, specify the order—random, fixed, or counterbalanced—in which subjects experience the treatment levels. If the design is neither a randomized block nor a repeated measures design, indicate by NA.

g. Compute the mean and variance for each treatment group.

h. If the design is a $CR\text{-}k$ design, perform the F_{max} test; if the design is $RB\text{-}k$ or $RM\text{-}k$, indicate by NA.

i. If independent samples, perform the most appropriate ANOVA on the basis of the F_{max} test and scale of measurement; if dependent samples, perform the most appropriate ANOVA on the basis of the scale of measurement.

j. State the null hypothesis for the ANOVA in words.

k. Use the appropriate *a priori* test at the 0.05 level of significance to compare groups with the largest and smallest means.

l. Determine if the experimental results support the research hypothesis.

1. At the undergraduate level, research often takes the form of attempting to replicate the results of classic experiments. An undergraduate psychology major who is interested in information processing attempts to replicate the findings of Stroop (1935). Stroop had demonstrated that observers had difficulty ignoring meaningful information that is irrelevant to a task. The student gives each member of a large experimental class a reaction-time test that involves identifying colors in pictures. On the basis of the results of the reaction-time test, the student forms three groups in which each member of a group has a corresponding member in the other groups with the same reaction-time score. Group 1 is measured on how long it takes to read a list of color names printed in black ink. Group 2 is measured on how long it takes to read a list of color names printed in ink that corresponds to the color, such as the color name *red* printed in red ink. Group 3 is measured on how long it takes to read a list of color names printed in ink that does not correspond to the color, such as the color name *yellow* printed in green ink. Assume that the three lists are randomly assigned to the three groups. Like Stroop, the student hypothesizes that irrelevant meaningful stimuli (ink color in the third group condition) can interfere with information processing, thereby producing longer reaction times. Table 15-C presents the reaction times to the nearest second for members of the three groups.

TABLE 15-C
Time in Seconds Needed to Read List of Color
Names Printed in Black, Corresponding, or
Different Color Inks

Group 1 (Black Ink)	Group 2 (Corresponding Color Ink)	Group 3 (Different Color Ink)
5	4	7
8	8	9
9	7	10
7	5	8
6	6	7
6	6	8
9	8	9
8	7	9

2. An investigator interested in the role familiarity plays in the spatial memory of aged individuals selects twelve residents of a nursing home by using a computer program to generate a random sample of names from the home roster. Models are constructed of the individuals' rooms, the dining hall where all residents eat three meals daily, and the infirmary in which each individual meets with a medical doctor once a week. Eight pieces of model furniture appropriate to each setting is used to assess spatial memory. Each resident is asked to place the model furniture in the corresponding space the real furniture occupies in the actual environmental settings. The investigator hypothesizes that the more familiar the room, the greater is the individual's spatial memory. The number of correctly placed pieces provides an index of an individual's spatial memory. Six different orders in which the model rooms can be presented are used with two residents experiencing the same order. Table 15-D presents the spatial memory indices for the twelve residents.

3. The term *neophobia* derives from the Greek word *neos* (meaning ''new'') and *phobos* (meaning ''fear''). Neophobia (fear of new things) is often observed in rats' eating and drinking behaviors. If a rat is presented with a novel flavor, it will generally sample only a small amount of the flavor in contrast to a rat sampling a familiar flavor. To determine if prior experience with novel flavors (novelty adaptation) decreases this neophobic tendency, an experimenter orders twenty-four rats from a commercial supplier and randomly assigns eight rats to each of three treatment groups: (1) a group for which the test solution is novel (novel-flavor group), (2) a group for which the test solution is familiar (familiar-flavor group), and (3) a group for which the test solution is novel except that the group had five previous experiences with different novel solutions (novelty-adaptation group). The researcher hypothesizes that this latter group will show less neophobia than the group for which the solution is novel. The animals are deprived of water for twelve hours and then given access to the test solution for one hour. The amount of the test solution drunk during the hour is recorded to the nearest milliliter and is the measure analyzed. These data are shown in Table 15-E.

TABLE 15-D
Number of Correctly Placed Pieces of Furniture by Nursing Home Residents in Three Model Rooms

Resident	Individual's Room	Dining Hall	Infirmary
1	7	5	3
2	8	6	1
3	7	7	5
4	8	6	5
5	6	5	3
6	5	5	2
7	6	4	3
8	7	7	4
9	6	5	3
10	5	4	4
11	4	3	1
12	5	4	2

TABLE 15-E
Amount in Milliliters of Test Solution Drunk by Each of Three Familiarity Groups

Novel-Flavor Group	Familiar-Flavor Group	Novelty-Adaptation Group
2	8	9
3	10	8
3	9	7
1	7	6
0	6	5
2	8	5
3	8	4
3	7	8

ANSWERS TO PROGRESS ASSESSMENTS

15.1   1. genetic
        2. mutual category
        3. repeated measures

15.2   1. a. a lighting condition
           b. *RB*-3
           c. age
        2. a. feelings of success and failure
           b. *RB*-3
           c. premeasurement of the dependent variable

15.3   1. a. type of handle
           b. *RM*-4
           c. counterbalance
        2. a. type of sound
           b. *RM*-3
           c. random assignment

15.4   1. See Table 15-F.
        2. Yes.
        3. H_0: $\mu_1 = \mu_2 = \mu_3 = \mu_4$; reject.
        4. The thresholds for different parts of the body are not the same.
        5. Yes, the threshold of the two most sensitive body parts differ significantly, $F(1, 15) = 10.3$, $p < 0.05$.

TABLE 15-F
Summary Table for the Hypothetical Two-Point Threshold Experiment

Source	SS	df	MS	F
Between subjects	33	5		
Within subjects	5993	18		
Body part	5922	3	1974	420
Error	71	15	4.7	
Total	6026	23		

15.5   **1.** *RM*-4

2. *F-R* = 13.68

3. The treatment populations do not differ.

4. Reject H_0.

5. $|T_-| = 1$

6. Lemon can be identified most readily

CHAPTER 16

Completely Randomized Factorial Designs and the Two-Way Analysis of Variance

*T*he completely randomized design discussed in Chapter 14 provides the foundation for the more complex class of designs introduced in this chapter called completely randomized factorial designs. **Completely randomized factorial (CRF) designs** are experimental designs that involve two or more treatment levels of two or more independent variables. The simplest case of these designs involves only two independent variables and is symbolized **CRF-pq** where the *p* and *q* refer to the number of treatment levels of the two independent variables.

Consider this example. An investigator of animal behavior is interested in the effects of time away from the nest and the magnitude of reinforcement on infant rats' performance on a specific learning task. The two independent variables are *time away from nest* and *magnitude of reinforcement*. If infant rats are kept away from the nest for either 1/2 hour or 1 hour and are reinforced for a correct response on the learning task by being allowed to remain with a lactating dam (reinforcement) for either 30 seconds or 60 seconds, then there are two treatment levels of each of the independent variables. If you let *p* equal the number of levels of one independent variable and *q* equal the number of levels of the other, then the design is symbolized *CRF-22*.

In the **factorial experiment,** each treatment level of any one variable is administered in conjunction with each and every treatment level of the other variables. Thus, in the hypothetical infant rat experiment, there are four treatment groups:

1. one that is out of the nest for 1/2 hour and is allowed to remain 30 seconds with a lactating dam after each correct response,
2. one that is out of the nest for 1/2 hour and is allowed to remain 60 seconds with a lactating dam after each correct response,
3. one that is out of the nest for 1 hour and is allowed to remain 30 seconds with a lactating dam after each correct response, and
4. one that is out of the nest for 1 hour and is allowed to remain 60 seconds with a lactating dam after each correct response.

Although each sample member is subjected to a treatment level of each of the independent variables, a single dependent measure taken on each sample member constitutes the data. The analysis performed on such data is the major topic of this chapter.

THE TWO-WAY ANOVA

The analysis used to evaluate the data from an experiment involving two independent variables and a single dependent measure taken on each sample member (*CRF-pq* design) is the **two-way ANOVA.**

The One-Way ANOVA versus the Two-Way ANOVA

Unlike the two-way ANOVA, the one-way ANOVA is easily applicable to experiments in which there are not equal numbers of sample members under each treatment level. Thus, in this chapter only those experiments in which there are equal numbers of sample members under the various combinations of treatment levels will be considered.

Another major difference between the one-way ANOVA and the two-way ANOVA has to do with the design requirements. The *CR-k* design requires a sample member to undergo only one level of the independent variable. The *CRF-pq* design, as previously mentioned, requires each sample member to jointly undergo one treatment level of each independent variable. Thus, the two-way ANOVA is used not only to evaluate **main effects,** which are the effects of the levels of individual independent variables on the dependent variable, but also to evaluate **interaction effects,** which are the effects on the dependent variable of one variable across levels of the other variable.

In the hypothetical infant rat experiment, for example, if infants kept away from the nest for 1 hour differ from infants kept away from the nest for 1/2 hour, then there exists *a main effect of time away from the nest.* If infant rats remaining with the lactating dam for 30 seconds do not differ from infants remaining with the dam for 60 seconds, then there exists *no main effect of magnitude of reinforcement.* If infant rats away from the nest for 1/2 hour differ with respect to time allowed to remain with the lactating dam, but infants away from the nest for 1 hour do not differ in this respect, then there exists an *interaction effect of time away from nest and magnitude of reinforcement.*

Terminology and Symbols

For the most part, the terminology of the one-way ANOVA is applicable to the two-way ANOVA. As in the one-way ANOVA, the total source of variation is partitioned into between-group and within-group sources. The sum of squares (*SS*) and mean squares (*MS*) for these two sources are computed and an *F*-ratio of the between-group *MS* to the within-group *MS* is obtained. In other words, the two-way ANOVA includes performing the one-way ANOVA. In addition, however, the between-group source of variation is partitioned into its component parts, the variation attributed to each of the independent variables and to the interaction of the variables.

The partitioning of a two-way ANOVA for the hypothetical infant rat experiment is diagramed in Figure 16.1. It is the partitioning of the between-group source of variation into its component parts that requires additional terminology and symbols.

Designating Variables, Levels, and Sums Necessary to Evaluate Main Effects.   The independent variables of a completely randomized factorial design are represented in a two-way ANOVA by the symbols *A*

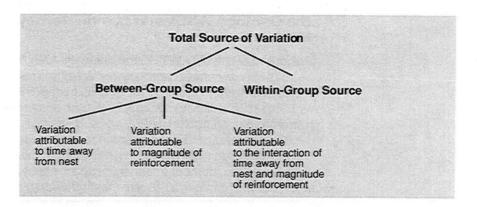

FIGURE 16.1 *The partititioning of variation in the two-way ANOVA of the hypothetical infant rat experiment.*

and **B**. The symbols A and B are arbitrarily assigned to the two independent variables. There are, then, p levels of A and q levels of B.

The individual p-levels of A are designated $a_1, a_2, \ldots a_p$. The individual q-levels of B are designated $b_1, b_2, \ldots b_q$. The symbol A_1 represents the *sum* of all the scores under treatment level a_1, A_2 represents the *sum* of all the scores under treatment level a_2, and so on for the other levels of A. These sums are needed to compute values for the computational symbols used in evaluating the main effect of the A-variable. The symbol B_1 represents the *sum* of all the scores under treatment level b_1, B_2 is the symbol for the *sum* of all the scores under treatment level b_2, and so on. These sums are needed to compute values for computational symbols used in evaluating the main effect of the B-variable.

Designating Interactions and Sums Necessary to Evaluate Their Effects.   The symbol **AB** refers to the combined treatments A and B and also to the interaction of variables A and B. If we let i symbolize the subscript number for any given level (a_i) of the A-variable and j symbolize the subscript number for any given level (b_j) of the B-variable, then the symbol AB_{ij} refers to the sum of all the scores of sample members treated with or receiving both the ith level of variable A and the jth level of variable B, that is ab_{ij}. For example, AB_{13} is the sum of the scores under the combined treatment levels a_1 and b_3. These AB_{ij}-sums are needed to compute values for computational symbols used in evaluating interaction effects.

PROGRESS ASSESSMENT 16.1

For the accompanying experiment complete the following steps:

1. Name and assign letter symbols to the independent variables in the design in the order in which they appear in the description of the experiment.

2. Assign a value to each of the letter designations for the number of levels of the independent variables in part 1.

3. Name and assign letter symbols to the individual treatment levels of each independent variable.

4. Symbolize the sum of the scores of the individuals tested for recall in the same context as the learning context twenty-five days after learning the list.

5. Symbolize the sum of the scores for individuals tested for recall one day after learning the list.

6. Symbolize the sum of the scores for individuals tested for recall in a context different from the learning context.

As a project for a course in experimental psychology, a psychology major decides to examine the effect that the environmental context has on recall of verbal material. Thirty randomly selected students who agreed to participate in the experiment learn a list of twenty words to one perfect recitation. Ten students are tested for recall of the list after one day, ten after ten days, and ten after twenty-five days. Half of the students at each of these intervals are tested in the room in which they learned the list. The remaining students are tested in a different room.

Computing *SS* and *df*

As for the one-way ANOVA, you will find it convenient to use a set of computational symbols to compute *SS* for the sources of variation in the two-way ANOVA. Again, the computational values needed to compute *SS* will be symbolized in terms of both numbers and monomials, and, again, it will be most convenient to use the number symbols in the computational formulas for *SS*.

Computational Symbols. The symbols (*1*) and (*2*) are the same as those in the one-way ANOVA. The symbol (*1*) refers to the squared sum of all the scores, G^2, divided by the total number of scores. In the two-way ANOVA, the total number of scores equals the number of scores per group (n) multiplied by the product of the treatment levels (pq). Thus, for the two-way ANOVA, the symbol (*1*) $= G^2/npq$. The symbol (*2*) refers to ΣX^2, the sum of all squared scores in the experiment.

The rest of the numbered symbols and the corresponding monomials refer to values needed in computational formulas used to compute *SS* for the component parts of the between-group sum of squares. To compute SS_A, $\Sigma A_i^2/nq$ is needed where $\Sigma A_i^2 = A_1^2 + A_2^2 + A_3^2 + \ldots + A_p^2$, n refers to group size, and q refers to number of levels of the *B*-variable. A similar computational monomial, $\Sigma B_j^2/np$, is needed to compute SS_B. Computational symbols for interaction *SS* are expressed similarly. For example, $\Sigma(AB_{ij})^2/n$ is the first computational monomial in the formula for computing SS_{AB} where $\Sigma(AB_{ij})^2 = (AB_{11})^2 + (AB_{12})^2 + \ldots + (AB_{pq})^2$.

If you understand the meaning of the number symbols and the corresponding monomials, you may find it convenient to drop the subscripts. For example, instead of writing ΣA_i^2, simply write ΣA^2. The computational number symbols and corresponding monomials (without subscripts) for the two-way ANOVA are as follows:

$$(1) = G^2/npq$$
$$(2) = \Sigma X^2$$
$$(3) = \Sigma A^2/nq$$
$$(4) = \Sigma B^2/np$$
$$(5) = \Sigma (AB)^2/n$$

Computational Formulas for SS. The computational symbols and computational formulas for SS and df for a two-way ANOVA are presented in Table 16.1.

In order to determine how to generate the formulas for SS and df for the two-way ANOVA, it is important to recognize the following three characteristics of the formulas in Table 16.1:

1. The computational formulas for SS_{bg}, SS_{wg}, and SS_{tot} in a two-way ANOVA correspond to the formulas for these SS in the one-way ANOVA. Note, however, that the computational number symbol (3) in the one-way ANOVA is replaced by (5) in the two-way ANOVA.

2. Any between-treatment variance can provide an unbiased estimate of σ^2 in a two-way ANOVA just as $n\Sigma(\bar{T} - \bar{G})^2/(k - 1)$ provides a between-treatment unbiased estimate of σ^2 in the one-way ANOVA. For example, $nq\Sigma(\bar{A} - \bar{G})^2/(p - 1)$ in a two-way ANOVA corresponds to $n\Sigma(\bar{T} - \bar{G})^2/(k - 1)$ in a one-way ANOVA and provides the between-A-treatment estimate of σ^2. Note that $\bar{A}$ designates the means of the treatment levels of the A-variable and nq is the number of scores for each treatment level. Similarly, $np\Sigma(\bar{B} - \bar{G})^2/(q - 1)$ provides the between-B-treatment estimate of σ^2. The numerators of these estimates can be shown to be algebraically equivalent to formulas (3) − (1) and (4) − (1), respectively, in Table 16.1. Thus, the formula for SS

TABLE 16.1
Summary Table of Symbols and Computational Formulas for Computing SS and df in a Two-Way ANOVA

Symbols	Source	SS	df
$(1) = G^2/npq$	Between groups	$(5) - (1)$	$pq - 1$
$(2) = \Sigma X^2$	A	$(3) - (1)$	$p - 1$
$(3) = \Sigma A^2/nq$	B	$(4) - (1)$	$q - 1$
$(4) = \Sigma B^2/np$	AB	$(5) - (4) - (3) + (1)$	$(p - 1)(q - 1)$
$(5) = \Sigma (AB)^2/n$	Within groups	$(2) - (5)$	$pq(n - 1)$
	Total	$(2) - (1)$	$npq - 1$

for the main effect of either treatment in a *CRF-pq*-designed experiment is obtained by subtracting computational symbol (*1*) from the computational number symbol in which the treatment alone is symbolized in the numerator of the corresponding monomial.

3. The computational formula for the *SS* for the interaction of variables *A* and *B* is easily generated. First of all, since SS_{bg} is partitioned into SS_A, SS_B, and SS_{AB}, these three *SS* sum to SS_{bg}. Thus, if SS_A and SS_B are subtracted from SS_{bg}, the remainder must equal SS_{AB}. In other words, the variation due to the interaction of treatments is the variation due to the combination of treatments (SS_{bg}) minus the variation due to the individual treatments alone, that is, $SS_{AB} = SS_{bg} - SS_A - SS_B$. Substituting the appropriate computational formulas for SS_{bg}, SS_A, and SS_B gives $SS_{AB} = [(5) - (1)] - [(3) - (1)] - [(4) - (1)]$. Changing the signs of symbols within brackets preceded by a minus sign and carrying out the operations yields the formula: $SS_{AB} = (5) - (4) - (3) + (1)$.

Computational Formulas for df.   The formulas for the *df* are also easily generated. Again, the formulas for the between-group, within-group, and total sources of variance in a two-way ANOVA correspond directly to the formulas for these sources of variance in the one-way ANOVA. The *df* associated with the between-group variance is the number of treatment combinations or groups minus one, that is, *pq*-1. The *df* for the within-group source of variance for each of the groups in the experiment is $n - 1$. The df_{wg}, then, is the number of groups times the *df* for each group or $pq(n - 1)$. The *df* for the total source of variance, the total number of scores minus one, is symbolized $npq - 1$.

When partitioning the between-group *df* into its component parts, the *df* associated with the variance attributable to any single variable is the number of levels of the variable minus 1. For variable *A* the *df* is $p - 1$ and for variable *B* the *df* is $q - 1$. The formula for the *df* associated with the variance attributable to the interaction of variables *A* and *B* is obtained by subtracting the *df* formulas for the individual variables from the *df* formula for between groups, that is, $(pq - 1) - (p - 1) - (q - 1) = pq - p - q + 1 = (p - 1)(q - 1)$. Thus, the *df* for the interaction of variables is the product of the *df* of the individual variables.

PROGRESS ASSESSMENT 16.2

1. List the computational number symbols and the corresponding monomials that would be used in a two-way ANOVA.
2. Construct a summary table of computational formulas for *SS* (in terms of number symbols) and *df* for the two-way ANOVA for the experiment described in Progress Assessment 16.1.

APPLICATION OF THE TWO-WAY ANOVA

An application of the two-way ANOVA can be illustrated through use of the data for the hypothetical infant rat experiment presented in section (i) of Table 16.2.

Section (i) presents the hypothetical data and the procedures used to obtain the sums of the scores for the individual treatment levels (a_1, a_2, b_1, and b_2) and the combinations of treatment levels (ab_{11}, ab_{12}, ab_{21}, and ab_{22}). These sums are used to compute the values for the computational symbols. In section (ii) the procedures for computing values for the computational symbols are illustrated. The values obtained in section (ii) are then used in section (iii) to compute values for SS for the different sources of variance.

TABLE 16.2
Hypothetical Data and Computational Procedures (i), Computational Symbols and Values (ii), SS Formulas and Procedures (iii), and Multifactor ANOVA Summary Table (iv) for the Infant Rat Experiment. Numerical Data (i) Represent the Number of Correct Responses in 25 Training Trials on a Specific Learning Task in Which 30 or 60 Seconds with a Lactating Dam Served as Reinforcement for 10-Day-Old Rats That Were Away from the Nest for 1/2 Hour or 1 Hour.

			Time Away from Nest		
			b_1 *(1/2 hour)*	b_2 *(1 hour)*	
			15	16	
			12	17	
		a_1 (30 Sec.)	13	15	
			10	16	
			14	14	
(i)	Time with		$AB_{11} =$ 64	$AB_{12} =$ 78	$A_1 = 64 + 78 = 142$
	Lactating Dam				
	(Reinforcement				
	Magnitude)		9	21	
			15	17	
		a_2 (60 Sec.)	11	18	
			14	21	
			12	20	
		$AB_{21} =$ 61	$AB_{22} =$ 97	$A_2 = 61 + 97 = 158$

$B_1 = 64 + 61 = 125 \quad B_2 = 78 + 97 = 175$

(continued)

TABLE 16.2 **(Continued)**

$$(1) = \frac{G^2}{npq} = \frac{300^2}{5(2)(2)} = \frac{90{,}000}{20} = 4500$$

$$(2) = \Sigma X^2 = 15^2 + 12^2 + 13^2 + \ldots + 18^2 + 21^2 + 20^2 = 4718$$

(ii)

$$(3) = \frac{\Sigma A^2}{nq} = \frac{(142^2 + 158^2)}{5(2)} = \frac{45{,}128}{10} = 4512.8$$

$$(4) = \frac{\Sigma B^2}{np} = \frac{(125^2 + 175^2)}{5(2)} = \frac{46{,}250}{10} = 4625$$

$$(5) = \frac{\Sigma (AB)^2}{n} = \frac{(64^2 + 61^2 + 78^2 + 97^2)}{5} = \frac{23310}{5} = 4662$$

(iii)

$SS_{bg} = (5) - (1) = 4662 - 4500 = 162$

$SS_A = (3) - (1) = 4512.8 - 4500 = 12.8$

$SS_B = (4) - (1) = 4625 - 4500 = 125$

$SS_{AB} = (5) - (4) - (3) + (1) = 4662 - 4625 - 4512.8 + 4500 = 24.2$

$SS_{wg} = (2) - (5) = 4718 - 4662 = 56$

$SS_{tot} = (2) - (1) = 4718 - 4500 = 218$

(iv)

	Source	SS	df	MS	F
	Between groups	162	3	54	15.43
A	(Magnitude of reinforcement)	12.8	1	12.8	3.66
B	(Time away from nest)	125	1	125	35.71
AB	(Interaction)	24.2	1	24.2	6.91
	Within groups	56	16	3.5	
	Total	218	19		

The mean squares in section (iv) of the summary table for the two-way ANOVA are obtained by dividing the SS by their corresponding df. The F-ratios are then obtained as in the one-way ANOVA by dividing the MS for a between-group source of variance by MS_{wg}.

Finally note in section (iv) that although the interaction is designated by the letter combination AB, it is, as indicated in parentheses, expressed in terms of the independent variables: Magnitude of Reinforcement × Time Away from Nest, where × is read as "by."

The significance of the F-ratios are determined in the same manner in which they are determined for the one-way ANOVA. You enter Appendix Table 6 with df associated with the numerator and denominator of the F-ratio at the preset level of significance. For the between-group F-ratio, df are 3 and 16, respectively. For the other F-ratios, df are 1 and 16. The decision rule is as follows:

$$\text{If } F_{calc} \geq F_{table}, \text{ reject } H_0.$$

With the significance level set at 0.05 for the hypothetical infant rat experiment, the between-group F, the F for the main effect of B (time away from nest), and the F for the interaction of A and B are significant.

How you interpret the results of the two-way ANOVA depends upon a number of factors. These include the conditions underlying the ANOVA, decisions made during the planning stage of the experiment, and the pattern of signficant effects, that is, whether there are significant main effects, interaction effects, or both.

PROGRESS ASSESSMENT 16.3

Table 16-A presents hypothetical data for the experiment in Progress Assessment 16.1. Apply the two-way ANOVA, put the results in a summary table, and indicate with an asterisk (*) which obtained F-values are significant at the 5 percent level of significance.

TABLE 16-A
Number of Items Recalled in a Testing Context That Was Either the Same or Different from the Training Context after One, Ten, and Twenty-five Days

		Recall Interval		
		1 day	10 days	25 days
Testing Context	Same	19	18	19
		20	18	18
		19	16	17
		18	17	17
		17	15	16
	Different	19	15	12
		17	13	11
		16	12	9
		18	12	13
		16	9	7

INTERPRETATION OF THE TWO-WAY ANOVA

As you already know, the outcome of a statistical test can be correctly interpreted only if certain conditions have been satisfied. The two-way ANOVA is no exception. In fact, certain decisions made during the planning stage of the experiment influence not only how the ANOVA is interpreted but also how it is performed.

Conditions Underlying the Two-Way ANOVA

The conditions underlying the two-way ANOVA are identical to those underlying the one-way ANOVA and the *t*-test for random independent samples. The dependent variable should be measured along an interval or ratio scale and the samples must be random independent samples from normal populations with equal variances. Recall from Chapter 14 that if these conditions are not satisfied, the distribution of the obtained *F*-values will be more variable than the theoretical *F*-distribution. This could result in rejecting a true H_0 and, hence, lead to faulty conclusions. It is especially important to select samples and take measures that meet the conditions underlying the two-way ANOVA because, unlike for the *CR-k* design, there is no alternative comparable nonparametric test for the *CRF* design.

Effects of Decisions Made When Planning the Experiment

In addition to the conditions just discussed, for the two-way ANOVA in this chapter assume that the treatment levels are selected on some predetermined nonrandom basis. For example, in the hypothetical infant rat experiment, the 1/2-hour and 1-hour times away from the nest may have been selected by the investigator because previous research indicated that these times were sufficient to increase the motor activity of the rat and yet not long enough to be distressful. If the levels had been chosen randomly from all possible time intervals, the times selected may have been so long as to be distressful or even debilitating for the infant rat, or so short as not to be sufficiently motivating.

Assume also that any replication of the experiment would necessarily include the same treatment levels. If another experimenter wishes to replicate the results of the hypothetical infant rat experiment, the times away from the nest and the times the infant rats are allowed to remain with a lactating dam for making a correct response would need to be the same.

While these assumptions reflect the kinds of decisions that are most often made in research, they are not the only decisions that can be made. You can, for example, decide to select the treatment levels of some or all of the independent variables randomly. Also, a replication of the experiment need not necessarily include the same treatment levels.

While the decisions that you make during the planning stages of your experiment do not affect how you derive your mean squares, they do affect how you obtain the *F*-ratios and the conclusions you draw from them. For example, when treatment levels of all factors are selected on some predetermined nonrandom basis, the factors are called **fixed factors.** With fixed factors, the analysis is simplified because the denominator of all *F*-ratios is the within-group mean square. The *F*-ratios can have different denominators if some or all of the treatment levels are selected randomly, that is, are **random factors.** Also, when you make the kind of decisions that have been assumed here, all treatment levels about which conclusions can be drawn on the basis of your analysis are included in the experimental design.

For the hypothetical infant rat experiment, no general statement can be made about either time away from nest or magnitude of reinforcement. All statements or conclusions are restricted to the two specific times away from the nest and the specific times allowed to remain with the lactating dam. Fixed factors, then, while they simplify the analysis, limit the generality of your results.

Pattern of Significant Effects

As you may have surmised from the number of *F*-ratios computed in section (iv) of Table 16.2, in a two-way ANOVA more than one null hypothesis is being tested. As in the one-way ANOVA there is a null hypothesis for the between-groups effect, H_0: $\mu_{ab_{11}} = \mu_{ab_{12}} = \ldots \mu_{ab_{1q}} = \mu_{ab_{21}} = \mu_{ab_{22}} = \ldots \mu_{ab_{pq}}$. There is also a null hypothesis for each main effect. The null hypothesis for the main effect of *A* is H_0: $\mu_{a_1} = \mu_{a_2} = \mu_{a_3} = \ldots \mu_{a_p}$; the null hypothesis for the main effect of *B* is H_0: $\mu_{b_1} = \mu_{b_2} = \mu_{b_3} = \ldots \mu_{b_q}$. In addition, there is a null hypothesis for the interaction which is H_0: *the interaction is additive.* The meaning of *additive* will be discussed shortly. In any given ANOVA all null hypotheses may be rejected or may fail to be rejected, or some may be rejected while others are not.

The obtained pattern of significance also influences how you perform and interpret the results of your analysis. The between-group *F* was found to be significant for the hypothetical infant rat experiment. This portion of the ANOVA is similar to the one-way ANOVA and, as in the one-way ANOVA, significance of the between-group *F* not only tells you that some or all of your experimental treatments are influencing your dependent variable but also that the data must be further analyzed. Had the between-group *F* not been significant, then chances are that there would be no main or interaction effects. Usually, when the between-group *F* is not significant, the analysis is discontinued.

When the between-group *F* is significant, then the pattern of significant main and interaction effects determine, in part, how you interpret the results of your ANOVA. In the numerical example of the two-factor ANOVA performed on the data from the hypothetical infant rat experiment reported in Table 16.2, there was a significant main effect of the B-variable (time away from the nest) and a significant interaction (Magnitude of Reinforcement × Time Away from Nest).

If the interaction effect were not significant, you could, simply by looking at the means of the B-levels, conclude that one level of B (b_2 = 1 hour away from the nest) was more effective than the other level (b_1 = 1/2 hour away from the nest). Since the B-variable (time away from the nest) interacted significantly with the A-variable (magnitude of reinforcement), a conclusion about the effect of the B-variable cannot be reached simply by looking at the means for the levels of B. The reason is that the significant interaction effect of variables A and B means that the levels of B may not be having the same effect across all levels of A. For example, it is possible that the effect of b_1 (1/2 hour away from the nest) differs from the effect of b_2 (1 hour away from the nest) when the magnitude of reinforcement is large (a_2) but not when it is small (a_1). The significant main effect of a variable with only two treatment levels can be simply interpreted from the means of the levels if and only if there is no significant interaction effect. If there is a significant interaction, then simple main effects may need to be assessed. **Simple main effects** are the effects of all levels of one variable at each level of another variable.

Also, if there are more than two treatment levels of a variable for which the main effect is significant, then, as for the one-way ANOVA, further analysis with *a priori* or *a posteriori* tests are required whether or not there is a significant interaction.

PROGRESS ASSESSMENT 16.4

1. State in symbols the null hypotheses for the main effects evaluated in Progress Assessment 16.3.
2. State in words the null hypothesis for interaction effects.
3. Which main effects, if any, in the ANOVA of Progress Assessment 16.3 can be interpreted without further analysis? Give the reason.

Interaction Effects

From the discussion on the pattern of significant effects it should be evident that a correct interpretation of the results of a two-way ANOVA requires a clear understanding of what is meant by interaction effects and when interaction effects are significant.

We have already alluded to the meaning of interaction effects. For example, in pointing out differences between the one-way ANOVA and the two-way ANOVA we mentioned that the two-way ANOVA is used to determine if the level of one variable has the same or a different effect across levels of the other variable (called interaction effects). When one variable

TABLE 16.3
Hypothetical Data Set for Subjects Assigned to Different Treatment Combinations of a *CRF*-23 Design before (i) and after (ii and iii) Introduction of the Experimental Treatments

	(i)			(ii) After Treatment That Produces Additive Effect			(iii) After Treatment That Produces Nonadditive Effect	
	Before Treatment							
	a_1	a_2		a_1	a_2		a_1	a_2
	X	X		$X + 1 + 1$	$X + 2 + 1$		$X + 1 + 1$	$X + 3 + 1$
b_1	X	X	b_1	$X + 1 + 1$	$X + 2 + 1$	b_1	$X + 1 + 1$	$X + 3 + 1$
	X	X		$X + 1 + 1$	$X + 2 + 1$		$X + 1 + 1$	$X + 3 + 1$
				(2)	(3)		(2)	(4)
	X	X		$X + 1 + 2$	$X + 2 + 2$		$X + 2 + 2$	$X + 2 + 2$
b_2	X	X	b_2	$X + 1 + 2$	$X + 2 + 2$	b_2	$X + 2 + 2$	$X + 2 + 2$
	X	X		$X + 1 + 2$	$X + 2 + 2$		$X + 2 + 2$	$X + 2 + 2$
				(3)	(4)		(4)	(4)
	X	X		$X + 1 + 3$	$X + 2 + 3$		$X + 3 + 3$	$X + 1 + 3$
b_3	X	X	b_3	$X + 1 + 3$	$X + 2 + 3$	b_3	$X + 3 + 3$	$X + 1 + 3$
	X	X		$X + 1 + 3$	$X + 2 + 3$		$X + 3 + 3$	$X + 1 + 3$
				(4)	(5)		(6)	(4)

has the same effect across levels of the other variable there is said to be an **additive interaction** and it is considered not significant. When one variable has a different effect across levels of the other variable there is said to be a **nonadditive interaction.** Nonadditive interaction effects are significant.

The hypothetical data set for a *CRF*-23 design in Table 16.3 is used to illustrate the difference between additive and nonadditive interaction effects.

In Table 16.3 the data (X's) in section (i) represent the scores of subjects on the characteristic of interest before the introduction of the experimental treatments. Values for X would be variable due to individual difference and various sources of error. Numerical values for these preexperimental data are not used so that the effects of the treatment combinations in section (ii) and (iii) will be seen more clearly.

In section (ii), it is assumed that levels of variable A have different effects but that each level of A has the same effect across all levels of B. In section (ii), a_1 has the effect of incrementing (first added number in the a_1 column) the X-value by 1 at b_1, b_2, and b_3 so that all the scores in the a_1 column begin with $X + 1$. Similarly, a_2 has the effect of incrementing (first added number in the a_2 column) the X-value by 2 at b_1, b_2 and b_3 so that all the scores in the a_2 column begin with $X + 2$. In section (ii), it is also assumed that the levels of the B variable have different effects but that each level of B has the same effect across both levels of A. Thus, b_1

has the effect of incrementing (second added number in the b_1 row) the scores by 1, b_2 has the effect of incrementing (second added number in the b_2 row) the scores by 2, and b_3 has the effect of incrementing (second number in the b_3 row) the scores by 3 in both the a_1 and a_2 columns. The value in parentheses is the average effect of the ab_{ij} treatment combination. The averages reflect an additive interaction effect.

In section (iii), it is also assumed that both the levels of A and the levels of B differ from each other and that each level of B has the same effect (second added number) across both levels of A. However, it is assumed that each A-level has a different effect (first added number) across the B-levels, that is a_1 adds 1 to b_1 scores, 2 to b_2 scores, and 3 to b_3 scores, and a_2 adds 3 to b_1 scores, 2 to b_2 scores, and 1 to b_3 scores. As in section (ii), the value in parentheses in section (iii) is the average effect of the ab_{ij} treatment combination. These mean values reflect a nonadditive interaction effect.

Plots of these average effects of the ab_{ij} treatment combinations for sections (ii) and (iii) as shown in Figure 16.2 more clearly illustrate the difference between additive and nonadditive interaction effects. The figure's left

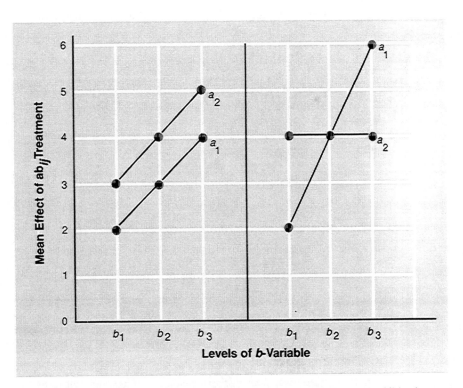

FIGURE 16.2 *Mean effect of ab_{ij} treatment. The left panel depicts an additive interaction. The right panel depicts a nonadditive interaction.*

panel, which depicts the average additive effect of the treatment combinations in Table 16.3, section (ii), shows two parallel lines. In contrast, the figure's right panel, which depicts the average nonadditive effect of the treatment combinations in Table 16.3, section (iii), shows a pair of lines that are clearly not parallel.

The plotted values in Figure 16.2 do not include the actual value of the X's but only the average effect of the experimental treatment combinations. Due to individual differences in the X-values and differences due to various sources of experimental error, interaction effects may result in data that, when plotted, do not resemble lines which are as clearly parallel or nonparallel as the lines in Figure 16.2. However, if the statistical analysis indicates that the interaction effect is significant, then the lack of parallelism is due to the combination of experimental treatments. If the interaction effect is not significant, then the lack of visual parallelism is due to individual differences or experimental error. For example, because the Time-Away-from-Nest- × -Magnitude-of-Reinforcement interaction was found to be significant in the analysis of the data from the hypothetical infant rat experiment, the lack of parallelism in the lines depicting this interaction in Figure 16.3 is attributed to the nonadditive interaction effects of the experimental treatments.

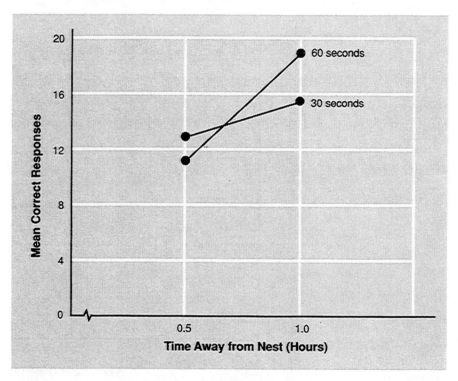

FIGURE 16.3 *A plot of the nonadditive interaction of the two independent variables, time away from nest and magnitude of reinforcement (time with lactating dam), for the hypothetical infant rat experiment.*

In contrast to the obviously nonparallel lines in Figures 16.3, observe the slight deviation from parallelism in the lines in Figure 16.4. Figure 16.4 depicts an *AB* (Gender of Model × Age of Model) interaction from a hypothetical experiment examining the effect of different model characteristics on children's (observers') imitative behavior. In this experiment, in which there is no significant interaction, the slight deviation from parallelism in the lines is attributed to individual differences and other sources of experimental error.

PROGRESS ASSESSMENT 16.5

1. Plot the *AB* interaction for the hypothetical recall experiment of Progress Assessment 16.1 from information given in Table 16-A.
2. Does the plot of the *AB* interaction suggest that it is or is not significant?
3. Does your answer to part 2 agree with your answer to Progress Assessment 16.3?

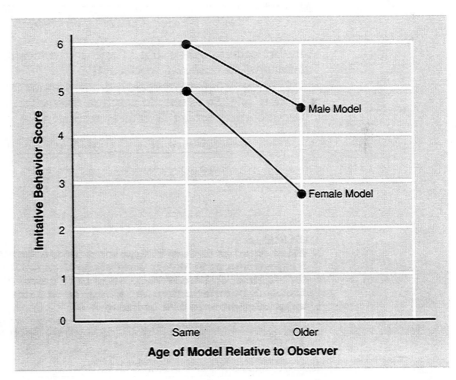

FIGURE 16.4 *A plot of the additive interaction of gender of model and age of model relative to observer for the hypothetical imitative behavior experiment.*

Tests for Simple Main Effects

When there is a significant interaction effect, a correct interpretation of the results of the two-way ANOVA requires tests for simple main effects. Simple main effects, you may recall, are the effects of all levels of one variable at each level of another variable. If a simple main effect is significant, then, comparisons among means for the simple main effect may also be necessary for a correct interpretation of the experimental results.

The F-test that you used to make comparisons following the one-way ANOVA can also be used to compare means for simple main effects when there are only two levels of the independent variable. If the number of treatment levels of an independent variable is greater than two, then a generalization of the F-test can be used to test for simple main effects.

Tests Used When There Are Only Two Levels of the Independent Variable.   In using the F-test we recommend replacing the $\overline{T}$-symbol for the mean of treatment effects with the appropriate symbolization from the two-way ANOVA. For example, for the hypothetical infant rat experiment in which there are only two levels of each independent variable, a test of the simple main effect of B across a_i is made with Formula 16.1:

Formula 16.1
$$F = \frac{(\overline{AB}_{ij} - \overline{AB}_{ij'})^2}{MS_{wg} \left(\frac{1}{n} + \frac{1}{n}\right)}$$

In this formula, $\overline{AB}_{ij}$ and $\overline{AB}_{ij'}$ refer to the means of the treatment combinations, ab_{ij} and $ab_{ij'}$, respectively.

The means for the hypothetical infant rat experiment are presented in Table 16.4. For a test of the simple main effect of B (magnitude of reinforcement) across a_1 (1/2 hour away from nest), you have the following:

$$F = \frac{(\overline{AB}_{11} - \overline{AB}_{12})^2}{MS_{wg} \left(\frac{1}{n} + \frac{1}{n}\right)} = \frac{(12.8 - 15.6)^2}{3.5 \left(\frac{1}{5} + \frac{1}{5}\right)} = \frac{7.84}{1.4} = 5.6$$

TABLE 16.4
Mean Number of Correct Responses for the Hypothetical Infant Rat Experiment in Which Infant Rats Kept Away from the Nest for 1/2 Hour or 1 Hour Were Allowed to Remain with a Lactating Dam for Either 30 Seconds or 60 Seconds after Making a Correct Response in a Learning Task

		Time Away from Nest	
		b_1 (1/2 hour)	b_2 (1 hour)
Time with	a_1 (30 seconds)	12.8	15.6
Dam	a_2 (60 seconds)	12.2	19.4

For the test of the simple main effect of B across a_2, F equals 37.03.

Similarly, for a test of the simple main effect of A (time away from nest) across b_j (magnitude of reinforcement) the general formula is as follows:

Formula 16.2
$$F = \frac{(\overline{AB}_{ij} - \overline{AB}_{i'j})^2}{MS_{wg} \left(\dfrac{1}{n} + \dfrac{1}{n}\right)}$$

For a test of the simple main effect of A (time away from nest) across b_1 (30 seconds with a lactating dam),

$$F = \frac{(\overline{AB}_{11} - \overline{AB}_{21})^2}{MS_{wg} \left(\dfrac{1}{n} + \dfrac{1}{n}\right)} = \frac{(12.8 - 12.2)^2}{3.5 \left(\dfrac{1}{5} + \dfrac{1}{5}\right)} = \frac{0.36}{1.4} = 0.26$$

For a test of the simple main effect of A across b_2, F equals 10.31.

The df associated with tests for simple main effects of A are $p - 1$ and df_{wg} for the numerator and denominator of the F-ratio, respectively. For tests of simple main effects of B, the comparable df are $q - 1$ and df_{wg}. Since in the hypothetical infant rat experiment there are only two levels of A and two levels of B, the df associated with all four tests of simple main effects are 1 and 16.

Although there has been considerable debate among statisticians about procedures controlling error rate for simple main effects, most researchers tend to set the same significance level for the simple main effects as they do for main and interaction effects. If you follow this procedure, then the table value, 4.49, (Appendix Table 6) for $F(1, 16)$ is the critical value used to determine if the F's for simple main effects in the infant rat experiment are significant at the 0.05 level of significance. Following is the decision rule for determining the significance of the simple main effects:

$$\text{If } F_{calc} \geq F_{table}, \text{ reject } H_0.$$

Since the F's for both simple main effects of B are greater than 4.49, it can be concluded that, as time with a lactating dam increases from 30 to 60 seconds, the number of correct responses made by infant rats increases regardless of whether amount of time spent away from the nest is 1/2 or 1 hour. The overall main effect of B (magnitude of reinforcement) is, then, meaningful even though the interaction is significant. In contrast, the simple main effect of A (time away from nest) at b_1 (30 seconds with a lactating dam) is not significant, $F(1, 16) = 0.36$; $p > 0.05$, but the simple main effect of A at b_2 (60 seconds with a lactating dam) is significant. No general statement about the effect of time away from nest can be made with respect to magnitude of reinforcement. In this case, this would be true even if the main effect of A were significant. It can only be concluded that 1 hour away from the nest leads to better performance than 1/2 hour away from the nest if the infant rat is allowed to remain with a lactating dam for 60 seconds but not if it is allowed to remain with the dam for only 30 seconds.

Tests Used When There Are More Than Two Levels of the Independent Variable.

When there are more than two levels of the independent variable, a test for simple main effects requires that you compute the SS and MS for the effect of one variable *at each level* of the other variable. You then compute the F-ratio for each simple main effect in the usual manner by dividing the MS for the treatment by the MS_{wg}. This, in effect, is what is accomplished with the *a priori* F-test.

The procedure for computing SS for simple main effects is the same as that for computing SS for main effects and is expressed by Formula 16.3. Although the number of levels of the independent variable, time away from nest, in the hypothetical infant rat experiment is only two, the data from that experiment is used to illustrate the application of Formula 16.3. The SS for the simple main effect of A (time away from nest) across b_2 (60 seconds with a lactating dam) is as follows:

Formula 16.3
$$SS_A \text{ at } b_2 = \frac{[(AB_{12})^2 + (AB_{22})^2]}{n} - \frac{B_2^2}{np}$$

$$= \frac{(78^2 + 97^2)}{5} - \frac{(175)^2}{10}$$

$$= 3098.6 - 3062.5 = 36.1$$

The df for the simple main effect of a variable is the same as the df for the main effect. The df for the simple main effect of A at b_2 is, therefore, $p - 1$. The MS, then, is

$$MS_A \text{ at } b_2 = \frac{(SS_A \text{ at } b_2)}{(p - 1)} = \frac{36.1}{1} = 36.1$$

The F for the simple main effect of A at b_2 is

$$F = \frac{(MS_A \text{ at } b_2)}{MS_{wg}} = \frac{36.1}{3.5} = 10.31$$

Since there are only two levels of the independent variable in the hypothetical infant rat experiment, the value obtained for F using this procedure is the same value obtained with Formula 16.2. The *a priori* F-test (Formula 16.2), in fact, is a derivation from a more general expression:

Formula 16.4
$$F_A \text{ at } b_j = \frac{\{[(AB_{1j})^2 + (AB_{2j})^2 + \ldots + (AB_{pj})^2]/n - (B_j^2/np)\}/(p - 1)}{MS_{wg}}$$

In this formula j is a constant level of the B-variable, B_j^2 represents the squared sum of treatment level b_j, n refers to the number of scores making up each AB_{ij} sum, and np represents the number of scores used in computing B_j.

More specifically,

$$F_A \text{ at } b_2 = \frac{\{[(AB_{12})^2 + (AB_{22})^2 + (AB_{32})^2 + \ldots + (AB_{p2})^2]/n - B_2^2/np\}/(p-1)}{MS_{wg}}$$

With the appropriate change in symbols, Formula 16.4 is applicable to the simple main effect of either variable at any level of the other variable.

PROGRESS ASSESSMENT 16.6

Using the information obtained in the solution of Progress Assessment 16.3, complete the following steps for the hypothetical recall experiment of Progress Assessment 16.1:

1. Perform a test for the simple main effect of testing context at the one-day recall interval.
2. Perform a test for the simple main effect of recall interval at the testing context that was different from the learning context.
3. Determine if the main effect of testing context is meaningful.

Mean Comparisons for Main Effects

When the interaction of two variables is not significant, tests for simple main effects are not required. If, however, the number of levels of an independent variable is greater than two *and* the main effect of that variable is significant, then comparisons of means for the main effect are necessary to interpret the results of the experiment. The formula used to compare means is a direct generalization of Formula 14.11, the *a priori* F-formula for making planned comparisons following the one-way ANOVA. Thus, the formula for comparing means of the *A*-variable is presented without illustrative application:

Formula 16.5
$$F = \frac{(\bar{A}_i - \bar{A}_{i'})^2}{MS_{wg}(\frac{1}{nq} + \frac{1}{nq})}$$

In this formula, i and i' denote different levels of A and $\bar{A}_i$ and $\bar{A}_{i'}$ are means of A-levels i and i', respectively. Note that nq is used instead of n for the fractions in the denominator of the F-ratio because the denominators of those fractions refer to the number of scores that make up the sum of the scores from which the means $\bar{A}_i$ and $\bar{A}_{i'}$ are computed.

The *df* associated with this F-ratio are 1 (for the numerator) and the df_{wg} (for the denominator).

When the number of mean comparisons is large, a critical value for the mean difference can be established in the same manner as for the *a priori* F-test following the one-way ANOVA. Following is the formula for a critical value (*CV*) for mean difference of a *B*-variable:

Formula 16.6 $\qquad CV = \sqrt{F_{\text{table}} \left[MS_{\text{wg}} \left(\frac{1}{np} + \frac{1}{np} \right) \right]}$

A similar formula can be written for the critical value for mean differences of the *A*-variable.

PROGRESS ASSESSMENT 16.7

1. Write the *F*-formula for comparing means for the main effect of the *B*-variable.
2. Write a formula for the critical value for mean differences of the *A*-variable.

The Extent of the Effect

When your analysis yields significant main or interaction effects, *effect* refers to the difference between the observed treatment mean and the mean of the sampling distribution. A significant effect means that the difference between the observed mean and the mean of the sampling distribution is larger than would be expected by chance.

Significant does not have the same meaning as it does in our everyday usage of the term. *Significant* does not indicate that the effect is meaningful or the extent to which the independent variables influence the dependent variable. You can, however, estimate the extent to which a dependent variable is influenced by an independent variable by calculating a value referred to as **eta-squared** (η^2). Although a Greek letter is used to designate this value, it is a statistic, not a parameter. In fact, it is a biased statistic because it tends to overestimate the value that you would obtain if you had access to all the population members. However, it is easy to calculate and gives you a rough idea of the extent to which your dependent variable is influenced by the independent variables.

Eta-squared is much like r^2, the coefficient of determination (Chapter 8). The coefficient of determination estimates the variability in one dependent variable that can be accounted for by the variation in another. Eta-squared estimates the percentage of variability in the dependent variable that can be attributed to an independent variable or an interaction of variables. Eta-squared is the ratio of the sum of squares for any given treatment or interaction of treatments to the total sum of squares (SS_{tot}) expressed as a percentage.

In the hypothetical infant rat experiment, for example, SS_B (where *B* refers to time away from nest) equals 125 and SS_{tot} equals 218. The percentage of variability in the performance measure of the infant rats that is attributable to time away from nest, then, is obtained by multiplying SS_B/SS_{tot} by 100 as follows:

$$\eta^2 = \frac{SS_B}{SS_{tot}} = \frac{125}{218} = 0.573$$

$$0.573 \times 100 = 57.3$$

Approximately 57 percent of the variability in performance can be attibuted to time away from nest. Similar percentages can be obtained for the reinforcement variable and the interaction of magnitude of reinforcement and time away from the nest.

PROGRESS ASSESSMENT 16.8

For the hypothetical infant rat experiment:

1. Determine how much variability in the dependent variable can be attributed to time with a lactating dam.
2. Determine the extent of the interaction effect.

SUMMARY

This chapter introduces you to a class of designs, called completely randomized factorial designs, in which there are two or more levels of each of two or more independent variables. It also introduces you to the two-way ANOVA, the procedure used to analyze the data of an experiment with two independent variables and a single dependent measure on each sample member. The two-way ANOVA is used to evaluate the individual effects of the independent variables, called main effects, and the combined effects of variables, called interaction effects. Terminology and symbols used to designate variables, levels, and sums necessary to evaluate main and interaction effects are explained. The formulas for evaluating these effects are applied in the analysis of an experiment in which there are two levels of each of two independent variables. How the pattern of significant effects and the decisions made when planning the experiment influence the way the data are analyzed and interpreted are discussed. Tests following the ANOVA that aid in its interpretation are also presented along with a statistic, η^2, that provides a rough measure of the extent of the effects of the independent variables on the dependent variable.

KEY DEFINITIONS

A, B   Symbols in a two-way ANOVA that are used to represent independent variables of a completely randomized factorial design.

A_1, A_2, B_1, B_2 Symbols used to designate sums of treatment levels a_1, a_2, b_1, b_2, respectively.

$a_1, a_2, \ldots a_p, b_1, b_2 \ldots b_q$ Symbols used to designate treatment levels of factors A, B.

AB   Symbol used to refer to the combined treatments A and B and also to the interaction of the two variables.

additive interaction   When one variable has the same effect across levels of the other variable.

completely randomized factorial design   An experimental design involving two or more levels of each of two or more independent variables.

CRF-pq   Symbols for a completely randomized factorial design where p and q refer to the number of treatment levels of the two independent variables.

$CV = \sqrt{F_{\text{table}} \, [MS_{\text{wg}} \, (1/np + 1/np)]}$ The formula for a critical value for mean differences of a B-variable.

eta-squared (η^2) A biased estimate of the extent to which a dependent variable is influenced by an independent variable. It is the ratio of SS for any given treatment or interaction of treatments to SS_{tot} expressed as a percentage.

$$F_A \text{ at } b_j = \frac{\{[(AB_{1j})^2 + (AB_{2j})^2 + \ldots + (AB_{pj})^2]/n - (B_j^2/np)\}/(p - 1)]}{MS_{wg}}$$

General expression for testing the simple main effect of A at b_j in a two-factor experiment.

factorial experiment   An experiment in which each treatment level of any one variable is administered in conjunction with each and every treatment level of the other variables.

$F = (\overline{AB}_{ij} - \overline{AB}_{i'j})^2/[MS_{\text{wg}}(1/n + 1/n)]$ Formula for testing the simple main effect of A across b_j when there are two levels of A in a *CRF-pq* design.

$F = (\overline{AB}_{ij} - \overline{AB}_{ij'})^2/[MS_{\text{wg}}(1/n + 1/n)]$ Formula for testing the simple main effect of B across a_i when there are two levels of B in a *CRF-pq* design.

$F = (\overline{A}_i - \overline{A}_{i'})^2/[MS_{\text{wg}}(1/nq + 1/nq)]$ Formula for comparing means for the main effect of A-variable in a *CRF-pq* design.

$F = (MS_A \text{ at } b_2)/MS_{\text{wg}}$ Formula for testing the simple main effect of A at b_2.

fixed factors Variables whose treatment levels have been selected on some predetermined nonrandom basis.

interaction effects The effects on the dependent variable of one independent variable across levels of another independent variable.

main effects The effects of levels of individual independent variables on the dependent variable.

nonadditive interaction When one variable has a different effect across levels of another variable.

p, q Letters used to designate the number of treatment levels of variables A and B, respectively.

random factors Variables whose treatment levels have been selected randomly.

simple main effects The effects of all levels of one variable at each level of another variable.

SS_A at b_2 $= \{[(AB_{12})^2 + (AB_{22})^2]/n\} - (B_2^2/np)$ The sum of squares for variable A at level b_2 in a factorial experiment with only two levels of A.

two-way ANOVA The analysis used to evaluate the data from an experiment involving two independent variables and a single dependent measure taken on each sample member (*CRF-pq* design).

REVIEW EXERCISES

It has been known for some time that electroconvulsive therapy (ECT) is effective in alleviating depression. This therapy involves passing a high-intensity current through the brain via electrodes placed on one side (unilateral) or both sides (bilateral) of the skull. Unfortunately, ECT has numerous behavioral side effects. Research indicates that retrograde amnmesia is the forgetting of events that preceded ECT with the greatest forgetting for events immediately preceding ECT.

To see which type of ECT (unilateral or bilateral) produces the greatest degree of retrograde amnesia, two researchers at a psychiatric institute had patients that were to receive ECT as a treatment for depression spend 30 seconds observing each of twenty novel scenes either immediately (0 hour), 1 hour, or 24 hours before therapy. The following day they recalled as many of the twenty scenes as they could. The data are shown in Table 16-B. One-third of the patients were randomly assigned to each of the observation-therapy intervals. A random half of the patients at each observation-therapy interval experienced the unilateral (uni) therapy and the remaining halves experienced the bilateral (bi) therapy.

a. Symbolize the design of the experiment.
b. Name the dependent and independent variables and assign letters to the independent variables.

TABLE 16-B
Number of Scenes Recalled by Patients Undergoing
Unilateral or Bilateral Electroconvulsive Therapy

Interval	Therapy	Scenes Recalled by Patients		
0 hour	uni	18	16	14
	uni	13	15	14
0 hour	bi	2	3	0
	bi	4	6	7
1 hour	uni	17	12	15
	uni	11	12	10
1 hour	bi	10	9	8
	bi	7	6	6
24 hour	uni	19	17	18
	uni	12	13	9
24 hour	bi	17	16	19
	bi	9	13	10

c. Assign symbols to the levels of the independent variables.

d. Name the scale on which the dependent variable is measured.

e. State if the dependent variable is continuous or discrete.

f. Determine if the samples are biased, random, or randomized.

g. Symbolize the sum of the scores for the patients receiving unilateral ECT.

h. Symbolize the sum of the scores for patients receiving bilateral ECT one hour after observing the scenes.

i. Symbolize the sum of the scores for the patients observing the scenes 24 hours before receiving unilateral therapy.

j. Construct a summary table of computational formulas for *SS* and *df*.

k. Plot the *AB* interaction.

l. Determine from the graphs if the interaction is significant.

m. Apply ANOVA to the data of Table 16-B and put the results in a summary table; indicate with an asterisk the *F*-values that are significant.

n. Does the ANOVA agree with your answer to part *l*?

o. Which main effect (if any) can be interpreted without further analysis?

p. Test for the simple main effects of type of therapy at the 0-hour observation-therapy interval.

q. Test for the simple main effects of observation-therapy interval at unilateral therapy.

r. How much variability in the number of scenes remembered can be attributed to the interaction of type of therapy and observation-therapy interval?

ANSWERS TO PROGRESS ASSESSMENTS

16.1   **1.** A = environmental context; B = recall interval.

       2. $p = 2$; $q = 3$.

       3. a_1 = same room; a_2 = different room; b_1 = 1 day; b_2 = 5 days; b_3 = 25 days

       4. AB_{13}

       5. B_1

       6. A_2

16.2   **1.** $(1) = G^2/npq$; $(2) = \Sigma X^2$; $(3) = \Sigma A^2/nq$; $(4) = \Sigma B^2/np$; $(5) = \Sigma(AB)^2/n$.

       2. See Table 16-C.

16.3   See Table 16-D.

TABLE 16-C
Summary Table of Computational Formulas for *SS* and *df* for the Two-Way ANOVA

Source	SS	df
Between groups	$(5) - (1)$	$pq - 1$
A(Test context)	$(3) - (1)$	$p - 1$
B(Recall interval)	$(4) - (1)$	$q - 1$
AB(Context × interval)	$(5) - (4) - (3) + (1)$	$(p - 1)(q - 1)$
Within groups	$(2) - (5)$	$pq(n - 1)$
Total	$(2) - (1)$	$npq - 1$

TABLE 16-D
Summary Table of a Two-Way ANOVA Performed on the Data from the Hypothetical Experiment on the Effect of Environmental Context on Recall of Verbal Material at Three Recall Intervals

Source	SS	df	MS	F
Between groups	273.37	5	54.67	19.88*
A(Test Context)	140.84	1	140.84	51.21*
B(Recall interval)	93.07	2	46.54	16.92*
AB(Context × interval)	39.46	2	19.73	7.17*
Within groups	66.00	24	2.75	
Total	339.37	29		

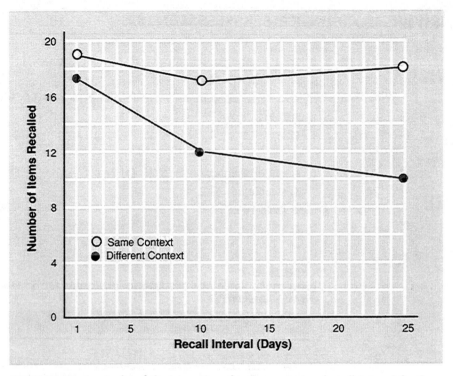

FIGURE 16-A *A plot of the interaction of testing context and recall interval for the hypothetical recall experiment.*

16.4   **1.** $H_0: \mu_{a_1} = \mu_{a_2}; H_0: \mu_{b_1} = \mu_{b_2} = \mu_{b_3}.$
       2. The interaction is additive.
       3. Neither main effect can be interpreted without further analysis because the interaction is significant.

16.5   **1.** See Figure 16-A.
       2. The graph suggests that the interaction is significant.
       3. Yes.

16.6   **1.** $F(1, 24) = 1.78$, not significant.
       2. $F(2, 24) = 22.57$, significant.
       3. The simple main effect of context is significant at the 10- and 25-day recall intervals $Fs(1, 24) > 19.2; p < 0.05$, but not at the 1-day recall interval (see answer to part 1 of this Progress Assessment). Therefore, the main effect of context is not meaningful.

16.7 **1.** $F = \dfrac{(\bar{B}_j - \bar{B}_{j'})^2}{MS_{wg} \left(\dfrac{1}{np} + \dfrac{1}{np}\right)}$

2. $CV = \sqrt{F_{table} \left[MS_{wg}(1/nq + 1/nq)\right]}$

16.8 **1.** You can attribute 5.9 percent of the variability in the dependent variable to time spent with the lactating dam (reinforcement).

2. You can attribute 11.1 percent of the variability in the dependent variable to the interaction of magnitude of reinforcement and time away from the nest.

CHAPTER 17

Analysis of Frequency Data Obtained for Specific Categories: Chi-Square

*T*he statistical tests that you have used so far in this text have dealt with data measured or ordered along a quantitative dimension—IQ scores, grade-point average, time to complete a maze, or ranks in a talent contest. There are times when an investigator does not have information about the *measured* amount of the characteristic of interest but, rather, has simply determined whether the event has or has not been observed. This chapter introduces a statistic that is used to evaluate hypotheses when observations are classified into mutually exclusive categories and the frequency of observations in each category is determined.

CHI-SQUARE AND ITS DISTRIBUTION

By now you should be very familiar with the fact that statistical hypothesis testing involves the use of a formula to calculate values of a specific statistic and a theoretical distribution to determine the probability of obtaining the values of a calculated statistic simply on the basis of chance. The statistic, **chi-square,** symbolized χ^2, is used to evaluate statistical hypotheses when frequency data are collected for different categories.

Chi-Square Formula

Computing chi-square requires an understanding of two new terms. One term, **expected frequencies (E),** refers to the number of observations that should be obtained based on statements given in the null hypothesis. The other term, **observed frequencies (O),** refers to the actual observations made by an investigator.

As an example of observed and expected frequencies, think of a population consisting of equal numbers of women, men, girls, and boys. Each age-gender group is a mutually exclusive category. Each individual can belong to only one of the four categories. The logical expectation is that randomly selecting 4 (or multiples of 4) individuals from this specified population will produce equal numbers in each category. Thus, if 40 individuals are selected from this specified population, then 10 members of each category, women, men, girls, boys, are expected. The individuals actually selected determine the *observed frequencies* in this example. As you surely have guessed, however, the observed frequency for each category is not guaranteed to be 10. Deviations from the *expected frequencies* of 10 are attributable to sampling error. In order to determine if your selected sample is representative of the population, you can determine the likelihood of obtaining the observed frequencies of each category on the basis of chance using the χ^2-statistic and its theoretical distribution. If it is likely that the observed frequencies are obtained on the basis of chance, then the selected sample can be considered representative of the population.

Given the definitions of observed and expected frequencies, the chi-square statistic is obtained on the basis of the following formula:

Formula 17.1

$$\chi^2 = \Sigma \frac{(O - E)^2}{E}$$

In Formula 17.1, O refers to the observed frequency of a particular category and E refers to the expected (or theoretical) frequency of a particular category.

Chi-Square (χ^2) Distribution

The chi-square distribution is a theoretical distribution whose shape changes in relation to degrees of freedom. The chi-square distribution can be used to determine the likelihood of obtaining a specific χ^2-value on the basis of chance. As for the t- and F-statistics, a table of critical values is used to determine whether or not the likelihood of obtaining specific values of χ^2 is less than or equal to a designated alpha level. Once df has been calculated, Appendix Table 10 can be used to determine critical values. In Table 10, the intersection of the column associated with a designated alpha level with the row associated with a specific df yields the critical value.

NECESSARY CONDITIONS FOR USING χ^2 AS A TEST STATISTIC

As is the case for every statistic discussed in this text, certain conditions must be met if the statistic is to be used to evaluate hypotheses. The use of χ^2 requires the following seven conditions to be fulfilled:

1. The observations must be obtained from a *random sample*. If a sample cannot be considered a random sample, then conclusions based on the χ^2-test are not valid.

2. The observations must be *frequency data*. Measures such as weight, IQ scores, or high-school class rank cannot be evaluated with χ^2. Determining the number of subjects that prefer magazine A versus magazine B versus no preference or the number of voting-age citizens who favor and the number who oppose capital punishment are two examples of frequency data that can be analyzed using χ^2.

3. The observations can only be assigned to one category, that is, categories must be *mutually exclusive*. For example, categorizing individuals as father/son and mother/daughter does *not* represent four mutually exclusive categories. Every father has to have been a son and any son might also be a father. In the previous example of categories based on age and gender, identifying individuals as women, men, girls, and boys represent mutually exclusive categories.

4. An observation must only increment a particular category by a *single frequency*. For example, you *cannot* compare the total frequency of errors made by each member of a sample of psychology majors versus

history majors on a memory task involving a list of ten words using χ^2. In such a case, a subject could contribute a value greater than 1 to any one category, for example, a subject who makes three errors. You can use χ^2, however, to evaluate whether or not the frequency of perfect scores versus imperfect scores, that is, scores with one or more errors, is similar between the two populations from which history and psychology majors were randomly selected. In this case, a perfect or imperfect score of a subject increments the particular category by a single frequency.

5. The categories must be *all-inclusive*. Every member of the sample must contribute a frequency to one of the categories. In the previous example comparing history majors and psychology majors, we had to include a category of imperfect scores as well as perfect scores. If this condition is fulfilled, then the sum of expected frequencies will equal the sum of observed frequencies.

6. Each observation must be *independent* of any other observation. In other words, any one observation must in no way influence the outcome of any other observation. For example, in a study of extrasensory perception, it would be *incorrect* to use χ^2 to determine if males and females differ in their ability to correctly predict which of three geometric figures would appear on each of three cards turned face downwards. In this case, the predictions about the figures on any one card would influence the prediction about any other card. Because these observed frequencies are dependent, a χ^2-test cannot be used.

7. The use of χ^2 requires that frequencies are *normally distributed*. Generally this condition is fulfilled. There are several situations, however, where this normality condition is violated and χ^2 should not be used. When observations are relatively few, the normality condition is not likely to be fulfilled. The exact conditions when this normality condition is seriously violated are debatable. We suggest that χ^2, as discussed in this text, only be used given one of the two following prerequisites:

(a) $df = 1$ and expected frequencies are equal to or greater than 10,

(b) $df \geq 2$ and all expected frequencies are 5 or more.

If the above seven conditions are fulfilled, χ^2 can be used to evaluate hypotheses.

PROGRESS ASSESSMENT 17.1

For each of the following, determine which, if any, of the seven conditions necessary for using χ^2 have not been fulfilled:

1. In order to examine whether or not a particular therapy treatment effectively decreases smoking behavior, a psychologist randomly

assigns ten clients who want to quit smoking to a therapy treatment group and eleven to a control treatment group. Following two weeks of treatment, the number of cigarettes smoked over a three-day period are recorded for each subject in the therapy treatment group and the control treatment group.

2. Instead of counting number of cigarettes smoked over three days, assume the investigator in part 1 organizes the data of individuals in both the therapy and control groups on the basis of those who did not smoke any cigarettes in the three-day interval and those who smoked one or more cigarettes.

3. In order to evaluate the effects a particular advertisement has on voting, a psychologist obtains a random sample of twenty subjects and asks them whether they are in favor of or opposed to a particular political issue. Half the subjects are then shown a 30-second advertisement biased in a direction that favors the political view and half are shown a 30-second advertisement biased in a direction that opposes the political view. The data for the two groups are organized as number of subjects in favor of the political view before and after the advertisement and number of subjects opposed to the political view before and after the advertisement.

TESTING GOODNESS OF FIT

The χ^2-**goodness-of-fit test** is a statistical test used to determine whether sampled category proportions of a population are equal to *hypothesized* population proportions. The hypothesized population proportions are described in the null hypothesis. As usual, the specific H_0 depends upon the investigator's specific research hypothesis and is obtained by negating H_1, the alternative hypothesis.

Most often the alternative hypothesis for χ^2 is expressed as follows: observed frequencies (O) will not equal the expected frequencies (E). The null hypothesis then is $O = E$. These hypotheses are more formally stated in relation to the expected frequencies expressed as proportions, symbolized as ***prop***. You will recall that frequencies of a specific category can be expressed as proportions in decimal form by dividing the specific frequency by the total frequency. When expected frequencies are expressed as proportions, note that the sum of the proportions equals 1.0.

In an example where equal frequencies are expected for two categories, the following statistical hypotheses can be written with the subscript *prop* referring to the category proportion; H_0: *prop*$_1$ = 0.5 and *prop*$_2$ = 0.5 and H_1: *prop*$_1$ ≠ 0.5 or *prop*$_2$ ≠ 0.5.

Because χ^2 can be used to evaluate hypotheses involving a large number of categories, the number of proportions symbolized in H_0 and H_1 can be very large. For statistical hypotheses involving more than two categories, we will describe the hypotheses in words rather than proportions. In such cases, we will use the less formal statement of the null and alternative hypotheses:

H_0: observed frequencies are equal to expected frequencies;

H_1: observed frequencies are *not* equal to expected frequencies.

Although not exhaustive, the following three examples demonstrate the versatility of the goodness-of-fit-test. In the first example, the use of χ^2 to evaluate the null hypothesis involving only two categories where expected frequencies are based on hypothesized values is discussed. In the second example, a situation involving hypothesis testing with four categories is demonstrated. In the third example, procedures used to evaluate whether a measured characteristic is normally distributed are presented.

Hypothesized Frequencies Involving Two Categories

Assume that the director of a counseling center at a large university is asked by the dean of students to determine whether students are in favor of maintaining the current quiet-hours policy enforced from 8:00 P.M. until 7:00 A.M., Sunday through Thursday. The director contacts 100 students randomly obtained from the college dormitory directory of students. Students are asked whether they are in favor of or opposed to maintaining this specific policy. The results of the survey are shown in Table 17.1. The 60 students in favor of these quiet hours are arbitrarily designated as Group 1 and the 40 opposed as Group 2.

Stating Research and Statistical Hypotheses. Assume that the director believes that there is a majority opinion among the students concerning maintenance of the current quiet-hours policy. The director does not know, however, whether the majority is opposed or in favor of maintaining the policy.

TABLE 17.1
Results and χ^2 Calculations from Hypothetical Survey of 100 Students concerning Their Support of Current Dormitory Quiet-Hours Policy. Note That $\chi^2 = \Sigma[(O - E)^2/E]$.

(a) View	(b) Observed frequency (O)	(c) Expected frequency (E)	(d) $O - E$	(e) $(O - E)^2$	(f) $(O - E)^2/E$
Favor	60	50	10	100	2
Opposed	40	50	-10	100	2
					$\chi^2 = 4$

Translation of this particular research hypothesis involving an even split of frequencies of two categories is a simple procedure. Because the director believes that the proportion of those in favor of the policy in the population of dormitory students is *not* equal to the proportion opposed to the policy, H_1 is written $prop_1 \neq 0.5$ or $prop_2 \neq 0.5$. Negating H_1 produces H_0: $prop_1 = 0.5$ and $prop_2 = 0.5$.

Performing the Statistical Test. In order to evaluate the null hypothesis, a specific decision rule for χ^2 is formed and a value for χ^2 is calculated.

In order to form a decision rule for χ^2, you must calculate *df*. When using χ^2 for testing goodness of fit, *df* is obtained by subtracting the number of categories used minus the number of mathematical restrictions imposed on the calculations for χ^2.

The only restriction placed on the calculations in the example involving two categories is that the sum of the expected frequencies must equal the sum of the observed frequencies. This restriction is *always* imposed on the calculation of χ^2 regardless of the purpose of the test. Thus, at least one restriction is always placed on the calculation of χ^2 from sample data. In the example, no other restrictions are involved in calculating χ^2. The *df* for goodness of fit involving hypothesized expected frequencies for one variable is written as $k - 1$, where k refers to number of categories. For the example in Table 17.1, $df = 2 - 1 = 1$.

The decision rule for this example is then determined by examining Appendix Table 10. As usual, alpha is set at 0.05 and $df = 1$. The value obtained in Table 10 is 3.84. The decision rule is written as follows:

$$\text{If } \chi^2_{calc} \geq \chi^2_{table}, \text{ reject } H_0.$$

Once a decsion rule is formed, χ^2 is calculated on the basis of Formula 17.1. The results of these calculations are shown in Table 17.1. Note in Table 17.1 that category labels are listed in column (a). In column (b) the observed frequencies are recorded. Expected frequencies, shown in column (c), are obtained by determining the proportion of scores expected in each category for the entire sample based on conditions described in the null hypothesis. In our case, since 100 students are surveyed and equal proportions are stated in the null hypothesis—0.5 in each category— expected frequencies for each category are 50 (0.5×100). Once expected and observed frequencies are obtained, the difference between each is determined and recorded in column (d). Squaring these differences gives the values in column (e). Each squared value is then divided by its appropriate expected frequency and listed in column (f). Finally the sum of these quotients is obtained as listed at the bottom of column (f). The calculated value of χ^2 in the example is 4.

Evaluating H_0 and the Research Hypothesis. Because 4.0, the calculated value of χ^2, is greater than the critical value, 3.84, H_0 is rejected.

The director of the counseling center may then conclude that a statistically significant majority of dormitory students is in favor of maintaining this policy of quiet hours, $\chi^2(1, N = 100) = 4.0$, $p < 0.05$. Note that for χ^2 it is recommended that total sample size be reported along with *df*, including the symbol N.

PROGRESS ASSESSMENT 17.2

Suppose the current library hours policy at a particular school was instituted because a two-thirds majority of students was in favor of such a policy. Using the standard steps for evaluating hypotheses, analyze the data collected from a random sample of 122 students where the null hypothesis tested is that a two-thirds (0.67) majority of the student population is in favor of maintaining the current library hours. Results of the survey are 80 in favor and 42 opposed.

Hypothesized Frequencies Involving Three or More Categories

The use of χ^2 frequently involves investigations where frequencies of several categories of a single variable have been observed. If frequencies are hypothesized, a goodness-of-fit test can be used to evaluate whether the observed frequencies come from a sample that represents a population having the hypothesized frequencies.

Suppose a psychology major believes that affiliation with recognized religious groups has changed for students currently enrolled at a particular university. Records kept by the dean of students at this school indicate that 80 percent of the past students reported belonging to traditional religious groups, such as Catholic, Jewish, Protestant, and so forth; 15 percent reported belonging to nontraditional religions, such as Hare Krishna or any religion other than those listed as traditional; and 5% reported having no religious affiliation. The psychology student uses this information to form the expected frequencies for the current population of students. Based on the results of a survey of a random sample of 150 students presented in Table 17.2, χ^2 can be used to determine if the current population of students at this school are affilated with religions according to the following proportions: traditional religions, *prop* = 0.8; nontraditional religions, *prop* = 0.15; no religious affiliations, *prop* = 0.05.

Stating Research and Statistical Hypotheses.   Since the psychology major believes that religious affiliation has changed at this university, H_1 is as follows: observed frequencies do not equal expected frequencies. Negation of H_1 gives H_0: observed frequencies equal expected frequencies of 120 for traditional religions, 22.5 for nontraditional, and 7.5 for no religious affiliation. Expected frequencies are obtained by multiplying the hypothesized proportions by N, sample size. For example, expected frequency for traditional religions is $150 \times 0.8 = 120$.

TABLE 17.2
Results and χ^2 Calculations of a Survey Assessing Religious Affiliation of 150 Students at Hypothetical University

Religious Category	Observed Frequency (O)	Expected Frequency (E)	$O - E$	$(O - E)^2$	$(O - E)^2/E$
Traditional	110	120.0	-10.0	100.0	0.83
Nontraditional	25	22.5	2.5	6.25	0.28
No Affiliation	15	7.5	7.5	56.25	7.50
					$\chi^2 = 8.61$

Stating the statistical hypotheses in this fashion means that if any one of the observed frequencies does not equal its expected frequency, H_0 is rejected. If H_0 is rejected, further analyses are needed to determine which of the observed and expected frequencies are not equal. If you are interested in exploring this subject further, refer to Marascuilo and McSweeney (1977) for a thorough discussion of such analyses.

Except for the statement of the statistical hypotheses, performing a χ^2-test for investigations involving three or more categories is identical to that used when only two categories are involved.

Performing the Statistical Test. Given there are three categories, df is equal to 2 (3 − 1). Appendix Table 10 for alpha = 0.05 and df = 2 shows a critical value of 5.99. The decision rule is thus written:

$$\text{If } \chi^2 \geq 5.99, \text{ reject } H_0.$$

The calculations used to determine a value of χ^2 are shown in Table 17.2 and are identical to those used in Table 17.1. The value of χ^2 in this example is 8.61.

Evaluating H_0 and the Research Hypothesis. In this example, H_0 is rejected since 8.61 is greater than the critical value, 5.99. The results suggest that religious affiliation is not described on the basis of the following proportions: traditional = 0.8, nontraditional = 0.15, and no affiliation = 0.05, $\chi^2(2, N = 150) = 8.61$, $p < 0.05$.

PROGRESS ASSESSMENT 17.3

A social psychologist is interested in determining whether or not the proportion of students admitted to a particular university reflect the proportions of different racial groups represented in the community where the college is located. The following community proportions are obtained from the city hall: Caucasian = 0.64, Afro-American = 0.21,

Hispanic = 0.08, Oriental = 0.04, Native North American Indian = 0.02, and Other = 0.01. The psychologist surveys a random sample of 500 students and obtains the following frequencies: Caucasian = 335, Afro-American = 100, Hispanic = 33, Oriental = 20, Native North American Indian = 7, and Other = 5. Using statistical hypothesis testing procedures, determine if the proportion of students in this random sample represents a population of students with proportions equal to the community population.

Testing for Normality

You will recall that the use of parametric statistics requires the measured characteristics of an observed sample to be normally distributed in the population from which the sample is randomly selected. The goodness-of-fit test can be used to determine whether data collected from a specific sample can be assumed to represent a population for which the characteristic of interest is normally distributed. The population that is evaluated for normality is defined on the basis of a mean and standard deviation estimated from the sample mean, $\bar{X}$, and sample standard deviation, s.

In order to demonstrate how χ^2 is used to test for normality, assume a psychologist has collected data from a random sample of fifty college students given a standard mathematical achievement test where scores can range between 1 and 150. In order to determine whether this sample represents a defined population where frequencies of mathematical achievement scores are normally distributed, a χ^2-goodness-of-fit test is performed.

Stating Research and Statistical Hypotheses. The low average score, 57.64, gives the psychologist reason to suspect that the sample comes from a population for which the characteristic is not normally distributed. This belief in the form of H_1 states that the measured characteristic is not normally distributed in the defined population. The H_0 then states that the measured characteristic is normally distributed.

Performing the Statistical Test. Determining the expected frequencies for the χ^2 used to evaluate whether a characteristic of interest is normally distributed requires some calculations different from those previously discussed.

Because χ^2 is performed on frequency data, the raw scores must be organized as a frequency distribution to complete the χ^2-test. The guidelines for organizing data as a grouped frequency distribution were discussed in Chapter 3. The results of such an organization for the hypothetical mathematical aptitude test scores are presented in columns (a) and (b) of Table 17.3.

Once organized as a grouped frequency distribution, expected frequencies are obtained using the following concepts. You will recall that the normal distribution table, Appendix Table 4, allows you to determine the

TABLE 17.3
Grouped Frequency Distribution and χ^2 Calculations Used to Perform a Goodness-of-Fit Test of Normality of Mathematical Aptitude Test Scores Where $\bar{X}$ = 57.64, s = 20.02, and N = 50

(a) Class interval	(b) Observed frequency	(c) LRL	(d) z-score $(LRL-\bar{X})/s$	(e) Propor. $-\infty$ to z	(f) Expected proportion	(g) Expected frequency
91–100	2	90.5	1.64	0.9495	0.0505	2.5
81–90	3	80.5	1.14	0.8729	0.0766	3.8
71–80	10	70.5	0.64	0.7389	0.1340	6.7
61–70	10	60.5	0.14	0.5557	0.1832	9.2
51–60	10	50.5	−0.36	0.3594	0.1963	9.8
41–50	4	40.5	−0.86	0.1949	0.1645	8.2
31–40	4	30.5	−1.36	0.0869	0.1080	5.4
21–30	5	20.5	−1.86	0.0314	0.0555	2.8
11–20	1	10.5	−2.35	0.0094	0.0220	1.1
1–10	1				0.0094	0.5

Class Interval	Observed (O)	Expected (E)	(O − E)	(O − E)²	(O − E)²/E
91–100	2	2.5	−0.5	0.25	0.10
81–90	3	3.8	−0.8	0.64	0.17
71–80	10	6.7	3.3	10.89	1.63
61–70	10	9.2	0.8	0.64	0.07
51–60	10	9.8	0.2	0.04	0.00
41–50	4	8.2	−4.2	17.64	2.15
31–40	4	5.4	−1.4	1.96	0.36
21–30	5	2.8	2.2	4.84	1.73
11–20	1	1.1	−0.1	0.01	0.01
1–10	1	0.5	0.5	0.25	0.50

$$6.72 = \Sigma[(O - E)^2/E] = 6.63$$

proportion of scores that fall between the mean and a given score of a normal distribution and the proportion of scores beyond a particular z-score. In column (c) the lower real limit for each class interval, except the last interval, is listed. These lower real limits (*LRL*) will be used as the specific X-value in the z-score formula. By obtaining a z-score for each class interval (category), the normal curve table can be used to determine the expected frequency of each class interval. In order to calculate z, estimates for μ and σ must be obtained. The best estimate for these parameters are $\bar{X}$ and s computed from the raw scores. In the example, $\bar{X}$ = 57.64 and s = 20.02. Once these values are obtained, they are used to convert the *LRL*'s to z-scores. These z-scores are listed in column (d).

In columns (e) through (g) in Table 17.3, the calculations used to obtain expected frequencies are presented. In order to determine the specific frequencies expected within a particular interval, the proportion of scores expected within the interval must be determined. This requires two steps:

1. Determine the proportion of scores between $-\infty$ and the z-score. For positive z-scores go to Appendix Table 4 and find the proportion of scores *between* the mean and the particular z-score and *add 0.5* to this table value. For negative z-scores go to Table 4 and find the proportion of scores *beyond* the particular z-score. If $z = 0$, simply list 0.5000. The proportions between $-\infty$ and z for each interval are listed in column (e).

2. Determine the expected proportions for each of the class intervals. For the lowest interval, find the proportion given in column (e) of the next higher interval and list it in column (f). In the example the expected proportion for the class interval 1–10 is 0.0094. Then for each successive interval subtract the proportion between $-\infty$ and z in column (e) from the next higher interval in column (e). This difference gives the expected proportion for the lower interval of the adjoining intervals and is listed in column (f). For example, the expected proportion for the class interval 11–20 is 0.0220, obtained by subtracting 0.0094 from 0.0314. For the highest interval of the grouped frequency distribution, subtract the proportion of $-\infty$ to z for this interval from the value 1.0. This difference produces the expected proportion within the highest interval. In the example, this proportion is 0.0505, $1 - 0.9495$.

Once the proportion expected within each interval is determined, expected frequency within each interval is obtained by multiplying the sample size, N, by the expected proportion within each interval. These values are listed in column (g). The sum of the expected values must equal N. In the example in Table 17.3, the sum of the expected frequencies equals 50, which is the value of N.

Assuming no computational mistakes, it is possible that the sum of expected frequencies does not exactly equal N, the sum of the observed frequencies. In order to compensate for this discrepancy due to rounding errors, one or two of the expected frequency values are randomly selected and adjusted by 0.1 so that the sum of the expected frequencies equals the sum of the observed frequencies. Formula 17.1 is then used to calculate χ^2 as demonstrated at the bottom of Table 17.3.

In forming a decision rule for a goodness-of-fit test in evaluating the normality of a distribution, **k − 3** is the adjusted degrees of freedom where k equals the number of categories (class intervals) in the grouped frequency distribution. Remember that *df* for χ^2 is defined as the number of categories minus the number of mathematical restrictions imposed on the calculations of χ^2. As usual, one restriction imposed is that the sum of the expected frequencies equals the sum of the observed frequencies. Whenever parameters need to be estimated to obtain expected frequencies for a theoretical distribution, as is the case here, it is customary to subtract a value of 1 from the degrees of freedom for each estimated parameter. In order to calculate z-scores in the example, two parameters, μ and σ, are estimated by $\bar{X}$ and s, respectively. The $k - 1$ degrees of freedom are adjusted, therefore, by subtracting 2 ($k - 1 - 2$ or $k - 3$). Thus in the example, the adjusted $df = 10 - 3 = 7$. Using Appendix Table 10, the specific decision rule with alpha = 0.05 and $df = 7$ is as follows:

$$\text{If } \chi^2_{calc} \geq 14.07, \text{ reject } H_0.$$

Evaluating H_0 and the Research Hypothesis. Since 6.72 is less than the critical value, 14.07, H_0 cannot be rejected. Thus, there is no evidence to indicate that the sample comes from a population in which mathematical aptitude test scores are not normally distributed, $\chi^2(7, N = 50) = 6.72$, p > 0.05.

PROGRESS ASSESSMENT 17.4

Assume that the grouped frequency distribution that follows represents test scores ranging from 51 through 108 and a psychologist needs to do further statistical analyses. Furthermore, assume that the analyses require that the data are collected from a sample that represents a population where the measured characteristic is normally distributed. Using χ^2, determine whether the psychologist has evidence to conclude that the data are collected from a sample where the measured characteristic is not normally distributed in the population. Note the following: $\bar{X} = 70.5$, $s = 10$, and $N = 100$.

TABLE 17-A
Grouped Frequency Distribution
of Test Scores Ranging from 51
through 108 Where $N = 100$

Class Interval	Frequency
106–110	2
101–105	2
96–100	2
91–95	5
86–90	4
81–85	8
76–80	19
71–75	18
66–70	10
61–65	9
56–60	10
51–55	11

TESTING INDEPENDENCE OF TWO VARIABLES

The χ^2 **test of independence** is used to determine whether the way observations are categorized on the basis of one variable influences the way they are categorized on the basis of a second variable. For example, use of the χ^2-statistic makes it possible to determine whether the way students are categorized with respect to major (variable 1) influences the way they are categorized with respect to political affiliation (variable 2).

Assume a random sample of 200 students is surveyed at a particular college having only the following four categories of general majors: (1) Social Sciences, (2) Natural Sciences, (3) Humanities, and (4) Engineering. Students are asked to report their major. In addition, they are asked to report their political affiliation from the following four categories: (1) Republican, (2) Democrat, (3) Independent, and (4) Other or No affiliation.

Stating Research and Statistical Hypotheses

Given there are no hypothesized values for how many majors fall into different political categories, the question asked in a test of independence is whether or not political affiliation is independent of a student's major. If the two categories are independent, then frequency of political affiliation should be proportionally distributed throughout the different college majors. Generally investigators believe that the two variables examined are not independent, and as a result, the alternative hypothesis is stated: political affiliation and college major are not independent. Negating H_1 produces H_0: political affiliation and college major are independent. In general, the logic used in stating statistical hypotheses for the χ^2 test of independence remains the same as the goodness-of-fit test in terms of the relationship between observed and expected frequencies. In H_0 it is stated that the observed and expected frequencies are equal, and in H_1 it is stated that they are not equal. Calculating expected frequencies, however, requires determining how the categories of each variable are proportioned throughout the entire sample. These proportions are then used to determine expected frequencies.

If college major and political affiliation are independent, you would expect that the proportion of individuals of any given major affiliated with a particular political party would be the same as the proportion of these majors in the entire sample. For example, if a proportion of 0.25 of the entire sample is engineering majors, then it is expected that for students affiliated with any particular party 0.25 would be engineering majors. Likewise, for any political affiliation, the proportion within any specific major should equal the proportion of that affiliation within the entire group.

In contrast, if college major and political affiliation are not independent, then the expected frequencies based on the entire sample would not be proportionately distributed throughout each major. Calculations for χ^2 are based on this logic and are discussed in the next section.

Performing the Statistical Test

Tables are generally used to summarize frequencies obtained for categories of two or more different variables. For example, the results of the hypothesized survey of college majors and political affiliation are presented in Table 17.4. Note that row and column totals are listed in the table. Both the summation of the row totals and the summation of the column totals should equal N. In Table 17.4 each sum equals 200.

TABLE 17.4
Summary Table and Calculations Used to Evaluate a χ^2 Test of Independence of College Major and Political Affiliation at a Hypothetical College

Political Affiliation	Social Sciences		Natural Sciences		Humanities		Engineers		Totals of Observed
	O	E	O	E	O	E	O	E	
Republican	24	(15.12)	15	(11.28)	6	(15.95)	10	(12.65)	55
Democrat	12	(15.95)	11	(11.89)	20	(16.82)	15	(13.34)	58
Independent	6	(11.28)	5	(8.40)	25	(11.89)	5	(9.43)	41
Other or No Affiliation	13	(12.65)	10	(9.43)	7	(13.34)	16	(10.58)	46
Totals of Observed	= 55		41		58		46		$N = 200$

Calculations of χ^2

O	E	$(O - E)$	$(O - E)^2$	$(O - E)^2/E$
24	15.12	8.88	78.85	5.22
15	11.28	3.72	13.84	1.23
6	15.95	− 9.95	99.00	6.21
10	12.65	− 2.65	7.02	0.55
12	15.95	− 3.95	15.60	0.98
11	11.89	− 0.89	0.79	0.07
20	16.82	3.18	10.11	0.60
15	13.34	1.66	2.76	0.21
6	11.28	− 5.28	27.88	2.47
5	8.40	− 3.40	11.56	1.38
25	11.89	13.11	171.87	14.46
5	9.43	− 4.43	19.62	2.08
13	12.65	0.35	0.12	0.01
10	9.43	0.57	0.32	0.03
7	13.34	− 6.34	40.20	3.01
16	10.58	5.42	29.38	2.78

$$\chi^2 = \Sigma[(O - E)^2/E] = 41.29$$

Calculating a Value for χ^2.   Listed in parenthesis in Table 17.4 are expected frequencies for each category. You recall that if the two variables are independent, then expected frequencies for one variable will be proportionately distributed throughout the categories of the other variable. For example, if Republicans are proportionately distributed throughout college majors, then it is expected that the proportion of natural sciences majors who are Republicans will be equal to the proportion of Republicans in the entire sample. To determine this expected frequency first divide the total number of Republicans observed, 55, (see row 1 total in Table 17.4) by 200 to determine the proportion of Republicans in the entire sample. Multiplying this proportion times the total number of natural sciences majors, 41, (see column 2 total in Table 17.4) produces the expected frequency (11.28) of natural sciences majors who are Republicans.

Repeating this process for each category produces corresponding expected frequencies. When calculating χ^2 with this table format, this process of using proportion of the entire sample to determine expected frequencies of a category can be condensed into a computational procedure: Simply multiply the specific column total by the specific row total and then divide this product by N. Report your expected frequencies to the nearest two decimal places. For example, $(41 \times 55)/200$ gives the expected frequency, 11.28, of natural sciences majors who are Republicans. You should verify the expected frequencies listed in Table 17.4 to determine if you understand this computational procedure. Note that expected frequencies summed over any row or column must equal the observed frequencies.

Once expected frequencies are obtained, Formula 17.1 is used to calculate a value for χ^2. The value of 41.29 is obtained for χ^2 in the example as shown at the bottom of Table 17.4.

Determining df **and Forming a Decision Rule.**   You will recall that the method for determining *df* for χ^2 is based on the computational procedures used to determine the χ^2-value. When data are arranged in table format, $(r - 1)(c - 1)$ is used to determine the *df* for the χ^2 test of independence where *r* refers to the number of categories of one variable (number of rows in the table) and *c* refers to the number of categories of the other variable (number of columns). This formula is based on the general concept of *df* for χ^2 where *df* is equal to the number of categories minus the number of mathematical restrictions imposed on the calculations. Because of having to estimate expected frequencies in the test of independence, the number of restrictions imposed on the calculation of χ^2 is this case is relatively large and changes as a function of the number of different categories examined. The formula $(r - 1)(c - 1)$ always gives the appropriate *df* for a test of independence for two variables no matter what the number of categories. In the example in Table 17.4, $df = 9$, $(4 - 1)(4 - 1)$.

With alpha $= 0.05$ and $df = 9$ the critical value obtained in Appendix Table 10 for our example is 16.92. The specific decision rule is as follows:

If $\chi^2_{calc} \geq 16.92$, reject H_0.

Evaluating H_0 and the Research Hypothesis

Since 41.29, the calculated value of χ^2 in Table 17.4, is greater than 16.92, H_0 is rejected. The results of this survey indicate that political affiliation and major at this college are not independent, $\chi^2(9, N = 200) = 41.29$, $p < 0.05$.

PROGRESS ASSESSMENT 17.5

In order to assess whether or not views about a school's current library hours are independent of year in college, a psychology student interviews thirty students selected randomly from each class—freshman, sophomore, junior, and senior. Based on the results given in Table 17-B, determine if views about the current library hours are independent of year in college.

TABLE 17-B
The Frequency of Freshman, Sophomore, Junior, and Senior Students
Who Are Opposed to or in Favor of the School's Current Library Hours

	Freshman	Sophomore	Junior	Senior
Oppose	20	16	6	6
Favor	10	14	24	24

CAUTIONS WHEN USING χ^2

As is always the case when planning research, consideration must be given to how the data will be collected. In projects where χ^2 is to be used to analyze frequencies of specific categories, the categories must be defined on some logical basis such as previously reported research hypotheses or generally accepted categories like Democrats, Republicans, and so on. It is pointless to collect data and then organize it in a way that will simply produce statistical significance.

A second caution when using χ^2 concerns the interpretation of a statistically significant χ^2-value involving three or more categories. For the test of both goodness of fit and independence, a significant χ^2 only allows rejection of a stated H_0. As is the case when a significant F is obtained with the analysis of variance, individual comparisons are needed to determine the source of the overall significance of χ^2. These individual comparison tests are not discussed in this text. You can, however, find a thorough discussion of these comparisons in books such as Siegel and Castellan (1988).

SUMMARY

The χ^2 statistic is discussed in this chapter in relation to its use as a goodness-of-fit test and a test of independence involving frequency data. The conditions that must be fulfilled in order to use χ^2, as well as cautions in interpreting the outcomes of a statistical test involving χ^2, are also discussed.

KEY DEFINITIONS

chi-square A statistic, symbolized χ^2, that is used to evaluate hypotheses when observations are classified into mutually exclusive categories and the frequency of observations in each category is determined.

$\chi^2 = \Sigma[(O - E)^2/E]$ Formula used to calculate χ^2 where O refers to the observed frequency of a particular category and E refers to the expected (or theoretical) frequency of a particular category.

χ^2-**goodness-of-fit test** A statistical test used to evaluate hypotheses that sampled category proportions of a population are equal to hypothesized population proportions. The hypothesized population proportions are described in the null hypothesis.

χ^2 **test of independence** A test performed on frequency data to determine whether the way observations are categorized on the basis of one variable influences the way they are categorized on the basis of a second variable.

expected frequencies (E) The number of observations that should be obtained for a defined category based on statements given in the null hypothesis for tests involving χ^2.

$k - 1$ Formula used to determine df for χ^2-goodness-to-fit test involving hypothesized expected frequencies for one variable where k refers to number of categories.

$k - 3$ Formula used to determine adjusted df for the χ^2-goodness-to-fit test of normality of a distribution, where k equals the number of categories (class intervals) in the grouped frequency distribution.

observed frequencies (O) The actual observations for a defined category made by an investigator.

prop Symbol for proportions given in χ^2 statistical hypotheses.

$(r - 1)(c - 1)$ Formula used to determine the df for the χ^2 test of independence when frequencies are in table format where r refers to the number of categories of one variable (number of rows in the table) and c refers to the number of categories of the other variable (number of columns).

REVIEW EXERCISES

Name the statistic, based on those discussed in this text, that would be used in the following problems if data were collected, statistical hypotheses tested and

a. assumptions for parametric statistics are fulfilled.

b. assumptions for parametric statistics are not fulfilled and a comparable non-parametric test exists.

1. In order to examine the effectiveness of two types of therapies on alleviating the symptoms of a specific phobic disorder, a group of patients with the disorder are randomly divided into two equal-size groups. Members of one group are given one type of therapy and members of the other group are given the other type of therapy. The symptoms of the disorder are measured following four therapy sessions on the basis of a test where scores are obtained along an interval scale.

2. In order to determine if mice change their behavior as a result of experience in a complex maze involving several choice points, a psychology student obtains a group of mice randomly selected from the university's animal colony. Each mouse is given ten trials and number of errors made is recorded for each trial. The student wants to determine if number of errors change over trials.

3. A social psychologist performs an experiment to evaluate the effects of two commercials on the attitude about smoking of high-school freshmen and seniors. One commercial involves the surgeon general and the other features an unknown actor. A random group of fifteen freshmen and a random group of fifteen seniors are shown one commerical where the surgeon general explains the hazards of cigarette smoking. Another randomly selected group of fifteen freshmen and another randomly selected group of fifteen seniors are shown the same commerical involving the unknown actor. Students are given a questionnaire where scores, which can range between 1 and 20, reflect change in attitude about smoking.

ANSWERS TO PROGRESS ASSESSMENTS

17.1
1. Any member of either sample can contribute a value greater than 1.

2. All conditions are fulfilled.

3. Since same subjects are involved in before and after conditions, observations are not independent.

17.2 *Research hypothesis:* Students in favor of current library hours do not make up two-thirds of the student population or students opposed do not make up one-third of the student population.
Statistical hypotheses: H_0: $prop_{favor} = 0.67$ and $prop_{opposed} = 0.33$, H_1: $prop_{favor} \neq 0.67$ or $prop_{opposed} \neq 0.33$.
Statistical test: If $\chi^2_{calc} \geq 3.84$, reject H_0; $\chi^2_{calc} = 0.12$.

Evaluation of H_0: Fail to reject H_0.

Interpretation: There is no evidence to indicate that the proportion of students' attitude about the current library hours is anything other than two-thirds in favor and one-third against, $\chi^2(1, N = 122) = 0.12, p > 0.05$.

17.3   *Research hypothesis:* Proportion of students based on race enrolled in the university is not equal to racial proportions existing in the community.

Statistical hypotheses: H_0: the observed frequencies are equal to the expected frequencies of 320 (Caucasian), 105 (Afro-American), 40 (Hispanic), 20 (Oriental), 10 (Native North American Indian) and, 5 (Other); H_1: observed frequencies are not equal to expected frequencies listed in H_0;

Statistical test: If $\chi^2_{calc} \geq 11.07$, reject H_0; $\chi^2_{calc} = 3.06$.

Evaluation of H_0: Fail to reject H_0:

Interpretation: The investigator has no evidence to indicate that the racial proportions are different from those that exist in the community, $\chi^2(5, N = 500) = 3.06, p > 0.05$.

17.4   *Research hypothesis:* The data do not come from a sample representative of a population where the measured characteristic is normally distributed.

Statistical hypotheses: H_0: scores are normally distributed within the population; H_1: scores are not normally distributed within the population.

Statistical test: If $\chi^2_{calc} \geq 16.92$, reject H_0; $\chi^2_{calc} = 250.70$.

Evaluation of H_0: Reject H_0.

Interpretation: Analysis indicates that scores are not normally distributed in the population, $\chi^2(9, N = 100) = 250.70, p > 0.05$..

17.5   *Research hypothesis:* Attitudes about current library policy are not independent of year in college.

Statistical hypotheses: H_0: observed frequencies of students in favor of or opposed to current library hours are equal to the expected frequencies that are proportionately distributed throughout freshmen, sophomores, juniors and seniors; H_1: observed frequencies are not equal to expected frequencies.

Statistical test: If $\chi^2_{calc} \geq 7.81$, reject H_0; $\chi^2_{calc} = 21.11$.

Evaluation of H_0: Reject H_0.

Interpretation: Attitude about current library hours at this school are not independent of year in college, $\chi^2(3, N = 120) = 21.11, p < 0.05$.

REFERENCES

American Psychological Association. (1983). *Publication manual of the American Psychological Association* (3rd ed.). Washington, D.C.: Author.

Cohen, J. (1988). *Statistical power analysis for the behaviorial sciences* (2nd ed.). Hillsdale, N.J.: Erlbaum.

Kirk, R. E. (1982). *Experimental design: Procedures for the behavioral sciences* (2nd ed.). Monterey, Calif.: Brooks/Cole.

Marascuillo, L. A., & McSweeney, M. (1977). *Nonparametric and distribution-free methods for the behavioral sciences.* Monterey, Calif.: Brooks/Cole.

Siegel, S., & Castellan, N. J. (1988). *Nonparametric statistics for the behavioral sciences* (2nd ed.). New York: McGraw-Hill.

Stroop, J. (1935). Studies of interference in serial verbal reactions. *Journal of Experimental Psychology, 18,* 624–643.

Tukey, J. W. (1977). *Exploratory data analysis.* Reading, Mass.: Addison-Wesley.

Winer, B. J. (1962). *Statistical Principles in Experimental Design.* New York: McGraw-Hill.

APPENDIX

TABLE 1
Table of Random Numbers

91225	47297	05208	09509	83287	98993	04792	82551	59606	88054
48832	04241	71986	08556	40419	69537	86871	54707	41149	16991
83516	35332	54964	28304	46934	61746	09772	20208	36456	51403
55814	15346	17425	41510	13329	09591	71725	31094	34654	45090
85716	12864	61976	24101	23601	62813	47996	57362	30232	35867
77799	89902	53499	34027	44773	91246	93487	85827	35988	31423
89346	94359	64580	88245	21215	78937	18180	62989	17247	96211
22821	26700	43247	48748	35591	77935	97016	92278	91298	23566
19651	46588	74048	25245	88242	89392	74849	23163	74727	89559
21738	10422	44197	57245	23564	05076	18267	27692	18681	49264
14439	16349	58690	24767	66401	63240	44038	15142	81338	70308
25482	05354	72238	80246	75754	88446	87496	92774	28165	06299
14606	94425	14315	64213	96364	29901	94156	13008	34784	34997
47291	66501	04111	98604	76249	16047	95252	69177	23764	57974
00097	39513	26145	50286	37804	95165	97489	83770	80511	71298
44474	18685	83439	63916	76277	87092	43999	65474	45455	17684
80188	55310	74084	41674	80282	46222	74965	69025	10428	30224
99909	70398	88267	96784	22232	74548	18681	71053	49820	54954
58968	12199	67836	95022	67725	67527	86541	97150	74569	90047
19893	22171	37003	03270	40464	39309	71950	31827	28303	62957
31180	66582	07814	48192	79581	82781	59678	20881	03922	96690
55358	46206	28790	27657	47210	39684	69566	95109	17541	67975
45265	25613	50103	93017	49489	63137	42899	46824	55305	68436
78752	50062	52099	49755	47455	85377	13404	12583	42142	94438
77026	65887	30936	69948	52651	44038	14192	65084	94240	30663
39276	97558	34925	86347	06528	94788	98409	12127	61672	09999
47532	77074	39717	09655	69029	12061	62872	18773	11799	42629
99298	62008	14744	81394	50813	60959	17941	99294	68438	54384
23713	29543	20617	02525	49301	62333	84918	38377	45095	89424
71025	93654	46311	61173	48844	38937	03812	05838	34285	08267
74948	69730	38268	45877	74220	17727	68357	92038	16486	72612
01975	51053	74679	33939	04308	29308	00031	52498	46210	21401
19636	08802	65859	83454	29762	95675	80618	46154	81250	49413
37063	11564	68775	32383	78364	35447	70729	31821	41957	96850
06570	48472	76950	25543	37661	13124	05752	28250	06892	32216
67187	70029	32276	51020	16715	26725	00374	24518	85007	95592
74318	16668	14616	51147	63823	28920	63506	67422	21521	62018
84658	32328	48257	69420	57437	18892	88152	43925	07585	13485
43578	54413	29390	82628	06420	48451	80697	68097	22577	12231
65336	91369	07765	92143	34215	96303	03353	71515	55424	68205
12297	99455	36506	53575	42859	03056	54436	72004	90550	24695
07592	19189	36976	54389	52519	88593	12640	63742	52863	57294
72348	55701	98604	75531	73266	45496	74386	51293	20682	99981
70909	48599	36829	27150	21839	05236	20499	47538	84775	44543
16013	75265	65054	51584	65837	44116	49457	46055	92802	10073
39954	51272	93372	19705	20047	81087	62993	40227	95610	75971
61131	59612	43759	27369	68613	88117	88168	62985	01794	51874
01608	31737	72572	47112	73336	86842	54882	81541	97497	42052
59312	10832	96622	32093	71354	71923	25833	55831	35692	71534
90697	91454	99243	74995	80926	93834	49471	55910	09853	12529

TABLE 1 (Continued)
Table of Random Numbers

72348	55701	98604	75531	73266	45496	74386	51293	20682	99981
70909	48599	36829	27150	21839	05236	20499	47538	84775	44543
16013	75265	65054	51584	65837	44116	49457	46055	92802	10073
39954	51272	93372	19705	20047	81087	62993	40227	95610	75971
61131	59612	43759	27369	68613	88117	88168	62985	01794	51874
01608	31737	72572	47112	73336	86842	54882	81541	97497	42052
59312	10832	96622	32093	71354	71923	25833	55831	35692	71534
90697	91454	99243	74995	80926	93834	49471	55910	09853	12529

TABLE 2
Critical Values of the Pearson Correlation Coefficient, *r*

Degrees of Freedom (df)	Two-Tailed Significance Levels	
	0.05	0.01
3	0.88	0.96
4	0.81	0.92
5	0.75	0.88
6	0.71	0.83
7	0.67	0.80
8	0.63	0.76
9	0.60	0.74
10	0.58	0.71
11	0.55	0.68
12	0.53	0.66
13	0.51	0.64
14	0.50	0.62
15	0.48	0.61
16	0.47	0.59
17	0.46	0.58
18	0.44	0.56
19	0.43	0.55
20	0.42	0.54
22	0.40	0.52
24	0.39	0.50
26	0.37	0.48
28	0.36	0.46
30	0.35	0.45
35	0.32	0.42
40	0.30	0.39
45	0.29	0.37
50	0.27	0.35

Adapted from Pearson, E.S., and Hartley, H.O., eds. (1966) Table 13. Percentage points for the distribution of the correlation coefficient, *r*, when ϱ = 0. *Biometrika Tables for Statisticians, 1,* 146 (3rd ed.). By permission of the Biometrika Trustees.

TABLE 3
Critical Values of the Spearman Rank-Order Correlation Coefficient, r_s

N	Two-Tailed Significance Levels	
	0.05	0.01
5	1.00	—
6	0.89	1.00
7	0.79	0.93
8	0.74	0.88
9	0.70	0.83
10	0.65	0.79
11	0.62	0.76
12	0.59	0.73
13	0.56	0.70
14	0.54	0.68
15	0.52	0.65
16	0.50	0.64
17	0.48	0.62
18	0.47	0.60
19	0.46	0.58
20	0.45	0.57
22	0.42	0.54
24	0.41	0.52
26	0.39	0.50
28	0.38	0.48
30	0.36	0.47
35	0.34	0.43
40	0.31	0.40
45	0.29	0.38
50	0.28	0.36

Adapted and abridged from Zar, J.H. (1972), Table 1. Significance testing of the Spearman rank correlation coefficient. *Journal of the American Statistical Association, 67,* 578–580, with kind permission of the author and publisher.

TABLE 4

Normal Distribution Table. Areas under the normal curve are listed for each z-score (column 1) in relation to the distance between the mean and the specific z-score (column 2) and the distance beyond the specific z-score (column 3).

1 z	2 between	3 beyond	1 z	2 between	3 beyond	1 z	2 between	3 beyond
0.00	0.0000	0.5000	0.39	0.1517	0.3483	0.78	0.2823	0.2177
0.01	0.0040	0.4960	0.40	0.1554	0.3446	0.79	0.2852	0.2148
0.02	0.0080	0.4920	0.41	0.1591	0.3409	0.80	0.2881	0.2119
0.03	0.0120	0.4880	0.42	0.1628	0.3372	0.81	0.2910	0.2090
0.04	0.0160	0.4840	0.43	0.1664	0.3336	0.82	0.2939	0.2061
0.05	0.0199	0.4801	0.44	0.1700	0.3300	0.83	0.2967	0.2033
0.06	0.0239	0.4761	0.45	0.1736	0.3264	0.84	0.2996	0.2004
0.07	0.0279	0.4721	0.46	0.1772	0.3228	0.85	0.3023	0.1977
0.08	0.0319	0.4681	0.47	0.1808	0.3192	0.86	0.3051	0.1949
0.09	0.0359	0.4641	0.48	0.1844	0.3156	0.87	0.3078	0.1922
0.10	0.0398	0.4602	0.49	0.1879	0.3121	0.88	0.3106	0.1894
0.11	0.0438	0.4562	0.50	0.1915	0.3085	0.89	0.3133	0.1867
0.12	0.0478	0.4522	0.51	0.1950	0.3050	0.90	0.3159	0.1841
0.13	0.0517	0.4483	0.52	0.1985	0.3015	0.91	0.3186	0.1814
0.14	0.0557	0.4443	0.53	0.2019	0.2981	0.92	0.3212	0.1788
0.15	0.0596	0.4404	0.54	0.2054	0.2946	0.93	0.3238	0.1762
0.16	0.0636	0.4364	0.55	0.2088	0.2912	0.94	0.3264	0.1736
0.17	0.0675	0.4325	0.56	0.2123	0.2877	0.95	0.3289	0.1711
0.18	0.0714	0.4286	0.57	0.2157	0.2843	0.96	0.3315	0.1685
0.19	0.0754	0.4246	0.58	0.2190	0.2810	0.97	0.3340	0.1660
0.20	0.0793	0.4207	0.59	0.2224	0.2776	0.98	0.3365	0.1635
0.21	0.0832	0.4168	0.60	0.2257	0.2743	0.99	0.3389	0.1611
0.22	0.0871	0.4129	0.61	0.2291	0.2709	1.00	0.3413	0.1587
0.23	0.0910	0.4090	0.62	0.2324	0.2676	1.01	0.3438	0.1562
0.24	0.0948	0.4052	0.63	0.2356	0.2644	1.02	0.3461	0.1539
0.25	0.0987	0.4013	0.64	0.2389	0.2611	1.03	0.3485	0.1515
0.26	0.1026	0.3974	0.65	0.2422	0.2578	1.04	0.3508	0.1492
0.27	0.1064	0.3936	0.66	0.2454	0.2546	1.05	0.3531	0.1469
0.28	0.1103	0.3897	0.67	0.2486	0.2514	1.06	0.3554	0.1446
0.29	0.1141	0.3859	0.68	0.2518	0.2482	1.07	0.3577	0.1423
0.30	0.1179	0.3821	0.69	0.2549	0.2451	1.08	0.3599	0.1401
0.31	0.1217	0.3783	0.70	0.2580	0.2420	1.09	0.3621	0.1379
0.32	0.1255	0.3745	0.71	0.2612	0.2388	1.10	0.3643	0.1357
0.33	0.1293	0.3707	0.72	0.2642	0.2358	1.11	0.3665	0.1335
0.34	0.1331	0.3669	0.73	0.2673	0.2327	1.12	0.3686	0.1314
0.35	0.1368	0.3632	0.74	0.2704	0.2296	1.13	0.3708	0.1292
0.36	0.1406	0.3594	0.75	0.2734	0.2266	1.14	0.3729	0.1271
0.37	0.1443	0.3557	0.76	0.2764	0.2236	1.15	0.3749	0.1251
0.38	0.1480	0.3520	0.77	0.2794	0.2206	1.16	0.3770	0.1230

(continued)

TABLE 4 (Continued)

1 z	2 between	3 beyond	1 z	2 between	3 beyond	1 z	2 between	3 beyond
1.17	0.3790	0.1210	1.58	0.4429	0.0571	1.99	0.4767	0.0233
1.18	0.3810	0.1190	1.59	0.4441	0.0559	2.00	0.4772	0.0228
1.19	0.3830	0.1170	1.60	0.4452	0.0548	2.01	0.4778	0.0222
1.20	0.3849	0.1151	1.61	0.4463	0.0537	2.02	0.4783	0.0217
1.21	0.3869	0.1131	1.62	0.4474	0.0526	2.03	0.4788	0.0212
1.22	0.3888	0.1112	1.63	0.4484	0.0516	2.04	0.4793	0.0207
1.23	0.3906	0.1094	1.64	0.4495	0.0505	2.05	0.4798	0.0202
1.24	0.3925	0.1075	1.65	0.4505	0.0495	2.06	0.4803	0.0197
1.25	0.3944	0.1056	1.66	0.4515	0.0485	2.07	0.4808	0.0192
1.26	0.3962	0.1038	1.67	0.4525	0.0475	2.08	0.4812	0.0188
1.27	0.3980	0.1020	1.68	0.4535	0.0465	2.09	0.4817	0.0183
1.28	0.3997	0.1003	1.69	0.4545	0.0455	2.10	0.4821	0.0179
1.29	0.4015	0.0985	1.70	0.4554	0.0446	2.11	0.4826	0.0174
1.30	0.4032	0.0968	1.71	0.4564	0.0436	2.12	0.4830	0.0170
1.31	0.4049	0.0951	1.72	0.4573	0.0427	2.13	0.4834	0.0166
1.32	0.4066	0.0934	1.73	0.4582	0.0418	2.14	0.4838	0.0162
1.33	0.4082	0.0918	1.74	0.4591	0.0409	2.15	0.4842	0.0158
1.34	0.4099	0.0901	1.75	0.4599	0.0401	2.16	0.4846	0.0154
1.35	0.4115	0.0885	1.76	0.4608	0.0392	2.17	0.4850	0.0150
1.36	0.4131	0.0869	1.77	0.4616	0.0384	2.18	0.4854	0.0146
1.37	0.4147	0.0853	1.78	0.4625	0.0375	2.19	0.4857	0.0143
1.38	0.4162	0.0838	1.79	0.4633	0.0367	2.20	0.4861	0.0139
1.39	0.4177	0.0823	1.80	0.4641	0.0359	2.21	0.4864	0.0136
1.40	0.4192	0.0808	1.81	0.4649	0.0351	2.22	0.4868	0.0132
1.41	0.4207	0.0793	1.82	0.4656	0.0344	2.23	0.4871	0.0129
1.42	0.4222	0.0778	1.83	0.4664	0.0336	2.24	0.4875	0.0125
1.43	0.4236	0.0764	1.84	0.4671	0.0329	2.25	0.4878	0.0122
1.44	0.4251	0.0749	1.85	0.4678	0.0322	2.26	0.4881	0.0119
1.45	0.4265	0.0735	1.86	0.4686	0.0314	2.27	0.4884	0.0116
1.46	0.4279	0.0721	1.87	0.4693	0.0307	2.28	0.4887	0.0113
1.47	0.4292	0.0708	1.88	0.4699	0.0301	2.29	0.4890	0.0110
1.48	0.4306	0.0694	1.89	0.4706	0.0294	2.30	0.4893	0.0107
1.49	0.4319	0.0681	1.90	0.4713	0.0287	2.31	0.4896	0.0104
1.50	0.4332	0.0668	1.91	0.4719	0.0281	2.32	0.4898	0.0102
1.51	0.4545	0.0655	1.92	0.4726	0.0274	2.33	0.4901	0.0099
1.52	0.4357	0.0643	1.93	0.4732	0.0268	2.34	0.4904	0.0096
1.53	0.4370	0.0630	1.94	0.4738	0.0262	2.35	0.4906	0.0094
1.54	0.4382	0.0618	1.95	0.4744	0.0256	2.36	0.4909	0.0091
1.55	0.4394	0.0606	1.96	0.4750	0.0250	2.37	0.4911	0.0089
1.56	0.4406	0.0594	1.97	0.4756	0.0244	2.38	0.4913	0.0087
1.57	0.4418	0.0582	1.98	0.4761	0.0239	2.39	0.4916	0.0084

(continued)

TABLE 4 (Continued)

z	between	beyond	z	between	beyond	z	between	beyond
2.40	0.4918	0.0082	2.67	0.4962	0.0038	2.94	0.4984	0.0016
2.41	0.4920	0.0080	2.68	0.4963	0.0037	2.95	0.4984	0.0016
2.42	0.4922	0.0078	2.69	0.4964	0.0036	2.96	0.4985	0.0015
2.43	0.4925	0.0075	2.70	0.4965	0.0035	2.97	0.4985	0.0015
2.44	0.4927	0.0073	2.71	0.4966	0.0034	2.98	0.4986	0.0014
2.45	0.4929	0.0071	2.72	0.4967	0.0033	2.99	0.4986	0.0014
2.46	0.4931	0.0069	2.73	0.4968	0.0032	3.00	0.4987	0.0013
2.47	0.4932	0.0068	2.74	0.4969	0.0031	3.01	0.4987	0.0013
2.48	0.4934	0.0066	2.75	0.4970	0.0030	3.02	0.4987	0.0013
2.49	0.4936	0.0064	2.76	0.4971	0.0029	3.03	0.4988	0.0012
2.50	0.4938	0.0062	2.77	0.4972	0.0028	3.04	0.4988	0.0012
2.51	0.4940	0.0060	2.78	0.4973	0.0027	3.05	0.4989	0.0011
2.52	0.4941	0.0059	2.79	0.4974	0.0026	3.06	0.4989	0.0011
2.53	0.4943	0.0057	2.80	0.4974	0.0026	3.07	0.4989	0.0011
2.54	0.4945	0.0055	2.81	0.4975	0.0025	3.08	0.4990	0.0010
2.55	0.4946	0.0054	2.82	0.4976	0.0024	3.09	0.4990	0.0010
2.56	0.4948	0.0052	2.83	0.4977	0.0023	3.10	0.4990	0.0010
2.57	0.4949	0.0051	2.84	0.4977	0.0023	3.20	0.4993	0.0007
2.58	0.4951	0.0049	2.85	0.4978	0.0022	3.30	0.4995	0.0005
2.59	0.4952	0.0048	2.86	0.4979	0.0021	3.40	0.4997	0.0003
2.60	0.4953	0.0047	2.87	0.4979	0.0021	3.50	0.4998	0.0002
2.61	0.4955	0.0045	2.88	0.4980	0.0020	3.60	0.4998	0.0002
2.62	0.4956	0.0044	2.89	0.4981	0.0019	3.70	0.4999	0.0001
2.63	0.4957	0.0043	2.90	0.4981	0.0019	3.80	0.4999	0.0001
2.64	0.4959	0.0041	2.91	0.4982	0.0018	3.90	0.49995	0.00005
2.65	0.4960	0.0040	2.92	0.4982	0.0018	4.00	0.49997	0.00003
2.66	0.4961	0.0039	2.93	0.4983	0.0017	4.10	0.49998	0.00002

Table 4 is taken from Table II of Fisher & Yates: *STATISTICAL TABLES FOR BIOLOGICAL, AGRICULTURAL AND MEDICAL RESEARCH* published by Longman Group UK Ltd., (previously published by Oliver and Boyd Ltd., Edinburgh) and by permission of the authors and publishers.

TABLE 5
Critical Values of the *t*-Statistic

Degrees of Freedom (*df*)	Two-Tailed Significance Levels	
	0.05	0.01
3	3.18	5.84
4	2.78	4.60
5	2.57	4.03
6	2.45	3.71
7	2.36	3.50
8	2.31	3.36
9	2.26	3.25
10	2.23	3.17
11	2.20	3.11
12	2.18	3.06
13	2.16	3.01
14	2.14	2.98
15	2.13	2.95
16	2.12	2.92
17	2.11	2.90
18	2.10	2.88
19	2.09	2.86
20	2.09	2.84
21	2.08	2.83
22	2.07	2.82
23	2.07	2.81
24	2.06	2.80
25	2.06	2.79
26	2.06	2.78
27	2.05	2.77
28	2.05	2.76
29	2.04	2.76
30	2.04	2.75
40	2.02	2.70
60	2.00	2.66
120	1.98	2.62
∞	1.96	2.58

Adapted from Pearson, E.S., and Hartley, H.O., eds. (1966) Table 12. Percentage points for the *t*-distribution. *Biometrika Tables for Statisticians, 1,* 146 (3rd ed.). By permission of the Biometrika Trustees.

TABLE 6
Critical Values of the *F*-Statistic at the 0.05 (Bold Type) and 0.01 (Roman Type)
Significance Levels

big

Denominator Degrees of Freedom (*df*)	Numerator Degrees of Freedom (*df*)								
	1	2	3	4	5	6	7	8	9
4	**7.71** 21.20	**6.94** 18.00	**6.59** 16.69	**6.39** 15.98	**6.26** 15.52	**6.16** 15.21	**6.09** 14.98	**6.04** 14.80	**6.00** 14.66
5	**6.61** 16.26	**5.79** 13.27	**5.41** 12.06	**5.19** 11.39	**5.05** 10.97	**4.95** 10.67	**4.88** 10.46	**4.82** 10.29	**4.77** 10.16
6	**5.99** 13.75	**5.14** 10.92	**4.76** 9.78	**4.53** 9.15	**4.39** 8.75	**4.28** 8.47	**4.21** 8.26	**4.15** 8.10	**4.10** 7.98
7	**5.59** 12.25	**4.74** 9.55	**4.35** 8.45	**4.12** 7.85	**3.97** 7.46	**3.87** 7.19	**3.79** 6.99	**3.73** 6.84	**3.68** 6.72
8	**5.32** 11.26	**4.46** 8.65	**4.07** 7.59	**3.84** 7.01	**3.69** 6.63	**3.58** 6.37	**3.50** 6.18	**3.44** 6.03	**3.39** 5.91
9	**5.12** 10.56	**4.26** 8.02	**3.86** 6.99	**3.63** 6.42	**3.48** 6.06	**3.37** 5.80	**3.29** 5.61	**3.23** 5.47	**3.18** 5.35
10	**4.96** 10.04	**4.10** 7.56	**3.71** 6.55	**3.48** 5.99	**3.33** 5.64	**3.22** 5.39	**3.14** 5.20	**3.07** 5.06	**3.02** 4.94
11	**4.84** 9.65	**3.98** 7.20	**3.59** 6.22	**3.36** 5.67	**3.20** 5.32	**3.09** 5.07	**3.01** 4.89	**2.95** 4.74	**2.90** 4.63
12	**4.75** 9.33	**3.89** 6.93	**3.49** 5.95	**3.26** 5.41	**3.11** 5.06	**3.00** 4.82	**2.91** 4.64	**2.85** 4.50	**2.80** 4.39
13	**4.67** 9.07	**3.81** 6.70	**3.41** 5.74	**3.18** 5.21	**3.03** 4.86	**2.92** 4.62	**2.83** 4.44	**2.77** 4.30	**2.71** 4.19
14	**4.60** 8.86	**3.74** 6.51	**3.34** 5.56	**3.11** 5.04	**2.96** 4.69	**2.85** 4.46	**2.76** 4.28	**2.70** 4.14	**2.65** 4.03
15	**4.54** 8.68	**3.68** 6.36	**3.29** 5.42	**3.06** 4.89	**2.90** 4.56	**2.79** 4.32	**2.71** 4.14	**2.64** 4.00	**2.59** 3.89
16	**4.49** 8.53	**3.63** 6.23	**3.24** 5.29	**3.01** 4.77	**2.85** 4.44	**2.74** 4.20	**2.66** 4.03	**2.59** 3.89	**2.54** 3.78
17	**4.45** 8.40	**3.59** 6.11	**3.20** 5.18	**2.96** 4.67	**2.81** 4.34	**2.70** 4.10	**2.61** 3.93	**2.55** 3.79	**2.49** 3.68
18	**4.41** 8.29	**3.55** 6.01	**3.16** 5.09	**2.93** 4.58	**2.77** 4.25	**2.66** 4.01	**2.58** 3.85	**2.51** 3.71	**2.46** 3.60
19	**4.38** 8.18	**3.52** 5.93	**3.13** 5.01	**2.90** 4.50	**2.74** 4.17	**2.63** 3.94	**2.54** 3.77	**2.48** 3.63	**2.42** 3.52
20	**4.35** 8.10	**3.49** 5.85	**3.10** 4.94	**2.87** 4.43	**2.71** 4.10	**2.60** 3.87	**2.51** 3.70	**2.45** 3.56	**2.39** 3.46
22	**4.30** 7.95	**3.44** 5.72	**3.05** 4.82	**2.82** 4.31	**2.66** 3.99	**2.55** 3.76	**2.46** 3.59	**2.40** 3.45	**2.34** 3.35

		Numerator Degrees of Freedom (df)							Denominator Degrees of Freedom (df)
10	12	15	20	24	30	40	60	120	
5.96	**5.91**	**5.86**	**5.80**	**5.77**	**5.75**	**5.72**	**5.69**	**5.66**	
14.55	14.37	14.20	14.02	13.93	13.84	13.75	13.65	13.56	4
4.74	**4.68**	**4.62**	**4.56**	**4.53**	**4.50**	**4.46**	**4.43**	**4.40**	
10.05	9.89	9.72	9.55	9.47	9.38	9.29	9.20	9.11	5
4.06	**4.00**	**3.94**	**3.87**	**3.84**	**3.81**	**3.77**	**3.74**	**3.70**	
7.87	7.72	7.56	7.40	7.31	7.23	7.14	7.06	6.97	6
3.64	**3.57**	**3.51**	**3.44**	**3.41**	**3.38**	**3.34**	**3.30**	**3.27**	
6.62	6.47	6.31	6.16	6.07	5.99	5.91	5.82	5.74	7
3.35	**3.28**	**3.22**	**3.15**	**3.12**	**3.08**	**3.04**	**3.01**	**2.97**	
5.81	5.67	5.52	5.36	5.28	5.20	5.12	5.03	4.95	8
3.14	**3.07**	**3.01**	**2.94**	**2.90**	**2.86**	**2.83**	**2.79**	**2.75**	
5.26	5.11	4.96	4.81	4.73	4.65	4.57	4.48	4.40	9
2.98	**2.91**	**2.85**	**2.77**	**2.74**	**2.70**	**2.66**	**2.62**	**2.58**	
4.85	4.71	4.56	4.41	4.33	4.25	4.17	4.08	4.00	10
2.85	**2.79**	**2.72**	**2.65**	**2.61**	**2.57**	**2.53**	**2.49**	**2.45**	
4.54	4.40	4.25	4.10	4.02	3.94	3.86	3.78	3.69	11
2.75	**2.69**	**2.62**	**2.54**	**2.51**	**2.47**	**2.43**	**2.38**	**2.34**	
4.30	4.16	4.01	3.86	3.78	3.70	3.62	3.54	3.45	12
2.67	**2.60**	**2.53**	**2.46**	**2.42**	**2.38**	**2.34**	**2.30**	**2.25**	
4.10	3.96	3.82	3.66	3.59	3.51	3.43	3.34	3.25	13
2.60	**2.53**	**2.46**	**2.39**	**2.35**	**2.31**	**2.27**	**2.22**	**2.18**	
3.94	3.80	3.66	3.51	3.43	3.35	3.27	3.18	3.09	14
2.54	**2.48**	**2.40**	**2.33**	**2.29**	**2.25**	**2.20**	**2.16**	**2.11**	
3.80	3.67	3.52	3.37	3.29	3.21	3.13	3.05	2.96	15
2.49	**2.42**	**2.35**	**2.28**	**2.24**	**2.19**	**2.15**	**2.11**	**2.06**	
3.69	3.55	3.41	3.26	3.18	3.10	3.02	2.93	2.84	16
2.45	**2.38**	**2.31**	**2.23**	**2.19**	**2.15**	**2.10**	**2.06**	**2.01**	
3.59	3.46	3.31	3.16	3.08	3.00	2.92	2.83	2.75	17
2.41	**2.34**	**2.27**	**2.19**	**2.15**	**2.11**	**2.06**	**2.02**	**1.97**	
3.51	3.37	3.23	3.08	3.00	2.92	2.84	2.75	2.66	18
2.38	**2.31**	**2.23**	**2.16**	**2.11**	**2.07**	**2.03**	**1.98**	**1.93**	
3.43	3.30	3.15	3.00	2.92	2.84	2.76	2.67	2.58	19
2.35	**2.28**	**2.20**	**2.12**	**2.08**	**2.04**	**1.99**	**1.95**	**1.90**	
3.37	3.23	3.09	2.94	2.86	2.78	2.69	2.61	2.52	20
2.30	**2.23**	**2.15**	**2.07**	**2.03**	**1.98**	**1.94**	**1.89**	**1.84**	
3.26	3.12	2.98	2.83	2.75	2.67	2.58	2.50	2.40	22

(continued)

TABLE 6   (Continued)

Denominator Degrees of Freedom (*df*)	Numerator Degrees of Freedom (*df*)								
	1	2	3	4	5	6	7	8	9
24	**4.26**	**3.40**	**3.01**	**2.78**	**2.62**	**2.51**	**2.42**	**2.36**	**2.30**
	7.82	5.61	4.72	4.22	3.90	3.67	3.50	3.36	3.26
26	**4.23**	**3.37**	**2.98**	**2.74**	**2.59**	**2.47**	**2.39**	**2.32**	**2.27**
	7.72	5.53	4.64	4.14	3.82	3.59	3.42	3.29	3.18
28	**4.20**	**3.34**	**2.95**	**2.71**	**2.56**	**2.45**	**2.36**	**2.29**	**2.24**
	7.64	5.45	4.57	4.07	3.75	3.53	3.36	3.23	3.12
30	**4.17**	**3.32**	**2.92**	**2.69**	**2.53**	**2.42**	**2.33**	**2.27**	**2.21**
	7.56	5.39	4.51	4.02	3.70	3.47	3.30	3.17	3.07
60	**4.00**	**3.15**	**2.76**	**2.53**	**2.37**	**2.25**	**2.17**	**2.10**	**2.04**
	7.08	4.98	4.13	3.65	3.34	3.12	2.95	2.82	2.72
120	**3.92**	**3.07**	**2.68**	**2.45**	**2.29**	**2.17**	**2.09**	**2.02**	**1.96**
	6.85	4.79	3.95	3.48	3.17	2.96	2.79	2.66	2.56

		Numerator Degrees of Freedom (*df*)							Denominator Degrees of Freedom (*df*)
10	**12**	**15**	**20**	**24**	**30**	**40**	**60**	**120**	
2.25	**2.18**	**2.11**	**2.03**	**1.98**	**1.94**	**1.89**	**1.84**	**1.79**	
3.17	3.03	2.89	2.74	2.66	2.58	2.49	2.40	2.31	24
2.22	**2.15**	**2.07**	**1.99**	**1.95**	**1.90**	**1.85**	**1.80**	**1.75**	
3.09	2.96	2.81	2.66	2.58	2.50	2.42	2.33	2.23	26
2.19	**2.12**	**2.04**	**1.96**	**1.91**	**1.87**	**1.82**	**1.77**	**1.71**	
3.03	2.90	2.75	2.60	2.52	2.44	2.35	2.26	2.17	28
2.16	**2.09**	**2.01**	**1.93**	**1.89**	**1.84**	**1.79**	**1.74**	**1.68**	
2.98	2.84	2.70	2.55	2.47	2.39	2.30	2.21	2.11	30
1.99	**1.92**	**1.84**	**1.75**	**1.70**	**1.65** _1.64_ **1.59**		**1.53**	**1.47**	
2.63	2.50	2.35	2.20	2.12	2.03	1.94	1.84	1.73	60
1.91	**1.83**	**1.75**	**1.66**	**1.61**	**1.55** _1.525_ **1.50**		**1.43**	**1.35**	
2.47	2.34	2.19	2.03	1.95	1.86	1.76	1.66	1.53	120

1.62

TABLE 7

Critical Values of the Mann-Whitney U-Statistic. If $U_{calc} \leq U_{table}$, reject H_0. An asterisk (*) indicates that no decision about H_0 can be made at the given level of significance. $p = 0.05$ $p = 0.01$

N_2	N_1	4	5	6	7	8	9	10	11	12	13	14	15	16	17	18	19	20
4		0	1	2	3	4	4	5	6	7	8	9	10	11	11	12	13	13
		*	*	0	0	1	1	2	2	3	3	4	5	5	6	6	7	8
5		1	2	3	5	6	7	8	9	11	12	13	14	15	17	18	19	20
		*	0	1	1	2	3	4	5	6	7	7	8	9	10	11	12	13
6		2	3	5	6	8	10	11	13	14	16	17	19	21	22	24	25	27
		0	1	2	3	4	5	6	7	9	10	11	12	13	15	16	17	18
7		3	5	6	8	10	12	14	16	18	20	22	24	26	28	30	32	34
		0	1	3	4	6	7	9	10	12	13	15	16	18	19	21	22	24
8		4	6	8	10	13	15	17	19	22	24	26	29	31	34	36	38	41
		1	2	4	6	7	9	11	13	15	17	18	20	22	24	26	28	30
9		4	7	10	12	15	17	20	23	26	28	31	34	37	39	42	45	48
		1	3	5	7	9	11	13	16	18	20	22	24	27	29	31	33	36
10		5	8	11	14	17	20	23	26	29	33	36	39	42	45	48	52	55
		2	4	6	9	11	13	16	18	21	24	26	29	31	34	37	39	42
11		6	9	13	16	19	23	26	30	33	37	40	44	47	51	55	58	62
		2	5	7	10	13	16	18	21	24	27	30	33	36	39	42	45	48
12		7	11	14	18	22	26	29	33	37	41	45	49	53	57	61	65	69
		3	6	9	12	15	18	21	24	27	31	34	37	41	44	47	51	54
13		8	12	16	20	24	28	33	37	41	45	50	54	59	63	67	72	76
		3	7	10	13	17	20	24	27	31	34	38	42	45	49	53	56	60
14		9	13	17	22	26	31	36	40	45	50	55	59	64	67	74	78	83
		4	7	11	15	18	22	26	30	34	38	42	46	50	54	58	63	67
15		10	14	19	24	29	34	39	44	49	54	59	64	70	75	80	85	90
		5	8	12	16	20	24	29	33	37	42	46	51	55	60	64	69	73
16		11	15	21	26	31	37	42	47	53	59	64	70	75	81	86	92	98
		5	9	13	18	22	27	31	36	41	45	50	55	60	65	70	74	79
17		11	17	22	28	34	39	45	51	57	63	67	75	81	87	93	99	105
		6	10	15	19	24	29	34	39	44	49	54	60	65	70	75	81	86
18		12	18	24	30	36	42	48	55	61	67	74	80	86	93	99	106	112
		6	11	16	21	26	31	37	42	47	53	58	64	70	75	81	87	92
19		13	19	25	32	38	45	52	58	65	72	78	85	92	99	106	113	119
		7	12	17	22	28	33	39	45	51	56	63	69	74	81	87	93	99
20		13	20	27	34	41	48	55	62	69	76	83	90	98	105	112	119	127
		8	13	18	24	30	36	42	48	54	60	67	73	79	86	92	99	105

Adapted and abridged from Table I of Mann, H. B., and Whitney, D. R. (1947). On a test of whether one of two random variables is stochastically larger than the other. *Annals of Mathematical Statistics, 18,* 50–60, from Table K of Siegel, S. (1956) *Nonparametric Statistics,* New York: McGraw Hill, pp. 274–277, and from Auble, D. (1953) Extended tables for the Mann-Whitney statistic. *Bulletin of the Institute of Educational Research of Indiana University, 1* (2), with the kind permission of the authors and publishers.

TABLE 8
Critical Values of the Wilcoxon Matched-Pairs Signed-Ranks Statistic, T. If $|T_-|$ or $|T_+| \leq T_{table}$, then reject H_0. An asterisk (*) indicates that no decision about H_0 can be made at the given level of significance. The N refers to the number of signed-ranks.

N	Two-Tailed Significance Levels	
	0.05	0.01
6	0	*
7	2	*
8	4	0
9	6	2
10	8	3
11	11	5
12	14	7
13	17	10
14	21	13
15	25	16
16	30	20
17	35	23
18	40	28
19	46	32
20	52	38
21	59	43
22	66	49
23	73	55
24	81	61
25	89	68

Adapted and abridged from Table II of Wilcoxon, F. (1949) *Some Rapid Approximate Statistical Procedures,* New York: American Cyanamid Company; p. 13, with the kind permission of the author and publisher.

TABLE 9
Critical Values of the F_{max} Statistic $p = 0.05$ $p = 0.01$

k df	2	3	4	5	6	7	8	9	10	11	12
4	9.60	15.50	20.60	25.20	29.50	33.60	37.50	41.10	44.60	48.00	51.40
	23.20	37.00	49.00	59.00	69.00	79.00	89.00	97.00	106.00	113.00	120.00
5	7.15	10.80	13.70	16.30	18.70	20.80	22.90	24.70	26.50	28.20	29.90
	14.90	22.00	28.00	33.00	38.00	42.00	46.00	50.00	54.00	57.00	60.00
6	5.82	8.38	10.40	12.10	13.70	15.00	16.30	17.50	18.60	19.70	20.70
	11.10	15.50	19.10	22.00	25.00	27.00	30.00	32.00	34.00	36.00	37.00
7	4.99	6.94	8.44	9.70	10.80	11.80	12.70	13.50	14.30	15.10	15.80
	8.89	12.10	14.50	16.50	18.40	20.00	22.00	23.00	24.00	26.00	27.00
8	4.43	6.00	7.18	8.12	9.03	9.78	10.50	11.10	11.70	12.20	12.70
	7.50	9.90	11.70	13.20	14.50	15.80	16.90	17.90	18.90	19.80	21.00
9	4.03	5.34	6.31	7.11	7.80	8.41	8.95	9.45	9.91	10.30	10.70
	6.54	8.50	9.90	11.10	12.10	13.10	13.90	14.70	15.30	16.00	16.60
10	3.72	4.85	5.67	6.34	6.92	7.42	7.87	8.28	8.66	9.01	9.34
	5.85	7.40	8.60	9.60	10.40	11.10	11.80	12.40	12.90	13.40	13.90
12	3.28	4.16	4.79	5.30	5.72	6.09	6.42	6.72	7.00	7.25	7.48
	4.91	6.10	6.90	7.60	8.20	8.70	9.10	9.50	9.90	10.20	10.60
15	2.86	3.54	4.01	4.37	4.68	4.95	5.19	5.40	5.59	5.77	5.93
	4.07	4.90	5.50	6.00	6.40	6.70	7.10	7.30	7.50	7.80	8.00
20	2.46	2.95	3.29	3.54	3.76	3.94	4.10	4.24	4.37	4.49	4.59
	3.32	3.80	4.30	4.60	4.90	5.10	5.30	5.50	5.60	5.80	5.90
30	2.07	2.40	2.61	2.78	2.91	3.02	3.12	3.21	3.29	3.36	3.39
	2.63	3.00	3.30	3.40	3.60	3.70	3.80	3.90	4.00	4.10	4.20
60	1.67	1.85	1.96	2.04	2.11	2.17	2.22	2.26	2.30	2.33	2.36
	1.96	2.20	2.30	2.40	2.40	2.50	2.50	2.60	2.60	2.70	2.70

Adapted and abridged from Pearson, E. S., and Hartley, H. O., eds. (1966) Table 31. Percentage points of the ratio, s^2_{max}/s^2_{min} *Biometrika Tables for Statisticians*, *1*, 146 (3rd ed.). By permission of the Biometrika Trustees.

TABLE 10
**Critical Values of the Kruskal-Wallis (K-W),
Friedman-Ranks (F-R), and Chi-Square (χ^2)
Statistics**

Degrees of Freedom (df)	Significance Levels 0.05	Significance Levels 0.01
1	3.84	6.63
2	5.99	9.21
3	7.81	11.34
4	9.49	13.28
5	11.07	15.09
6	12.59	16.81
7	14.07	18.48
8	15.51	20.09
9	16.92	21.67
10	18.31	23.21
11	19.68	24.72
12	21.03	26.22
13	22.36	27.69
14	23.68	29.14
15	25.00	30.58
16	26.30	32.00
17	27.59	33.41
18	28.87	34.81
19	30.14	36.19
20	31.41	37.57
21	32.67	38.93
22	33.92	40.29
23	35.17	41.64
24	36.42	42.98
25	37.65	44.31
26	38.89	45.64
27	40.11	46.96
28	41.34	48.28
29	42.56	49.59
30	43.77	50.89

ANSWERS TO REVIEW EXERCISES

Chapter 1

1. **a.** refers to group characteristics
    b. completing research
    c. descriptive statistics
    d. sample of students in U.S. colleges
    e. average number of books is a statistic.
2. **a.** group characteristics and branch of mathematics
    b. completing research and problem solving
    c. inferential statistics
    d. sample of subscribers
    e. statistic
3. **a.** analyzing data, using statistics as a branch of mathematics
    b. completing research
    c. inferential statistics
    d. sample; selected from Introductory Psychology class
    e. statistics

Chapter 2

1. **a.** inferential statistics
    b. samples
    c. statistics
    d. randomized samples
    e. dependent
    f. experimental design
    g. *independent variable:* reward—levels are reward and no reward.
    h. *dependent variable:* maze learning
    dependent measure: time to move down the maze recorded to nearest second

i. Time is a continuous quantitative measure.
j. True limits are ± 0.5 seconds.
k. ratio scale
l. *operational definitions:* independent variable: reward condition—levels are presence of mother and suckling (reward) and absence of mother and no suckling (no reward); dependent variable: no reference to operational definition
m. *hypothesis:* very young rats can learn to run down a maze if rewarded for doing so.

2. **a.** inferential
    b. samples
    c. statistics
    d. randomized samples
    e. independent samples
    f. experimental design
    g. *independent variable:* type of tablet—levels are cold tablet and placebo.
    h. *dependent variable:* reaction time;
    dependent measure: score on video game in units
    i. discrete quantitative
    j. true limits not appropriate
    k. interval scale
    l. *operational definitions:* independent variable: type of tablet—levels are cold tablet and placebo; dependent variable; reaction time; dependent measure; score on video game measured in whole units.
    m. *hypothesis:* The cold tablet will change reaction time.
3. **a.** inferential statistics
    b. samples
    c. statistics

d. biased, in that the results are applicable only to college students willing to send back the questionnaire; also there is no evidence that students at the university are representative of all college students.

e. not appropriate, as only one sample is selected

f. correlational design

g. no independent variable

h. *dependent variables:* habit of cigarette smoking and habit of marijuana smoking; *dependent measures:* number of tobacco cigarettes and number of marijuana cigarettes smoked each month

i. Both are discrete quantitative variables.

j. True limits not appropriate.

k. ratio scales

l. *operational definitions:* habit of cigarette smoking—reported number of tobacco cigarettes smoked each month; habit of marijuana cigarette smoking—reported number of marijuana cigarettes each month

m. The habit of tobacco smoking is related to habit of marijuana smoking.

Chapter 3

1. a. sample, whose population is college students who will take a statistics course comparable to the one taught in question

b. inferential statistics since inferences are to be made about all students

c. statistics

d. randomized samples

e. dependent samples matched on midterm scores

f. experimental design since manipulation is involved

g. independent variable is the CAI program; two levels: program A and program B

h. *dependent variable:* mastery of statistics; *dependent measure:* exam score

i. continuous quantitative dependent measure

j. interval scale if exam score is taken to indicate mastery of statistics; ratio scale if exam score only reflects number of items correct

k. *operational definitions:* independent variable: the two specific CAI programs used; dependent variable: score on instructor's exam

l. Several research hypotheses can be stated. An example is that one of the two specific CAI programs is better than the other.

m. relative frequency distribution

n. range for program A is 165; range for program B is 150

o. f's for the lowest class intervals of programs A and B are 1

p. Cumulative f's for the second highest class intervals of programs A and B are 31 and 30, respectively.

q. program A: 149.5 and 134.5; program B: 164.5 and 149.5

r. program A: 299 and 285; program B: 299 and 285

2. a. sample whose population is children living in Kingston, Ontario

b. inferential since the psychologist hopes to generalize to all children in Kingston, Ontario

c. statistics

d. biased sample

e. not applicable since there is only one sample

f. correlational design

g. no independent variable

h. *dependent measures:* number of hours of TV exposure and age in weeks when first word is uttered

i. The number of hours is quantitative continuous; the age in weeks is quantitative discrete.

j. Both dependent measures are along a ratio scale.

k. *operational definitions:* TV exposure—parents report of average daily hours of TV exposure; age at which first word is uttered—age in weeks based on birth records

l. *research hypothesis:* Age at which first word is uttered is (or is not) related to TV exposure.

m. grouped frequency distribution

n. 20.0

o. 1

p. 44

q. 2.5 and 0.5

r. 20 and 19

Chapter 4

1. a. experimental method

   b. *independent variable:* type of picture; two levels: line figures and faces; *dependent variable:* picture preference

   c. *dependent measure:* time in seconds spent looking at drawings of faces and figures

   d. dependent—each infant is observed under both conditions.

   e. preference defined as time looking at figures; specific pictures used for faces and specific pictures used for squares and triangles are operational definitions of figures.

   f. Time is a continuous variable; both face and line drawings are discrete variables.

   g. Time is a ratio scale.

   h. bar graph; Y-axis, average time in seconds; X-axis, type of picture: faces and figures—independent variable is discrete

2. a. frequency count

   b. not appropriate

   c. no dependent measures, only frequency count

   d. random sample

   e. political affiliation operationally defined as person's verbal report

   f. Political affiliation is discrete.

   g. Political affiliation is a qualitative variable not involving numbers.

   h. bar graph with frequency on Y-axis and political affiliation on X-axis because data are collected as frequencies and political affiliation is a discrete variable.

3. a. frequency count of different incomes

   b. not appropriate

   c. not appropriate

d. random samples

e. income operationally defined as subject's report on questionnaire

f. Income is continuous.

g. The scale of measurement for income is ratio, zero represents absence of income.

h. histogram or frequency polygon where X-axis has real limits for histogram and midpoints for frequency polygon. Either is appropriate as frequency is to be plotted on Y-axis as a function of the continuous variable, income.

4. a. correlational method

   b. no independent variable; dependent variables: amount of exercise and academic success

   c. dependent measures: grade point average based on a 100 percentage point system and hours of exercise per week

   d. random sample

   e. *operational definition of academic success:* based on report of average percent grade; exercise is defined by subjects' reported average weekly exercise

   f. Academic success is continuous; 0–100 hours of exercise is continuous.

   g. The scale for academic success is an interval scale; for exercise, the scale is ratio.

   h. scatter plot where scale of measurement for one of the measures is placed on X-axis and remaining scale is placed on the Y-axis as you are looking for a relationship of two continuous variables

5. a. frequency count

   b. no independent variable; dependent variable: none

   c. *dependent measure:* none

   d. population

   e. *operational definition of academic aptitude:* score on Scholastic Aptitude Test

   f. Test scores are considered continuous.

   g. The scale of measurement on the Scholastic Aptitude Test is interval.

h. percent cumulative frequency polygon where percent cumulative frequency is on the Y-axis and the upper real limits of the class intervals are on the X-axis.

6. a. frequency count
   b. no independent variable; dependent variable: level of achievement
   c. *dependent measure:* none
   d. population
   e. achievement defined on the basis of test score
   f. Test scores are considered continuous.
   g. The scale for test score is interval.
   h. stem-and-leaf display where division of digits determine stem-and-leaf, stem serves as base, and each leaf is displayed to form the height of the bar over stem reflecting frequency. Stem-and-leaf is used because you want group patterns and individual scores.

TABLE 5-F
The Number of Hours Worked Daily During the Month of April by a College Student in a Work-Study Program

Hours X	f
7	2
6	2
5	3
4	5
3	6
2	8
1	4
	$\Sigma f = 30$

Chapter 5

1. a. 47, 46, 46, 46, 45, 44, 43, 43, 42, 41
   b. 10
   c. line
   d. mean = 44.3, median = 44.5, mode = 46
   e. left
   f. 177.2

2. a. See Table 5-F.
   b. See Figure 5-A. *(see page 432)*
   c. right
   d. 2
   e. 3
   f. 3.3
   g. right
   h. 8.3

3. a. See Table 5-G.
   b. See Figure 5-B. *(see page 432)*
   c. 164.5
   d. 174.7
   e. 181.17

TABLE 5-G
The Number of Hours of TV Watched by Each of Ninety Students During the Fall Semester

Hours Class	f
330–359	1
300–329	2
270–299	6
240–269	8
210–239	10
180–209	14
150–179	25
120–149	10
90–119	7
60–89	4
30–59	3

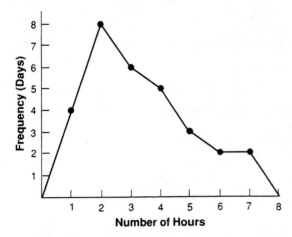

FIGURE 5-A *Frequency polygon of the number of hours worked daily during the month of April by a college student in a work-study program*

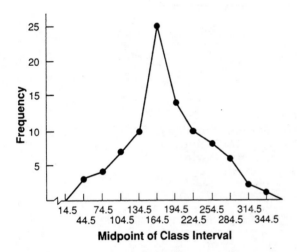

FIGURE 5-B *Frequency polygon of the number of hours of TV watched by each of 90 students during the fall semester*

Chapter 6

1. **a.** (1) 9.33 (2) 10 (3) 3 and 12 (4) 18
      (5) 36 (6) 6
   b. See Figure 6-A.
   c. between-group

2. **a.** See Table 6-E.
   b. (1) 14.10 (2) 7.31 (3) 4.5 (4) 100
      (5) 314.12 (6) 17.72

   c. median
   d. quartile deviation
   e. within-group
   f. right

3. **a.** mean: open-ended interval
   b. average deviation, range, standard deviation, variance—open-ended interval
   c. open-ended interval; k < 10

TABLE 6-E
The Number of Hazardous Waste Sites in Each of Fifty States in the U.S.A.

| Sites | |
Class	f
90–99	1
80–89	0
70–79	0
60–69	0
50–59	2
40–49	1
30–39	3
20–29	5
10–19	6
0–9	32

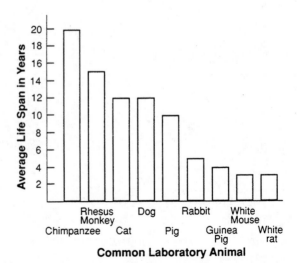

FIGURE 6-A *Bar graph of the average life span in years of some common laboratory animals*

Chapter 7

1. **a.** See Displays 7-A and 7-B.

DISPLAY 7-A
Stem-and-Leaf Display of Grades on an Abnormal Psychology Comprehensive Midterm Examination. Unit = 1 such that 4   9 equals 49.

Stem	Leaf
4	9
5	45
6	0147
7	1235566667778889999
8	111333344455778
9	000222358

DISPLAY 7-B
Stem-and-Leaf Display of Grades on an Abnormal Psychology Comprehensive Final Examination. Unit = 1 such that 3   6 equals 36.

Stem	Leaf
3	6
4	07
5	79
6	13789
7	000011111123355777789999
8	0113334556789
9	0112

    b. See Table 7-C.
    c. See Table 7-D.
    d. median = 79; Interquartile Range = 86 − 75 = 11.
    e. 42

2. **a.** midterm, 79; final, 74.26
    b. midterm, 79.19; final, 75.5
    c. midterm, 77; final, 68.5
    d. midterm, 116.33; final, 154.23
    e. midterm, 10.79; final 12.42
    f. midterm, 5.36; final, 7.22
    g. midterm, 73; final, 82

3. **a.** 65.75
    b. 83.93
    c. 90.4
    d. 57

TABLE 7-C
Grouped Frequency Distribution of Grades on an Abnormal Psychology Comprehensive Midterm Examination ($N = 50$)

Grades Class	f
95–99	2
90–94	7
85–89	5
80–84	10
75–79	16
70–74	3
65–69	1
60–64	3
55–59	1
50–54	1
45–49	1

TABLE 7-D
Grouped Frequency Distribution of Grades on an Abnormal Psychology Comprehensive Final Examination ($N = 50$)

Grades Class	f
90–95	4
84–89	7
78–83	11
72–77	9
66–71	12
60–65	2
54–59	2
48–53	0
42–47	1
36–41	2

Chapter 8

1. **a.** See Figure 8-A.
   b. positive
   c. (1) See Table 8-E   (2) 13.33   (3) 23.33   (4) 4.83
   d. (1) 99, 92, 90, 90, 87, 87, 85, 80, 80, 75, 70, 60   (2) 82.92   (3) 113.72   (4) 10.66
   e. (1) 0.88   (2) Yes
   f. Yes
   g. $Y' = 1.94X + 57.06$
   h. 86
   i. 5.12
   j. (1) 0.77   (2) 0.23
2. **a.** X-ranks: 11.5, 11.5, 10, 9, 8, 6, 6, 6, 3.5, 3.5, 2, 1; Y-ranks: 12, 9.5, 11, 7.5, 9.5, 4.5, 6, 3, 7.5, 4.5, 2, 1
   b. 0.87
   c. 0.87
   d. Yes

TABLE 8-E
The Number of Hours (X) Spent Preparing for a Final Biology Exam by Twelve Biology Majors

Hours X	Frequency f
20	2
19	0
18	1
17	1
16	1
15	0
14	0
13	0
12	3
11	0
10	2
9	0
8	1
7	0
6	0
5	1

   e. No
3. **a.** no effect
   b. Since adding a constant has no effect upon the standard deviation and affects the mean by the addition of the constant, the z-scores will remain the same as they were before the addition of the constants. Hence, *r* will also remain the same.

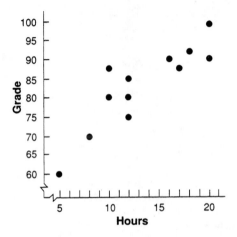

FIGURE 8-A   *Scatter plot relating the exam grade achieved (Y) by twelve biology majors to the number of hours (X) spent preparing for the exam*

Chapter 9

1. **a.** mean = 75.5; median = 75.5; mode = 75.5
   b. normal as all three measures of central tendency are equal to each other
   c. See Figure 9-A.
   d. normal distribution as indicated by symmetry and bell shape
   e. $\sigma = 24.8$ (transformed σ of 2.48 × 10)
   f. See Figure 9-B.
   g. Shape remains the same as the only change was converting the X-scale from raw scores to Z-scores.
2. **a.** 107.94
   b. 21
3. **a.** 107.24
   b. 21
   c. The answers are similar as the two methods used to estimate values in parts *a* and *b* of

problems 2 and 3 are based on the same mathematical concepts.

   d. 26.89 and 124.11

   e. 0.1109 (0.0708 + 0.0401)

4. **a.** $H_0: \varrho = 0$, $H_1: \varrho \neq 0$

   b. Fail to reject the null hypothesis.

   c. Type II or beta error

5. **a.** $H_0: \mu_{air} = \mu_{college}$; $H_1: \mu_{air} \neq \mu_{college}$

   b. Reject the null hypothesis.

   c. Type I or alpha error

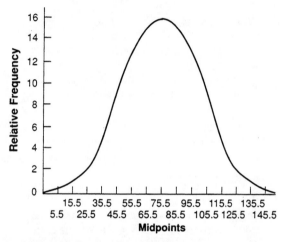

FIGURE 9-A *Relative frequency polygon of time to report boredom by air-traffic controllers described for Review Exercise 1, part c*

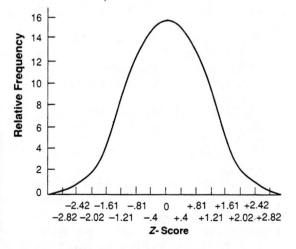

FIGURE 9-B *Relative frequency polygon of time to report boredom converted to z-scores for air-traffic controllers described in Review Exercise 1, part f*

Chapter 10

1. **a.** $\bar{X} = 94.2$

   b. $\bar{X} = 102.9$ and $\bar{X} = 77.10$

   c. 102.9

2. **a.** an alpha or Type I error where a true H_0 is incorrectly rejected

   b. The investigator would have incorrectly assumed that the skeletal remains represent a unique species of ground finch which has become extinct on the island.

3. **a.** a beta or Type II error where a false H_0 is not rejected

   b. The investigator would have missed discovering an extinct species of ground finch.

Chapter 11

1. **a.** The purpose is to examine the psychologist's belief that the average capacity of short-term memory for students of this college is not 7 items or bits of information.

   b. Hypothesis testing procedures are required as the specific value of $\mu = 7$ items is to evaluated.

   c. The event measured is the number of items recalled.

   d. The number of items recalled is a ratio scale since 0 indicates the absence of items recalled.

   e. The one-sample t where $t = \bar{X} - \mu_0/s_{\bar{X}}$ as μ is hypothesized and σ has to be estimated on the basis of $s/\sqrt{N}$ from one sample.

   f. With $df = 15$ ($16 - 1$), the decision rule is, reject H_0 if $|t_{calc}| \geq 2.13$

   g. One-sample $t = (8 - 7)/0.48 = 2.08$

   h. Fail to reject H_0 as t_{calc} equal to 2.08 is less than 2.13.

   i. The results fail to support the psychologist's belief that the short-term memory capacity of students at this college is not seven items or bits of information, $t(15) = 2.08$, $p > 0.05$.

2. **a.** The purpose is to calculate the probability of obtaining a random sample from a population whose μ and σ are known.

   b. Neither hypothesis testing nor interval estimation procedures are needed.

c. The event measured is the score on the IQ test.

d. The scale of measurement is interval since the score of 0 is an arbitrary zero point.

e. $z = (\bar{X} - \mu)/\sigma_{\bar{X}}$ as μ and σ are known.

f. A decision rule is not needed.

g. Probability $= 0.2302$ $(0.1151 + 0.1151)$ as $z = (103 - 100)/2.5$ and $z = (97 - 100)/2.5 = -1.2$.

h. not appropriate

i. not applicable

3. a. The purpose is to estimate average daily consumption of caffeine by all students at this university.

b. The interval estimation procedure is needed to estimate probable values of μ.

c. The event measured is the daily number of ounces of coffee consumed as reported by the students surveyed.

d. The scale of measurement is ratio as zero indicates the absence of coffee consumption.

e. The t-statistic is used where upper limit $\bar{X} + t_{table}$ $(s_{\bar{X}})$ and lower limit is $\bar{X} - t_{table}$ $(s_{\bar{X}})$.

f. not appropriate

g. 95% CI: $26.8 \leq \mu \leq 33.2$.

h. not appropriate

i. Based on the collected data, the student can be 95 percent confident that the interval 26.8 through 33.2 contains the average amount of coffee consumed by all students at this university.

Chapter 12

1. a. to determine if removal of brain structure affects learning

b. two randomized independent samples

c. total number of maze errors

d. ratio scale

e. t-test for two random independent samples since two randomized independent samples are used where the scale of measurement is a ratio scale and a statistical hypothesis is to be evaluated

f. *statistical hypotheses for testing for homogeneity of variance:* H_0: $\sigma^2 = \sigma^2$, H_1: $\sigma^2 \neq \sigma^2$ *statistical test:* decision rule is reject H_0 if F_{calc} ≥ 3.79 and calculations reveal that $F = 1.31$ is less than 3.79; *interpretation:* there is no evidence that variances are heterogeneous; *statistical test:* use t-test for two random independent samples; *research hypothesis:* brain surgery will affect learning; *statistical hypotheses:* H_0: $\mu_{diff} = 0$, H_1: $\mu_{diff} \neq 0$; *decision rule:* reject H_0 if $|t_{calc}| \geq 2.14$; *calculations:* $t = (37.25 - 32)/3.72 = 1.41$; *evaluation of H_0:* fail to reject H_0 since 1.41 is less than 2.14; *interpretation:* no evidence to suggest that brain surgery affects maze learning, $t(14) = 1.41$, $p > 0.05$.

2. a. to determine if new weight program affects performance during a cross-country race

b. two randomized independent samples

c. placement in race

d. ordinal scale

e. Mann-Whitney U-test as random independent samples are used, scale of measurement is ordinal, and a statistical hypothesis is to be evaluated

f. *research hypothesis:* the two different weight training programs will affect race performance differently; *statistical hypotheses:* H_0: population distributions of runners using the weight programs do not differ, H_1: population distributions of runners using the weight programs are different; *statistical test:* Mann-Whitney U-test; *decision rule:* reject H_0 if $U_{calc} \leq 15$; *calculation:* U_{calc} equals 21; *evaluation of H_0:* fail to reject H_0 since $U_{calc} > U_{table}$; *interpretation:* no evidence to support notion that weight programs differentially affect race performance, $U(9, 8) = 21$, $p > 0.05$

3. a. to determine if there is a relationship between hours spent studying and reading for enjoyment

b. one random sample selected from population of school's students

c. hours spent studying and hours spent reading for enjoyment

d. both measures obtained along a ratio scale

e. correlation coefficient, r

f. *research hypothesis:* there is a relationship between hours spent studying and hours spent reading for enjoyment;
statistical hypotheses: $H_0\ \varrho = 0$, $H_1: \varrho \neq 0$;
statistical test: Pearson correlation; decision rule: reject H_0 if $r_{calc} \geq 0.71$;
calculations: $r = 0.95$;
evaluation of H_0: reject H_0 since 0.95 is greater than 0.71;
interpretation: there is a relationship between hours spent studying and hours spent reading for enjoyment, $r(6) = 0.95$, $p < 0.05$.

4. a. estimate average number of visits to physicians in this community where problem is behavioral not physiological

b. one random sample of family physicians from the population of family physicians in this community

c. number of patients judged to have behavorial problems

d. ratio scale

e. 95 percent confidence interval is needed

f. Apply formulas: lower limit 95% $CI = \bar{X} - t_{table}(s_{\bar{X}})$ and upper limit 95% $CI = \bar{X} + t_{table}(s_{\bar{X}})$ such that 95% CI: $1395 \leq \mu \leq 1822$. Note that the values are rounded to whole numbers since number of patients is a discrete variable.

Chapter 13

1. a. *dependent variable:* reaction time;
independent variable: type of stimuli

b. ratio

c. continuous

d. dependent

e. random

f. $r = 0.52$

g. repeated measures

h. $\bar{X}_{sim} = 674.67$, $\bar{X}_{dissim} = 771$; $s^2_{sim} = 6764.5$, $s^2_{dissim} = 14444$

i. not applicable

j. $t(8) = 2.77$

k. The means of the treatment populations are equal; $\mu_{sim} = \mu_{dissim}$

l. reject

m. supports research hypothesis

2. a. *dependent variable:* items recalled;
independent variable: instructions

b. ratio

c. discrete

d. dependent

e. randomized

f. $r = 0.73$

g. matching by mutual category

h. $\bar{X}_{label} = 9.6$, $\bar{X}_{category} = 11.9$; $s^2_{label} = 8.49$; $s^2_{category} = 3.43$

i. not applicable

j. $t(9) = 3.65$

k. The means of the populations from which the samples were drawn are equal; $\mu_{label} = \mu_{category}$

l. reject

m. supports research hypothesis

3. a. *dependent variable:* items recalled;
independent variable: interpolated learning

b. ratio

c. discrete

d. independent

e. randomized

f. NA

g. NA

h. $\bar{X}_{exp} = 9.62$, $\bar{X}_{con} = 13.25$; $s^2_{exp} = 4.27$, $s^2_{con} = 1.07$

i. $F(7, 7) = 3.99$

j. $U = 2$

k. The populations from which the samples were drawn are similar.

l. reject

m. supports teacher's expectations

Chapter 14

1. **a.** *dependent variable:* fear of dogs as measured by distance from dog in feet; *independent variable:* type of model

    b. ratio

    c. continuous

    d. randomized

    e. CR-4

    f. *7–9 yr. olds:* $\bar{X} = 10.17$, $s^2 = 5.28$; *14–16 yr. olds:* $\bar{X} = 12.50$, $s^2 = 10.94$; *adults:* $\bar{X} = 12.92$, $s^2 = 3.85$; *no model:* $\bar{X} = 18.67$, $s^2 = 4.33$

    g. $F_{max} = 2.84$

    h. not significant

    i. parametric ANOVA, $F(3, 20) = 12.83$, $p < 0.05$

    j. The means of the populations from which the samples were drawn are equal.

    k. $\mu_1 = \mu_2 = \mu_3 = \mu_4$.

    l. F (7–9 vs. con) $= 35.59$, F(14–16 vs. con) $= 18.75$, F(adult vs. con) $= 16.29$.

    m. $CV = 2.97$; See Table 14-N.

    n. seven-to-nine year-old boys would be most influenced by models their own age.

    o. not supported

2. **a.** *dependent variable:* interference with memory as measured by the number of nonsense syllables recalled; *independent variable:* type of interference determined by the temporal position of list A relative to list B

    b. ratio

    c. discrete

    d. randomized

    e. CR-3

    f. *proactive:* $\bar{X} = 12.6$, $s^2 = 11.37$; *retroactive:* $\bar{X} = 14.2$, $s^2 = 16.4$; *control:* $\bar{X} = 20.4$, $s^2 = 2.71$

    b. $F_{max} = 6.05$

    h. significant

    i. $K\text{-}W = 15.4$

    j. The populations from which the samples were drawn do not differ.

    k. nonapplicable

    l. Mann-Whitney U-test: *Proactive vs. Con:* $U(10, 10) = 2.5$, $p < 0.05$; *Retroactive vs. Con:* $U(10, 10) = 12.5$, $p < 0.05$

    m. nonapplicable

    n. proactive interference with memory of verbal material is greater than retroactive interference

    o. not supported—*Proactive vs. Retroactive:* $U(10, 10) = 39.5$, $p > 0.05$

3. **a.** *problems:* $\bar{X} = 86.2$, median $= 89$, mode $= 89$; *multiple choice:* $\bar{X} = 78.6$, median $= 78$, mode $= 78$

    b. *problems:* range $= 25$, $s^2 = 58.18$, $s = 7.63$; *multiple choice:* range $= 22$, $s^2 = 35.16$, $s = 5.93$

    c. *problems:* $z = 0.37$; *multiple choice:* $z = -0.10$

    d. $F(9, 9) = 1.65$, $p > 0.05$

    e. t(independent samples) $= 2.488$

    f. reject H_0

    g. $\mu_1 = \mu_2$

    h. $F(1, 18) = 6.19$, $p < 0.05$

    i. $t^2 = F$

TABLE 14-N
Absolute Values of Mean Differences for the Data (Median Distance from Dog in Feet) in Table 14-F in Review Exercise 14.1

	$\bar{T}_{7-9}$	$\bar{T}_{14-16}$	$\bar{T}_{Adult}$
$\bar{T}_{14-16}$	2.33		
$\bar{T}_{Adult}$	2.75	0.42	
$\bar{T}_{No\ Model}$	8.50*	6.17*	5.75*

Chapter 15

1. **a.** *dependent variable:* reaction time; *independent variable:* condition of color name

    b. ratio

    c. continuous

    d. RB-3

    e. blocking

    f. premeasurement of reaction times

    g. *black:* $\bar{X} = 7.25$, $s^2 = 2.21$; *corresponding color:* $\bar{X} = 6.38$, $s^2 = 1.98$; *different color:* $\bar{X} = 8.38$, $s^2 = 1.12$

    h. NA

i. See Table 15-G.

j. The means of the populations from which the samples were drawn are equal.

k. $F(1, 14) = 50$, $p < 0.05$

l. $F(1, 14) = 15.8$, $p < 0.05$; Yes, the outcome of the experiment supported the research hypothesis.

2. a. *dependent variable:* spatial memory as measured by the number of correctly placed pieces of model furniture;
   independent variable: type of model room

   b. ratio

   c. discrete

   d. RM-3

   e. repeated measures

   b. counterbalance

   g. *individual's room:* $\overline{X} = 6.17$, $s^2 = 1.61$;
   dining hall: $\overline{X} = 5.08$, $s^2 = 1.54$;
   infirmary: $\overline{X} = 3$, $s^2 = 1.82$

   h. NA

   i. See Table 15-H.

   j. The means of the treatment populations are equal.

   k. $F(1, 22) = 87.4$, $p < 0.05$

   l. Yes, $F(1, 22) = 37.6$, $p < 0.05$, (dining hall vs. infirmary)

3. a. *dependent variable:* neophobia as measured by the amount of test solution drunk;
   independent variable: relative novelty of test solution

   b. ratio

   c. continuous

   d. CR-3

   e. NA

   f. NA

   g. *novel flavor:* $\overline{X} = 2.12$, s^2 1.27;
   familiar: $\overline{X} = 7.88$, $s^2 = 1.55$;
   novelty adaptation: $\overline{X} = 6.5$, $s^2 = 3.14$

   h. $F_{max} = 2.47$

   i. See Table 15-I.

   j. The means of the populations from which the samples were drawn are equal.

   k. $F(1, 21) = 66.36$, $p < 0.05$

   l. Yes, $F(1, 21) = 38.37$, $p < 0.05$ (*novel vs. novelty adaptation*).

TABLE 15-G
Summary Table for ANOVA Performed on Time to Read a List of Color Names Printed in Black Ink, Ink Corresponding to the Color Name, or Ink Color Not Corresponding to the Color Name

Source	SS	df	MS	F
Between blocks	32.66	7		
Within blocks	20.67	16		
Color condition	16.08	2	8.04	24.36
Error	4.59	14	0.33	
Total	53.33	23		

TABLE 15-H
Summary Table for ANOVA Performed on the Number of Pieces of Model Furniture Placed Correctly in Model Rooms by Residents of a Nursing Home as a Function of Familiarity with the Room Setting

Source	SS	df	MS	F
Between subjects	39.42	11		
Within subjects	77.33	24		
Type of room	62.17	2	31.08	45.04
Error	15.16	22	0.69	
Total	116.75	35		

TABLE 15-I
Summary Table for ANOVA Performed on the Amount of a Test Solution Drunk by Rats as a Function Familiarity with the Solution (Familiar with the Solution, Familiar with Similar Solutions, or Unfamiliar with the Solution or Similiar Solutions)

Source	SS	df	MS	F
Between groups	144.25	2	72.12	36.24
Within groups	41.75	21	1.99	
Total	186.00	23		

Chapter 16

a. *CRF*-23

b. *dependent variable:* retrograde amnesia as measured by the number of scenes recalled; *independent variables:* A = type of therapy, B = observation-therapy interval

c. a_1 = unilateral therapy, a_2 = bilateral therapy; b_1 = 0 hour interval, b_2 = 1 hour interval, b_3 = 24 hour interval

d. ratio

e. discrete

f. randomized

g. A_1

h. AB_{22}

i. AB_{13}

j. See Table 16-E.

k. See Figure 16-B.

l. The interaction is significant.

m. See Table 16-F.

n. Yes.

o. Neither.

p. F_A at b_1 = 45.39 (significant)

q. SS_B at a_1
$$= [(AB_{11}^2 + AB_{12}^2 + AB_{13}^2)/n] - [(A_1^2)/npr]$$
$$= [(90^2 + 77^2 + 88^2)/6] - (255^2/18) =$$
$3628.8 - 3621.5 = 16.33$. MS_B at $a_1 = (SS_B$ at $a_1)/df_B = 16.33/2 = 8.16$. F_B at $a_1 = (MS_B$ at $a_1)/MS_{wg} = 8.16/8.49 = 0.96$ (not significant).

r. 19.3 percent

TABLE 16-E
Summary Table of Computational Formulas for a 2 × 2 Factorial ANOVA on the Effect of Type of Electroconvulsive Therapy (Unilateral or Bilateral) on Recall of Scenes Observed Either 0, 1, or 24 Hours before Therapy

Source	SS	df
Between groups	(5) − (1)	$pq - 1$
A(Therapy)	(3) − (1)	$p - 1$
B(Interval)	(4) − (1)	$q - 1$
AB(T × I)	(5) − (4) − (3) + (1)	$(p - 1)(q - 1)$
Within groups	(2) − (5)	$pq(n - 1)$
TOTAL	(2) − (1)	$npq - 1$

TABLE 16-F
Summary Table of a Two-Way ANOVA Performed on Number of Scenes Recalled as a Function of Type of Electroconvulsive Therapy (Unilateral or Bilateral) Administered to Patients 0, 1, or 24 Hours after They Observed the Scenes.

Source	SS	df	MS	F
Between groups	636.81	5	127.36	15.00*
A(Therapy)	294.70	1	294.70	34.71*
B(Interval)	170.06	2	85.03	10.01*
AB(T × I)	172.05	2	86.02	10.13*
Within groups	254.83	30	8.49	
TOTAL	891.64	35		

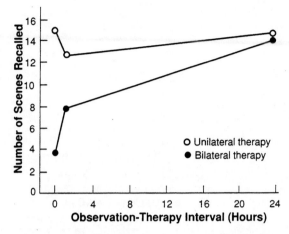

FIGURE 16-B *Line graphs depicting the interaction of type of therapy and observation-therapy interval for the hypothetical electroconvulsive therapy experiment*

Chapter 17

1. **a.** *t*-statistic for two independent samples

   b. Mann-Whitney *U*-statistic

2. **a.** *F* based on the parametric dependent samples ANOVA

   b. *F-R* (Friedman ranks ANOVA)

3. **a.** *F* based on a two-way ANOVA

   b. no comparable nonparametric test available

INDEX